Modern
MANDARIN CHINESE
Grammar
WORKBOOK

The *Modern Mandarin Chinese Grammar Workbook* is a book of exercises and language tasks for all learners of Mandarin Chinese. Divided into two sections, the *Workbook* initially provides exercises based on essential grammatical structures, and moves on to practice everyday functions such as making introductions, apologizing and expressing needs.

With an extensive answer key at the back to enable students to check on their progress, main features include:

* exercises at various levels of challenge for a broad range of learners
* cross-referencing to the related *Modern Mandarin Chinese Grammar*
* a comprehensive index to exercises alphabetically arranged in terms of structures, functions, and key Chinese structure vocabulary.

This second edition also offers a revised and expanded selection of exercises including new task-based exercises.

The *Modern Mandarin Chinese Grammar Workbook* is ideal for all learners of Mandarin Chinese, from beginner to intermediate and advanced students. It can be used both independently and alongside the *Modern Mandarin Chinese Grammar* (978-0-415-82714-0), which is also published by Routledge.

Claudia Ross is Professor of Chinese at the College of the Holy Cross in Worcester, Massachusetts.

Jing-heng Sheng Ma is Professor Emeritus of Chinese at Wellesley College, Massachusetts.

Baozhang He is Associate Professor of Chinese at the College of the Holy Cross in Worcester, Massachusetts.

Pei-Chia Chen is Lecturer in Chinese at the University of California, San Diego.

Routledge Modern Grammars

Series concept and development – Sarah Butler

Other books in the series

Modern MANDARIN CHINESE Grammar WORKBOOK

SECOND EDITION

Claudia Ross
Jing-heng Sheng Ma
Baozhang He
Pei-Chia Chen

 Routledge
Taylor & Francis Group

LONDON AND NEW YORK

First published 2006
by Routledge

Second edition published 2015
by Routledge
2 Park Square, Milton Park, Abingdon, Oxon OX14 4RN

and by Routledge
711 Third Avenue, New York, NY 10017

Routledge is an imprint of the Taylor & Francis Group, an informa business

© 2006, 2015 Claudia Ross, Jing-heng Sheng Ma, Baozhang He and Pei-Chia Chen

The right of Claudia Ross, Jing-heng Sheng Ma, Baozhang He and Pei-Chia Chen to be identified as authors of this work has been asserted by them in accordance with sections 77 and 78 of the Copyright, Designs and Patents Act 1988.

British Library Cataloguing in Publication Data
A catalogue record for this book is available from the British Library

Library of Congress Cataloging in Publication Data
Ross, Claudia.
  Modern Mandarin grammar workbook / Claudia Ross, Jing-heng Sheng Ma, Baozhang He, Pei-Chia Chen. – Second Edition.
     pages cm. – (Routledge Modern Grammars)
  Text in English and Chinese.
  Includes bibliographical references and index.
  1. Chinese language–Textbook for foreign speakers–English.   2. Mandarin dialects.
I. Ma, Jing-heng Sheng.   II. He, Baozhang, 1955–   III. Chen, Pei-Chia.   IV. Title.
  PL1129.E5R6783 2014
  495.182′421–dc23

                                                                                    2014002768

ISBN: 978-0-415-83488-9 (pbk)
ISBN: 978-1-315-76435-1 (ebk)

Typeset in ITC Stone Serif
by Graphicraft Limited, Hong Kong

Contents

Contents

Introduction

The *Modern Mandarin Chinese Grammar Workbook* is a companion to *Modern Mandarin Chinese Grammar* and is designed to help you to strengthen your command of Mandarin Chinese. It can be used alongside a Chinese language textbook in a regular language program, or as review material for self study. The Answer Key at the end of the book allows you to check your answers as you work through the exercises. Exercises in the *Workbook* are graded in terms of level of difficulty, making the book appropriate for near-beginners as well as Mandarin learners at the advanced level in a high school or university program. Instructions are written in English, and all exercises are presented in simplified and traditional characters and Pinyin romanization.

The *Workbook* focuses on the major structural patterns and communication strategies used in Mandarin Chinese. Exercises focusing on structure are presented in Part A 'Structures' and those focusing on communication are presented in Part B 'Situations and functions.' Since successful communication is built in part on structural accuracy, there is overlap between the two sections. We recommend that as you work on situations and functions in Part B, you also practice the related structure exercises in Part A. For example, when working on Chapters 47 'Expressing location and distance' and 48 'Talking about movement, directions, and means of transportation,' you should also work through the structure exercises involving prepositions in Part A. Use the table of contents to find exercises for specific structures or general communication tasks. Consult the Index for exercises focusing on specific topics such as illness, or the weather, or reciting telephone numbers. Follow the cross-references to *Modern Mandarin Chinese Grammar* for explanations about structure and usage.

Chinese language study is an interesting journey. We hope that the *Modern Mandarin Chinese Grammar Workbook* and *Modern Mandarin Chinese Grammar* are helpful in your navigation, and wish you enjoyment and success as you develop your language skills.

Claudia Ross
Jing-heng Sheng Ma
Baozhang He
Pei-Chia Chen
January 2014

How to use this book

We have written this book as a companion to *Modern Mandarin Chinese Grammar* to provide practice with the major structures and functions of Mandarin Chinese. Use it to strengthen your grammatical skills and your ability to communicate in Mandarin.

The presentation of material follows the order of presentation in *Modern Mandarin Chinese Grammar*. You can work on the chapters in any order, selecting chapters that focus on the structures and functions that address your specific needs.

This *Workbook* is divided into two parts. Part A focuses on structures. If you want to focus on basic structures such as the formation of numbers, or noun modification, or the phrase order of the Mandarin sentence, you should select exercises in Part A. Part A also includes some practice with Pinyin romanization, and some activities involving Chinese characters that will help you to use a Chinese dictionary. Part B, 'Situations and functions,' focuses on communication. When you want to practice giving an opinion, or politely refusing a request, or to talk about the past, you should select exercises from Part B. You can work on related structures as you practice communicative tasks. For example, when practicing talking about the past you may wish to consult the chapters on verbs in Part A.

Each exercise in the *Modern Mandarin Chinese Grammar Workbook* is followed by one or more numbers indicating the section(s) of the *Grammar* in which the relevant structures or functions are discussed. For example, the number 30.2 following an exercise indicates that the exercise targets the material presented in Chapter 30, section 2. You should study the presentation in the *Grammar* before completing the relevant activities in the *Workbook*.

This *Workbook* includes an alphabetical Index to help you to locate exercises that focus on particular structures or functions. The numbers following each item in the Index indicate the sections of the *Workbook* in which activities are presented.

Finally, an Answer Key is provided at the end of the book. Check the answer key *only after* you have completed each activity!

Part A

Structures

1

Overview of pronunciation and Pinyin romanization

1 Put the tone mark over the appropriate vowel.

a. **xian** (1)   e. **tou** (2)
b. **bie** (2)   f. **huai** (4)
c. **xuan** (3)   g. **chui** (1)
d. **yue** (4)   h. **zao** (3)

⇨ 1.2.1

2 Rewrite these sentences and phrases to indicate the changed tones in natural speech.

Example: **nǐ hǎo** → **ní hǎo**

a. **Xiǎo Lǐ**
b. **wǔ bǎ yǐzi**
c. **Nǐ yǒu gǒu ma?**
d. **Wǒ hěn hǎo.**
e. **Tā yě xiǎng mǎi bǐ.**
f. **Wǒ xiǎng mǎi shū.**
g. **Tā yǒu jiǔ gè péngyou.**
h. **wǔshíwǔ běn shū**

⇨ 1.1.3

3 Correct the Pinyin spelling for each of the following words and syllables.

a. **kwai**   f. **üe**
b. **uan**   g. **shuesheng**
c. **pengyow**   h. **jungguo**
d. **quian**   i. **hsiao**
e. **dwo**   j. **iao**

⇨ 1.1.1, 1.1.2, 1.2.2

2
Syllable, meaning, and word

1 Rewrite these sentences and phrases to indicate the changed tones in natural speech.

    Example: **yī tiáo** → **yì tiáo**

a. **yī tiáo lù**   f. **yī gè rén**

b. **bù tài guì**   g. **yī shù huār**

c. **yī kuài qián**   h. **yī háng**

d. **yī mén kè**   i. **yī bù diànyǐng**

e. **yī suǒ fángzi**   j. **bù cuò**

⇨ 2.3

3
The Chinese writing system: an overview

1 Using a traditional character dictionary as your reference, circle the radical in each of the following characters.

     Example: 嗎 → ⑩馬

a. 好   f. 錢
b. 們   g. 這
c. 說   h. 漢
d. 筆   i. 從
e. 紅

➪ 3.2.1

2 Using a simplified character dictionary as your reference, circle the radical in each of the following characters.

a. 过   f. 对
b. 房   g. 楚
c. 闻   h. 聪
d. 情   i. 治
e. 救

➪ 3.2.1

3 Consult a dictionary to find the simplified radical that corresponds to each of the following traditional radicals.

     Example: 言 = 讠

a. 門   e. 馬
b. 車   f. 貝
c. 糸   g. 金
d. 食   h. 魚

4

Sometimes a simplified character is formed by taking one part of its traditional form. Match the traditional character in the column on the left with its simplified form in the column on the right. Consult a dictionary if necessary.

Example: 從 = 从

a.	飛	A.	亲
b.	習	B.	丽
c.	雖	C.	电
d.	電	D.	飞
e.	麗	E.	业
f.	業	F.	习
g.	廣	G.	虽
h.	親	H.	广

⇨ 3.1

5

Consult a dictionary to find the simplified character that corresponds to each of the following traditional characters. Write each simplified character beside the corresponding traditional character.

Example: 對 = 对

a.	講	f.	歐
b.	塊	g.	學
c.	樣	h.	認
d.	蘭	i.	聽
e.	連	j.	曆

⇨ 3.1

6

Look up the following characters in a dictionary and identify the shared pronunciation in each group. Arrange the characters according to their common phonetic.

爸，站，吧，占，城，誠，綱，战，把，剛，東，棟，成，凍，鋼

Group 1	Group 2	Group 3	Group 4	Group 5

⇨ 3.2.2

7

Indicate the total number of strokes in each of the following characters.

Example: 我 = 7

a.	中	e.	张
b.	走	f.	寫
c.	去	g.	写
d.	張		

⇨ 3.4

4
Phrase order in the Mandarin sentence

1

Underline the main verb and bracket the main nouns (the ones that serve as subject and direct object) in the following Mandarin sentences.

> Example: ［他］给 ［我］［一本书］。
>
> ［他］給 ［我］［一本書］。
>
> [Tā] gěi [wǒ] [yī běn shū].
>
> [He] gave (gives) [me] [one book].

a. 我昨天跟朋友吃午饭了。

我昨天跟朋友吃午飯了。

Wǒ zuótiān gēn péngyou chī wǔfàn le.

Yesterday I ate lunch with friends.

b. 我的弟弟每天看电视。

我的弟弟每天看電視。

Wǒ de dìdi měitiān kàn diànshì.

My younger brother watches television every day.

c. 中国的大学生也上网吗？

中國的大學生也上網嗎？

Zhōngguó de dàxuéshēng yě shàng wǎng ma?

Do Chinese university students also surf the web?

d. 城里的书店有很多外国书。

城裏的書店有很多外國書。

Chéng lǐ de shūdiàn yǒu hěn duō wàiguó shū.

The bookstore in the city has a lot of foreign books.

e. 我今天下午在公园的门口等你。

我今天下午在公園的門口等你。

Wǒ jīntiān xiàwǔ zài gōngyuán de ménkǒu děng nǐ.

I'll wait for you at the park gate this afternoon.

⇨ 4.1

2 Underline the prepositional phrases in the following Mandarin sentences.

Example: 他<u>跟他的女朋友</u>吃晚饭。

他<u>跟他的女朋友</u>吃晚飯。

Tā <u>gēn tā de nǚ péngyou</u> chī wǎnfàn.

He eats dinner <u>with his girlfriend</u>.

a. 我给奶奶写信了。

我給奶奶寫信了。

Wǒ gěi nǎinai xiě xìn le.

I wrote a letter to my grandma.

b. 我对心理学很有兴趣。

我對心理學很有興趣。

Wǒ duì xīnlǐxué hěn yǒu xìngqù.

I am very interested in psychology.

c. 我很喜欢跟朋友去玩。

我很喜歡跟朋友去玩。

Wǒ hěn xǐhuan gēn péngyou qù wán.

I really like to go out with my friends.

d. 要是你忙，我可以替你做这件事。

要是你忙，我可以替你做這件事。

Yàoshi nǐ máng, wǒ kěyǐ tì nǐ zuò zhè jiàn shì.

If you are busy I can do that for you.

e. 你什么时候到我家来？

你甚麼時候到我家來？

Nǐ shénme shíhòu dào wǒ jiā lái?

When are you coming to my house?

⇨ 4.3

3 The following sentences and phrases include 'time when' expressions, location expressions, and prepositional phrases. Rewrite the Mandarin sentences, putting the phrases in the correct order to convey the meanings in the English translations.

a. 我学了中文去年在中国。

我學了中文去年在中國。

Wǒ xué le Zhōngwén qùnián zài Zhōngguó.

I studied Chinese last year in China.

b. 每天都我碰到他在学生中心。

每天都我碰到他在學生中心。

Měitiān dōu wǒ pèngdào tā zài xuésheng zhōngxīn.

I run into him every day in the student center.

c.　你想结婚跟什么样的人将来？

你想結婚跟甚麼樣的人將來？

Nǐ xiǎng jiéhūn gēn shénme yàng de rén jiānglái?

What kind of person do you plan to marry in the future?

d.　他打了电话昨天晚上给我。

他打了電話昨天晚上給我。

Tā dǎ le diànhuà zuótiān wǎnshang gěi wǒ.

Last night he phoned me.

e.　跟他他请我去看电影礼拜六。

跟他他請我去看電影禮拜六。

Gēn tā tā qǐng wǒ qù kàn diànyǐng lǐbài liù.

He invited me to go see a movie with him on Saturday.

⇨　4.3, 4.4, 4.5, 4.6

4　Insert the phrase in parentheses into the appropriate location in the sentence based on the English translation.

a.　我 ＿＿＿＿＿＿ 在日本住了 ＿＿＿＿＿＿。（五年）

Wǒ ＿＿＿＿＿＿ zài Rìběn zhùle ＿＿＿＿＿＿. (wǔ nián)

I lived in Japan <u>for five years</u>.

b.　我 ＿＿＿＿＿＿ 喜欢看电影 ＿＿＿＿＿＿。（也）

我 ＿＿＿＿＿＿ 喜歡看電影 ＿＿＿＿＿＿。（也）

Wǒ ＿＿＿＿＿＿ xǐhuān kàn diànyǐng ＿＿＿＿＿＿. (yě)

I like to watch movies <u>too</u>.

c.　我 ＿＿＿＿＿＿ 都回家 ＿＿＿＿＿＿。（每个周末）

我 ＿＿＿＿＿＿ 都回家 ＿＿＿＿＿＿。（每個週末）

Wǒ ＿＿＿＿＿＿ dōu huí jiā ＿＿＿＿＿＿. (měi gè zhōumò)

I go home <u>every weekend</u>.

d.　我 ＿＿＿＿＿＿ 工作 ＿＿＿＿＿＿。（在图书馆）

我 ＿＿＿＿＿＿ 工作 ＿＿＿＿＿＿。（在圖書館）

Wǒ ＿＿＿＿＿＿ gōngzuò ＿＿＿＿＿＿. (zài túshūguǎn)

I work <u>at the library</u>.

e.　你要不要 ＿＿＿＿＿＿ 去看电影 ＿＿＿＿＿＿？（跟我）

你要不要 ＿＿＿＿＿＿ 去看電影 ＿＿＿＿＿＿？（跟我）

Nǐ yào bu yào ＿＿＿＿＿＿ qù kàn diànyǐng ＿＿＿＿＿＿? (gēn wǒ)

Would you like to go to the movies with me?

f.　我 ＿＿＿＿＿＿ 没有兴趣 ＿＿＿＿＿＿。（对外国电影）

我 ＿＿＿＿＿＿ 沒有興趣 ＿＿＿＿＿＿。（對外國電影）

Wǒ ＿＿＿＿＿＿ méi yǒu xìngqù ＿＿＿＿＿＿. (duì wàiguó diànyǐng)

I'm not interested in foreign movies.

⇨　4.4, 4.5, 4.6. 4.7, 4.9

5

Rewrite these sentences, adding the negation word provided in parentheses into the sentence in the appropriate location.

a. 我喜欢吃臭豆腐。（不）

我喜歡吃臭豆腐。（不）

Wǒ xǐhuān chī chòu dòufu. (bù)

I don't like to eat stinky bean curd.

b. 我们想跟你一起去看电影。（不）

我們想跟你一起去看電影。（不）

Wǒmen xiǎng gēn nǐ yīqǐ qù kàn diànyǐng. (bù)

We don't want to go with you to see a movie.

c. 他在餐厅工作，他在宿舍工作。（不）

他在餐廳工作，他在宿舍工作。（不）

Tā zài cāntīng gōngzuò, tā zài sùshè gōngzuò. (bù)

He doesn't work in the cafeteria; he works in the dorm.

d. 他给我打电话。（没）

他給我打電話。（沒）

Tā gěi wǒ dǎ diànhuà. (méi)

He didn't phone me.

e. 他在法国念书，他在德国念书。（不）

他在法國唸書，他在德國唸書。（不）

Tā zài Fǎguó niànshū, tā zài Déguó niànshū. (bù)

He doesn't study in France, he studies in Germany.

⇨ 4.8

5
Nouns

1

Complete these sentences with the appropriate pronouns to match the English translations.

a. ＿＿＿＿＿＿ 得想办法解决这个问题。

＿＿＿＿＿＿ 得想辦法解決這個問題。

＿＿＿＿＿＿ **děi xiǎng bànfǎ jiějué zhège wèntí.**

We should think of a way to solve this problem.

b. ＿＿＿＿＿＿ 想请 ＿＿＿＿＿＿ 吃晚饭。

＿＿＿＿＿＿ 想請 ＿＿＿＿＿＿ 吃晚飯。

＿＿＿＿＿＿ **xiǎng qǐng** ＿＿＿＿＿＿ **chī wǎnfàn.**

We want to invite you to dinner.

c. ＿＿＿＿＿＿ 六点钟吃晚饭。

＿＿＿＿＿＿ 六點鐘吃晚飯。

＿＿＿＿＿＿ **liù diǎn zhōng chī wǎnfàn.**

They eat dinner at 6 p.m.

d. ＿＿＿＿＿＿ 不认识 ＿＿＿＿＿＿。

＿＿＿＿＿＿ 不認識 ＿＿＿＿＿＿。

＿＿＿＿＿＿ **bù rènshi** ＿＿＿＿＿＿.

I don't know them.

e. ＿＿＿＿＿＿ 听说 ＿＿＿＿＿＿ 很喜欢 ＿＿＿＿＿＿。

＿＿＿＿＿＿ 聽說 ＿＿＿＿＿＿ 很喜歡 ＿＿＿＿＿＿。

＿＿＿＿＿＿ **tīngshuō** ＿＿＿＿＿＿ **hěn xǐhuān** ＿＿＿＿＿＿.

I heard that he likes her a lot.

⇨ 5.2

2

Complete these sentences with the appropriate expressions to indicate possession.

a. ＿＿＿＿＿＿ 宿舍离图书馆很近。

＿＿＿＿＿＿ 宿舍離圖書館很近。

＿＿＿＿＿＿ **sùshè lí túshūguǎn hěn jìn.**

Her dorm is close to the library.

b. 这是 ＿＿＿＿＿＿ 朋友。

这是 ＿＿＿＿＿＿ 朋友。

Zhè shì ＿＿＿＿＿＿ péngyou.

This is my friend.

c. 他是 ＿＿＿＿＿＿ 弟弟。

Tā shì ＿＿＿＿＿＿ dìdi.

He is my younger brother.

d. ＿＿＿＿＿＿ 宿舍很大，＿＿＿＿＿＿ 很小。

＿＿＿＿＿＿ **sùshè hěn dà, ＿＿＿＿＿＿ hěn xiǎo.**

Your dormitory is very big. Ours is very small.

e. 那个手机是 ＿＿＿＿＿＿ 吗？

那個手機是 ＿＿＿＿＿＿ 嗎？

Nàge shǒujī shì ＿＿＿＿＿＿ ma?

Is that cell phone yours?

⇨ 5.2, 5.2.4

3

What does George say in these situations? Complete the sentences with the appropriate pronouns to match the English translations.

a. George introduces his friends from Chinese class to his mother:

＿＿＿＿＿＿ 都是 ＿＿＿＿＿＿ 的同学。＿＿＿＿＿＿ 是在中文课认识的。

＿＿＿＿＿＿ 都是 ＿＿＿＿＿＿ 的同學。＿＿＿＿＿＿ 是在中文課認識的。

＿＿＿＿＿＿ **dōu shì ＿＿＿＿＿＿ de tóngxué. ＿＿＿＿＿＿ shì zài Zhōngwén kè rènshi de.**

They are all my friends. I met them in Chinese class.

b. George is telling his friend about getting his girlfriend some flowers for her birthday today.

今天是 ＿＿＿＿＿＿ 的生日，＿＿＿＿＿＿ 很喜欢花，所以 ＿＿＿＿＿＿ 想买花送给

＿＿＿＿＿＿。＿＿＿＿＿＿ 可以陪我一起去买吗？

今天是 ＿＿＿＿＿＿ 的生日，＿＿＿＿＿＿ 很喜歡花，所以 ＿＿＿＿＿＿ 想買花送給

＿＿＿＿＿＿。＿＿＿＿＿＿ 可以陪我一起去買嗎？

Jīntiān shì ＿＿＿＿＿＿ de shēngrì, ＿＿＿＿＿＿ hěn xǐhuān huā, suǒyǐ ＿＿＿＿＿＿

xiǎng mǎi huā sòng gěi ＿＿＿＿＿＿. ＿＿＿＿＿＿ kěyǐ péi wǒ yīqǐ qù mǎi ma?

Today is her birthday, she likes flowers a lot, so I want to buy flowers to give to her. Can you go with me (accompany me) to buy flowers?

c. George wants to borrow Kevin's Chinese textbook but Kevin refuses.

George: ＿＿＿＿＿＿ 可以跟 ＿＿＿＿＿＿ 借中文课本吗？＿＿＿＿＿＿ 忘了带。

＿＿＿＿＿＿ 可以跟 ＿＿＿＿＿＿ 借中文課本嗎？＿＿＿＿＿＿ 忘了帶。

＿＿＿＿＿＿ **kěyǐ gēn ＿＿＿＿＿＿ jiè zhōngwén kèběn ma? ＿＿＿＿＿＿**

wàngle dài.

Can you loan me a Chinese textbook? I forgot to bring it.

Kevin: 不行！明天 ＿＿＿＿＿＿ 有考试，你 ＿＿＿＿＿＿ 去图书馆借！

不行！明天 ＿＿＿＿＿＿ 有考試，你 ＿＿＿＿＿＿ 去圖書館借！

Bù xíng! míngtiān ＿＿＿＿＿＿ yǒu kǎoshì, nǐ ＿＿＿＿＿＿ qù túshūguǎn jiè!

I can't. Tomorrow I have a test. Go to the library yourself to borrow it.

⇨ 5.2

6
Numbers

1 Write these numbers in Chinese characters or Pinyin.

Example: 72 → 七十二

a. 6   c. 11   e. 23   g. 55
b. 15   d. 36   f. 84   h. 97

⇨ 6.1

2 Rewrite these phone numbers in Chinese characters and Pinyin.

a. 6505-7823   c. 911   e. 852-2609-5498
b. 781-283-2191   d. 032-457-7639 f. 8529-6688

⇨ 6.1.1

3 Fill in the blank with 二 **èr** or 两/兩 **liǎng** as appropriate.

a. _____ 把椅子

   _____ **bǎ yǐ zi**
   two chairs

b. 十 _____ 张桌子
   十 _____ 張桌子
   shí _____ **zhāng zhuōzi**
   twelve tables

c. _____ 十个学生
   _____ 十個學生
   _____ **shí gè xué shēng**
   twenty students

d. _____ 天

   _____ **tiān**
   two days

e. _____ 年

   _____ **nián**
   two years

f. _____ 个星期
   _____ 個星期
   _____ **gè xīng qī**
   two weeks

g. _____ 個月

   _____ **gè yuè**
   two months

h. _____ 次

   _____ **cì**
   two times

i. 零点 _____
   零點 _____
   líng diǎn _____
   0.2

j. _____ 三百块钱
   _____ 三百塊錢
   _____ **sān bǎi kuài qián**
   two or three hundred dollars

⇨ 6.1

13

4 Complete the table by writing the Arabic numerals in Chinese and the Chinese numbers as Arabic numerals.

	Arabic numeral	Chinese number
a.	1,276	
b.		三万五千六百三十四
		三萬五千六百三十四
		sānwàn wǔqiān liùbǎi sānshísì
c.	256,758	
d.		九百六十万
		九百六十萬
		jiǔbǎi liù shí wàn
e.	1,893,683	
f.	3,027	
g.		三十七万零三十五
		三十七萬零三十五
		sānshí qī wàn líng sānshí wǔ
h.	279,005	
i.		三百零七万九千零一
		三百零七萬九千零一
		sānbǎi líng qī wàn jiǔqiān líng yī
j.		六千六百二十万九千三百八十
		六千六百二十萬九千三百八十
		liùqiān liùbǎi èrshí wàn jiǔqiān sānbǎi bāshí

⇨ 6.2

5 Complete the table by adding the corresponding ordinal numbers in English and Mandarin.

	English ordinal	Mandarin ordinal
a.	20th	
b.		第九
		dì jiǔ
c.	3rd	
d.		第十七
		dì shíqī
e.		第一
		dì yī
f.	12th	
g.	48th	
h.		第三十六
		dì sānshíliù

⇨ 6.4

6   Complete the table, expressing the Mandarin phrases in English and the English phrases in Mandarin.

	English	Mandarin
a.	50 more or less	
b.		两百以下
		兩百以下
		liǎng bǎi yǐxià
c.	almost 100	
d.		两三个学生
		兩三個學生
		liǎng sān gè xuésheng
e.	nine or ten students	
f.	less than 10	
g.		五十以上
		wǔshí yǐshàng
h.	more than a month	

⇨ 6.5

7   Complete the table by adding the corresponding fractions and percentages in Mandarin and English.

	English	Mandarin
a.	5/8	
b.		三分之一
		sān fēn zhīyī
c.	0.75	
d.		百分之三十
		bǎi fēn zhī sānshí
e.	8.33	
f.		零点零零三
		零點零零三
		líng diǎn líng líng sān
g.	4/5	
h.		七分之一
		qī fēn zhī yī

⇨ 6.6

8 Put 半 **bàn** in the right location in each phrase to express the English meaning.

> Example: 3½ minutes → 三分半 **sān fēn bàn**

a. 9½ hours [钟头/鐘頭 **zhōngtóu** hour]

b. 1½ cups of coffee [咖啡 **kāfēi** coffee, 杯/盃 **bēi** cup]

c. ½ month [月 **yuè** month]

d. 1½ months

e. ½ year [年 **nián** year]

f. 3½ years

g. ½ book

h. 2½ semesters [学期/學期 **xuéqī** semester]

i. 3½ bowls of rice [碗 **wǎn** bowl]

j. ½ glass of beer [啤酒 **píjiǔ** beer]

⇨ 6.6.4

9 Write out the discount in Chinese.

> Example: 20% off = 打八折 **dǎ bāzhé**

a. 30% off

b. 10% off

c. 50% off

d. 25% off

⇨ 6.6.6

10 Here is the original price and the discount. Compute the final price.

> Example: 100 元 **yuán** 1 折 **zhé** → 10 元 **yuán**

Original price	*Discount*	*Final price*
a. 30 元 **yuán**	9 折 **zhé**	
b. 160 元 **yuán**	8 折 **zhé**	
c. 80 元 **yuán**	5 折 **zhé**	
d. 500 元 **yuán**	2 折 **zhé**	
e. 1000 元 **yuán**	7.5 折 **zhé**	
f. 24000 元 **yuán**	6 折 **zhé**	

⇨ 6.6.6

7
Specifiers and demonstratives

1

Fill in each blank with a word from the following list to complete each sentence according to its English translation.

这/這 zhè, 这儿/這兒 zhèr, 这里/這裏 zhèlǐ
那 nà, 那儿/那兒 nàr, 那里/那裏 nàlǐ
哪儿/哪兒 nǎr, 哪里/哪裏 nǎlǐ

a. _____ 是我的, _____ 是你的。

_____ shì wǒ de, _____ shì nǐ de.

This is mine, that is yours.

b. 你周末去 _____ 了?

Nǐ zhōumò qù _____ le?

Where did you go this weekend?

c. 你知道我的中文书在 _____ 吗?

你知道我的中文書在 _____ 嗎?

Nǐ zhīdào wǒ de Zhōngwén shū zài _____ ma?

Do you know where my Chinese book is?

d. _____ 是我今天买的字典，很不错。

_____ 是我今天買的字典，很不錯。

_____ shì wǒ jīntiān mǎi de zìdiǎn, hěn bù cuò.

This is the dictionary I bought today. It's not bad.

e. 请问, 在 _____ 可以买到中国的邮票?

請問, 在 _____ 可以買到中國的郵票?

Qǐng wèn, zài _____ kěyǐ mǎidào Zhōngguo de yóupiào?

Excuse me, where can you buy Chinese stamps?

f. 下课以后我们都去小张 _____ , 你去吗?

下課以後我們都去小張 _____ , 你去嗎?

Xià kè yǐhòu wǒmen dōu qù xiǎo Zhāng _____ , nǐ qù ma?

After class we are all going to Xiao Zhang's. Are you going?

g. _____ 很安静, 地方也很大, 你可以搬过来。

_____ 很安靜, 地方也很大, 你可以搬過來。

_____ hěn ānjìng, dìfāng yě hěn dà, nǐ kěyǐ bānguòlái.

It is very peaceful here and also spacious. You can move in.

h.   _____ 是谁的电脑？怎放在 _____ 了？

      _____ 是誰的電腦？怎放在 _____ 了？

      _____ shì shéi de diànnǎo? Zěnme fàng zài _____ le?

      Whose computer is this? Why is it here?

i.   你 _____ 比我 _____ 安静。我们去你 _____ 学习吧。

      你 _____ 比我 _____ 安靜。我們去你 _____ 學習吧。

      Nǐ _____ bǐ wǒ _____ ānjìng. Wǒmen qù nǐ _____ xuéxí ba.

      Your place is more peaceful than mine. Let's go to your place to study.

j.   请问，图书馆在 _____，离 _____ 远吗？

      請問，圖書館在 _____，離 _____ 遠嗎？

      Qǐng wèn, túshūguǎn zài _____, lí _____ yuǎn ma?

      Excuse me, where is the library? Is it far from here?

⇨ 7

2

Complete the following dialogue by filling in each blank with a word from the list presented in (1) above.

George is talking to Kevin in Kevin's dorm.

George: 你周末去 (a)_____ 了？我给你打电话你不在。

          你週末去 (a)_____ 了？我給你打電話你不在。

          Nǐ zhōumò qù (a)_____ le? Wǒ gěi nǐ dǎ diànhuà nǐ bù zài.

          Where did you go this weekend? I phoned you but you weren't home.

Kevin: 我爸妈从北加州到 (b)_____ 来看我。我带他们出去玩，晚上在我女朋友 (c)_____ 吃饭。有事吗？

          我爸媽從北加州到 (b)_____ 來看我。我帶他們出去玩，晚上在我女朋友 (c)_____ 吃飯。有事嗎？

          Wǒ bà-mā cóng běi Jiāzhōu dào (b)_____ lái kàn wǒ. Wǒ dài tāmen chūqu wán, wǎnshang zài wǒ nǚ péngyou (c)_____ chī fàn. Yǒu shì ma?

          My dad and mom came here from northern California to see me. I took them out, and in the evening we ate at my girlfriend's place. What's up?

George: 你不是要找房子吗？我帮你找了一个，你看看。(George shows Kevin the housing ad.)

          你不是要找房子嗎？我幫你找了一個，你看看。

          Nǐ bù shì yào zhǎo fángzi ma? Wǒ bāng nǐ zhǎole yīgè, nǐ kàn kàn.

          Aren't you looking for a place to live? I've helped you to find one. Look.

Kevin: (d)_____ 个房子看起来不错，在 (e)_____？

          (d)_____ 個房子看起來不錯，在 (e)_____？

          (d)_____ gè fángzi kànqilai bùcuò, zài (e)_____?

          This house looks pretty good. Where is it?

George: 离 (f)_____ 很近，只要十分钟，现在就去吧！

離 (f)_____ 很近，只要十分鐘，現在就去吧！

Lí (f)_____ hěn jìn, zhǐ yào shí fēn zhōng, xiànzài jiù qù ba!

It's very near here, only 10 minutes away. Let's go now!

Kevin: 好。上次我去看的 (g)_____ 个房子太小了，希望 (h)_____ 个房子够大。

好。上次我去看的 (g)_____ 個房子太小了，希望 (h)_____ 個房子夠大。

Hǎo. Shàngcì wǒ qù kàn de (g)_____ gè fángzi tài xiǎo le, xīwàng (h)_____ gè fángzi gòu dà.

Okay. The house I went to look at last time was too small. I hope this house is big enough.

George: 那我们走吧。

那我們走吧。

Nà wǒmen zǒu ba.

Well then, let's go.

Kevin: 等一下，我怎么找不到我的手机，啊，我可能把手机忘在我女朋友 (i)_____ 了，我们先去拿。

等一下，我怎麼找不到我的手機，啊，我可能把手機忘在我女朋友 (i)_____ 了，我們先去拿。

Děng yīxià, wǒ zěnme zhǎobudào wǒ de shǒujī, a, wǒ kěnéng bǎ shǒujī wàng zài wǒ nǚ péngyou (i)_____ le, wǒmen xiān qù ná.

Wait a minute. How come I can't find my cell phone? I may have forgotten it at my girlfriend's place. First, let's go and get it.

George: 可是从 (j)_____ 去看房子比较方便，别拿手机了。

可是從 (j)_____ 去看房子比較方便，別拿手機了。

Kěshì cóng (j)_____ qù kàn fángzi bǐjiào fāngbiàn, bié ná shǒujī le.

But it's more convenient to go look at the house from here. Don't take your cell phone.

(George sees a cell phone across the room next to the TV.)

你說你的手機不見了，那，電視旁邊的 (k)_____ 個手機是誰的？

你说你的手机不见了，那，电视旁边的 (k)_____ 个手机是谁的？

Nǐ shuō nǐ de shǒujī bùjiàn le, nǎ, diànshì pángbiān de (k)_____ gè shǒujī shì shéi de?

You say your cell phone is lost. Then, whose cell phone is next to the television?

Kevin: (l)_____ 个？喔，太好了，(m)_____ 是我的手机！我们走吧。

(l)_____ 個？喔，太好了，(m)_____ 是我的手機！我們走吧。

(l)_____ gè? O, tài hǎo le, (m)_____ shì wǒ de shǒujī! Wǒmen zǒu ba.

Which one? Oh, great, that's my cell phone! Let's go.

⇨ 7

19

8
Classifiers

1
Rewrite these noun phrases, putting the specifiers, numbers, classifiers, and nouns in the correct order.

Example: 那学生三个 → 那三个学生
那學生三個   那三個學生
nà xuésheng sān gè   **nà sān gè xuésheng**

a. 这桌子两张
这桌子两张
這桌子兩張
zhè zhuōzi liǎng zhāng
these two desks

b. 这教授三位
這教授三位
zhè jiàoshòu sān wèi
these three professors

c. 两双那鞋子
兩雙那鞋子
liǎng shuāng nà xiézi
those two pairs of shoes

d. 啤酒那瓶四
píjiǔ nà píng sì
those four bottles of beer

e. 那中文三本书
那中文三本書
nà Zhōngwén sān běn shū
those three Chinese books

f. 毛衣这件两
毛衣這件兩
máoyī zhè jiàn liǎng
these two sweaters

g. 这两个学生英国

這兩個學生英國

zhè liǎng gè xuésheng Yīngguó

these two English students

h. 四文学那课门

四文學那課門

sì wénxué nà kè mén

those four literature classes

⇨ 8.1

2

Write these noun phrases in Chinese, using the appropriate classifier in each phrase.

. Example: those three students = 那三个学生/那三個學生

nà sān gè xuésheng

a. those ten students

b. these three days

c. that cell phone

d. those five photographs

e. this cup of coffee

f. that piece of paper

⇨ 8.1

3

A. Select the appropriate classifier from the following list in each scenario to complete these dialogues.

B. Translate the dialogues into English.

Scenario 1

张/張 zhāng, 件 jiàn, 把 bǎ, 个/個 gè, 条/條 tiáo, 枝 zhī, 本 běn

Kevin: 快开学了，我去买一些学校要用的东西，你看，这家店的东西真便宜：
我买了十 (a)_____ 铅笔、两 (b)_____ 字典、一 (c)_____ 背包，
两 (d)_____ 衣服、一 (e)_____ 裤子，一共才三十五块。他们的纸更
便宜，五百 (f)_____ 才四块五。

Kevin: 快開學了，我去買一些學校要用的東西，你看，這家店的東西真便宜：
我買了十 (a)_____ 鉛筆、兩 (b)_____ 字典、一 (c)_____ 背包，
兩 (d)_____ 衣服、一 (e)_____ 褲子，一共才三十五塊。他們的紙更
便宜，五百 (f)_____ 才四塊五。

Kevin: **Kuài kāixué le, wǒ qù mǎi yīxiē xuéxiào yào yòng de dōngxi,
nǐ kàn, zhè jiā diàn de dōngxi zhēn piányi: wǒ mǎile shí** (a)_____
qiānbǐ、liǎng (b)_____ **zìdiǎn、yī** (c)_____ **bēibāo, liǎng** (d)_____
yīfu、yī (e)_____ **kùzi, yīgòng cái sānshíwǔ kuài. Tāmen de zhǐ
gèng piányi, wǔbǎi** (f)_____ **cái sì kuài wǔ.**

Scenario 2: Tina and Lily are preparing for a dinner party in their backyard tonight.

张/張 zhāng, 件 jiàn, 把 bǎ, 个/個 gè, 条/條 tiáo, 枝 zhī, 本 běn, 瓶 píng

Tina: 桌椅都准备好了吗？你要的五 (a)_____ 面包、四 (b)_____ 酒我都买回来了。

Lily: 一共有十 (c)_____ 人，可能坐不下，我们还需要一 (d)_____ 桌子。还有，再拿三 (e)_____ 椅子过来。另外，每 (f)_____ 桌子上都要放一 (g)_____ 花。

Tina: 好。今天晚上你穿什么？我要穿我的红裙子。

Lily: 我打算穿我新买的那 (h)_____ 裙子，配那 (i)_____ 白色的上衣正好。

Tina: 桌椅都準備好了嗎？你要的五 (a)_____ 麵包、四 (b)_____ 酒我都買回來了。

Lily: 一共有十 (c)_____ 人，可能坐不下，我們還需要一 (d)_____ 桌子。還有，再拿三 (e)_____ 椅子過來。另外，每 (f)_____ 桌子上都要放一 (g)_____ 花。

Tina: 好。今天晚上你穿什麼？我要穿我的紅裙子。

Lily: 我打算穿我新買的那 (h)_____ 裙子，配那 (i)_____ 白色的上衣正好。

Tina: **Zhuōyǐ dōu zhǔnbèi hǎole ma? Nǐ yào de wǔ** (a)_____ **miànbāo, sì** (b)_____ **jiǔ wǒ dōu mǎi huílai le.**

Lily: **Yīgòng yǒu shí** (c)_____ **rén, kěnéng zuòbuxià, wǒmen hái xūyào yī** (d)_____ **zhuōzi. hái yǒu, zài ná sān** (e)_____ **yǐzi guòlái. lìngwài, měi** (f)_____ **zhuōzi shàng dōu yào fàng yī** (g)_____ **huā.**

Tina: **Hǎo. Jīntiān wǎnshang nǐ chuān shénme? Wǒ yào chuān wǒ de hóng qúnzi.**

Lily: **Wǒ dǎsuan chuān wǒ xīn mǎi de nà** (h)_____ **qúnzi, pèi nà** (i)_____ **báisè de shàngyī zhènghǎo.**

⇨ 8.2

4

Rewrite these prices in Chinese.

Example: $34.56 → 三十四块五毛六
三十四塊五毛六
sānshísì kuài wǔ máo liù

a. $13,459   d. $450.02

b. $2,850   e. $1,222

c. $.75   f. $96,457.45

⇨ 6, 8.5

5   Rewrite these prices in Arabic numerals.

Example: 三十四块五毛六   → $34.56

三十四塊五毛六

sānshísì kuài wǔ máo liù

a.   九十三块八毛一

九十三塊八毛一

jiǔshísān kuài bā máo yī

b.   四十五块〇三分

四十五塊〇三分

sì shí wǔ kuài líng sān fēn

c.   八块一

八塊一

bā kuài yī

d.   两千七百零三块钱

兩千七百零三塊錢

liǎng qiān qī bǎi líng sān kuài qián

e.   六块〇九分

六塊〇九分

liù kuài líng jiǔ fēn

f.   六毛六分

liù máo liù fēn

⇨   8.5

9
Noun phrases

1
Insert 的 **de** following each modifier in these noun phrases where possible.

Example: 我朋友小狗 → 我 (的) 朋友的小狗
wǒ péngyou xiáogǒu   wǒ (de) péngyou de xiáogǒu
my friend's puppy

a. 这三本书
  這三本書
  zhè sān běn shū
  these three books

b. 五本很有意思小说
  五本很有意思小說
  wǔ běn hěn yǒu yìsī xiǎoshuō
  five very interesting novels

c. 五张很便宜飞机票
  五張很便宜飛機票
  wǔ zhāng hěn piányi fēijī piào
  five very cheap airplane tickets

d. 那条蓝色裤子
  那條藍色褲子
  nà tiáo lánsè kùzi
  that pair of blue trousers

e. 那门中文课
  那門中文課
  nà mén Zhōngwén kè
  that Chinese class

f. 那六把很漂亮椅子
  nà liù bǎ hěn piàoliang yǐzi
  those six pretty chairs

g. 一瓶五十块钱葡萄酒
  一瓶五十塊錢葡萄酒
  yī píng wǔshí kuài qián pútao jiǔ
  one $50 bottle of wine

⇨ 9.1, 9.2

2 Put these words in the correct order to form Mandarin noun phrases that express the English translations.

a. 五 / 铅笔 / 我 / 枝 / 的
五 / 鉛筆 / 我 / 枝 / 的
wǔ / qiānbǐ / wǒ / zhī / de
my five pencils

b. 我的 / 朋友 / 一个
我的 / 朋友 / 一個
wǒ de / péngyou / yī gè
a friend of mine

c. 两个 / 他的 / 同学
兩個 / 他的 / 同學
liǎng gè / tā de / tóngxué
two classmates of his

d. 三位 / 的 / 老师 / 我们
三位 / 的 / 老師 / 我們
sān wèi / de / lǎoshī / wǒmen
our three teachers

e. 四本书 / 我的
四本書 / 我的
sì běn shū / wǒ de
my four books

f. 椅子 / 那把 / 他的
yǐzi / nà bǎ / tā de
that chair of his

g. 女孩子 / 的 / 喜欢 / 旅游
女孩子 / 的 / 喜歡 / 旅游
nǚháizi / de / xǐhuan / lǚyóu
a girl who likes to travel

h. 两张飞机票 / 的 / 很贵
兩張飛機票 / 的 / 很貴
liǎng zhāng fēijī piào / de / hěn guì
two expensive airplane tickets

i. 那位 / 的 / 很高 / 老师 / 德文
那位 / 的 / 很高 / 老師 / 德文
nà wèi / de / hěn gāo / lǎoshī / Déwén
that tall German language teacher

j. 很好的朋友 / 的 / 我
    hěn hǎo de / péngyou / de / wǒ
    a good friend of mine

k. 毛衣 / 一件 / 的 / 黄颜色
    毛衣 / 一件 / 的 / 黃顏色
    máoyī / yījiàn / de / huáng yánsè
    a yellow sweater

l. 中国地图 / 一块钱的
    中國地圖 / 一塊錢的
    Zhōngguó dìtú / yīkuài qián de
    a $1 Chinese map

⇨ 5.1, 9.1, 9.2

3 Translate the following into English.

a. 谁的中文书?
    誰的中文書?
    Shéi de Zhōngwén shū?

b. 谁写的中文书?
    誰寫的中文書?
    Shéi xiě de Zhōngwén shū?

c. 你什么时候买的中文书?
    你甚麼時候買的中文書?
    Nǐ shénme shíhòu mǎi de Zhōngwén shū?

d. 你在哪儿买的中文书?
    你在哪兒買的中文書?
    Nǐ zài nǎr mǎi de Zhōngwén shū?

e. 马老师写的哪本书?
    馬老師寫的哪本書?
    Mǎ lǎoshī xiě de nǎ běn shū?

f. 你喜欢的什么书?
    你喜歡的甚麼書?
    Nǐ xǐhuan de shénme shū?

g. 多少钱的书?
    多少錢的書?
    Duōshǎo qián de shū?

⇨ 9.2.1

4 Translate these noun phrases into Mandarin.

a. these three books
f. these newspapers
b. those two students
g. this pair of pants
c. those five pens
h. these three chairs
d. these ten notebooks
i. those five desks
e. this piece of paper
j. that man

⇨ 5.1, 9.1, 9.2.1

5 Translate these noun phrases into Mandarin.

a. three people who study Chinese

b. the movie that I saw yesterday

c. Chinese characters that I can write

d. the man who was talking with you

e. the man who was talking with you this morning

f. the man who was talking with you in the cafeteria this morning

g. the shoes that I bought

h. the shoes that I bought in Italy

⇨ 9.2.1.5, 9.2.1.6, 9.2.1.7, 9.4

6 Explain each of the following phrases in Mandarin using a noun with a modifier.

> Example: '司机' 是什么？ '司机' 就是开车的人。
> '司機' 是什麼？ '司機' 就是開車的人。
> 'Sījī' shì shénme? 'Sījī' jiù shì kāi chē de rén.
> A 'sījī' is a person who drives cars.

a. '图书馆' 是什么地方？ / '圖書館' 是什麼地方？ 'Túshūguǎn' (library) shì shénme dìfang?

b. '同屋' 是什么？ / '同屋' 是什麼？ 'Tóngwū' (roommate) shì shénme?

c. '厨师' 是什么？ / '廚師' 是什麼？ 'Chúshī' (chef, cook) shì shénme?

d. '医生' 是什么？ / '醫生' 是什麼？ 'Yīshēng' (doctor) shì shénme?

e. '学校' 是什么地方？ / '學校' 是什麼地方？ 'Xuéxiào' (school) shì shénme dìfang?

⇨ 9.2

10
Adjectival verbs

Ask yes–no questions using these subjects and adjectival verbs.

Example: 你累。　→　你累不累？　　or　你累吗？
　　　　　　　　　　　　　　　　　　　你累嗎？

　　　　　Nǐ lèi.　　**Nǐ lèi bù lèi?**　　**Nǐ lèi ma?**

a.　他很忙。
　　Tā hěn máng.
　　He's busy.

b.　那本书有意思。
　　那本書有意思。
　　Nà běn shū yǒu yìsi.
　　That book is interesting.

c.　飞机票很贵。
　　飛機票很貴。
　　Fēijī piào hěn guì.
　　Airplane tickets are expensive.

d.　那件事情很复杂。[事情 **shìqing** situation, 复杂/複雜 **fùzá** complicated]
　　那件事情很複雜。
　　Nà jiàn shìqing hěn fùzá.
　　That situation is complicated.

e.　她的男朋友很好看。
　　Tā de nán péngyou hěn hǎo kàn.
　　Her boyfriend is good-looking.

f.　他们很用功。
　　他們很用功。
　　Tāmen hěn yònggōng.
　　They are hardworking.

g.   他很有钱。

他很有錢。

Tā hěn yǒu qián.

He is rich.

h.   那辆车很快。

那輛車很快。

Nà liàng chē hěn kuài.

That car is fast.

⇨   10.2

2   Answer 'no' to each of the questions you have formed in (1) above.

⇨   10.2

3   Describe 王明 **Wáng Míng** in Mandarin using intensifiers and the adjectival verbs provided. The Mandarin translations of the adjectival verbs follow each sentence.

Example: He is somewhat lazy.   →   他相当懒。

他相當懶。

Tā xiāngdāng lǎn.

a.   He is very <u>tall</u>. [高 **gāo**]

b.   He is extremely <u>good looking</u>. [帅 **shuài**]

c.   He is rather <u>smart</u>. [聪明/聰明 **cōngming**]

d.   He is too <u>fat</u>. [胖 **pàng**]

e.   He is quite <u>polite</u>. [客气/客氣 **kèqi**]

f.   He is really <u>interesting</u>. [有意思 **yǒu yìsī**]

⇨   10.3

4   周利 **Zhōu Lì** exceeds 王明 **Wáng Míng** in every property listed below. Describe 周利 **Zhōu Lì** and 王明 **Wáng Míng**, using the example as your model.

Example: 快 **kuài** fast   →   王明很快。周利更快。

Wáng Míng hěn kuài. Zhōu Lì gèng kuài.

a.   聪明/聰明 **cōngming** smart

b.   有本事 **yǒu běnshi** talented

c.   帅/帥 **shuài** handsome

d.   和气/和氣 **héqi** nice

⇨   10.3, 10.5

5 王大明 Wáng Dàmíng, 李家同 Lǐ Jiātóng and 张天一/張天一 Zhāng Tiānyī are best friends at school. Complete the following information about them based on the chart below.

	Height	GPA	Size of their rooms	Distance – home to school
王大明 Wáng Dàmíng	5'11"	4.00	150 sq. ft.	2 miles
李家同 Lǐ Jiātóng	6'2"	3.86	200 sq. ft.	1.5 miles
张天一/張天一 Zhāng Tiānyī	5'11"	3.50	200 sq. ft	5 miles

a. 王大明和张天一 _____ 高。

　　王大明和张天一 _____ 高。

　　Wáng Dàmíng hé Zhāng Tiānyī _____ gāo.

b. 李家同 _____ 高。

　　Lǐ Jiātóng _____ gāo.

c. 張天一的家离学校 _____。[学校/學校 xuéxiào school]

　　張天一的家離學校 _____。

　　Zhāng Tiānyī de jiā lí xuéxiào _____.

d. 王大明的房间 _____。

　　王大明的房間 _____。

　　Wáng Dàmíng de fángjiān _____.

e _____ 一样大。

　　_____ 一樣大。

　　_____ yīyàng dà.

⇨ 10.3, 10.5, 10.6

11
Stative verbs

1 Negate these sentences.

    Example: 我喜欢他。   →   我不喜欢他。

              我喜歡他。   我不喜歡他。

              Wǒ xǐhuan tā.   **Wǒ bù xǐhuan tā.**

a.   他想吃中国饭。

     他想吃中國飯。

     Tā xiǎng chī Zhōngguó fàn.

     He wants to eat Chinese food.

b.   他怕陌生人。

     Tā pà mòshēng rén.

     He is very afraid of strangers.

c.   我懂他的意思。

     Wǒ dǒng tā de yìsi.

     I understand what he means.

d.   我很爱他。我愿意嫁给他。

     我很愛他。我願意嫁給他。

     Wǒ hěn ài tā. Wǒ yuànyi jià gěi tā. (negate both sentences)

     I love him. I am willing to marry him.

e.   他像他爷爷。

     他像他爺爺。

     Tā xiàng tā yéye.

     He resembles his grandfather.

⇨   11.1

2

Introduce 张小春小姐/張小春小姐 **Miss Zhāng Xiǎo Chūn** in complete Mandarin sentences including the following information.

a. family name
b. given name
c. age: 18 years old
d. occupation: student, studies at the university
e. possessions: doesn't have a car, has a cat
f. likes history a lot
g. fears dogs
h. really wants to go to China

⇨ 11.1, 11.2, 11.4, 11.5, 11.6, 11.7

3

Complete each sentence with 是 **shì**, 姓 **xìng**, 有 **yǒu**, or 在 **zài** as appropriate.

a. 图书馆 _____ 公园的北边。
   圖書館 _____ 公園的北邊。
   Túshūguǎn _____ gōngyuán de běibiān.
   The library is north of the park.

b. 图书馆里 _____ 很多外文字典。
   圖書館裏 _____ 很多外文字典。
   Túshūguǎn lǐ _____ hěn duō wàiwén zìdiǎn.
   In the library there are a lot of foreign language dictionaries.

c. 她 _____ 张。
   她 _____ 張。
   Tā _____ Zhāng.
   Her name is Zhang.

d. 她 _____ 张校长。
   她 _____ 張校長。
   Tā _____ Zhāng xiàozhǎng.
   She is Principal Zhang.

e. 她 _____ 她的办公室。
   她 _____ 她的辦公室。
   Tā _____ tā de bàngōngshì.
   She is in her office.

f. 这本书很 _____ 意思。
   這本書很 _____ 意思。
   Zhè běn shū hěn _____ yìsi.
   This book is very interesting.

g. 这本书 _____ 我的。要是你 _____ 兴趣我可以借给你。
   這本書 _____ 我的。要是你 _____ 興趣我可以借給你。
   Zhè běn shū _____ wǒ de. Yàoshi nǐ _____ xìngqù wǒ kěyǐ jiè gěi nǐ.
   This book is mine. If you are interested I can loan it to you.

⇨ 11.4, 11.5, 11.6, 11.7

4

Talking about past states. Mr. Wang and Ms. Li went to their 20 year high school reunion and had a great time catching up. Complete the dialogue based on the English translation.

王先生：　　　　　　　我记得你以前 (a)_____

　　　　　　　　　　　_____

王先生：　　　　　　　我記得你以前 (a)_____

　　　　　　　　　　　_____

Wáng Xiānsheng:　　**Wǒ jìdé nǐ yǐqián** (a)_____

　　　　　　　　　　　_____

Mr. Wang:　　　　　　I remember you used to <u>have a dog right? Your house was next to our school. Also you like chemistry and history a lot.</u>

李小姐：　　　　　　　你怎么还记得？那是二十多年前的事情了。

李小姐：　　　　　　　你怎麼還記得？那是二十多年前的事情了。

Lǐ Xiǎojiě:　　　　**Nǐ zěnme hái jìdé? Nà shì èrshíduō nián qián de shìqing le.**

Ms. Li:　　　　　　　How can you still remember? It was more than 20 years ago.

王先生：　　　　　　　我当然记得！我还记得你从前 (b)_____，
　　　　　　　　　　　现在呢？

王先生：　　　　　　　我當然記得！我還記得你從前 (b)_____，
　　　　　　　　　　　現在呢？

Wáng Xiānsheng:　　**Wǒ dāngrán jìdé! Wǒ hái jìdé nǐ cóngqián**
　　　　　　　　　　　(b)_____**, xiànzài ne?**

Mr. Wang:　　　　　　Of course I do! I also remember that you used to <u>be really afraid of driving [you most feared driving]</u>. How about now?

李小姐(大笑)：　　　　那是从前，现在当然 (c)_____。

李小姐(大笑)：　　　　那是從前，現在當然 (c)_____。

Lǐ Xiǎojiě (Dà xiào):　　**Nà shì cóngqián, xiànzài dāngrán**
　　　　　　　　　　　(c)_____.

Ms. Li (Laughing out loud):　That was before. Of course (I'm) <u>not afraid anymore.</u>

12
Modal verbs

1 Fill in the blanks with 会/會 **huì**, 能 **néng**, or 可以 **kěyǐ** as appropriate.

a. 明天 _____ 不 _____ 下雪?

   Míngtiān _____ bù _____ xià xuě?

   Will it snow tomorrow?

b. 你想她明天 _____ 来吗?

   你想她明天 _____ 來嗎?

   Nǐ xiǎng tā míngtiān _____ lái ma?

   Do you think she will come tomorrow?

c. 你 _____ 不 _____ 跑马拉松?

   你 _____ 不 _____ 跑馬拉松?

   Nǐ _____ bù _____ pǎo mǎlāsōng?

   Are you able to run a marathon?

d. 你 _____ 不 _____ 打中文字?

   Nǐ _____ bù _____ dǎ Zhōngwén zì?

   Can you type in Chinese?

e. 我 _____ 借你的车吗?

   我 _____ 借你的車嗎?

   Wǒ _____ jiè nǐ de chē ma?

   Can I borrow your car?

f. 你 _____ 不 _____ 帮我的忙?

   你 _____ 不 _____ 幫我的忙?

   Nǐ _____ bù _____ bāng wǒ de máng?

   Can you help me?

g. 我 _____ 看电视吗?

   我 _____ 看電視嗎?

   Wǒ _____ kàn diànshì ma?

   Can I watch television?

h. 你 _____ 说法语吗?

   你 _____ 說法語嗎?

   Nǐ _____ shuō Fáyǔ ma?

   Can you speak French?

⇨ 12.1, 12.2, 12.3

2

Select the most appropriate expression of obligation or prohibition from the following list to complete each sentence.

应该/應該 yīnggāi, 应当/應當 yīngdāng, 得 děi, 必得 bìděi,
必须/必須 bìxū, 不应该/不應該 bù yīnggāi, 不必 bù bì, 不许/不許 bù xǔ

a. 你们今天晚上 _____ 作功课。
你們今天晚上 _____ 作功課。
Nǐmen jīntiān wǎnshang _____ zuò gōngkè.
You don't have to do homework tonight.

b. 你 _____ 每天晚上睡八个小时的觉。
你 _____ 每天晚上睡八個小時的覺。
Nǐ _____ měitiān wǎnshang shuì bā gè xiǎoshí de jiào.
You should sleep for eight hours every night.

c. 你 _____ 边吃东西边说话。
你 _____ 邊吃東西邊說話。
Nǐ _____ biān chī dōngxi biān shuō huà.
You shouldn't talk while eating.

d. 你 _____ 八月二十日以前付学费。
你 _____ 八月二十日以前付學費。
Nǐ _____ bāyuè èrshí rì yǐqián fù xuéfèi.
You have to pay tuition by August 20th.

e. 你 _____ 马上回家。
你 _____ 馬上回家。
Nǐ _____ mǎshàng huí jiā.
You must go home immediately.

f. 你 _____ 看那本书。
你 _____ 看那本書。
Nǐ _____ kàn nà běn shū.
You don't have to read that book.

g. 你 _____ 在这儿停车。
你 _____ 在這兒停車。
Nǐ _____ zài zhèr tíng chē.
You can't park here.

h. 在饭馆 _____ 抽烟。
在飯館 _____ 抽煙。
Zài fànguǎn _____ chōu yān.
Smoking is not permitted in restaurants.

⇨ | 12.4, 12.5

3

Complete each sentence to match the English translation by adding the appropriate expression of obligation and prohibition.

Example: 请你的朋友吃晚饭　→　你应该请你的朋友吃晚饭。

請你的朋友吃晚飯　　　你應該請你的朋友吃晚飯。

qǐng nǐ de péngyou　　**Nǐ yīnggāi qǐng nǐ de péngyou chī**

chī wǎnfàn　　**wǎnfàn.**

You should invite your friends to dinner.

a. 对老师客气

對老師客氣

duì lǎoshī kèqi

You should be polite to your teachers.

b. 每天上课

每天上課

měitiān shàng kè

You have to attend class every day.

c. 每天晚上学中文

每天晚上學中文

měitiān wǎnshang xué Zhōngwén

You ought to study Chinese every night.

d. 买一本中文字典

買一本中文字典

mǎi yī běn Zhōngwén zìdiǎn

You must buy a Chinese dictionary.

e. 看那个电影

看那個電影

kàn nàge diànyǐng

You don't have to see that movie.

⇨ 12.4, 12.5

4

Express these obligations and prohibitions in Mandarin.

a. You should eat breakfast every morning.

b. You must lock the door. [锁门/鎖門 **suǒ mén** to lock the door]

c. You should not drink too much coffee.

d. You should not read other people's letters.

e. You do not have to wait for me.

f. You have to find a job.

g. You don't have to go home early.

h. You are not permitted to smoke in a hospital.

⇨ 12.4, 12.5

5 Jack's family recently became the host family for Meiling, an exchange student from China. Today, Jack is showing Meiling around in the neighborhood. He tries to explain in Mandarin the signs that they pass. Fill in the blanks with the appropriate modal verb to complete his sentences.

a. Tuition must be paid by the 5th of the month.

每个月五号以前 _____ 交学费。

每個月五號以前 _____ 交學費。

Měi ge yuè wǔ hào yǐqián _____ jiāo xué fèi.

b. Cell phone use prohibited while driving.

开车的时候 _____ 用手机。

開車的時候 _____ 用手機。

Kāi chē de shíhou _____ yòng shǒujī.

c. Do not touch.

_____ 碰。

_____ **pèng.**

d. No food allowed.

_____ 吃东西。

_____ 吃東西。

_____ **chī dōngxi.**

e. Free parking with any purchase.

买东西就 _____ 免费停车。

買東西就 _____ 免費停車。

Mǎi dōngxi jiù _____ miǎnfèi tíng chē.

f. French native speaker needed.

我们需要 _____ 说法语的人。

我們需要 _____ 說法語的人。

Wǒmen xūyào _____ shuō Fǎyǔ de rén.

6 Middle schooler 茉莉 **Mòlì** Molly has invited some friends to her house tomorrow. Too bad some of them can't make it. Fill in the blanks with appropriate modal verbs to complete their replies.

a. 杰克： 对不起，茉莉，明天我 _____ 去，我有足球比赛。

傑克： 對不起，茉莉，明天我 _____ 去，我有足球比賽。

Jiékè: Duìbuqǐ, Mòlì, míngtiān wǒ _____ qù, wǒ yǒu zúqiú bǐsài.

Jake: Sorry, Molly, I can't go tomorrow. I have a soccer game.

b. 海伦： 对不起，茉莉，我觉得我 _____ 去，因为我的报告还没有写完。

海倫： 對不起，茉莉，我覺得我 _____ 去，因為我的報告還沒有寫完。

Hǎilún: Duìbuqǐ, Mòlì, wǒ juéde wǒ _____ qù, yīnwèi wǒ de bàogào hái méi yǒu xiě wán.

Helen: Sorry, Molly, I don't think I should go because I haven't finished my report.

c. 艾米： 对不起，茉莉，我妈妈 _____ 我出去，因为我上个考试考得
太糟糕了。

艾米： 對不起，茉莉，我媽媽 _____ 我出去，因為我上個考試考得
太糟糕了。

Àimǐ: **Duìbuqǐ, Mòlì, wǒ māma _____ wǒ chūqù, yīnwèi shàng gè
kǎoshì kǎo de tài zāogāo le.**

Amy: Sorry, Molly. My mom isn't letting me go out because I did very
poorly on my last test.

13
Action verbs

1

Complete these sentences by adding 过/過 **guo** or 了 **le** according to the English translation.

a. 我去 _____ 中国，没去 _____ 日本。
   我去 _____ 中國，沒去 _____ 日本。
   Wǒ qù _____ Zhōngguó, méi qù _____ Rìběn.
   I've been to China, I haven't been to Japan.

b. 我骑 _____ 一次摩托车。
   我騎 _____ 一次摩托車。
   Wǒ qí _____ yīcì mótuō chē.
   I've ridden on a motorcycle once before.

c. 我们已经看 _____ 那个电影，不要再看了。
   我們已經看 _____ 那個電影，不要再看了。
   Wǒmen yǐjing kàn _____ nàge diànyǐng, bù yào zài kàn le.
   We've seen that movie before. We don't have to see it again.

d. 我从来没喝 _____ 酒。
   我從來沒喝 _____ 酒。
   Wǒ cónglái méi hē _____ jiǔ.
   I've never drunk alcohol before.

e. 他跟他朋友谈 _____ 一个小时。
   他跟他朋友談 _____ 一個小時。
   Tā gēn tā péngyou tán _____ yī gè xiǎoshí.
   He and his friends talked for an hour.

f. 我吃 _____ 一次日本饭。
   我吃 _____ 一次日本飯。
   Wǒ chī _____ yīcì Rìběn fàn.
   I've eaten Japanese food once.

g. 你大学毕业 _____ 没有？
   你大學畢業 _____ 沒有？
   Nǐ dàxué bìyè _____ méi yǒu?
   Have you graduated from university?

⇨ 13.1, 13.2, 33.1, 33.6

2 Describe 周利 **Zhōu Lì**'s day in complete Mandarin sentences, using 了 **le** or 没 **méi** as appropriate.

a. He didn't eat breakfast.

b. He went to class.

c. He studied in the library.

d. He ate lunch.

e. He didn't see his girlfriend.

f. He saw a movie.

g. He went to the bookstore.

h. He didn't buy a book.

⇨ 13.1, 13.3.2, 33.1, 33.3

3 周利 **Zhōu Lì** asked his friends what they did last night. Translate their answers into Mandarin. Be sure to include the object of the verb in your translations.

> 周利：你昨天晚上作了什么？
>
> 周利：你昨天晚上作了甚麼？
>
> **Zhōu Lì: Nǐ zuótiān wǎnshang zuò le shénme?**
>
> Example: 小郭 **xiǎo Guō**: I danced. → 我跳舞了。
>
> **Wǒ tiào wǔ le.**

a. 小王 **Xiǎo Wáng**: I read.

b. 小高 **Xiǎo Gāo**: I sang with friends.

c. 小毛 **Xiǎo Máo**: I studied at the library.

d. 小林 **Xiǎo Lín**: I painted two paintings.

e. 小何 **Xiǎo Hé**: I watched TV for two hours.

⇨ 13.4.2, 13.5.1, 39.1.2

4 莊雄 **Zhuāng Xióng** explains to his friend how hectic his life has been and what he did last night, which is why he slept through the alarm and missed this morning's classes. Write a paragraph based on the English translation of his explanation. Below is a list of verbs you can use.

Verbs: 工作 **gōngzuò** 'work,' 开车/開車 **kāi chē** 'drive a car,'

洗衣服 **xǐ yīfu** 'wash clothes,' 做功课/做功課 **zuò gōngkè** 'do homework,'

学习/學習 **xuéxí** 'study,' 睡觉/睡覺 **shuì jiào** 'sleep'

Zhuang Xiong: I've been very busy every day recently. I work four hours a day after class and drive an hour to go back home every day. Last night after I got home, I did laundry for half an hour, did my homework for three hours and studied for 2 hours. I only slept 2½ hours last night. I'm extremely tired now!

莊雄：我最近每天都很忙。

Zhuāng Xióng: Wǒ zuì jìn měitiān dōu hěn máng.

_____

_____

_____

_____

_____

_____

➪ 13.4.2, 13.5.1

5

Mike has some very interesting friends. Translate the following sentences about his friends into Mandarin using the durative aspect particle 着/著 **zhe.**

Amy eats standing up:_____

Beth sleeps with the door open: _____

There's a long coat (长大衣/長大衣 **cháng dàyī**) hanging on Carmen's bedroom wall: _____

There are 12 stone lions (石狮子/石獅子 **shí shīzi**) on Derek's desk:

_____

Emily can only sing sitting down: _____

Frank only wears pajamas (睡衣 **shuì yī**) to school: _____

➪ 13.6.1

14
Prepositions and prepositional phrases

1 Complete each sentence by supplying the appropriate preposition.

a.　陈老师有事。张老师 _____ 她教课。

　　陳老師有事。張老師 _____ 她教課。

　　Chén lǎoshī yǒu shì. Zhāng lǎoshī _____ tā jiāo kè.

　　Teacher Chen had something to do. Teacher Zhang taught a class for her.

b.　从宿舍门口 _____ 南走。

　　從宿舍門口 _____ 南走。

　　Cóng sùshè ménkǒu _____ nán zǒu.

　　Go south from the entrance to the dormitory.

c.　你应该 _____ 客人很客气。

　　你應該 _____ 客人很客氣。

　　Nǐ yīnggāi _____ kèren hěn kèqi.

　　You should be polite to guests.

d.　别 _____ 我开玩笑。

　　别 _____ 我開玩笑。

　　Bié _____ wǒ kāi wánxiào.

　　Don't play a joke on me.

e.　我 _____ 环境保护很有兴趣。

　　我 _____ 環境保護很有興趣。

　　Wǒ _____ huánjìng bǎohù hěn yǒu xìngqù.

　　I am very interested in environmental protection.

f.　他 _____ 家吃饭，不愿意 _____ 饭馆去吃饭。

　　他 _____ 家吃飯，不願意 _____ 飯館去吃飯。

　　Tā _____ jiā chī fàn, bù yuànyi _____ fànguǎn qù chī fàn.

　　He eats at home. He isn't willing to go to a restaurant to eat.

g.　你 _____ 她说什么了？

　　你 _____ 她說甚麼了？

　　Nǐ _____ tā shuō shénme le?

　　What did you say to her?

h.　他站在门口 _____ 外看。
　　他站在門口 _____ 外看。
　　Tā zhàn zài ménkǒu _____ wài kàn.
　　He stands at the doorway looking out.

⇨　14.2

2

Rewrite each sentence to include the prepositional phrase.

　　Example: 我跳舞了。 [with friends]　→　我跟朋友跳舞了。
　　　　　　 Wǒ tiào wǔ le.　　　　　　　**Wǒ gēn péngyou tiào wǔ le.**

a.　我打电话了。 [to my friend]
　　我打電話了。
　　Wǒ dǎ diànhuà le.
　　I called my friend.

b.　她请我来吃饭。 [to her house]
　　她請我來吃飯。
　　Tā qǐng wǒ lái chī fàn.
　　She invited me to come to her house to eat.

c.　我念书了。 [at the library]
　　我念書了。
　　Wǒ niàn shū le.
　　I studied at the library.

d.　我到她家去了。 [from the library]
　　Wǒ dào tā jiā qù le.
　　I went from the library to her house.

e.　我买了糖。 [for her]
　　我買了糖。
　　Wǒ mǎi le táng.
　　I bought her candy.

f.　她介绍她的父母。 [to me]
　　她介紹她的父母。
　　Tā jièshào tā de fùmǔ.
　　She introduced me to her parents.

g.　后来，我看电影了。 [with her]
　　後來，我看電影了。
　　Hòulái, wǒ kàn diànyǐng le.
　　Afterwards, I saw a movie with her.

h.　我们看电影了。 [in the study]
　　我們看電影了。
　　Wǒmen kàn diànyǐng le.
　　We watched the movie in the study.

⇨　14.1, 14.2

3

Introduce the new English teacher to your classmates. Use a preposition in each sentence except (a).

a. Say that this is our new teacher.

b. Say that you want to introduce him to you.

c. Say that he has just come from the United States.

d. Say that he is teaching English at our school this year.

e. Say that he is very interested in Chinese culture.

f. Say that he wants to travel everywhere [各地 **gè dì** everywhere].

g. Say that he also hopes to interact with Chinese people. [来往/來往 **láiwǎng** to interact]

⇨ 14.1, 14.2

4

My roommate is really mad today. He won't do anything I ask him. Here are my requests. Provide my roommate's responses, as in the example.

Example: A: 今天跟我们去看电影吧。

今天跟我們去看電影吧。

Jīntiān gēn women qù kàn diànyǐng ba.

How about going to watch a movie with us today.

B: 今天我不跟你们去看电影。

今天我不跟你們去看電影。

Jīntiān wǒ bù gēn nǐmen qù kàn diànyǐng.

I am not going to watch a movie with you today.

a. A: 下课以后，请你给我打电话。

下課以後，请你給我打電話。

Xià kè yǐhòu, qǐng nǐ gěi wǒ dǎ diànhuà.

Call me when class is over.

B: _____。

b. A: 替我把书还给图书馆。

替我把書還給圖書館。

Tì wǒ bǎ shū huángěi túshūguǎn.

Return the book to the library for me.

B: _____。

c. A: 跟老师说我病了。

跟老師說我病了。

Gēn lǎoshī shuō wǒ bìng le.

Tell the teacher I am sick.

B: _____。

d. A: 你在餐厅等我好吗？

你在餐廳等我好嗎？

Nǐ zài cāntīng děng wǒ hǎo ma?

Will you please wait for me at the dining hall?

B: _____。

e. A: 你把你的书拿走。

你把你的書拿走。

Nǐ bǎ nǐ de shū názǒu.

Move your book away.

B: _____。

f. A: 请你给我买午饭。

請你給我賣午飯。

Qǐng nǐ gěi wǒ mǎi wǔfan.

Please buy lunch for me.

B: _____。

⇨ 14.1, 14.2

15
Adverbs

1

Complete these sentences by filling in the blanks with 也 yě, 都 dōu, 还/還 hái, 就 jiù, 只 zhǐ, or 才 cái.

a. 小王会说英国话，＿＿＿＿＿ 会说日本话。

小王會說英國話，＿＿＿＿＿ 會說日本話。

Xiǎo Wáng huì shuō Yīngguó huà, ＿＿＿＿＿ huì shuō Rìběn huà.

Little Wang can speak English and he can also speak Japanese.

b. 他去过英国 ＿＿＿＿＿ 没去过日本。

他去過英國 ＿＿＿＿＿ 沒去過日本。

Tā qùguò Yīngguó ＿＿＿＿＿ méi qùguò Rìběn.

He has been to Britain but he has not yet been to Japan.

c. 他在英国 ＿＿＿＿＿ 住了一个月。

他在英國 ＿＿＿＿＿ 住了一個月。

Tā zài Yīngguó ＿＿＿＿＿ zhù le yī gè yuè.

He has only lived in Britain for a month.

d. 他说英国，日本 ＿＿＿＿＿ 有意思。

他說英國，日本 ＿＿＿＿＿ 有意思。

Tā shuō Yīngguó, Rìběn ＿＿＿＿＿ yǒu yìsī.

He says that Britain and Japan are both interesting.

e. 日本人会写汉字 ＿＿＿＿＿ 会看中文报纸。

日本人會寫漢字 ＿＿＿＿＿ 會看中文報紙。

Rìběn rén huì xiě Hàn zì ＿＿＿＿＿ huì kàn Zhōngwén bàozhǐ.

Japanese people can write Chinese characters and they can read Chinese newspapers.

f. 英文不用汉字，＿＿＿＿＿ 用罗马字。

英文不用漢字，＿＿＿＿＿ 用羅馬字。

Yīngwén bù yòng Hàn zì, ＿＿＿＿＿ yòng Luómǎ zì.

English does not use Chinese characters, it only uses the Roman alphabet.

g. 他 ＿＿＿＿＿ 学了两个外语。

他 ＿＿＿＿＿ 學了兩個外語。

Tā ＿＿＿＿＿ xué le liǎng gè wàiyǔ.

He has only studied two foreign languages.

h. 他上了中学 _____ 开始学英文。

他上了中學 _____ 開始學英文。

Tā shàng le zhōngxué _____ kāishǐ xué Yīngwén.

When he started middle school he began to study English.

i. 他上大学以后 _____ 开始学日文。

他上大學以後 _____ 開始學日文。

Tā shàng dàxué yǐhòu _____ kāishǐ xué Rìwén.

Only after he started college did he begin to study Japanese.

j. 日本人喜欢旅游。英国人不 _____ 喜欢旅游。

日本人喜歡旅游。英國人不 _____ 喜歡旅游。

Rìběn rén xǐhuan lǚyóu. Yīngguó rén bù _____ xǐhuan lǚyóu.

Japanese people like to travel. Not all British people like to travel.

⇨ 15

2 小李 **Xiǎo Lǐ** is a high school student in China who is being interviewed because of his excellent foreign language skills. Translate his replies into Mandarin, using an adverb in each sentence. Translate the interviewer's questions into Mandarin.

a. Interviewer: What foreign languages do you study?

Xiao Li: I study English and I also study Japanese.

b. Interviewer: How old are you?

Xiao Li: I am only 16 years old.

c. Interviewer: Have you ever been to a foreign country?

Xiao Li: Not yet. I have still not left China.

d. Interviewer: Do you plan to go abroad?

Xiao Li: Yes. After I graduate, only then will I have the chance to go abroad.

e. Interviewer: Where will you go?

Xiao Li: I plan to go to Britain and I plan to go to the United States.

f. Interviewer: Will you also go to Japan?

Xiao Li: After I go to England and the United States I plan to go to Japan.

⇨ 15

3

Here is a short dialog between two classmates with some adverbs omitted. Fill in the appropriate adverbs based on the English translations.

A: 昨天 _____ 开学，明天中文课 _____ 有小考， _____ 让人受不了。
昨天 _____ 開學，明天中文課 _____ 有小考， _____ 讓人受不了。
Zuótiān _____ kāi xué, míngtiān Zhōngwén kè _____ yǒu xiǎokǎo, _____ ràng rén shòubùliǎo.
School only just started yesterday and tomorrow we have a quiz in Chinese class. I can't stand it.

B: _____ 开学你 _____ 受不了了，你 _____ 学不学了？
_____ 開學你 _____ 受不了了，你 _____ 學不學了？
_____ kāi xué nǐ _____ shòubùliǎo le, nǐ _____ xué bù xué le?
School has just started and you can't stand it. Do you want to continue?

A: 学 _____ 要学，我 _____ 抱怨一下 _____ 。
學 _____ 要學，我 _____ 抱怨一下 _____ 。
Xué _____ yào xué, wǒ _____ bàoyuàn yīxià éryǐ.
Sure I want to continue. I just want to complain (and that's all).

B: 抱怨有什么用， _____ 能让你自己不高兴。
抱怨有甚麼用， _____ 能讓你自己不高興。
Bàoyuàn yǒu shénme yòng, _____ néng ràng nǐ zìjǐ bù gāoxìng.
Complaining is not helpful. It only makes you unhappy.

A: 你 _____ 常常抱怨呀。
Nǐ _____ chángcháng bàoyuàn ya.
You also often complain.

B: 我 _____ 抱怨你抱怨得 _____ 多。
Wǒ _____ bàoyuàn nǐ bàoyuàn de _____ dūo.
I only complain that you complain too much.

⇨ 15

16
Conjunctions

Pick the appropriate conjunction from the following list to complete each sentence: 和 **hé**/跟 **gēn**, 还是/還是 **háishi**, 或者 **huòzhě**.

a. 足球队 _____ 网球队，今天都有比赛。

   足球隊 _____ 網球隊，今天都有比賽。

   Zúqiú duì _____ wǎngqiú duì, jīntiān dōu yǒu bǐsài.

   The soccer team and the tennis team both have competitions today.

b. 你要看足球比赛 _____ 看网球比赛？

   你要看足球比賽 _____ 看網球比賽？

   Nǐ yào kàn zúqiú bǐsài _____ kàn wǎngqiú bǐsài?

   Would you rather watch the soccer game or the tennis match?

c. 足球比赛 _____ 网球比赛，我都愿意看。

   足球比賽 _____ 網球比賽，我都願意看。

   Zúqiú bǐsài _____ wǎngqiú bǐsài, wǒ dōu yuànyi kàn.

   I'll watch either the soccer game or the tennis match.

d. 你打棒球 _____ 打网球？

   你打棒球 _____ 打網球？

   Nǐ dǎ bàngqiú _____ dǎ wǎngqiú?

   Do you play soccer or tennis?

e. 棒球 _____ 网球我都打。

   棒球 _____ 網球我都打。

   Bàngqiú _____ wǎngqiú wǒ dōu dǎ.

   I play both soccer and tennis.

f. 美国人 _____ 英国人都踢足球吗？

   美國人 _____ 英國人都踢足球嗎？

   Měiguó rén _____ Yīngguó rén dōu tī zúqiú ma?

   Do Americans and the British both play soccer?

g. 美国人踢足球 _____ 美式足球。

   美國人踢足球 _____ 美式足球。

   Měiguó rén tī zúqiú _____ Měishì zúqiú.

   Americans play soccer and American football.

h. 明天的天气好的话，我们打网球 _____ 踢足球。

明天的天氣好的話，我們打網球 _____ 踢足球。

Míngtiān de tiānqì hǎo de huà, wǒmen dǎ wǎngqiú _____ tī zúqiú.

If the weather is good tomorrow, let's play soccer or tennis.

⇨ 16.1, 16.2

2 Xiao Wang is not helpful.

Xiao Li and Xiao Wang are roommates. They are discussing the courses they are going to take next semester. Translate their dialogue into Mandarin, paying attention to the conjunctions used in each of their exchanges. Remember that Mandarin does not use conjunctions everywhere that English does.

Xiao Li: I don't know whether it is better to take a Chinese language class or a Chinese history class. (Literally, I don't know whether taking a Chinese class is better or a Chinese history class is better.)

Xiao Wang: Which one do you like more, Chinese language or Chinese history?

Xiao Li: I like them both, Chinese language and Chinese history. (Chinese language and Chinese history, I like them both.)

Xiao Wang: Then just take both Chinese language and Chinese history.

Xiao Li: I do not have that much time.

Xiao Wang: Then you can choose either Chinese language or Chinese history.

Xiao Li: So you also don't know whether I should take Chinese language or Chinese history.

Xiao Wang: Of course not, because it has nothing to do with me.

Xiao Li: Thanks a lot!

⇨ 16

17
Aspect

1 Write a sentence for each action describing what Li did yesterday.

a. read two books
b. had coffee with friends
c. watched television for an hour
d. went shopping with his roommate.
e. bought an expensive pair of sneakers. [运动鞋/運動鞋 **yùndòng xié** sneakers, athletic shoes]

⇨ 17.1

2 Negate these actions and translate your sentences into English.

a. 学校开学了。
   學校開學了。
   Xuéxiào kāi xué le.
   School has started.

b. 我买课本了。
   我買課本了。
   Wǒ mǎi kèběn le.
   I bought textbooks.

c. 我买了三本中文书。
   我買了三本中文書。
   Wǒ mǎi le sān běn Zhōngwén shū.
   I bought three Chinese books.

d. 我做功课了。
   我做功課了。
   Wǒ zuò gōngkè le.
   I did my homework.

e. 我的同屋白天睡觉。
   我的同屋白天睡觉。
   Wǒ de tóngwū báitiān shuì jiào.
   My roommate sleeps during the day.

f. 我学过中文。

我學過中文。

Wǒ xuéguo Zhōngwén.

I have studied Chinese before.

g. 我在中国学过中文。

我在中國學過中文。

Wǒ zài Zhōngguó xuéguo Zhōngwén.

I have studied Chinese in China.

h. 我妹妹学中文。

我妹妹學中文。

Wǒ mèimei xué Zhōngwén.

My younger sister studies Chinese.

i. 我跟朋友去买东西了。

我跟朋友去買東西了。

Wǒ gēn péngyou qù mǎi dōngxi le.

I went shopping with my friends.

⇨ 17.1

3

It's Sunday night and you've phoned your sister to ask her about her week. What do you say in Mandarin to find out about each of these activities?

a. Did you see a movie this week?

b. Did you have dinner with mom and dad on Friday night?

c. Did you go to that new coffee shop?

d. Did you buy a new coat? [外套 **wàitào**]

e. Did you finish reading that history book? [看完 **kànwán** finish reading, 历史/歷史 **lìshǐ** history]

⇨ 17.1

4

Write a sentence for each action describing what 小李 **Xiǎo Lǐ** is doing right now.

a. Xiao Li is doing her homework.

b. Xiao Li is getting dressed.

c. Xiao Li is cleaning up her room. [收拾屋子 **shōushi wūzi**]

d. Xiao Li is driving.

e. Xiao Li is eating dinner.

⇨ 17.2

5 Complete this narrative by adding the appropriate aspect marker in each blank. In one of the blanks, the word that you should include indicates a new situation.

上个周末我跟我的朋友小王去城里看 _____(a) 一个电影。在电影院的门口，小王看到 _____(b) 他的一个同事。他的同事手里拿 _____(c) 一束花，_____(d) 等他的女朋友。小王跟他说 _____(e) 几句话我们就进去 _____(f)。看完电影以后，我们去 _____(g) 一家我们很喜欢的中国饭馆去吃晚饭。可能是餐馆换 _____(h) 师傅，我们都觉得饭不如以前好吃。我想不会再来这个饭馆吃饭 _____(i)。吃 _____(j) 饭我就马上回家 _____(k)，因为家里还有很多事等 _____(l) 我做呢。

上個周末我跟我的朋友小王去城裡看 _____(a) 一個電影。在電影院的門口，小王看到 _____(b) 他的一個同事。他的同事手裡拿 _____(c) 一束花，_____(d) 等他的女朋友。小王跟他說 _____(e) 幾句話我們就進去 _____(f)。看完電影以後，我們去 _____(g) 一家我們很喜歡的中國飯館去吃晚飯。可能是餐館換 _____(h) 師傅，我們都覺得飯不如以前好吃。我想不會再來這個飯館吃飯 _____(i)。吃 _____(j) 飯我就馬上回家 _____(k)，因為家裡還有很多事等 _____(l) 我做呢。

Shàng gè zhōumò wǒ gēn wǒ de péngyǒu Xiǎo Wáng qù chénglǐ kàn
_____(a) **yīgè diànyǐng. Zài diànyǐngyuàn de ménkǒu, Xiǎo Wáng kàndào**
_____(b) **tā de yīge tóngshì. Tā de tóngshì shǒulǐ ná** _____(c) **yīshù huā,**
_____(d) **děng tā de nǚ péngyǒu. Xiǎo Wáng gēn tā shuō** _____(e) **jǐ jù**
huà wǒmen jiù jìnqù _____(f). **Kànwán diàn yǐng yǐhòu, wǒmen qù**
_____(g) **yī jiā wǒmen hěn xǐhuān de Zhōngguó fànguǎn qù chī wǎnfàn.**
Kěnéng shì cānguǎn huàn _____(h) **shīfù, wǒmen dōu juéde fàn bùrú**
yǐqián hǎo chī. Wǒ xiǎng bù huì zài lái zhège fànguǎn chī fàn _____(i).
Chī _____(j) **fàn wǒ jiù mǎshàng huí jiā** _____(k), **yīnwéi jiālǐ hái yǒu**
hěn duō shì děng _____(l) **wǒ zuò ne.**

⇨ 17.1, 17.2, 38.1

6 方琴 **Fāng Qín** and some of her classmates are hosting Tommy, an exchange student, for a weekend, and she has made a list of things to do and places to see. It isn't Tommy's first visit to Beijing, though, and 方琴 **Fāng Qín** has asked Tommy whether he has already done each thing on the list. His replies are indicated here. Write them up in a paragraph that 方琴 **Fāng Qín** can email to her classmates, using Verb 过/過 as appropriate and incorporating other information that Tommy has provided.

a.	登长城 / 登長城 **dēng Chángchéng** / climb the Great Wall	No
b.	去圆明园 / 去圓明園 **qù Yuánmíngyuán** / visit the Old Summer Palace	No
c.	吃北京烤鸭 / 吃北京烤鴨 **chī Běijīng Kǎoyā** / eat Beijing roast duck (Peking duck)	No
d.	吃饺子 / 吃餃子 **chī jiǎozi** / eat dumplings	Yes
e.	看京剧 / 看京劇 **kàn Jīngjù** / watch Beijing opera	No (not interested)
f.	逛胡同 **guàng hútòng** / visit *Hutongs*, Beijing's traditional narrow streets	yes (wants to go again)

⇨ 17.3

7 You are the receptionist at a law firm. A client calls and asks for Mr. Wang, who is at a meeting [开会/開會/**kāi huì**] right now. Explain why Mr. Wang can't come to the phone right now, and tell the client that he will call back after the meeting. [正在 + Verb]

8 You are giving your friends directions to your house. To help them locate the right house, tell them that there's a wreath [花圈 **huāquān**] hanging on the door and there's a flower pot [一盆花 **yī pén huā**] at the entrance, using the structure Verb 着/著 where appropriate.

9 Tell your friend that you're not going over to his house tonight because you are exhausted. List a few of your accomplishments today. For example, you wrote five pages of characters, washed tons of dishes and tidied up [整理 **zhěnglǐ**] three bookshelves. Add at least three more activities that you did today. Use Verb 了 as appropriate.

18

Resultative verbs

Complete these sentences by adding the appropriate resultative suffix based on the English translations.

a. 我听 _____ 了。

    我聽 _____ 了。

    Wǒ tīng _____ le.

    I understood through listening.

b. 功课做 _____ 了。

    功課做 _____ 了。

    Gōngkè zuò _____ le.

    The homework is finished.

c. 那本书我找 _____ 了。

    那本書我找 _____ 了。

    Nà běn shū wǒ zhǎo _____ le.

    I found that book.

d. 那本书我还没有看 _____。

    那本書我還沒有看 _____。

    Nà běn shū wǒ hái méiyǒu kàn _____.

    I still have not finished reading that book.

e. 现在我能看 _____ 中国电影了。

    現在我能看 _____ 中國電影了。

    Xiànzài wǒ néng kàn _____ Zhōngguó diànyǐng le.

    Now I can understand Chinese movies.

f. 我的手机在路上丢 _____ 了。真麻烦!

    我的手機在路上丢 _____ 了。真麻煩!

    Wǒ de shǒujī zài lùshang diū _____ le. Zhēn máfan!

    I lost my cell phone on the road. How annoying!

g. 饭做 _____ 了，可以吃了。

    飯做 _____ 了，可以吃了。

    Fàn zuò _____ le, kěyǐ chī le.

    The food is ready, we can eat.

h.　他每个字都写 _____ 了。

　　他每個字都寫 _____ 了。

　　Tā měi gè zì dōu xiě _____ le.

　　He wrote every character wrong.

⇨　18.3, 18.4

2

Rewrite these sentences in Mandarin, using the correct form of the resultative verb.

a.　I can't remember his name. [名字 **míngzi** name, 记 **jì** remember]

b.　We've already finished today's homework. [功课/功課 **gōngkè** homework, 做 **zuò** do]

c.　Can you finish today's homework in an hour? [一个钟头/一個鐘頭 **yī ge zhōngtou** an hour]

d.　Not in an hour. (In an hour, I can't finish it.)

e.　I can't open the window. Can you open it? [窗户 **chuānghu** window, 打（开）/打（開）**dǎ (kāi)** open]

f.　I still haven't finished washing the clothes. [衣服 **yīfu** clothing, 洗 **xǐ** wash]

g.　This shirt is really dirty. Do you think you can wash it clean? [衬衫/襯衫 **chènshān** shirt, 脏/髒 **zāng** dirty, 干净/乾淨 **gānjìng** clean]

h.　I didn't hear clearly what you just said. Could you say it again?

　　[听/聽 **tīng** hear, 你说的话/你說的話 **nǐ shuō de huà** what you said]

i.　I don't understand (by listening) what the teacher says.

j.　Can you afford an airplane ticket? [买/買 **mǎi** buy, 飞机票/飛機票 **fēijī piào** airplane ticket]

⇨　18.5, 18.6, 18.7

3

Turn these sentences into yes–no questions.

Example:

我吃不完。　　　→　你吃得完吃不完？　　　or　你吃得完吗？

　　　　　　　　　　　　　　　　　　　　　　　　你吃得完嗎？

Wǒ chībùwán.　　**Nǐ chīdewán chībùwán?**　　**Nǐ chī de wán ma?**

a.　我來不及了。

　　Wǒ láibùjí le.

　　I can't make it.

b.　这些书这么重，我拿不动。

　　這些書這麼重，我拿不動。

　　Zhè xiē shū zhème zhòng, wǒ nábùdòng.

　　These books are so heavy. I can't lift them.

c. 我找到工作了。

Wǒ zhǎodào gōngzuò le.

I found a job.

d. 这么黑我看不见。

這麼黑我看不見。

Zhème hēi wǒ kànbùjiàn.

It's so dark I can't see it.

⇨ 18.5, 18.6.1

4 Chen Li and Wang Xiaoming are roommates. Complete their conversation, adding in the correct resultative verbs in the correct form.

a. 陈：花生酱在哪儿？我 _____ 。

陳：花生醬在哪兒？我 _____ 。

Chén: Huāshēngjiàng zài nǎr? Wǒ _____.

Chen: Where is the peanut butter? I can't find it.

b. 王：噢，我昨天 _____ 了。

Wáng: Ò wǒ zuótiān _____ le.

Wang: Oh, I finished it yesterday.

c. 陈：你昨天 _____ 了吗？

陳：你昨天 _____ 了嗎？

Chén: Nǐ zuótiān _____ le ma?

Chen: You ate it up yesterday?

d. 王：对。我去商店买，可是 _____ （花生酱）都 _____ 了。

王：對。我去商店買，可是 _____ （花生醬）都 _____ 了。

Wáng: Duì. Wǒ qù shāngdiàn mǎi, kěshì _____ (huāshēngjiàng) dōu _____ le.

Wang: Yes, I went to the store to buy some, but I couldn't buy any (couldn't obtain it by shopping). Peanut butter was all sold out.

⇨ 18.3, 18.4, 18.5, 18.6

5 Choose one of the following resultative complements to complete each sentence.

住 zhù	掉 diào	饱/飽 bǎo	会/會 huì	到 dào	完 wán

a. 骑自行车不难，一个下午就学 _____ 了。

騎自行車不難，一個下午就學 _____ 了。

Qí zìxíngchē bù nán, yīge xiàwǔ jiù xué _____ le.

Riding a bike is not hard. You can learn it in one afternoon.

b. 我写 _____ 功课就来帮你。

我寫 _____ 功課就來幫你。

Wǒ xiě _____ gōngkè jiù lái bāng nǐ.

I'll come help you as soon as I finish doing my homework.

c. 我已经吃 _____ 了，别再给我了。

我已經吃 _____ 了，別再給我了。

Wǒ yǐjīng chī _____ le, bié zài gěi wǒ le.

I'm full already. Stop giving me (food).

d. 我教书教了三十多年，哪里记得 _____ 所有学生的名字呢？

我教書教了三十多年，哪裡記得 _____ 所有學生的名字呢？

Wǒ jiāo shū jiāo le sānshí duō nián, nǎli jìde _____ suǒyǒu xuésheng de míngzi ne?

I've been teaching for more than 30 years. How can I remember all students' names?

e. 那个洗衣机坏 _____ 了，用另外一个吧。

那個洗衣機壞 _____ 了，用另外一個吧。

Nàge xǐyījī huài _____ le, yòng lìngwài yī ge ba.

That washing machine is broken. Use the other one.

f. 他找了半年都没找 _____ 工作，只好搬回家跟父母住。

他找了半年都沒找 _____ 工作，只好搬回家跟父母住。

Tā zhǎo le bànnián dōu méi zhǎo _____ gōngzuò, zhǐ hǎo bān huí jiā gēn fùmǔ zhù.

He looked for half a year but he couldn't find a job, so he had to move back to his parents' house.

⇨ 18.3, 18.4, 18.5, 18.6

6 王方 **Wáng Fāng** can't function well lately because he has been under a lot of stress. In Mandarin, describe what he probably can't do right now.

Example: He can't sleep. → 他睡不着。

他睡不著。

Tā shuìbùzháo.

a. He can't eat anything.

b. He can't remember what he needs to do everyday.

c. He can't see (things) clearly.

d. He can't find his cell phone.

e. He can't understand what other people are saying.

⇨ 18.6

7

李美 **Lǐ Měi** is texting all her girlfriends to see if they can come over tonight. Everyone is texting back saying that they will come as soon as they finish what they are doing right now. Translate their texts into Mandarin using the appropriate resultative verbs.

> Example: I'll be there as soon as   →   我做完功课就来。
>   I finish doing homework   我做完功課就來。
>
>   **Wǒ zuòwán gōngkè jiù lái.**

a. I'll be there as soon as I find my shoes.

b. I'll be there as soon as I take a shower.

c. I'll be there as soon as I buy the book I need.

d. I'll be there as soon as I throw away some clothes.
    [扔掉 **rēngdiào** throw away]

e. I'll be there as soon as I fix my alarm clock.
    [闹钟/鬧鐘 **nàozhōng** alarm clock]

⇨ 18.3

19
Directional verbs

1 邱羽 **Qiū Yǔ** is putting together a manual for his dog training school. Below is a list of tricks included in the training session. Translate them into Mandarin with the appropriate directional verbs/suffix.

> Example: Sit (down) → 坐下
> **zuò xià**

a. Stand up

b. Go in

c. Come out

d. Lie down

e. Lie down on your stomach

f. Jump over (jump past) it

g. Come here (come towards me)

⇨ 19.2, 19.3

2 王太太 **Wáng tàitai** Mrs. Wang is a mom to four toddlers. Today she has taken them shopping at a furniture store. Oh no! Her children see the furniture store as a big jungle gym! Help Mrs. Wang get them under control by translating her sentences into Mandarin, using the correct combination of verb and directional suffixes.

> Example: You can't stand on that! → 不可以站上去
> **Bù kěyǐ zhàn shàngqù.**

a. Don't lie down!

b. Don't run out!

c. Don't climb up!

d. Don't jump down!

⇨ 19.2, 19.3, 19.4

3 Fill in the blanks with either 起来/起來 **qǐlái** or 下去 **xiàqù**.

a. 把干净的衣服收 _____ 吧。
把乾淨的衣服收 _____ 吧。
Bǎ gānjìng de yīfu shōu _____ ba.
Put away the clean clothes.

b. 她笑 _____ 真可爱。

她笑 _____ 真可爱。

Tā xiào _____ zhēn kě'ài.

She looks really cute when she smiles.

c. 他的歌声那么糟糕，你怎么还听得 _____？

他的歌聲那麼糟糕，你怎麼還聽得 _____？

Tā de gēshēng name zāogāo, nǐ zěnme hái tīng de _____?

His voice is so bad. How could you continue to listen to it?

d. 失业加上太太孩子离开他，他觉得自己快活不 _____ 了。

失業加上太太孩子離開他，他覺得自己快活不 _____ 了。

Shīyè jiā shàng tàitai háizi líkāi tā, tā juéde zìjǐ kuài huó bù _____ le.

Being unemployed plus the fact that his wife and children left him, he felt like he almost couldn't keep on living anymore.

e. 这件事情说 _____ 容易做 _____ 困难。

這件事情說 _____ 容易做 _____ 困難。

Zhèjiàn shìqing shuō_____ róngyì, zuò _____ kùnnán.

This is easier said than done.

f. 她觉得很委屈，忍不住哭了 _____。

她覺得很委屈，忍不住哭了 _____。

Tā juéde hěn wěiqū, rěnbuzhù kū le _____.

Feeling misunderstood, she couldn't help but cry.

⇨ 19.7

4

Fill in the blanks with 起来/起來 qǐlái、出来/出來 chūlái、上去 shàngqù、下去 xiàqu、下来/下來 xiàlái

a. 你的名字我想不 _____ 了。

你的名字我想不 _____ 了。

Nǐde míngzi wǒ xiǎng bù _____ le.

I can't remember your name.

b. 这个办法是他想 _____ 的。

這個辦法是他想 _____ 的。

Zhège bànfǎ shì tā xiǎng _____ de.

It is he who came up with this method.

c. 这个电影太没意思了，我看不 _____ 了。

這個電影太沒意思了，我看不 _____ 了。

Zhège diànyǐng tài méi yìsi le, wǒ kàn bù _____ le.

This movie is really not interesting. I can't keep on watching.

d. 阴天了。看 _____ 要下雨了。

陰天了。看 _____ 要下雨了。

Yīntiān le. Kàn _____ yào xiàyǔ le.

It's very cloudy now. It looks like it will rain soon.

e.　孩子们高兴得唱 _____ 了。

　　孩子們高興得唱 _____ 了。

　　Háizimen gāoxìng de chàng _____ le.

　　The children were so happy that they began singing.

f.　你的想法听 _____ 很不错。

　　你的想法聽 _____ 很不錯。

　　Nǐde xiǎngfǎ tīng _____ bùcuò.

　　Your idea is not bad at all.

g.　他看 _____ 四十多岁的样子。

　　他看 _____ 四十多歲的樣子。

　　Tā kànshàngqù sìshí duō suì de yàngzi.

　　He looks like [he's] in his forties.

h.　你说得很好，说 _____。

　　你說得很好，說 _____。

　　Nǐ shuōde hěn hǎo, shuō _____.

　　You've said it very well. Go on.

i.　从他的话里我听 _____ 了他不喜欢我。

　　從他的話裡我聽 _____ 了他不喜歡我。

　　Cóng tāde huà lǐ wǒ ting _____ le tā bù xǐhuān wǒ.

　　From the way he talks I can tell that he doesn't like me.

j.　我想把省 _____ 的钱存 _____。

　　我想把省 _____ 的錢存 _____。

　　Wǒ xiǎng bǎ shengxiàlái de qián cúnqǐlái.

　　I want to put the money I saved in the bank.

⇨　19.7

5

Use the directional expression in a sentence, saying that you are running in that direction towards your friend, as in the example.

上楼	我跑上楼来。
上樓	我跑上樓來。
shàng lóu	**Wǒ pǎoshàng lóu lái.**
come upstairs	I will run upstairs (to him).

a.　回学校

　　回學校

　　huí xuéxiào

　　return to school

b.　回家

　　huí jiā

　　return home

c. 下楼
    下樓
    xià lóu
    go downstairs

d. 上山
    shàngshān
    go up the hill

e. 出图书馆
    出圖書館
    chū túshūguǎn
    exit the library

f. 回宿舍
    huí sùshè
    return to the dorm

g. 进教室
    進教室
    jìn jiàoshì
    enter the classroom

h. 过马路
    過馬路
    guò mǎlù
    cross the street

⇨ | 19.4.2

20
把 bǎ sentences: the 'disposal' construction

1

Use these phrases to form 把 bǎ sentences, as in the example.

Example:

我	拿书	到学校	→	我把书拿到学校了。
我	拿書	到學校		我把書拿到學校了。
Wǒ	ná shū	dào xuéxiào		Wǒ bǎ shū ná dào xuéxiào le.
I	take book	to school		I took the book to school.

a.
小王	还书	给图书馆
	還書	給圖書館
Xiǎo Wàng	huán shū	gěi túshūguǎn
Xiao Wang	return book	to library

b.
大伟	开车	回家
大偉	開車	回家
Dà Wěi	kāi chē	huí jiā
David	drive	go home

c.
小李	洗衣服	衣服干净
		衣服乾淨
Xiǎo Lǐ	xǐ yīfu	yīfu gānjing
Xiao Li	wash clothes	clothes clean

d.
老师	开窗户	窗户开开了
老師	開窗戶	窗戶開開了
lǎoshī	kāi chuānghu	chuānghu kāikāi le
teacher	open window	window open

e.
我	买课本	课本买到了
	買課本	課本買到了
wǒ	mǎi kèběn	kèběn mǎidào le
I	buy textbook	textbook bought

f. 弟弟　　　　　　做功课　　　　　　功课做完了
　　　　　　　　　　做功課　　　　　　功課做完了

　　dìdi　　　　　**zuò gōngkè**　　　**gōngkè zuòwán le**
　　younger brother　do homework　　homework finished

g. 张明　　　　　　用我的电脑　　　　我的电脑坏了
　　張明　　　　　　用我的電腦　　　　我的電腦壞了

　　Zhāng Míng　**yòng wǒde diànnǎo**　**wǒde diànnǎo huài le**
　　Zhang Ming　　　use my computer　　my computer is broken

h. 他　　　　　　　卖他的汽车　　　　汽车卖了
　　他　　　　　　　賣他的汽車　　　　汽車賣了

　　ta　　　　　　**mài tāde qìchē**　　**qìchē mài le**
　　he　　　　　　　sell his car　　　　car sold

⇨ 20.1

2   Negation: Rewrite the sentences you formed in (1) in negative form.

⇨ 20.4

3   Rewrite the following topic-comment sentences as 把 **bǎ** sentences as in the example, and translate your 把 **bǎ** sentences into English.

Example: 窗户，我关上了。　　　　　我把窗户关上了。
　　　　　窗戶，我關上了。　　　　　我把窗戶關上了。
　　　　　Chuānghu, wǒ guānshang le.　**Wǒ bǎ chuānghu guānshang le.**
　　　　　As for the window, I closed it.　I closed the window.

a. 我的书，他借走了。
　　我的書，他借走了。
　　Wǒde shū, tā jièzǒu le.
　　As for my book, he borrowed it.

b. 饺子，他吃完了。
　　餃子，他吃完了。
　　Jiǎozi, tā chīwán le.
　　As for the dumplings, he ate them all.

c. 手机，我忘在教室了。
　　手機，我忘在教室了。
　　Shǒujī, wǒ wàngzài jiāoshì le.
　　As for my cell phone, I forgot it in the classroom.

d. 电脑，我带来了。
　　電腦，我帶來了。
　　Diànnǎo, wǒ dàilái le.
　　As for the computer, I brought it over.

e. 电影，学生们看完了。

電影，學生們看完了。

Diànyǐng, xuéshēngmen kànwán le.

As for the movie, the students finished watching it.

f. 宿舍，我的同屋整理好了。

宿舍，我的同屋整理好了。

Sùshè, wǒde tóngwū zhěnglǐhǎo le.

As for my dorm, my roommate tidied it up.

g. 我的衣服，妈妈给洗干净了。

我的衣服，媽媽給洗乾淨了。

Wǒde yī fú, māma gěi xǐgānjìng le.

As for my clothes, my mom washed them clean.

h. 你的椅子，我给搬到门外边去了。

你的椅子，我給搬到門外邊去了。

Nǐde yǐzi, wǒ gěi bāndào mén wàibiān qù le.

As for your chair, I moved it outside of the door.

⇨ 20.1, 20.2, 20.3

4 Rewrite these sentences, adding the phrase in parentheses in the correct location, as in the example.

Example:

把脏衣服丢在地上。	（别）	→	别把脏衣服丢在地上。
把髒衣服丢在地上。	（别）	→	别把髒衣服丢在地上。
Bǎ zāng yīfu diū zài dishing.	**(bié)**	→	**Bié bǎ zāng yīfu diū zài dishing.**
Throw dirty clothes on the floor.	(don't)	→	Don't throw dirty clothes on the floor.

a. 把这里的书拿走。（不可以）

把這裡的書拿走。（不可以）

Bǎ zhèlǐ de shū ná zǒu. (bù kěyǐ)

Take away the books from here. (cannot)

b. 他们把外套穿好了。（都）

他們把外套穿好了。（都）

Tāmen bǎ wàitào chuān hǎo le. (dōu)

They put on their coats. (all)

c. 我把所有的功课写好了。（都）

我把所有的功課寫好了。（都）

Wǒ bǎ suǒyǒu de gōngkè xiě hǎo le. (dōu)

I finish the homework. (all)

d. 把水果吃光。(不要)

Bǎ shuǐguǒ chī guāng. (bù yào)

Eat all the fruit. (don't)

e. 明天把雨伞带着。(得)

明天把雨傘帶著。(得)

Míngtiān bǎ yǔsǎn dàizhe. (děi)

Bring an umbrella tomorrow. (have to)

⇨ 20.4, 20.5

5 白太太 **Bái tàitai** Mrs. Bai is giving the housekeeper a list of chores to do today. Fill in the blanks with the appropriate verb phrase to complete her instructions, as in the example

Example: 把碗 _____   → 把碗洗干净

把碗 _____   → 把碗洗乾淨

把碗 _____ Bǎ wǎn _____   → bǎ wǎn xǐ gānjìng

Wash the dishes clean.

把床单 _____ 一 _____, 把垃圾 _____。把冬天的衣服 _____, 把鞋子 都 _____, 顺便把鞋柜 _____。再把晚餐的材料 _____。对了, 如果你有 时间, 可以帮我把裙子 _____ 吗? 我把裙子 _____ 了。你走之前, 别忘了把 钥匙 _____。

把床單 _____ 一 _____, 把垃圾 _____。把冬天的衣服 _____, 把鞋子 都 _____, 順便把鞋櫃 _____。再把晚餐的材料 _____。對了, 如果你有 時間, 可以幫我把裙子 _____ 嗎? 我把裙子 _____ 了。你走之前, 別忘了把 鑰匙 _____。

Bǎ chuángdān _____ yī _____, bǎ lājī _____. Bǎ dōngtiān de yīfu _____, bǎ xiézi dōu _____, shùnbiàn bǎ xiéguì _____. Zài bǎ wǎncān de cáiliào _____. Duìle, rúguǒ nǐ yǒu shíjiān, kěyǐ bang wǒ bǎ _____ ma? Wǒ bǎ qúnzi _____ le. Nǐ zǒu zhīqián, bié wàng le bǎ yàoshǐ _____.

Wash the bedsheets. *Take out* the trash. *Put away* the winter clothes. Put the shoes *back into the shoe closet* and *tidy up* the shoe closet at the same time. Then *prepare* the ingredients for dinner. By the way, if you have time, could you *shorten the length* of my skirt? I left the skirt on my bed. Before you go, don't forget to *leave* the keys.

⇨ 20.3

6

When 黄太太 **Huáng Tàitai** Mrs. Huang arrived home today, her children all complained about what their younger brother did while she was gone. Translate their complaints into Mandarin, as in the example.

Example: He threw all my books → 他把我的书都丢在地上!
on the floor!   他把我的書都丢在地上!

                                Tā bǎ wǒde shū dōu diū zài dìshang.

a.   He broke my favorite vase. [vase: 花瓶 **huāpíng**]

b.   He put my homework into the washing machine. [washing machine: 洗衣机/洗衣機 **xǐyījī**]

c.   He ate all my cookies. [cookies: 饼干/餅乾 **bǐnggān**]

⇨   20.3

21
The passive

Little Wang has had a bad day. These are the things that have happened to him. Express these situations in the passive form as in the example.

Example: *subject*   *verb*   *object*

孩子   吃完了   饼干/餅乾

Háizi   **chīwán le**   **bǐnggān.**

The children   ate up   the cookies.

→

Passive: 饼干让孩子吃完了。

餅乾讓孩子吃完了。

Bǐnggān ràng háizi chīwán le.

The cookies were eaten up by the children.

	subject	*verb*	*object*
a.	他的同屋	打破了	台灯 臺燈
	Tā de tóngwū	**dǎpò le**	**táidēng.**
	His roommate	broke	the desk lamp.
b.	小偷	偷走了	他的电脑 他的電腦
	Xiǎotōu	**tōuzǒule**	**tā de diànnǎo.**
	A thief	stole	his computer.
c.	他的朋友	弄丢了	他的钥匙 他的鑰匙
	Tā de péngyou	**nòngdiū le**	**tā de yàoshi.**
	His friend	lost	his keys.
d.	他的狗	吃掉了	他的三明治
	Tā de gǒu	**chīdiào**	**tā de sānmíngzhì.**
	His dog	ate up	his sandwich.
e.	他	用坏 用壞	字典
	Tā	**yònghuài**	**zìdiǎn.**
	He	used until ruined	the dictionary.

(He used the dictionary so much it fell apart.)

	subject	*verb*	*object*
f.	人家	碰坏了	他的自行车
		碰壞了	他的自行車
	Rénjiā	**pènghuài le**	**tā de zìxíngchē.**
	Someone	hit and destroyed	his bike.
g.	他的教练	骂了	他
	他的教練	罵了	
	Tā de jiàoliàn	**mà le**	**tā.**
	His coach	scolded	him.
h.	猫	撕破了	他的衣服
	貓		
	Māo	**sīpò le**	**tā de yīfu.**
	The cat	tore	his clothing.

⇨ 21.1

2 Express the situations in (1) in complete Mandarin sentences using 把 **bǎ**.

Example: *subject*　　　*verb*　　　*object*

孩子　　　　吃完了　　　饼干/餅乾

Háizi　　　**chīwán le**　　　**bǐnggān.**

The children　　ate up　　　the cookies.

→

孩子把饼干都吃完了。

孩子把餅乾都吃完了。

Háizi bǎ bǐnggān dōu chīwán le.

⇨ 20.1, 57.2.1

3 Four friends got together at the end of the day and compared their misfortunes. Translate what they said in Mandarin using 被/**bèi**.

Example: My car was stolen.　我的车被偷走了。

我的車被偷走了。

Wǒ de chē bèi tōu zǒu le.

a. I got laid off. [解雇 **jiěgù** lay off from work]

b. My house was on fire.

c. My window was broken.

d. I was robbed on the way here. [抢/搶 **qiǎng** rob]

⇨ 21.3

Situations and functions

22

Names, kinship terms, titles, and terms of address

1

Here is the Zhao family:

Mr. Zhao 赵先生/趙先生 **Zhào xiānsheng**   45 years old

Mrs. Zhao 赵太太/趙太太 **Zhào tàitai**   43 years old

Miss Zhao Xijie 赵西杰/趙西杰 **Zhào Xījié**   18 years old

Mr. Zhao Mingzhi 赵明智/趙明智 **Zhào Míngzhì**   20 years old

Miss Zhao Xiqing 赵西清/趙西清 **Zhào Xīqīng**   16 years old

Mr. Zhao Mingyi 赵明义/趙明義 **Zhào Míngyì**   14 years old

a. You are a hotel clerk.

   (i)   Address Mr. Zhao

   (ii) Address Miss Zhao Xijie

   (iii) Address Mrs. Zhao

⇨ 22.1, 22.3.1

b. You are a good friend of Mr. Zhao, 40 years old. Address Mr. Zhao.

c. You are Zhao Xijie's best friend. Address her.

⇨ 22.4.1

d. You are Zhao Xiqing.

   (i) Address Zhao Xijie.

   (ii) Address Zhao Mingzhi.

e. You are Zhao Xijie. Introduce yourself and your family members to your teacher, giving their ages.

f. You are Zhao Xiqing. Introduce your siblings using kinship terms.

g. You are Zhao Mingyi. Introduce yourself and your siblings using kinship terms.

⇨ 22.2, 22.4.2

h. You refer to someone as 叔叔 **shūshu**. Is 叔叔 **shūshu** male or female, and what is 叔叔 **shūshu**'s age in relation to your father's age?

i. You hear a child describing someone as 奶奶 **nǎinai**. Is 奶奶 **nǎinai** male or female, and what is 奶奶 **nǎinai**'s age in relationship to the child?

⇨ 22.4.2

j. You meet Miss Zhao Ailing for the first time.

    (i)   Ask her for her family name politely.

    (ii)   Assume you are Miss Zhao Ailing and answer the question.

    (iii) Ask her for her full name.

    (iv) Ask her how she would like to be addressed by you.

⇨ 22.5

2

Provide the information requested in English below based on this name card.

金山国际花园
金山國際花園
Jīnshān Guójì Huāyuán
郭明智
Guō Míngzhì
地址：北京市朝阳区建国路   电话：010-65666557
21号
北京市朝陽區建國路   电传：010-6566555
21號
Běijīng shì   手机：13196118888
Cháoyáng qū
Jiànguó lù 21 hào

a. name

b. phone number

c. employer

d. fax number

3

Design your own name card. (*No answer is provided in the Answer Key.*)

⇨ 22.6

23
Introductions

1

Here is information about 王明 **Wáng Míng** and 周利 **Zhōu Lì**.

王明 **Wáng Míng**	周利 **Zhōu Lì**

- student
- your classmate
- studies economics
- speaks English

- student
- your younger male cousin on your father's side
- studies linguistics
- speaks Japanese

Introduce them to each other in an informal manner and have them greet each other.

You:

王明 **Wáng Míng:**

周利 **Zhōu Lì:**

⇨ 22.2.2, 23.1, 23.2, 23.3

2

Introduce the famous Professor Lin [林教授 **Lín jiàoshòu**] to the famous Dr. Zhang [张医生/張醫生 **Zhāng yīshēng**] in a formal manner. Have them greet each other formally after the introductions.

You:

林教授 **Lín jiàoshòu:**

张医生/張醫生 **Zhāng yīshēng:**

⇨ 23.1, 23.2

3

周利 **Zhōu Lì** has just moved into the dormitory and has met 王明 **Wáng Míng** for the first time.

Complete 周利 **Zhōu Lì**'s part of the conversation in Mandarin.

王明 **Wáng Míng:**	我是王明，是上海人。
	Wǒ shì Wáng Míng, shì Shànghǎi rén.
周利 **Zhōu Lì:**	(a) Hi. I am Zhou Li. I'm from Shandong.
王明 **Wáng Míng:**	真高兴。我们今年是同屋。
	真高興。我們今年是同屋。
	Zhēn gāoxìng. Wǒmen jīnnián shì tóngwū.
周利 **Zhōu Lì:**	(b) I'm glad to meet you. I hope we get along and can give each other a hand this year.

王明 **Wáng Míng:** 你是学什么的？

你是學甚麼的？

Nǐ shì xué shénme de?

周利 **Zhōu Lì:** (c) I'm studying chemistry.

王明 **Wáng Míng:** 我也是。

Wǒ yě shì.

周利 **Zhōu Lì:** (d) What a lucky coincidence!

⇨ 23.1, 23.2, 23.3

24
Greetings and goodbyes

1 Match these greetings with the appropriate situation.

	Greeting		*Situation*
a.	来吃饭吗？ 來吃飯嗎？ **Lái chī fàn ma?**	1	You see an acquaintance going home.
b.	老陈！ 老陳！ **Lǎo Chén!**	2	It is 7 a.m.
c.	上哪儿去？ 上哪兒去？ **Shàng nǎr qù?**	3	You see your professor on the subway.
d.	早。 **Zǎo.**	4	You run into your good friend at a restaurant.
e.	回家呀。 **Huí jiā ya.**	5	You pass your neighbor on the street at noon.
f.	上班去吗？ 上班去嗎？ **Shàng bān qù ma?**	6	You are at your front door and see your neighbor leaving the house.
g.	王老师好。 王老師好。 **Wáng lǎoshī hǎo.**	7	You are at your car at 7:30 a.m. and see your neighbor walk by.

⇨ 24.1

2 Provide the equivalent Mandarin expressions.

a. See you again.

b. See you in a while.

c. See you soon.

d. See you tomorrow.

e. See you next week.

⇨ 24.2

3 Provide the appropriate greetings and goodbyes for the following letters.

a. An informal letter to your friend 许伟强/許偉強 Xǔ Wěiqiáng.

Greeting: As if talking to you face to face

Goodbye: Expressing good wishes for a Happy New Year, Your 'younger brother,' 刘绪武/劉緒武 Liú Xùwǔ

b. A formal letter to your teacher 唐老师/唐老師 Táng lǎoshī.

Greeting: Please read this letter.

Goodbye: I respectfully extend my good wishes with concern about your welfare in this summer season, I bow to you. Respectfully written by your student, 张晓春/張曉春 Zhāng Xiǎochūn.

⇨ 24.3

4 You call your friend 王明 Wáng Míng on the phone. Translate your part of the conversation into Mandarin.

a. I am looking for Wang Ming.

b. Wang Ming, long time no see. [好久不见/好久不見 hǎo jiǔ bù jiàn] What have you been busy with lately?

c. You are going to Australia [澳大利亚/澳大利亞 Aòdàlìyà]? Have a good trip.

d. See you *when you get back*. [See if you can figure out how to say this.]

⇨ 24.1, 24.2

25

Basic strategies for communication

1 Match each phrase with its function:

Phrase

a. 我想打听一下/我想打聽一下
   wǒ xiǎng dǎting yīxià

b. 对不起/對不起
   duìbuqǐ

c. 清楚吗?/清楚嗎?
   qīngchu ma?

d. 行。
   xíng

e. 怎么写?/怎麼寫?
   zěnme xiě?

f. 例如
   lìrú

g. 劳驾/勞駕
   láojià

h. 第一
   dìyī

i. 然后/然後
   ránhòu

Function

1 indicating that the situation is acceptable

2 making a list

3 formal apology before asking for assistance or information

4 making an inquiry

5 describing a sequence

6 neutral apology before asking for assistance or information

7 inquiring about writing something

8 asking for confirmation

9 giving an example

⇨ 25.1, 25.5

2

Sheila is studying Chinese in Beijing and wants to go to Wangfujing [王府井 **Wángfǔjǐng**] to shop. She asks a cab driver for information. Translate her conversation into Mandarin.

a. Sheila: Driver, sorry for bothering you. Is Wangfujing far from here?
    Driver: _____

b. Sheila: I'm sorry. I didn't understand. Can you say it again please?
    Driver: _____

c. Sheila: I'm very sorry. Please say it again slower.
    Driver: _____

d. Sheila: Yes, I understand. Thank you.

⇨ 25.1, 25.5, 47.4

3

Write the character described by each of the following phrases.

> Example: [四] [維] Luó → 羅 Luó
> 'sì' 'wéi' Luó
> The character pronounced **Luó** is composed of the characters
> 四 and 維.

NOTE | This description only works for the traditional form of this character. The simplified form is not composed of 四 and 維.

a. [兄弟]的 **dì** 'xiōngdì' de dì 'the "di" of older and younger brother'

b. [三点]水 / [三點] **shuǐ** 'sāndiǎn' shuǐ 'three dot' water

c. [木子] **Lǐ** 'mù zǐ' Lǐ 'wood child' Li

d. [立早] **Zhāng** 'lì zǎo' Zhāng 'stand up early' Zhang

e. [耳东] **Chén** / [耳東] **Chén** 'ěr dōng' Chén 'ear east' Chen

f. [三横一竖]的 **Wáng** / [三橫一豎]的 **Wáng** 'sān héng yī shù' de Wáng
    'three horizontal one vertical' Wang

⇨ 25.7

4

志雄 **Zhìxióng** and 姍姍 **Shānshān** discuss housing options for school with their friend 美玲 **Měilíng**, an incoming college freshman. 志雄 **Zhìxióng** prefers living in a dorm while 姍姍 **Shānshān** thinks renting an apartment near campus is better. Read their dialogue and fill in the blanks with words that introduce further points (25.11.2), establish sequence or reference (25.11.3, 25.11.4) or give examples (25.11.5).

志雄 **Zhìxióng**: 当然是宿舍好！ _____(first of all)，宿舍就在学校里，不必买车，
走路就可以去上课。

当然是宿舍好！ _____(first of all)，宿舍就在學校裡，不必買車，
走路就可 以去上課。

Dāngrán shì sùshè hǎo! _____(first of all), **sùshè jiù zài**
xuéxiào lǐ, bù bì mǎi chē, zǒulù jiù kěyǐ qù shàngkè.

————(In addition)，宿舍里什么都有，非常方便。

————(In addition)，宿舍裡甚麼都有，非常方便。

————(In addition)，**sùshè lǐ shénme dōu yǒu, fēicháng fāngbiàn.**

姍姍 **Shānshān:** 谁说宿舍什么都有？————(For example)，如果你想吃中国饭，还是得到外边的饭馆。

誰說宿舍甚麼都有？————(For example)，如果你想吃中國飯，還是得到外邊的飯館。

Shéi shuō sùshè shénme dōu yǒu? ————(For example)，**rúguǒ nǐ xiǎng chī zhōngguó fàn, háishì děi dào wàibian de fànguǎn.**

————(as for) 交通问题，如果你在学校附近租房子，可以坐公车去学校，一样方便。

————(as for) 交通問題，如果你在學校附近租房子，可以坐公車去學校，一樣方便。

————(as for) **jiāotōng wèntí, rúguǒ nǐ zài xuéxiào fùjìn zū fángzi, kěyǐ zuò gōng chē qù xuéxiào, yīyàng fāngbiàn.**

————(To put it another way)，租房子真的不错！

————(To put it another way)，租房子真的不錯！

————(To put it another way)，**zū fángzi zhēn de bù cuò!**

5 Imagine you are there giving 美玲 **Měilíng** your advice on the housing too. Write a few sentences telling her which is better, renting or living in a dorm, with supporting evidence. Be sure to introduce your evidence with 'for example,' 'in addition,' etc.

_____

_____

_____

_____

26

Telecommunications and e-communications: telephones, the internet, and faxes

1

Write these phone numbers in Chinese (characters or Pinyin).

a. 62191074
b. 13651281180
c. 67179469

⇨ 6.1.1, 26.5

2

You are placing a phone call to your friend 王明 **Wáng Míng**. You speak with his roommate, 周利 **Zhōu Lì**. Complete the conversations by translating the English into Mandarin.

Conversation A

周利 **Zhōu Lì**: 喂? **Wéi?**

You: I'm looking for Wang Ming.

周利 **Zhōu Lì**: 他不在。**Tā bù zài.**

You: Please tell him to return my phone call. My cell phone number is 13501327806.

Conversation B

周利 **Zhōu Lì**: 喂? **Wéi?**

You: Is Wang Ming in?

周利 **Zhōu Lì**: 他不在。**Tā bù zài.**

You: Please tell him to email me.

Conversation C

周利 **Zhōu Lì**: 喂? **Wéi?**

You: I'd like to speak with Wang Ming.

周利 **Zhōu Lì**: 他不在。**Tā bù zài.**

You: Okay. I'll send him a text message.

⇨ 26.1, 26.4

3 Solve these problems by giving advice in Mandarin.

a. The line is busy. → Dial again.

b. No one is picking up the phone. → Leave a message.

c. I don't have a computer. → Go to an internet café to get on the web.

d. How can I let you know when you are in class? → Send me a text message.

e. Mr. Wang is not at home. → Call his cell phone.

f. Where is the information? → Open the attachment.

g. How can I interview an international student? → Make a video call.

⇨ 26.1

4 Mr. Zhou told his secretary to do the following this morning. Fill in the blanks to complete Mr. Zhou's order.

麻烦你把昨天开会的纪录用电子邮件 _____ 给王经理。另外，给张先生 _____ 一个电话问他我今天下午会晚一点到。桌上有好几张我昨天 _____ 的传真，你看看有什么需要处理的。

麻煩你把昨天開會的紀錄用電子郵件 _____ 給王經理。另外，給張先生 _____ 一個電話告訴他我今天下午會晚一點到。桌上有好幾張我昨天 _____ 的傳真，你看看有甚麼需要處理的。

Máfán nǐ bǎ zuótiān kāi huì de jìlù yòng diànzǐ yóujiàn _____ gěi Wáng Jīnglǐ. Lìngwài, gěi Zhāng Xiānsheng _____ yīgè diànhuà gàosu tā wǒ jīntiān xiàwǔ huì wǎn yīdiǎn dào. Zhuō shàng yǒu hǎo jǐ zhāng wǒ zuótiān _____ de chuánzhēn, nǐ kàn kàn yǒu shénme xūyào chǔlǐ de.

5 45 minutes later. Mr. Zhou's secretary reported on her progress. Fill in the blanks to complete the paragraph.

昨天开会的纪录已经用 _____(attachment) 寄给王经理了。我给张先生打电话他没 _____，所以我 _____ 了话。等一下我可以再 _____ 一封短信提醒他。那几张传真也处理好了。对了，刚才我在帮您 *报帐*(file reimbursement)，有一个部分需要 _____(enter) 详细日期，麻烦您看一下对不对。

昨天開會的紀錄已經用 _____(attachment) 寄給王經理了。我給張先生打電話他沒 _____，所以我 _____ 了話。等一下我可以再 _____ 一封短信提醒他。那幾張傳真也處理好了。對了，剛才我在幫您報帳(file reimbursement)，有一個部分需要 _____(enter) 詳細日期，麻煩您看一下對不對。

Zuótiān kāi huì de jìlù yǐjīng yòng _____(attachment) jì gěi Wáng Jīnglǐ le. Wǒ gěi Zhāng Xiānsheng dǎ diànhuà tā méi _____, suǒyǐ wǒ _____ le huà. Děng yīxià wǒ kěyǐ zài _____ yī fēng duǎnxìn tíxǐng tā. Nà jǐ zhāng chuánzhēn yě chǔlǐ hǎo le. Duìle, gāngcái wǒ zài bāng nín bàozhàng(file reimbursement), yǒu yīgè bùfèn xūyào _____(enter) xiángxì rìqī, máfan nín kàn yīxià duì bù duì.

27
Negating information

1

Put the negation word in the right place in the following sentences to match the English translations.

Example: 我要跟他说话。（不）　　　　→　　我不要跟他说话。
　　　　　我要跟他說話。（不）　　　　　　我不要跟他說話。
　　　　　Wǒ yào gēn tā shuō huà. (bù)　**Wǒ bù yào gēn tā shuō huà.**
　　　　　　　　　　　　　　　　　　　I don't want to talk with him.

a.　我要跟他们吃饭。（不）
　　我要跟他們吃飯。（不）
　　Wǒ yào gēn tāmen chī fàn. (bù)
　　I don't want to eat with them.

b.　我听懂他的话。（不）
　　我聽懂他的話。（不）
　　Wǒ tīngdǒng tā de huà. (bù)
　　I don't understand what he says.

c.　我愿意跟他结婚。（不）
　　我願意跟他結婚。（不）
　　Wǒ yuànyi gēn tā jiéhūn. (bù)
　　I am not willing to marry him.

d.　我还决定买什么。（没）
　　我還決定買甚麼。（沒）
　　Wǒ hái juédìng mǎi shénme. (méi)
　　I still haven't decided what to buy.

e.　我常来这里。（不）
　　我常來這裏。（不）
　　Wǒ cháng lái zhèlǐ. (bù)
　　I don't come here often.

f.　我根本有钱。（没）
　　我根本有錢。（沒）
　　Wǒ gēnběn yǒu qián. (méi)
　　I have absolutely no money.

g. 我在餐厅吃饭。(不)

我在餐廳吃飯。(不)

Wǒ zài cāntīng chī fàn. (bù)

I don't eat in the cafeteria.

h. 我们都会说广东话。(不)

我們都會說廣東話。(不)

Wǒmen dōu huì shuō Guǎngdōng huà. (bù)

None of us can speak Cantonese.

i. 我听懂他的话。(没)

我聽懂他的話。(没)

Wǒ tīngdǒng tā de huà. (méi)

I did not understand what he said.

⇨ 10.1, 11.1, 12, 13.3, 17, 27.1, 27.2

2 Rewrite these sentences in Mandarin, using 不 **bù** or 没 **méi** as appropriate.

a. I don't like noodles. [面条/麵條 **miàntiáo** noodles]

b. I don't have any friends.

c. I didn't do my homework.

d. I am not tall.

e. I was not busy yesterday.

f. I haven't ever heard that song before.

g. There's no one home.

h. It didn't rain yesterday.

i. I can't drive a car.

j. I haven't graduated from university.

⇨ 27.1

3 Match these expressions with 无/無 **wú** and 非 **fēi** with equivalent Mandarin expressions.

a. 无论如何/無論如何   1 必须/必須
   wúlùn rúhé   **bìxū**

b. 无故/無故   2 非凡
   wúgù   **fēifán**

c. 非常   3 不管怎么样/不管怎麼樣
   fēicháng   **bù guǎn zěnmeyàng**

d. 非得   4 没有原故
   fēiděi   **méi yǒu yuángù**

e. 无比/無比   5 特别
   wúbǐ   **tèbié**

f. 非 (verb) 不可   6   不合法
    fēi (verb) bù kě   bù héfǎ

g. 非法   7   一定
    fēifǎ   yīdìng

⇨ 27.5

4

Some friends are having lunch together and they all want the last brownie
[布朗尼蛋糕 bùlǎngnì dàngāo] on the dessert tray. Each one says something
to convince the others that s/he is the most in need of that last brownie.
Translate their sentences into Mandarin.

Tom: I <u>don't</u> have a girlfriend. I don't know <u>ANY</u> girls.

Collins: I <u>have never been</u> to a prom. [舞会/舞會 wǔhuì]

Jackie: I'm 35 years old but I <u>don't know how to</u> drive.

Abby: I've been learning Chinese for two years but I <u>absolutely do not
         understand</u> what the teacher says.

Dennis: I'm broke. <u>Without a doubt,</u> I should get that brownie.

Sophia: I'm 42 years old, <u>jobless</u> and still live with my parents. <u>No matter
         what,</u> I should get that brownie.

Imagine you are there. Say something to fight for the last brownie!

YOU:

28
Asking questions and replying to questions

Turn these statements into yes–no questions with 吗/嗎 **ma**. Be careful to change the pronouns when appropriate. Translate your questions into English.

Example: 我会说中文。 → 你会说中文吗？
我會說中文。 你會說中文嗎？
Wǒ huì shuō Zhōngwén. **Nǐ huì shuō Zhōngwén ma?**
I can speak Chinese. Can you speak Chinese?

a. 我想去中国。
我想去中國。
Wǒ xiǎng qù Zhōngguó.
I want to go to China.

b. 她有男朋友。
Tā yǒu nán péngyou.
She has a boyfriend.

c. 我吃过生鱼片。
我吃過生魚片。
Wǒ chīguò shēngyúpiàn.
I've eaten sashimi before.

d. 他们会说中国话。
他們會說中國話。
Tāmen huì shuō Zhōngguó huà.
They can speak Chinese.

e. 他是英国人。
他是英國人。
Tā shì Yīngguó rén.
He is English.

f. 我喜欢旅行。
我喜歡旅行。
Wǒ xǐhuan lǚxíng.
I like to travel.

g. 中国人爱唱歌儿。

中國人爱唱歌兒。

Zhōngguó rén ài chàng gēr.

Chinese people love to sing.

h. 他每天在公园跑步。

他每天在公園跑步。

Tā měitiān zài gōngyuán pǎo bù.

He jogs in the park every day.

⇨ 28.1.1

2   Turn the statements in (1) into yes–no questions with *verb-not-verb* structure.

Example: 你会说中文吗?   → 你会不会说中文?

你會說中文嗎?   你會不會說中文?

Nǐ huì shuō Zhōngwén ma?   **Nǐ huì bù huì shuō Zhōngwén?**

Can you speak Chinese?   Can you speak Chinese?

⇨ 28.1.2

3   Turn the statements in (1) into yes–no questions with 是否 **shìfǒu** structure.

Example: 你会说中文吗?   → 你是否会说中文?

你會說中文嗎?   你是否會說中文?

Nǐ huì shuō Zhōngwén ma?   **Nǐ shìfǒu huì shuō Zhōngwén?**

Can you speak Chinese?   Can you speak Chinese?

⇨ 28.1.3

4   Reply 'yes' to the following questions. Translate your responses into English.

Example: 你去过中国吗?   → 去过。我去过中国。

你去過中國嗎?   去過。我去過中國。

Nǐ qùguò Zhōngguó ma?   **Qùguò. Wǒ qùguò Zhōngguó.**

Have you been to China?   Yes. I have been to China before.

a. 你是学生吗?

你是學生嗎?

Nǐ shì xuésheng ma?

Are you a student?

b. 你会开车吗?

你會開車嗎?

Nǐ huì kāi chē ma?

Can you drive a car?

c. 你喝过中国茶吗?

你喝過中國茶嗎?

Nǐ hēguò Zhōngguó chá ma?

Have you drunk Chinese tea before?

d. 你吃过北京烤鸭吗？

你吃過北京烤鴨嗎？

Nǐ chīguò Běijīng kǎoyā ma?

Have you eaten Beijing roast duck (Peking duck) before?

e. 你喜欢看电影吗？

你喜歡看電影嗎？

Nǐ xǐhuan kàn diànyǐng ma?

Do you like to watch movies?

f. 台北有地铁吗？

臺北有地鐵嗎？

Táiběi yǒu dìtiě ma?

Does Taipei have a subway?

g. 桂林的山水漂亮吗？

桂林的山水漂亮嗎？

Guìlín de shānshuǐ piàoliang ma?

Is Guilin's scenery pretty?

h. 你用筷子吃饭吗？

你用筷子吃飯嗎？

Nǐ yòng kuàizi chī fàn ma?

Do you use chopsticks to eat?

⇨ | 28.1.4.1

5

Reply 'no' to each of the questions in (4).

Example: 你去过中国吗？	→	没去过。我没去过中国。
		沒去過。我沒去過中國。
Nǐ qùguò Zhōngguó ma?		**Méi qùguò. Wǒ méi qùguò Zhōngguó.**
Have you been to China?		No, I haven't. I have never been to China.

⇨ | 28.1.4.2

6

Ask 王明 **Wáng Míng** either–or questions with 还是/還是 **háishi** about the following topics. Use the verb in parentheses for each question. Translate your questions into English.

Example: [是 **shì**] 中国人/中國人	→	你是中国人还是美国人？
Zhōngguó rén –		你是中國人還是美國人？
美国人/美國人		**Nǐ shì Zhōngguó rén háishi**
Měiguó rén		**Měiguó rén?**
		Are you Chinese or American?

a. [喜欢/喜歡 xǐhuan] 中餐 Zhōngcān – 西餐 xīcān

b. [是 shì] 学生/學生 xuésheng – 老师/老師 lǎoshī

c. [学/學 xué] 中国文学/中國文學 Zhōngguó wénxué – 英国文学/英國文學
    Yīngguó wénxué

d. [是 shì] 二十一岁/二十一歲 èrshíyī suì – 二十二岁/二十二歲 èrshí'èr suì

e. [喜欢/喜歡 xǐhuan] 看电视/看電視 kàn diànshì – 听收音机/聽收音機
    tīng shōuyīnjī [电视/電視 diànshì television, 收音机/收音機 shōuyīnjī radio]

f. [上 shàng] 高中 gāo zhōng – 大学/大學 dàxué

⇨ 28.3

7

Rewrite the following 呢 **ne** questions as full Mandarin questions.

Example: 我会说中国话。你呢？　　　→　你会说中国话吗？
　　　　　我會說中國話。你呢？　　　　　你會說中國話嗎？
　　　　　Wǒ huì shuō Zhōngguo　　　　Nǐ huì shuō Zhōngguo
　　　　　huà. Nǐ ne?　　　　　　　　　huà ma?

a. 我喜欢吃西餐。你呢？
    我喜歡吃西餐。你呢？
    Wǒ xǐhuan chī xīcān. Nǐ ne?

b. 我是学生。你呢？
    我是學生。你呢？
    Wǒ shì xuésheng. Nǐ ne?

c. 我学中国文学。你呢？
    我學中國文學。你呢？
    Wǒ xué Zhōngguó wénxué. Nǐ ne?

d. 我喜欢看电视。你呢？
    我喜歡看電視。你呢？
    Wǒ xǐhuan kàn diànshì. Nǐ ne?

e. 我上大学。你呢？
    我上大學。你呢？
    Wǒ shàng dàxué. Nǐ ne?

f. 我爱看中国电影。你呢？
    我愛看中國電影。你呢？
    Wǒ ài kàn Zhōngguó diànyǐng. Nǐ ne?

g. 我不抽烟。你呢？
    我不抽煙。你呢？
    Wǒ bù chōu yān. Nǐ ne?

h. 我去过中国。你呢？
    我去過中國。你呢？
    Wǒ qùguò Zhōngguó. Nǐ ne?

⇨ 28.5

8

Turn each of the following statements into a content question in which you ask about the underlined word or phrase.

Example: 他是<u>小王</u>的弟弟。 → 他是<u>谁</u>的弟弟？

他是<u>誰</u>的弟弟？

Tā shì <u>Xiǎo Wáng</u> de dìdi.　　**Tā shì <u>shéi</u> de dìdi?**

He is <u>little Wang</u>'s younger brother.　　<u>Whose</u> younger brother is he?

a.　地铁票<u>三块钱</u>。

地鐵票<u>三塊錢</u>。

Dìtiě piào <u>sān kuài</u> qián.

A subway ticket is <u>$3</u>.

b.　哥哥特别喜欢吃<u>饺子</u>。

哥哥特別喜歡吃<u>餃子</u>。

Gēge tèbié xǐhuan chī <u>jiǎozi</u>.

Older brother particularly likes to eat <u>dumplings</u>.

c.　现在<u>五点钟</u>。

現在<u>五點鐘</u>。

Xiànzài <u>wǔ</u> diǎn zhōng.

It's now <u>5</u> o'clock.

d.　他在美国住了<u>十年</u>。

他在美國住了<u>十年</u>。

Tā zài Měiguó zhù le <u>shí nián</u>.

He lived in America for <u>ten years</u>.

e.　她是<u>法国</u>人。

她是<u>法國</u>人。

Tā shì <u>Fǎguó</u> rén.

She is <u>French</u>. (lit.: a <u>French</u> person)

f.　北海公园在<u>地安门大街</u>。

北海公園在<u>地安門大街</u>。

Běihǎi gōngyuán zài <u>Dì'ānmén dàjiē</u>.

Beihai Park is on <u>Di'Anmen street</u>.

g.　我有<u>三个</u>同屋。

我有<u>三個</u>同屋。

Wǒ yǒu <u>sān</u> gè tóngwū.

I have <u>three</u> roommates.

h.　我跟<u>我的朋友</u>一起租一个房子。

我跟<u>我的朋友</u>一起租一個房子。

Wǒ gēn <u>wǒ de péngyou</u> yīqǐ zū yī gè fángzi.

I am renting a house with <u>my friends</u>.

⇨　28.6

9   Place these phrases in the correct order to correspond to the English translations.

a. 高跟鞋　　　为什么　　　不愿意　　　你　穿？
高跟鞋　　　爲甚麽　　　不願意　　　你　穿？
gāogēnxié　wèishénme　bù yuànyi　nǐ　chuān?
Why aren't you willing to wear high-heeled shoes?

b. 几点钟　　　　昨天　　晚上　　　回家的　　你？
幾點鐘　　　　昨天　　晚上　　　回家的　　你？
jǐdiǎn zhōng　zuótiān　wǎnshang　huí jiā de　nǐ?
What time did you return home last night?

c. 在哪儿　你　大学　　上？
在哪兒　你　大學　　上？
zài nǎr　nǐ　dàxué　shàng?
Where do you attend university?

d. 多少　　　学生　　　有　　你的　　中文班？
多少　　　學生　　　有　　你的　　中文班？
duōshao　xuésheng　yǒu　nǐ de　Zhōngwén bān?
How many students are in your Chinese class?

e. 什么地方　　　每天　　你　在　停车？
甚麽地方　　　每天　　你　在　停車？
shénme dìfang　měitiān　nǐ　zài　tíng chē?
Where do you park your car every day?

f. 多远　　　巴黎　离　伦敦　　　有？
多遠　　　巴黎　離　倫敦　　　有？
duō yuǎn　Bālí　lí　Lúndūn　yǒu?
How far is it from Paris to London?

g. 几个人　　能　　这个车　　　坐？
幾個人　　能　　這個車　　　坐？
jǐ gè rén　néng　zhège chē　zuò?
How many people can this car seat?

h. 几号　　几月　　今天　　是？
幾號　　幾月　　今天　　是？
jǐ hào　jǐ yuè　jīntiān　shì?
What is today's date? (What is today's month and date?)

⇨ 4, 28.6, 47.4

10   Translate these questions into Mandarin.

a.   Where do you study Chinese?

b.   When do you eat dinner?

c.   What time does this store open for business?

d.   How long have you studied Chinese?

e.   How many people have you invited to dinner?

f.   Who do you know?

g.   Why do you want to see that movie?

h.   How many children do they have?

⇨   28.6

11   An American movie star, who reportedly studied Chinese just for this role, is here in Shanghai to promote her new film. As a reporter, you are compiling a list of questions that you can ask at the press conference. Translate the first five questions into Mandarin and write three additional questions in Mandarin based on the cues in parentheses.

a.   How long are you staying in Shanghai?

b.   Have you ever been to China before?

c.   Is Chinese difficult to learn? Why?

d.   What Chinese food do you most want to try?

e.   Can you tell us more about this role [角色 **juésè** role]?

f.   _____ (ask about her future plans)

g.   _____ (ask about her co-stars)

h.   _____ (ask about her acting history)

29
Expressing identification, possession, and existence

Complete each of the following sentences with 是 **shì**, 有 **yǒu**, or 在 **zài** to best match the English translation.

a. 北湖 _____ 公园里。

  北湖 _____ 公園裏。

  Běi Hú _____ **gōngyuán lǐ.**

  North Lake is in the park.

b. 我家 _____ 五个人。

  我家 _____ 五個人。

  Wǒ jiā _____ **wǔ gè rén.**

  There are five people in my family.

c. 院子里都 _____ 花。

  院子裏都 _____ 花。

  Yuànzi lǐ dōu _____ **huā.**

  The courtyard is full of flowers.

d. 机场 _____ 城外。

  機場 _____ 城外。

  Jīchǎng _____ **chéngwài.**

  The airport is outside of the city.

e. 他 _____ 张老师。

  他 _____ 張老師。

  Tā _____ **Zhāng lǎoshī.**

  He is teacher Zhang.

f. 万里长城 _____ 中国吗?

  萬里長城 _____ 中國嗎?

  Wànlǐ Chángchéng _____ **Zhōngguó ma?**

  Is the Great Wall in China?

g. 城外 _____ 一个机场。

  城外 _____ 一個機場。

  Chéngwài _____ **yī gè jīchǎng.**

  Outside of the city there is an airport.

h. 城西边 _____ 大学城。

城西邊 _____ 大學城。

Chéng xībian _____ dàxué chéng.

The west side of the city is the university district.

i. 那个大学 _____ 一万学生。

那個大學 _____ 一萬學生。

Nàge dàxué _____ yī wàn xuésheng.

That university has ten thousand students.

j. 电影院 _____ 图书馆的对面。

電影院 _____ 圖書館的對面。

Diànyǐng yuàn _____ túshūguǎn de duìmiàn.

The movie theater is right across from the library.

⇨ 29.1, 29.2, 29.3

2 Translate these noun phrases into English.

Example: 爸爸做的饭 → food that dad cooked

爸爸做的飯

bàba zuò de fàn

a. 我哥哥的女朋友

wǒ gēge de nǔ péngyou

b. 你的新车

你的新車

nǐ de xīn chē

c. 我们的外语老师

我們的外語老師

wǒmen de wàiyǔ lǎoshī

d. 孩子的妈妈

孩子的媽媽

háizi de māma

e. 我弟弟的同屋的朋友

wǒ dìdi de tóngwū de péngyou

f. 我朋友的同屋的弟弟

wǒ péngyou de tóngwū de dìdi

g. 张老师的妹妹的学生

張老師的妹妹的學生

Zhāng lǎoshī de mèimei de xuésheng

h. 张老师的学生的妹妹

張老師的學生的妹妹

Zhāng lǎoshī de xuésheng de mèimei

⇨ 29.2.2

3   Unscramble these noun phrases to correspond to their English translations.

a.   她的女孩子很的漂亮

    tā de nǚ háizi hěn de piàoliang

    her very pretty daughter

b.   课本的中文我

    課本的中文我

    kèběn de Zhōngwén wǒ

    my Chinese textbook

c.   你的朋友外国

    你的朋友外國

    nǐ de péngyou wàiguó

    your foreign friends

d.   我房子城里的

    我房子城裏的

    wǒ fángzi chénglǐ de

    my house in the city

e.   和气的朋友的她

    和氣的朋友的她

    héqi de péngyou de tā

    her very nice friend

f.   鞋子我的很舒服的

    xiézi wǒ de hěn shūfu de

    my very comfortable shoes

⇨   29.2.2

4   Henry is on a business trip to a city in China. On Saturday he decided to explore the city himself. The concierge at the hotel was very helpful, showing him the neighborhood on the map. Complete the dialogue for them by filling in 有 **yǒu**, 是 **shì** or 在 **zài** as appropriate.

Concierge: 您看，我们的旅馆 _____ 这儿。您想去哪儿？

           您看，我們的旅館 _____ 這兒。您想去哪兒？

           Nín kàn, women de lǚguǎn _____ zhèr. Nín xiǎng qù nǎr?

           You see, our hotel is here. Where do you want to go?

Henry: 听说附近 _____ 一个公园，现在 _____ 圣诞花灯展，我想去看看。

           聽說附近 _____ 一个公園，現在 _____ 聖誕花燈展，我想去看看。

           Tīngshuō fùjìn _____ yī ge gōngyuán, xiànzài _____

           Shèngdàn huādēng zhǎn, wǒ xiǎng qù kànkan.

           I heard there's a park nearby. There's a Christmas light show right now. I'd like to check it out.

Concierge: 我知道，您说的 _____ 中山公园吧。中山公园 _____ 这儿，您可以坐六号车。车站就 _____ 对面。上车买票。

我知道，您說的 _____ 中山公園吧。中山公園 _____ 這兒，
您可以坐六號車。車站就 _____ 對面。上車買票。

**Wǒ zhīdào, nín shuō de _____ Zhōngshān gōngyuán ba.
Zhōngshān gōngyuán _____ zhèr. Nín kěyǐ zuò liù hào chē.
Chēzhàn jiù _____ duìmiàn. Shàng chē mǎi piào.**

I know. What you said is Zhongshan Park right? Zhongshan Park
is here. You can take Bus #6. The bus stop is right across the street.
Tickets are purchased onboard.

Henry: 车站附近 _____ 可以换零钱的地方吗？

车站附近 _____ 可以換零錢的地方嗎？

fùjìn _____ kěyǐ huàn língqián de dìfāng ma?

Is there a place near the stop that I can get some change?

Concierge: 车站旁边就 _____ 那家有名的早餐店，建议您可以去吃个早餐，
顺便换钱。

車站旁邊就 _____ 那家有名的早餐店，建議您可以去吃個早餐，
順便換錢。

**Chēzhàn pángbiān jiù _____ nà jiā yǒumíng de zǎocān diàn,
jiànyì nín kěyǐ qù chī ge zǎocān, shùnbiàn huàn qián.**

Right next to the stop is that famous breakfast place. I suggest that
you can eat breakfast there and get some change.

Henry: 好，谢谢你，再见！

好，謝謝你，再見！

Hǎo, xièxie nǐ, zài jiàn!

Great. Thanks. Goodbye!

Concierge: 不客气，祝您玩得愉快！

不客氣，祝您玩得愉快！

Bù kèqi, zhù nín wán de yúkuài!

You are welcome. Have fun!

5 Your classmate is describing how messy the professor's office is. Draw a picture
of the office based on the description below.

屋子里有一张大沙发。沙发靠着墙，就在窗户的下边。沙发上都是报纸。沙发的
左边是老师的书桌，桌上放着很多书，还有好几个杯子。沙发右边有一个书架，
书架旁边的墙上挂着一幅画。书架上只有两三本书，可是地上都是书。

屋子裡有一張大沙發。沙發靠著牆，就在窗戶的下邊。沙發上都是報紙。沙發的
左邊是老師的書桌，桌上放著很多書，還有好幾個杯子。沙發右邊有一個書架，
書架旁邊的牆上掛著一幅畫。書架上只有兩三本書，可是地上都是書。

**Wūzi li yǒu yī zhāng dà shāfā. Shāfā kàozhe qiáng, jiù zài chuānghu
de xiàbian. Shāfā shàng dōu shì bàozhǐ. Shāfā de zuǒbian shì lǎoshī de
shūzhuō, zhuōshàng fàngzhe hěn duō shū, hái yǒu hǎo jǐ gè bēizi. Shāfā
yòubian yǒu yīgè shūjià, shūjià pángbiān de qiáng shàng guàzhe yī fú
huà. Shūjià shàng zhǐ yǒu liǎng sān běn shū, kěshì dìshang dōu shì shū.**

30
Describing people, places, and things

1   Describe 王明 **Wáng Míng** in complete sentences in terms of these attributes.

a.   18 years old
b.   a student
c.   intelligent
d.   tall
e.   Canadian

⇨   30.1, 30.2

2   Ask content questions about 王明 **Wáng Míng** in complete Mandarin sentences based on the following information. Each question should focus on the underlined information.

> Example: He studies <u>in China</u>.   →   他在哪儿念书？
> 他在哪兒念書？
> **Tā zài nǎr niàn shū?**

a.   He is <u>18 years old</u>.
b.   He speaks <u>Chinese</u>.
c.   He is <u>Canadian</u>.
d.   He likes <u>foreign</u> movies.
e.   His birthday is <u>June 15</u>.
f.   He has <u>two</u> younger brothers.
g.   He goes to <u>France</u> every year.
h.   He bought a <u>Chinese</u> dictionary.

⇨   28.6, 30.4, 30.7

3   In complete Mandarin sentences, explain what the following things are made of.

> Example: ice cream – cream   →   冰淇淋是用奶油做的。
> 冰淇淋是用奶油做的。
> **Bīngqilín shì yòng nǎiyóu zuò de.**

a.   books – paper
b.   candy [糖果 **táng guǒ**] – sugar [糖 **táng**]

c. steamed buns [馒头/饅頭 **mántou**] – flour [面粉/麪粉 **miànfěn**]

d. ice cubes [冰块/冰塊 **bīngkuài**] – water

e. houses – wood [木头/木頭 **mùtou**]

⇨ | 30.5

4

You are a weather forecaster. Describe the weather for these three cities in complete sentences in Mandarin.

a. *New York*	b. *Beijing*	c. *Taipei*
cold	partly cloudy	sunny
snowing	windy	humid
15 °F	–2 °C	30 °C

⇨ | 30.8

5

You are feeling ill and have a doctor's appointment. Express the conversation in Mandarin.

a. Tell the doctor that you are not feeling well, that you have a cough and a headache and that you also have a runny nose.

b. Have the doctor ask you if you have a fever.

c. Tell the doctor you don't have a fever.

d. Have the doctor ask if you have diarrhea.

e. Tell the doctor that you do.

f. Have the doctor ask you if you have a stomachache.

g. Tell her that you don't.

h. Have the doctor tell you that you have a cold. She will write you a prescription, and you should take the medicine every four hours. You should sleep a lot, and you should drink a lot of water. It would be best if you did not eat any spicy food [辣的 **là de** spicy things]. You will feel better in a couple of days.

⇨ | 30.9, 50.1.3

6

If you were to write a personal ad in Mandarin for your best friend, what would you say? Write a paragraph with no less than 50 words that includes his/her personal background, personality and appearance.

(*No answer is provided in the Answer Key.*)

7

You are telling your neighbor's children the story of 'Hansel and Gretel' in Mandarin. Describe the candy house in the story. For example, 'the roof is made of cookies'. Here's a beginning for you:

他们看到一个很奇怪的房子，_____

他們看到一個很奇怪的房子，_____

Tāmen kàndào yī ge hěn qíguài de fángzi, _____

They see a very strange house, _____

(*No answer is provided in the Answer Key.*)

31

Describing how actions are performed

1 In complete Mandarin sentences, describe how 唐玫玲 **Táng Méilíng** does each of the following actions.

> Example: walks *slowly* → 她走得很慢。
>
> 她走得很慢。
>
> **Tā zǒu de hěn màn.**

a. speaks *slowly*

b. writes *clearly*

c. eats *a lot*

d. drives *too fast*

e. studies *too little*

f. runs *very fast*

g. cooks *well*

h. sings *a lot*

⇨ 31.1

2 In complete Mandarin sentences, describe how 唐玫玲 **Táng Méilíng** does each of the following actions. Be sure to include the object of the verb in each of your sentences.

> Example: sleeps *a lot* → 她睡觉睡得很多。
>
> 她睡覺睡得很多。
>
> **Tā shuì jiào shuì de hěn duō.**

a. speaks Japanese *slowly*

b. writes Chinese characters *clearly*

c. drinks *a lot* of tea

d. drives a car *too fast*

e. studies Chinese *too little*

f. plays tennis *a lot* [打网球/打網球 **dǎ wǎngqiú** play tennis]

g. cooks Chinese food *well*

h. sings karaoke *a lot* [卡拉 OK **kǎlā** OK karaoke]

⇨ 31.1.1, 31.1.2

3 王明 **Wáng Míng** is thinking about asking 高蕾 **Gāo Lěi** for a date, but he wants to know a few things about her first. Translate his questions into English.

a. 她学得怎么样？

    她學得怎麼樣？

    Tā xué de zěnmeyàng?

b. 她做菜做得怎么样？

    她做菜做得怎麼樣？

    Tā zuò cài zuò de zěnmeyàng?

c. 她开车开得怎么样？

    她開車開得怎麼樣？

    Tā kāi chē kāi de zěnmeyàng?

d. 她唱歌儿唱得怎么样？

    她唱歌兒唱得怎麼樣？

    Tā chàng gēr chàng de zěnmeyàng?

e. 她跳舞跳得怎么样？

    她跳舞跳得怎麼樣？

    Tā tiào wǔ tiào de zěnmeyàng?

f. 她说英文说得怎么样？

    她說英文說得怎麼樣？

    Tā shuō Yīngwén shuō de zěnmeyàng?

⇨   31.2

4

This is what you tell 王明 **Wáng Míng** about 高蕾 **Gāo Lěi**. Express your opinions in Mandarin.

a. She studies well.

b. She cooks extremely well.

c. She drives (a car) a little slowly.

d. She is not bad at singing. (In Chinese: She sings not bad.)

e. She doesn't dance too well. (In Chinese: She dances not too well.)

f. She speaks English particularly accurately.

⇨   31.1

5

Rewrite these sentences in Mandarin, inserting the parenthesized adverbial modifier in the appropriate position to express the English meaning.

    Example: 孩子在玩。(高高兴兴地)

              孩子在玩。(高高興興地)

              Háizi zài wán. (gāogāo xīngxīng de)

              The children are playing. (happily)

              →

              孩子在高高兴兴地玩。

              孩子在高高興興地玩。

              Háizi zài gāogāo xīngxīng de wán.

              The children are playing happily.

a.　唐玫玲把门开开了。

唐玫玲把門開開了。

Táng Méilíng bǎ mén kāikai le.

Tang Meiling opened the door slowly. [慢慢地 **mànmān de**]

b.　唐玫玲把饭吃完了。

唐玫玲把飯吃完了。

Táng Méilíng bǎ fàn chīwán le.

Tang Meiling finished eating quickly. [快快地 **kuàikuāi de**]

c.　唐玫玲把同屋的光碟借走了。

Táng Méilíng bǎ tóngwū de guāngdié jiè zǒu le.

Tang Meiling secretly borrowed her roommate's CDs. [偷偷儿地/偷偷兒地

tōutōur de]

d.　唐玫玲帮助了妹妹。

唐玫玲幫助了妹妹。

Táng Méilíng bāngzhù le mèimei.

Tang Meiling willingly helped her younger sister. [自愿地/自願地 **zìyuàn de**]

e.　唐玫玲洗了盘子。

唐玫玲洗了盤子。

Táng Méilíng xǐ le pánzi.

Tang Meiling hurriedly washed the dishes. [匆忙地/匆忙地 **cōngmáng de**]

f.　唐玫玲叫了朋友。

Táng Méilíng jiào le péngyou.

Tang Meiling greeted her friends loudly. [大声地/大聲地 **dàshēng de**]

g.　唐玫玲写了作文。

唐玫玲寫了作文。

Táng Méilíng xiě le zuòwén.

Tang Meiling carefully wrote the essay. [用心地 **yòngxīn de**]

h.　唐玫玲听了报告。

唐玫玲聽了報告。

Táng Méilíng tīng le bàogào.

Tang Meiling listened attentively to the announcement. [认真地/認真地

rènzhēn de]

⇨　31.3

6 You are the agent of John Lee, an aspiring actor, and you are on the phone trying to set up an audition for him. Use John's resumé below to talk him up.

> ....
> a. Fluent in Chinese; conversational French
> b. Regional champion in car racing
> c. Finalist in national dance competition
> d. Two years training in classical piano [弹钢琴/彈鋼琴 **tán gāngqín**]
> ....

7 As a casting director, you want to know if this actor is worthy of an audition for the role. Find out if he has the following talents.

a. Does he run fast?

b. Does he have perfect handwriting?

c. Does he have a beautiful voice? (Is his voice nice to listen to?)

d. Does he speak clearly?

8 Ms. Annie, an elementary school teacher, is preparing her students for a 'Meet-the-Author' event with Mr. Will. Fill in the blanks with the proper adverbial modifiers to complete her talk.

安安静静地 ānān jìngjing de quietly	急急忙忙地 jíjí mángmáng de hurriedly	大声地/大聲地 dàshēng de in a loud voice	悄悄地 qiǎoqiǎo de quietly, without being noticed	认真地/認真地 rènzhēn de conscientiously

明天早上 9:50 我们就 _____ 排队(line up)准备去大礼堂(auditorium)。我知道你们都很兴奋，可是，可以 _____ 说话吗？(students: 不可以！) 到了大礼堂坐下来，要 _____ 听 Mr. Will 说话。如果听到一半你需要去厕所，请你 _____ 告诉我，然后快去快回。结束以后，排好队慢慢地走回教室，可不可以 _____ 跑？(students: 不可以！)

明天早上 9:50 我們就 _____ 排隊(line up)準備去大禮堂(auditorium)。我知道你們都很興奮，可是，可以 _____ 說話嗎？(students: 不可以！) 到了大禮堂坐下來，要 _____ 聽 Mr. Will 說話。如果聽到一半你需要去廁所，請你 _____ 告訴我，然後快去快回。結束以後，排好隊慢慢地走回教室，可不可以 _____ 跑？(students: 不可以！)

Míngtiān zǎoshang 9:50 wǒmen jiù _____ **páiduì**(line up) **zhǔnbèi qù dà lǐtáng**(auditorium)**. Wǒ zhīdào nǐmen dōu hěn xīngfèn, kěshì, kěyǐ** _____ **shuō huà ma?** (students: **Bù kěyǐ!**) **Dào le dà lǐtáng zuò xialái, yào** _____ **tīng Mr. Will shuō huà. Rúguǒ tīngdào yībàn nǐ xūyào qù cèsuǒ, qǐng nǐ** _____ **gàosu wǒ, ránhòu kuài qù kuài huí. Jiéshù yǐhòu, páihǎo duì mànmànde zǒu huí jiàoshì, kě bù kěyǐ** _____ **pǎo?** (students: **Bù kěyǐ!**)

32

Indicating result, conclusion, potential, and extent

1 Insert the right resultative verb ending to complete the meaning of each sentence.

a. 我吃 _____ 了。
   Wǒ chī _____ le.
   I'm full.

b. 我吃 _____ 了。

   Wǒ chī _____ le.
   I ate enough.

c. 我吃 _____ 了。
   Wǒ chī _____ le.
   I've finished eating.

d. 我找 _____ 了。
   Wǒ zhǎo _____ le.
   I've finished looking.

e. 我找 _____ 了。
   Wǒ zhǎo _____ le.
   I've found it.

f. 我记 _____ 了。
   我記 _____ 了。
   Wǒ jì _____ le.
   I've memorized it.

g. 我看 _____ 了。
   Wǒ kàn _____ le.
   I saw it.

h. 我看 _____ 了。
   Wǒ kàn _____ le.
   I read it wrong.

⇨ 18.3, 32.1.1

2 Translate these sentences into Mandarin, selecting the appropriate form of the parenthesized resultative verb.

a. I learned the lesson. [学会/學會 **xuéhuì** *or* 学得会/學得會 **xuédehuì**]

b. I can't memorize these characters. [没记住/沒記住 **méi jìzhu** *or* 记不住/記不住 **jìbuzhù**]

c. I didn't hear the sound. [没听见/沒聽見 **méi tīngjian** *or* 听不见/聽不見 **tīngbujiàn**]

d. I was unable to buy the book. [没买到/沒買到 **méi mǎidào** *or* 买不到/買不到 **mǎibùdào**]

e. I bought the dictionary. [买到了/買到了 **mǎidào le** *or* 买得到/買得到 **mǎidedào**]

f. I am able to understand Chinese (by listening). [听懂了/聽懂了 **tīngdǒng le** *or* 听得懂/聽得懂 **tīngdedǒng**]

g. I didn't understand (by listening). [没听懂/沒聽懂 **méi tīngdǒng** *or* 听不懂/聽不懂 **tīngbudǒng**]

h. I can't finish eating (this food). [没吃完 **méi chīwán** *or* 吃不完 **chībùwán**]

⇨ 32.1, 32.2, 32.3

3 Translate these sentences into Mandarin using the parenthesized verb with the appropriate resultative ending.

a. I bought the wrong book. [买/買 **mǎi**]

b. Can you see the subway station? [地鐵站 **dìtiě zhàn**] [看 **kàn**]

c. Have you bought that book? [买/買 **mǎi**]

d. I have bought it. [买/買 **mǎi**]

e. Have you finished reading it? [看 **kàn**]

f. No. I haven't finished reading it. [看 **kàn**]

g. Do you understand it (by reading it)? [看 **kàn**]

h. Yes (I understand it by reading it.) [看 **kàn**]

⇨ 32.1.1, 32.1.2

4 These sentences all involve the potential suffix 得了 **deliǎo** or 不了 **buliǎo**. Translate them into English.

a. 下雪了，我们走不了了。
下雪了，我們走不了了。
Xià xuě le, wǒmen zǒubuliǎo le.

b. 我的车坏了，开不了了。
我的車壞了，開不了了。
Wǒ de chē huài le, kāibuliǎo le.

c. 这么多饭，你吃得了吗？
這麼多飯，你吃得了嗎？
Zhème duō fàn, nǐ chīdeliǎo ma?

d. 他说他的手很疼，写不了字。
他說他的手很疼，寫不了字。
Tā shuō tā de shǒu hěn téng, xiěbùliǎo zì.

e. 你的花都冻死了，活不了了。[花 **huā** flower, 冻/凍 **dòng** to freeze]
你的花都凍死了，活不了了。
Nǐ de huā dōu dòngsǐle, huóbuliǎo le.

f. 你明天来得了吗？
你明天來得了嗎？
Nǐ míngtiān láideliǎo ma?

g. 听我的，一定错不了。
聽我的，一定錯不了。
Tīng wǒ de, yīdìng cuòbuliǎo.

h. 我今天有事，参加不了你们的晚会。
我今天有事，參加不了你們的晚會。
Wǒ jīntiān yǒu shì, cānjiābuliǎo nǐmen de wǎnhuì.

⇨ 18.6.2, 32.4

5 Select the correct resultative or potential expression to match the English meanings.

a. 他 _____ 大学。[考不了 – 考不上]

他 _____ 大學。[考不了 – 考不上]

Tā _____ dàxué. [kǎobùliǎo – kǎobushàng]

He can't pass the university entrance exam.

b. 我 _____ 新车。[买不了 – 买不起]

我 _____ 新車。[買不了 – 買不起]

Wǒ _____ xīnchē. [mǎibuliáo – mǎibuqǐ]

I can't afford to buy a new car.

c. 我 _____ 你。[忘不了 – 忘不掉]

Wǒ _____ nǐ. [wàngbuliǎo – wàngbudiào]

I can never forget you.

d. 我们 _____ 看电影。[来不了 – 来不及]

我們 _____ 看電影。[來不了 – 來不及]

Wǒmen _____ kàn diànyǐng. [láibuliǎo – láibují]

We won't be in time to see the movie.

e. 他已经把作业 _____ 了。[做得完 – 做完]

他已經把作業 _____ 了。[做得完 – 做完]

Tā yǐjing bǎ zuòyè _____ le. [zuòdewán – zuòwán]

He already finished his homework.

f. 我 _____ 那种事。[做不了 – 做不到]

我 _____ 那種事。[做不了 – 做不到]

Wǒ _____ nà zhǒng shì. [zuòbuliǎo – zuòbudào]

I can't do that kind of work.

g. 普通的人 _____。[进不了 – 进不去]

普通的人 _____。[進不了 – 進不去]

Pǔtōng de rén _____. [jìnbuliǎo – jìnbuqù]

Ordinary people can't go in.

h. 你不应该 _____ 你的父母。[对得起 – 对不起]

你不應該 _____ 你的父母。[對得起 – 對不起]

Nǐ bù yīnggāi _____ nǐ de fùmǔ. [duìdeqǐ – duìbuqǐ]

You must not embarrass (show disrespect for) your parents.

⇨ 32.2, 32.4

6 Use a resultative verb to complete each of the following sentences to express the English meanings.

Example: 他怎么吃 (也)　　→　他怎么吃也吃不饱。
他怎麼吃 (也)　　　　 他怎麼吃也吃不飽。
Tā zěnme chī (yě)　**Tā zěnme chī yě chī bùbǎo.**
No matter how much he eats he can't get full.

a. 我怎么吃 (也)
我怎麼吃 (也)
Wǒ zěnme chī (yě)
No matter how much I eat I can't finish.

b. 他怎么学 (也)
他怎麼學 (也)
Tā zěnme xué (yě)
No matter how much he studies he can't master (it).

c. 我怎么看 (也)
我怎麼看 (也)
Wǒ zěnme kàn (yě)
No matter how I read (it) I can't understand (it).

d. 他怎么做 (也)
他怎麼做 (也)
Tā zěnme zuò (yě)
No matter how he does (it) he does it wrong.

e. 我怎么做 (也)
我怎麼做 (也)
Wǒ zěnme zuò (yě)
No matter how I try to do (it) I can't do it.

f. 我怎么找 (也)
我怎麼找 (也)
Wǒ zěnme zhǎo (yě)
No matter how (much) I look I can't find (it).

⇨ 32.2.2.1

7 Complete these sentences in Mandarin to match the English meaning, using the phrases provided to express the result or extent of the situation.

Example: He was so tired that he could not lift his head.

[抬不起头来了/抬不起頭來了 **táibuqǐtóu lái**]

→

他累得抬不起头来了。

他累得抬不起頭來了。

Tā lèi de táibuqǐtóu lái le.

a. He was so happy that he began to sing.
[唱起歌儿来/唱起歌兒來 **chàng qǐ gēr lái**]

b. I was so tired that I slept for two days.
[睡了两天/睡了兩天 **shuì le liǎng tiān**]

c. They were so busy that they forgot to eat.
[把吃饭都忘了/把吃飯都忘了 **bǎ chī fàn dōu wàng le**]

d. He was so hungry that he ate all of the dumplings.
[把饺子都吃完了/把餃子都吃完了 **bǎ jiǎozi dōu chīwán le**]

e. He sang so much that his throat was sore.
[嗓子都疼了 **sǎngzi dōu téng le**]

f. We walked so much that our legs got swollen.
[腿都肿了/腿都腫了 **tuǐ dōu zhǒng le**]

g. I ate so much that I couldn't walk.
[走不动了/走不動了 **zǒubudòng le**]

h. The book was so interesting that I couldn't put it down.
[我简直放不下/我簡直放不下 **wǒ jiǎnzhí fàngbuxià**]

⇨ 32.6

8 王明 **Wáng Míng** is studying hard for college entrance exams. He is explaining his progress to his parents. Express this in Mandarin.

a. I've already finished studying math.

b. I have not finished studying chemistry.

c. No matter how hard I study, I can't memorize all of the chemistry formulas. [记住/記住 **jìzhù** memorize, 公式 **gōngshì** formula]

d. I can't understand the English poems (by reading).

e. I have learned (studied and mastered) all of the English vocabulary.
[词汇/詞彙 **cíhuì** vocabulary]

f. I am so nervous that I can't sleep and I can't eat.

g. No matter how I try to sleep I can't fall asleep.

h. I am so tired that I can't study anymore.

⇨ 32.1–32.6

9 Mrs. Peng is telling the nanny what needs to be done while they are away. Read the following paragraph and provide the relevant information in English.

我们回来以前三个小孩都得做完功课、洗好澡。老大写了十个法文句子，你看一下，写错的地方让她重写。老二说她找不到她的字典。请你帮她找找看。找不到的话帮她上网买一本。我煮了一锅汤。如果没有喝完要放进冰箱里。吃完晚饭才可以看电视。老三今天穿的那件上衣弄脏了，你能不能帮她用水洗一下。洗不干净的话就丢进洗衣机里。我们大约十点到家。如果有事就给我打电话，要是我没听到你就留言吧。谢谢你。

我們回來以前三個小孩都得做完功課、洗好澡。老大寫了十個法文句子，你看一下，寫錯的地方讓她重寫。老二說她找不到她的字典。請你幫她找找看。找不到的話幫她上網買一本。我煮了一鍋湯。如果沒有喝完要放進冰箱里。吃完晚飯才可以看電視。老三今天穿的那件上衣弄髒了，你能不能幫她用水洗一下。洗不乾淨的話就丟進洗衣機里。我們大約十點到家。如果有事就給我打電話，要是我沒聽到你就留言吧。謝謝你。

Wǒmen huí lai yǐqián sān gè xiǎohái dōu děi zuòwán gōngkè, xǐhǎo zǎo. Lǎo dà xiěle shí gè Fǎwén jùzi, nǐ kàn yīxià, xiěcuò de dìfang ràng tā chóng xiě. Lǎo'èr shuō tā zhǎobudào tā de zìdiǎn. Qǐng nǐ bāng tā zhǎozhǎo kàn. Zhǎobudào de huà bāng tā shàng wǎng mǎi yī běn. Wǒ zhǔ le yī guō tang. Rúguǒ méi yǒu hē wán yào fàng jìn bīngxiāng lǐ. Chīwán wǎnfàn cái kěyǐ kàn diànshì. Lǎo sān jīntiān chuān de nà jiàn shàngyī nòngzāng le, nǐ néng bù néng bāng tā yòng shuǐ xǐ yīxià? Xǐ bù gānjìng de huà jiù diū jìn xǐyījī lǐ. Wǒmen dàyuē shídiǎn dào jiā. Rúguǒ yǒu shì jiù gěi wǒ dǎ diànhuà, yàoshi wǒ méi tīngdào nǐ jiù liúyán ba. Xièxie nǐ.

Things the children need to do before Mr. and Mrs. Peng come back tonight:

a.

b.

c.

Things that the nanny needs to take care of:

d. 10 French sentences:

e. Dictionary:

f. T-shirt:

g. Soup:

h. Phone call:

33
Making comparisons

1

Compare 王明 **Wáng Míng** and 周利 **Zhōu Lì** in complete Mandarin sentences using 比 **bǐ**, 没/沒有 **méi yǒu**, or 跟 (和) …一样/一樣 **gēn (hé)** . . . **yīyàng** as appropriate.

Example: equally hardworking → 王明跟周利一样用功。
王明跟周利一樣用功。
Wáng Míng gēn zhōulì yīyàng yònggōng.

王明 Wáng Míng		周利 Zhōu Lì
a.		equally tall (the same height)
b. smarter [聪明/聰明 cōngming]		
c.		not as fast
d. more handsome [帅/帥 shuài]		
e.		not as hardworking [用功 yònggōng]
f.	equally interesting [有意思 yǒu yìsī]	
g. lazier [懒/懶 lǎn]		
h.		not as friendly [和气/和氣 héqi]
i. thinner [瘦 shòu]		
j.	equally happy	

⇨ 33.1.3, 33.3.1, 33.4

2 Ask the following yes–no questions about 王明 **Wáng Míng** and 周利 **Zhōu Lì** in Mandarin.

    a. Are Wang Ming and Zhou Li equally smart?

    b. Is Zhou Li taller than Wang Ming?

    c. Is Wang Ming lazier than Zhou Li?

    d. Are Wang Ming and Zhou Li equally interesting?

    e. Is Wang Ming better looking than Zhou Li?

⇨ 28.1, 33.1–33.3

3 In complete Mandarin sentences, say that 王明 **Wáng Míng** outperforms 周利 **Zhōu Lì** in each of the following actions. Include the object of the comparison in your sentences.

    Example: takes tests – better → 王明比周利考试考得好。

                                    王明比周利考試考得好。

                                    Wáng Míng bǐ Zhōu Lì kǎo shì kǎo de hǎo.

    a. sings songs – better [唱歌兒 **chàng gēr**]

    b. writes Chinese – better

    c. works – faster [做事 **zuò shì**]

    d. cooks food – better [做菜 **zuò cài**]

    e. speaks English – better

    f. dances – better [跳舞 **tiào wǔ**]

    g. studies – more

    h. reads books – more

    i. sees more movies

    j. plays ball – better [打球 **dǎ qiú**]

⇨ 33.3.5

4 In complete Mandarin sentences, say that 周利 **Zhōu Lì** is not as good as 王明 **Wáng Míng** in performing each of the actions listed in (3) above. Include the object of the comparison in your sentences.

    Example: taking tests → 周利没有王明考试考得好。

                                周利沒有王明考試考得好。

                              Zhōu Lì méi yǒu Wáng Míng kǎo shì kǎo de hǎo.

⇨ 33.4.3

5 In complete Mandarin sentences, say that 王明 **Wáng Míng** and 周利 **Zhōu Lì** are identical in their performance of the actions listed in (3). Include the object of the comparison in your sentences. For (5) say that they study equally well.

    Example: taking tests → 王明跟周利考试考得一样好。

                                王明跟周利考試考得一樣好。

                              Wáng Míng gēn Zhōu Lì kǎo shì kǎo de

                              yīyàng hǎo.

⇨ 33.1.6

6   Put these Mandarin phrases in the correct order to match the English translations.

a.   周利的薪水一倍多比王明的薪水。

Zhōu Lì de xīnshui yī bèi duō bǐ Wáng Míng de xīnshui.

Zhou Li's salary is twice as much as Wang Ming's salary.

b.   比周利的朋友得王明的朋友多多。

bǐ Zhōu Lì de péngyou de Wáng Míng de péngyou duō duō.

Zhou Li has a lot more friends than Wang Ming.

c.   周利高一点比王明。

周利高一點比王明。

Zhōu Lì gāo yīdiǎn bǐ Wáng Míng.

Zhou Li is a little taller than Wang Ming.

d.   林伟学更高比周利。

林偉學更高比周利。

Lín Wěixué gèng gāo bǐ Zhōu Lì.

Lin Weixue is even taller than Zhou Li.

e.   王明写得最写汉字漂亮。

王明寫得最寫漢字漂亮。

Wáng Míng xiě de zuì xiě Hàn zì piàoliang.

Wang Ming writes Chinese characters the prettiest (of everyone).

⇨ 33.3.4.1, 33.3.4.2, 33.3.4.3, 33.3.4.4, 33.5, 33.6

7   Translate the following into English.

a.   周利比王明大两岁。

周利比王明大兩歲。

Zhōu Lì bǐ Wáng Míng dà liǎng suì.

b.   周利的车比王明的车贵五千块钱。

周利的車比王明的車貴五千塊錢。

Zhōu Lì de chē bǐ Wáng Míng de chē guì wǔ qiān kuài qián.

c.   周利的车比王明的车大一点。

周利的車比王明的車大一點。

Zhōu Lì de chē bǐ Wáng Míng de chē dà yīdiǎn.

d.   林伟学的车更大。

林偉學的車更大。

Lín Wěixué de chē gèng dà.

e.   这本书比那本书贵得多。

這本書比那本書貴得多。

Zhè běn shū bǐ nà běn shū guì de duō.

f.   周利比王明吃得多得多。

Zhōu Lì bǐ Wáng Míng chī de duō de duō.

g.　林伟学吃饭吃得最多。

林偉學吃飯吃得最多。

Lín Wěixué chī fàn chī de zuì duō.

h.　王明写汉字写得没有周利那么漂亮。

王明寫漢字寫得沒有周利那麼漂亮。

Wáng Míng xiě Hàn zì xiě de méi yǒu Zhōu Lì nàme piàoliang.

⇨　33.3.4.1, 33.3.4.2, 33.3.4.3, 33.3.4.4, 33.5, 33.6

8　Translate these sentences into Mandarin. The Mandarin translations of underlined words are provided in brackets.

a.　My younger brother <u>works</u> a lot faster than I. [做事 **zuò shì**]

b.　My younger brother eats a lot more food than I do.

c.　My younger brother doesn't <u>earn</u> as much <u>money</u> as I do. [赚钱/賺錢 **zhuàn qián**]

d.　I earn a lot more money than him.

e.　I am eleven years older than my younger brother.

f.　This movie is not as <u>interesting</u> as that movie. [有意思 **yǒu yìsī**]

g.　I like that movie the most.

h.　This book is twice as expensive as that book.

⇨　6.6.5, 33.3.4.1, 33.3.4.2, 33.3.5, 33.4.1, 33.4.3, 33.6

9　Translate these sentences with 不如 **bùrú**, 比较/比較 **bǐjiào**, and 相当/相當 **xiāngdāng** into English.

a.　这课的生词相当多。

這課的生詞相當多。

Zhè kè de shēngcí xiāngdāng duō.

b.　这个学期我选的课都比较容易。

這個學期我選的課都比較容易。

Zhège xuéqī wǒ xuǎn de kè dōu bǐjiào róngyì.

c.　学日文不如学中文。

學日文不如學中文。

Xué Rìwén bùrú xué Zhōngwén.

d.　这种字典比较难买。

這種字典比較難買。

Zhè zhǒng zìdiǎn bǐjiào nán mǎi.

e.　他觉得所有的人都不如他。

他覺得所有的人都不如他。

Tā juédé suóyǒu de rén dōu bùrú tā.

f.　那个学生学得相当努力。

那個學生學得相當努力。

Nàge xuéshēng xué de xiāngdāng nǔlì.

⇨　33.4.2, 33.7

10 You are planning to buy a house in China and are asking a Chinese friend for advice. Express this conversation in Mandarin.

a. Ask your friend how much houses sell for in China.

b. Your friend tells you the following:

(i) Houses outside the city are less expensive than houses inside the city.

(ii) Houses outside the city are also a lot bigger than houses in the city.

(iii) However, living outside the city is not as convenient as living inside the city.

c. Ask your friend, if you buy a house in the city, what kind of house is the cheapest.

d. Your friend tells you the following:

(i) A house that faces south is more expensive than a house that faces north.

(ii) A house that faces east is a little cheaper than a house that faces west.

⇨ 33.3, 33.4, 47.3, 54.2

11 美如 Měirú and 美芸/美蕓 Měiyún are sisters. Compare them by completing each sentence based on the following information.

	Age	Height	Driving record	Grades	Parent–child resemblance
美如 Měirú	20	5'5"	perfect	B+ average	looks like mom
美芸/美蕓 Měiyún	17	5'5"	speeding tickets	straight A's	looks like dad

a. _____ 是姐姐，_____ 是妹妹。姐姐比妹妹大 _____。

_____ 是姐姐，_____ 是妹妹。姐姐比妹妹大 _____。

_____ shì jiějie, _____ shì mèimei. Jiějie bǐ mèimei dà _____.

b. _____ 高。

_____ 高。

_____ gāo.

c. 美如开车 _____。

美如開車 _____。

Měirú kāi chē _____.

d. 美如的成绩 _____。

美如的成績 _____。

Měirú de chéngjì _____.

e. 美芸不象 _____，跟爸爸 _____。

美蕓不像 _____，跟爸爸 _____。

Měiyún bù xiàng _____, gēn bàba _____.

12 Do you have any siblings? If so, use the above as your inspiration and write a short passage comparing you and your sibling. If you don't have a sibling, write about you and your cousin, best friend, etc.

34
Talking about the present

1

In complete Mandarin sentences describe what 王明 **Wáng Míng** is doing at each of the times indicated below. Use the time expressions provided in your sentences. Translate your sentences into English.

Example: today –

买东西	→	王明今天买东西。
買東西		王明今天買東西。
mǎi dōngxi		**Wáng Míng jīntiān mǎi dōngxi.**
		Wang Ming is shopping today.

a. this year – 学中文/學中文 xué **Zhōngwén**

b. this month – 放假 **fàng jià**

c. this week – 在意大利旅行 **zài Yìdàlì lǚxíng**

d. now – 跟朋友吃饭/跟朋友吃飯 **gēn péngyou chī fàn**

e. presently – 洗澡 **xǐ zǎo**

⇨ 34.1

2

What are the following people doing now? Describe their activities in complete Mandarin sentences using 在 **zài** or 正在 **zhèngzài**.

Example: 高蕾 **Gāo Lěi** – sleeping → 高蕾在睡觉。
　　　　　　　　　　　　　　　　　　高蕾在睡覺。
　　　　　　　　　　　　　　　Gāo Lěi zài shuì jiào.

a. 王明 **Wáng Míng** – watching television

b. 周利 **Zhōu Lì** – singing

c. 林伟学/林偉學 **Lín Wěixué** – playing ball

d. 唐玫玲 **Táng Méilíng** – writing a letter

⇨ 17.2, 34.2

3

Translate the following into English.

a. 门外头站着一个人。
　门外頭站著一個人。
　Mén wàitou zhànzhe yī gè rén.

b. 桌子上放着很多书。
　桌子上放著很多書。
　Zhuōzi shàng fàngzhe hěn duō shū.

   c.   孩子在床上躺着。

        孩子在床上躺著。

        Háizi zài chuángshàng tǎngzhe.

   d.   医院里等着很多病人。

        醫院裏等著很多病人。

        Yīyuàn lǐ děngzhe hěn duō bìngrén.

   e.   教室里坐着很多学生。

        教室裏坐著很多學生。

        Jiàoshì lǐ zuòzhe hěn duō xuésheng.

⇨ 17.2, 34.4

4

Translate the following sentences into Mandarin to describe 王明 **Wáng Míng**'s activities and to indicate that he intends to continue doing each one.

a.   Wang Ming has already eaten thirty dumplings. [饺子/餃子 **jiǎozi**]

b.   Wang Ming has already walked five miles.

c.   Wang Ming has already studied one hundred Chinese characters.

d.   Wang Ming has already sung three songs.

e.   Wang Ming has already slept for ten hours.

⇨ 34.7

5

You are a Chinese student writing to a university abroad to apply for admission to their doctoral program in economics. You have written the first draft in Mandarin. Translate it into English.

a.   我是大学四年级的学生。

       我是大學四年級的學生。

       Wǒ shì dàxué sì niánjí de xuésheng.

b.   我现在在写毕业论文，是有关现代中国经济环境的。

       我現在在寫畢業論文，是有關現代中國經濟環境的。

       Wǒ xiànzài zài xiě bìyè lùnwén, shì yǒuguān xiàndài Zhōngguó jīngjì huánjìng de.

c.   我在申请读贵校的经济学系的研究生。

       我在申請讀貴校的經濟學系的研究生。

       Wǒ zài shēnqǐng dú guì xiào de jīngjìxué xì de yánjiūshēng.

d.   我对经济特别感兴趣，希望能读博士学位。

       我對經濟特別感興趣，希望能讀博士學位。

       Wǒ duì jīngjì tèbié gǎn xìngqu, xīwàng néng dú bóshì xuéwèi.

e.   目前我正在为我的论文做市场调查。

       目前我正在爲我的論文做市場調查。

       Mùqián wǒ zhèngzài wéi wǒ de lùnwén zuò shìchǎng diàochá.

f. 同时我还在准备托福考试。

同時我還在準備托福考試。

Tóngshí wǒ hái zài zhǔnbèi tuōfú kǎoshì. [托福 **tuōfú** the Test of English as a Foreign Language]

g. 其他成功申请者应具备哪些条件请告知。

其他成功申請者應具備哪些條件請告知。

Qítā chénggōng shēnqǐng zhě yīng jùbèi nǎ xiē tiáojiàn qǐng gàozhī.

h. 另外，有关外国学生的经济资助等事宜亦请告知。

另外，有關外國學生的經濟資助等事宜亦請告知。

Lìngwài, yǒu guān wàiguó xuésheng de jīngjì zīzhù děng shìyí yì qǐng gàozhī.

⇨ 9.2, 34

6

You are hosting an open house for a new art gallery in Chinatown. Below is a list of special guests who will be present tonight. Prepare to introduce them in Mandarin.

a. Mr. **Zhìmíng Liào** 廖志明:
   - has lived in New York [纽约 **Niǔyuē**] for 30 years.
   - is himself a famous artist [画家/畫家 **huàjiā**]
   - is now the owner of three galleries [画廊/畫廊 **huàláng**] in New York.

b. Professor Richard Yamaguchi:
   - has been teaching Chinese literature [文学/文學 **wénxué**] for over 20 years.
   - currently teaches at NYU [纽约大学/紐約大學 **Niǔyuē Dàxué**].
   - has written five books on Chinese art and literature and is currently working on his sixth book.

c. Ms. Catherine Simon:
   - has been studying Chinese for over seven years.
   - is studying art history [艺术史/藝術史 **yìshù shǐ**] at NYU right now.

35

Talking about habitual actions

1 Rewrite the Mandarin sentences, adding the adverb that is provided in parentheses after each English translation.

Example: 她在那个饭馆吃饭。　　→　她平常在那个饭馆吃饭。
她在那個飯館吃飯。　　　　她平常在那個飯館吃飯。
Tā zài nàge fànguǎn　　　**Tā píngcháng zài nàge fànguǎn**
chī fàn.　　　　　　　　**chī fàn.**
She eats at that restaurant. (often)

a. 我早上跑步。
Wǒ zǎoshang pǎo bù.
I jog in the morning. (often)

b. 他们吃中国饭。
他們吃中國飯。
Tāmen chī Zhōngguó fàn.
They eat Chinese food. (often)

c. 我七点钟吃晚饭。
我七點鐘吃晚飯。
Wǒ qīdiǎn zhōng chī wǎnfàn.
I eat dinner at 7 p.m. (usually)

d. 我们去法国旅行。
我們去法國旅行。
Wǒmen qù Fǎguó lǚxíng.
In the past we used to go to France for vacation. (always)

e. 我早上喝咖啡。
Wǒ zǎoshang hē kāfēi.
I drink coffee in the morning. (always)

f. 我们下班以后打网球。
我們下班以後打網球。
Wǒmen xià bān yǐhòu dǎ wǎngqiú.
We play tennis after work. (often)

g. 你在那个饭馆吃饭吗?

你在那個飯館吃飯嗎?

Nǐ zài nàge fànguǎn chī fàn ma?

Do you eat at that restaurant? (frequently)

h. 我看那个电视节目。

我看那個電視節目。

Wǒ kàn nàge diànshì jiémù.

I watch that television program. (regularly)

i. 我晚上遛狗。

Wǒ wǎnshang liù gǒu.

I walk my dog at night. (always)

j. 我看电影。

我看電影。

Wǒ kàn diànyǐng.

I see a movie. (every week)

⇨ 35.3

2

You are writing to your Chinese pen pal in Mandarin, telling her about your typical activities.

a. Say that except for the weekends, you go to class every day.

b. Tell her that you begin class at 8:30 a.m. every day.

c. Say that you usually get out of class at 4, but on Fridays you get out of class at 1.

d. Say that you work in a hospital every Friday afternoon.

e. Tell her that when the weather is nice, you usually take a walk in the park on Saturday afternoon.

f. Say that you always go to see a movie with your friends on Saturday night.

g. Say that you used to always eat at a restaurant on Sunday with your family.

h. Tell her that you often stay in the dormitory on Sunday and do homework.

⇨ 35.1, 35.3

3

You are a detective working with someone from Interpol to conduct a stakeout in order to catch a suspect in action. Explain in Mandarin to your new partner the routine of this suspect based on the information you have gathered so far:

a. leaves the house <u>every</u> morning at 7:30.

b. <u>Always</u> buys a cup of coffee at the shop next to the bus stop.

c. <u>Often</u> goes to the gym [健身房/**jiànshēnfáng**] during lunch break (at noon).

d. <u>Always</u> goes straight home after work. <u>Never</u> goes out for dinner with co-workers.

e. Works part-time at a bookstore <u>every</u> Sunday.

⇨ 35.1, 35.2, 35.3

4 Marge's father is a billionaire. She grew up living in luxury. Imagine her lifestyle and complete the sentences below.

a. Marge 从来不在 _____ 买东西，也从来没去过 _____。

Marge 從來不在 _____ 買東西，也從來沒去過 _____。

Marge cónglái bù zài _____ mǎi dōngxi, yě cónglái méi qùguò _____.

b. Marge 出门 _____ 有司机开车，_____ 坐过公共汽车。

Marge 出門 _____ 有司機開車，_____ 坐過公共汽車。

Marge chū mén _____ yǒu sījī kāi chē, _____ zuò guò gōnggòng qìchē.

c. Marge 跟朋友去吃饭，_____ 是她请客。

Marge 跟朋友去吃飯，_____ 是她請客。

Marge gēn péngyǒu qù chī fàn, _____ shì tā qǐng kè.

d. Marge 的爸爸 _____ 送她很贵的礼物。(regularly)

Marge 的爸爸 _____ 送她很貴的禮物。

Marge de bàba _____ sòng tā hěn guì de lǐwù.

e. Marge 从来没自己 _____。

Marge 從來沒自己 _____。

Marge cónglái méi zìjǐ _____.

⇨ 35.1, 35.2, 35.3

36
Talking about the future

Rewrite these sentences, putting the Mandarin time words in the appropriate location in the sentence. Translate your completed sentences into English.

Example: 我们打球。(明天)   →   我们明天打球。

我們打球。(明天)   我們明天打球。

Wǒmen dǎ qiú. (míngtiān)   **Wǒmen míngtiān dǎ qiú.**

We are playing ball tomorrow.

a. 你要去哪儿跳舞？(今天)

你要去哪兒跳舞？(今天)

Nǐ yào qù nǎr tiào wǔ? (jīntiān)

b. 他一定会有很多钱。(将来)

他一定會有很多錢。(將來)

Tā yīdìng huì yǒu hěn duō qián. (jiānglái)

c. 我请你去看电影。(明天晚上)

我請你去看電影。(明天晚上)

Wǒ qǐng nǐ qù kàn diànyǐng. (míngtiān wǎnshang)

d. 谁去中国学习？(明年)

誰去中國學習？(明年)

Shéi qù Zhōngguó xuéxí? (míngnián)

e. 我们放假。(下个星期)

我們放假。(下個星期)

Wǒmen fàng jià. (xià gè xīngqī)

f. 我们打算去意大利旅行。(下个月)

我們打算去意大利旅行。(下個月)

Wǒmen dǎsuan qù Yìdàlì lǚxíng. (xià gè yuè)

g. 天气预报说会下雪。(后天)

天氣預報說會下雪。(後天)

Tiānqì yùbào shuō huì xià xuě. (hòutiān)

h. 我想给奶奶打电话。(明天早上)

我想給奶奶打電話。(明天早上)

Wǒ xiǎng gěi nǎinai dǎ diànhuà. (míngtiān zǎoshang)

⇨ 36.1

2 Complete these sentences with the Mandarin words or phrases that best express the English translations.

a. 我 _____ 结婚了。

    我 _____ 結婚了。

    Wǒ _____ jiéhūn le.

    I will get married soon.

b. 请你明天 _____ 来。

    請你明天 _____ 來。

    Qǐng nǐ míngtiān lái.

    Please come again tomorrow.

c. 明天 _____ 下雨。

    明天 _____ 下雨。

    Míngtiān _____ xià yǔ.

    It may rain tomorrow.

d. 他今天 _____ 不来上课了。

    他今天 _____ 不來上課了。

    Tā jīntiān _____ bù lái shàng kè le.

    He probably won't come to class today.

e. 你 _____ 跟他结婚吗？

    你 _____ 跟他結婚嗎？

    Nǐ _____ gēn tā jiéhūn ma?

    Are you willing to marry him?

f. 你 _____ 将来住在哪儿？

    你 _____ 將來住在哪兒？

    Nǐ _____ jiānglái zhù zài nǎr?

    Where do you plan to live in the future?

g. 我 _____ 早一点下课。

    我 _____ 早一點下課。

    Wǒ _____ zǎo yīdiǎn xià kè.

    I am thinking about leaving class a little early.

h. 我不要 _____ 看那个电影了。

    我不要 _____ 看那個電影了。

    Wǒ bù yào _____ kàn nàge diànyǐng le.

    I don't want to see that movie again.

⇨ 36.1, 36.2, 36.3, 36.4

3

王明 **Wáng Míng** has made a list of things that he has to do. Rewrite the list in complete Mandarin sentences.

Example: this morning: → 我今天早上要给我的女朋友打电话。
        call girlfriend   我今天早上要給我的女朋友打電話。
                      Wǒ jīntiān zǎoshang yào gěi wǒ de
                      nǚ péngyou dǎ diànhuà.

a. this afternoon: borrow money from roommate
b. tomorrow morning: buy girlfriend a birthday present
c. the day after tomorrow: make reservation at restaurant
d. next week: return money to roommate
e. next Tuesday: borrow money from roommate again
f. next month: definitely look for a job

⇨ 36.1, 36.2, 36.4

4

Mr. Wang is discussing his schedule with his personal assistant, George. Translate their conversation into Mandarin, incorporating the following schedule.

2/5 (today)	2/6	2/7
12:30 p.m. lunch with Mr. Chen	9–11:00 a.m. conference call	1:30 p.m. flight
2:30 p.m. meeting with Mr. Li	1–3:00 p.m. meeting with	UA 360 to Tokyo
3:30 p.m. meeting with R & D	Marketing	[UA 联合/聯合
4:30 p.m. meeting with PR team	3–4:00 p.m. conference call	**liánhé**]
6:00 p.m. dinner with Director Cao		

George: 李先生 (a)_____ 会来跟您见面。
Mr. Wang: 我不是上个星期才和他见面吗？怎么今天 (b)_____ 要见面了？
George: 他说他 (c)_____(plan) 今天跟您讨论合作细节。
Mr. Wang: 我中午有什么事？
George: 您今天中午 (d)_____。(e)_____ 开始连着有三个会。
Mr. Wang: 给李先生打电话，说我中午有事，下午 (f)_____(possibly) 回不来。
           问他 (g)_____ _____(willing) 改成 (h) _____(the day after tomorrow) 见面。
George: 您 (i)_____ 的飞机去日本，只有 (j)_____ 有空。我可以给他打电话
          问问。如果不行，您明天 (k)_____ 以后就没有事了，那时候也可以吧？
Mr. Wang: 好。让司机 (l)_____(get ready) 车，我 (m)_____ 出去一下。
George: 我马上去。

George: 李先生(a)_____ 會來跟您見面。
Mr. Wang: 我不是上個星期才和他見面嗎？怎麼今天 (b)_____ 要見面了？
George: 他說他 (c)_____(plan) 今天跟您討論合作細節。
Mr. Wang: 我中午有甚麼事？
George: 您今天中午 (d)_____。(e)_____ 開始連著有三個會。

Mr. Wang: 給李先生打電話，說我中午有事，下午 (f)————(possibly) 回不來。

問他 (g)———— ————(willing) 改成 (h)————(the day after tomorrow) 見面。

George: 您 (i)———— 的飛機去日本，只有 (j)———— 有空。我可以給他打電話

問問。如果不行，您明天 (k)———— 以後就沒有事了，那時候也可以吧？

Mr. Wang: 好。讓司機 (l)————(get ready) 車，我 (m)———— 出去一下。

George: 我馬上去。

George: Lǐ Xiānsheng (a)———— huì lái gēn nín jiàn miàn.

Mr. Wang: Wǒ bù shì shàng ge xīngqī cái gēn tā jiàn miàn? Zěnme jīntiān

(b)———— yào jiàn miàn le?

George: Tā shuō tā (c)————(plan) jīntiān gēn nín tǎolùn hézuò xìjié.

Mr. Wang: Wǒ zhōngwǔ yǒu shénme shì? Xiàwǔ ne?

George: Nín jīntiān zhōngwǔ (d)————. (e)———— kāishǐ lián zhe yǒu

sān gè huì.

Mr. Wang: Gěi Lǐ Xiānsheng dǎ diànhuà, shuō wǒ zhōngwǔ yǒu shì, xiàwǔ

(f)————(possibly) huí bù lái. Wèn tā (g)————(willing) gǎi chéng

(h)————(the day after tomorrow) jiàn miàn.

George: Nín (i)———— de fēijī qù Rìběn, zhǐ yǒu (j)———— yǒu kòng.

Wǒ kěyǐ gěi tā dǎ diànhuà wènwen. Rúguǒ bù xíng, nín míngtiān

(k)———— yǐhòu jiù méi yǒu shì le, nà shíhòu yě kěyǐ ba?

Mr. Wang: Hǎo. Ràng sījī (l)————(get ready) chē, wǒ (m)———— chūqù yīxià.

George: Wǒ mashing qù.

37

Indicating completion and talking about the past

1 Describe my older brother's dinner party in complete sentences in Mandarin. Pay attention to the position of time and location phrases in your sentences.

a. My older brother bought a house last month.
b. Last week he invited some friends to his house to eat dinner.
c. He cooked five dishes.
d. He also made a soup.
e. His friends gave him a bottle of wine. [送⋯一瓶酒 **sòng . . . yīpíng jiǔ**]
f. They ate the food and drank the wine.

⇨ 17.1, 37.1

2 Describe the sequence of events at the dinner party in complete Mandarin sentences using 了 **le**, 以后/以後 **yǐhòu**, and 就 **jiù**.

> Example: After my brother → 我哥哥下了班以后就回家了。
> got out of work, 我哥哥下了班以後就回家了。
> he went home. **Wǒ gēge xià le bān yǐhòu jiù huí jiā le.**

a. After the guests arrived, my older brother invited them to drink tea.
b. After they drank tea, my older brother invited them to eat dinner.
c. After they ate, they all sang some songs.
d. After they sang, they went home.
e. After they left, my older brother began to wash the dishes. [洗 **xǐ** wash, 盘子/盤子 **pán zi** dishes]
f. After he washed the dishes he went to sleep.

⇨ 17.1.2, 37.2, 42.2

3 王明 **Wáng Míng** is getting ready for the new semester. Here is a list of things he has done and things that he has not yet done. Translate the list into Mandarin in complete sentences.

> Example: *Done* → 王明已经买电脑了。
> bought a computer 王明已經買電腦了。
> **Wáng Míng yǐjing mǎi diànnǎo le.**
>
> *Not yet done* → 王明还没看他的朋友。
> see his friends 王明還沒看他的朋友。
> **Wáng Míng hái méi kàn tā de péngyou.**

Done	*Not yet done*
a. select classes [选课/選課 **xuǎn kè**]	d. buy textbooks
b. buy notebooks	e. review Chinese characters [复习汉字/復習漢字 **fùxí Hàn zì**]
c. pay tuition [付学费/付學費 **fù xuéfèi**]	f. find classrooms [找教室 **zhǎo jiàoshì**]

⇨ 17.1, 37.1, 37.3

4 王明 **Wáng Míng**'s mother asks him whether he has done the following. Translate her questions into Mandarin.

a. Have you cleaned your room? [收拾屋子 **shōushí wūzi**]

b. Have you done your homework? [做作业/做作業 **zuò zuòyè**]

c. Have you finished your essay? [写作文/寫作文 **xiě zuòwén**]

d. Have you looked for a job? [找工作 **zhǎo gōngzuò**]

e. Have you selected your classes?

f. Have you bought your textbooks?

⇨ 17.1.1.2, 17.1.1.3, 37.4

5 Rewrite these sentences in Mandarin, adding 又 **yòu** to indicate that the action happened again in the past. Translate your sentences into English.

Example: 我们昨天考试了。 → 我们昨天又考试了。
我們昨天考試了。　　　　我們昨天又考試了。
Wǒmen zuótiān kǎo shì le.　　**Wǒmen zuótiān yòu kǎo shì le.**
We took a test yesterday.　　We took a test again yesterday.

a. 我父母去日本了。
我父母去日本了。
Wǒ fùmǔ qù Rìběn le.
My parents went to Japan.

b. 你出错误了。
你出錯誤了。
Nǐ chū cuòwù le.
You made a mistake.

c. 我给了他二十块钱。
我給了他二十塊錢。
Wǒ gěi le tā èrshí kuài qián.
I gave him $20.

d. 我跟朋友看了那个电影。
我跟朋友看了那個電影。
Wǒ gēn péngyou kàn le nàge diànyǐng.
I saw a movie with friends.

e. 我打篮球了。

    我打籃球了。

    Wǒ dǎ lánqiú le.

    I played basketball.

f. 我给她打电话了。

    我給她打電話了。

    Wǒ gěi tā dǎ diànhuà le.

    I gave her a phone call. (I called her on the phone.)

⇨ 37.5

6 Using the cues in parentheses, answer the following questions in complete Mandarin sentences.

Example: 你吃过中国饭没有？ (no) → 我没吃过中国饭。

你吃過中國飯沒有？   我沒吃過中國飯。

Nǐ chīguò Zhōngguó   **Wǒ méi chīguò Zhōngguó fàn.**
fàn méi yǒu?

a. 你看过没看过中国电影？ (yes)

    你看過沒看過中國電影？

    Nǐ kànguo méi kànguo Zhōngguó diànyǐng?

b. 你今年检查过身体吗？ (no)

    你今年檢查過身體嗎？

    Nǐ jīnnián jiǎncháguo shēntǐ ma? [检查身体/檢查身體 **jiǎnchá shēntǐ**

    have a physical exam]

c. 你学过英文吗？ (yes)

    你學過英文嗎？

    Nǐ xuéguo Yīngwén ma?

d. 我没吃过这个菜。你呢？ (never)

    我沒吃過這個菜。你呢？

    Wǒ méi chīguo zhège cài. Nǐ ne?

e. 你看过这本书吗？ (no)

    你看過這本書嗎？

    Nǐ kànguò zhè běn shū ma?

f. 你学过经济学吗？ [经济学/經濟學 **jīngjì xué** economics] (yes)

    你學過經濟學嗎？

    Nǐ xuéguò jīngjìxué ma?

g. 你唱过卡拉OK吗？ [卡拉 OK **kǎlā** OK karaoke] (not yet)

    你唱過卡拉OK嗎？

    Nǐ chàngguo kǎlā OK ma?

h. 你吃过日本饭吗？ (yes)

    你吃過日本飯嗎？

    Nǐ chīguò Rìběn fàn ma?

⇨ 17.3, 37.6

127

7 Fill in the blanks, using either 过/過 **guo**, 了 **le**, or 过了/過了 **guo le** as appropriate.

a. 我妹妹跟她朋友去 _____ 中国。

我妹妹跟她朋友去 _____ 中國。

Wǒ mèimei gēn tā péngyou qù _____ Zhōngguó.

My younger sister and her friend went to China.

b. 我从来没去 _____ 日本，可是我哥哥在那儿住 _____ 两年。

我從來沒去 _____ 日本，可是我哥哥在那兒住 _____ 兩年。

Wǒ cónglái méi qù _____ Rìběn, kěshì wǒ gēge zài nàr zhù _____

liǎng nián.

I have never been to Japan, but my older brother lived there for two years.

c. 你吃没吃 _____ 泰国饭？

你吃沒吃 _____ 泰國飯？

Nǐ chī méi chī _____ Tàiguó fàn?

Have you eaten Thai food before?

d. 我们老师给我们介绍 _____ 以后就是好朋友 _____。

我們老師給我們介紹 _____ 以後就是好朋友 _____。

Wǒmen lǎoshī gěi wǒmen jièshào _____ yǐhòu jiù shì hǎo péngyou

_____.

After our teacher introduced us we became good friends.

e. 我们以前都没有见 _____ 这个人。

我們以前都沒有見 _____ 這個人。

Wǒmen yǐqián dōu méi yǒu jiàn _____ zhège rén.

None of us have ever met this person before.

⇨ 17.1, 17.3, 37.1, 37.3, 37.6, 37.7

8 Translate the following sentences into Mandarin using adverbs to indicate past time.

a. He was my boyfriend.

b. I used to drink coffee every morning.

c. When I was young I liked to talk a lot.

d. Gasoline was 19 cents a gallon in 1962. [加仑 **jiālún** gallon]

e. This used to be a park.

f. Previously, I was not interested in China.

⇨ 37.8

9   Rewrite these sentences in Mandarin, adding 是 **shì** . . . 的 **de** to focus on the underlined detail of each past event.

     Example: 我<u>在上海</u>长大。   →   我是<u>在上海</u>长大的。

             我<u>在上海</u>長大。   我是<u>在上海</u>長大的。

             Wǒ <u>zài Shànghǎi</u> zhǎngdà.   **Wǒ shì <u>zài Shànghǎi</u> zhǎngdà de.**

             I grew up <u>in Shanghai</u>.

a.   他们<u>一九七零年</u>结婚。

    他們<u>一九七零年</u>結婚。

    Tāmen <u>yī jiǔ qī líng nián</u> jiéhūn.

    They got married <u>in 1970</u>.

b.   我们<u>在</u>中国认识。

    我們<u>在</u>中國認識。

    Wǒmen <u>zài Zhōngguó</u> rènshi.

    We met <u>in China</u>.

c.   弟弟<u>一九九八年</u>毕业。

    弟弟<u>一九九八年</u>畢業。

    Dìdi <u>yī jiǔ jiǔ bā nián</u> bìyè.

    Younger brother graduated <u>in 1998</u>.

d.   这件毛衣<u>我父母</u>给我买。

    這件毛衣<u>我父母</u>給我買。

    Zhè jiàn máoyī <u>wǒ fùmǔ</u> gěi wǒ mǎi.

    This sweater was bought for me by <u>my parents</u>.

e.   那本书<u>王老师</u>写。

    那本書<u>王老師</u>寫。

    Nà běn shū <u>Wáng lǎoshī</u> xiě.

    That book was written <u>by Professor Wang</u>.

f.   这本字典<u>在书店</u>买。

    這本字典<u>在書店</u>買。

    Zhè běn zìdiǎn <u>zài shūdiàn</u> mǎi.

    This dictionary was purchased <u>at the library</u>.

g.   <u>他</u>告诉我。

    <u>Tā</u> gàosu wǒ.

    <u>It was he who</u> told me.

h.   我<u>坐公共汽车</u>去。

    我<u>坐公共汽車</u>去。

    Wǒ <u>zuò gōnggòng qìchē</u> qù.

    I went <u>by bus</u>.

⇨   37.9

10

小张/小張 Xiǎo Zhāng and 小王 Xiǎo Wáng are having dinner at a restaurant in Chinatown. Complete their dialogue using the information supplied in parentheses. Think carefully about when to use 了 **le**, 过/過 **guò**, and 是…的 **shì . . . de** in your sentences.

小张：这儿的豆腐没有北京的好吃。服务员的中文，也没有北京人的中文好听。
小王：你好像知道很多北京的事，为什么？

a.　小张：因为 _____。 (I've been to Beijing.)
b.　小王：真的吗？你 _____? (When did you go?)
c.　小张：_____。 (I went in 2004, with my mother.)
d.　小王：北京有意思吗？你们 _____? (Where did you go?)
e.　小张：我们去 _____ 很多地方，也吃 _____ 很多好吃的东西。
　　　　我还买 _____ 一些便宜的衣服。
f.　小王：你在北京 _____? (How long did you stay in Beijing?)
g.　小张：两个月，然後我们 _____。 (Then we went to Shanghai.)
h.　小王：你们 _____? (How did you get there?)
　　　　小张：坐火车。
i.　小王：_____? (How long was the train ride?)
　　　　小张：我忘了，好象八个钟头吧。
j.　小王：我 _____。 (I've never been to China.) 你再多说一点儿吧。
k.　小张：当然！2010年，我们 _____。 (We went to China again.)

小張：這兒的豆腐沒有北京的好吃。服務員的中文，也沒有北京人的中文好聽。
小王：你好像知道很多北京的事，為甚麼？

a.　小張：因為 _____。 (I've been to Beijing.)
b.　小王：真的嗎？你 _____? (When did you go?)
c.　小張：_____。 (I went in 2004, with my mother.)
d.　小王：北京有意思嗎？你們 _____? (Where did you go?)
e.　小張：我們去 _____ 很多地方，也吃 _____ 很多好吃的東西。
　　　　我還買_____一些便宜的衣服。
f.　小王：你在北京 _____? (How long did you stay in Beijing?)
g.　小張：兩個月，然後我們 _____。 (Then we went to Shanghai.)
h.　小王：你們 _____? (How did you get there?)
　　　　小張：坐火車。
i.　小王：_____? (How long was the train ride?)
　　　　小張：我忘了，好像八個鐘頭吧。
j.　小王：我 _____。 (I've never been to China.) 你再多說一點兒吧！
k.　小張：當然！2010年，我們 _____。 (We went to China again.)

    Xiǎo Zhāng: Zhèr de dòufu méi yǒu Běijīng de hǎo chī. Fúwùyuán de
                   Zhōngwén, yě méi yǒu Běijīngrén de Zhōngwén hǎo tīng
    Xiǎo Wáng: Nǐ hǎoxiàng zhīdào hěnduō Běijīng de shì, wèishénme?

a. Xiǎo Zhāng: Yīnwèi _____. (I've been to Beijing.)

b. Xiǎo Wáng: Zhēnde ma? Nǐ _____? (When did you go?)

c. Xiǎo Zhāng: _____. (I went in 2004, with my mother.)

d. Xiǎo Wáng: Běijīng yǒu yìsi ma? Nǐmen _____? (Where did you go?)

e. Xiǎo Zhāng: Wǒmen qù _____ hěn duō dìfāng, yě chī _____
                   hěn duō hǎo chī de dōngxi. Wǒ hái mǎi _____
                   yī xiē piányi de yīfu.

f. Xiǎo Wáng: Nǐ zài Běijīng _____? (How long did you stay in Beijing?)

g. Xiǎo Zhāng: Liǎng ge yuè. Ránhòu wǒmen _____.
                   (Then we went to Shanghai.)

h. Xiǎo Wáng: Nǐmen _____? (How did you get there?)
    Xiǎo Zhāng: Zuò huǒchē.

i. Xiǎo Wáng: _____? (How long was the train ride?)
    Xiǎo Zhāng: Wǒ wàng le. Hǎoxiàng bā ge zhōngtou ba.

j. Xiǎo Wáng: Wǒ _____. (I've never been to China.)
                  Nǐ zài duō shuō yīdiǎr ba.

k. Xiǎo Zhāng: Dāngrán! 2010 nián, wǒmen _____.
                   (We went to China again.)

38
Talking about change, new situations, and changing situations

1

王小妹 **Wáng Xiǎomèi** is training to run a marathon. Her coach is giving her a pep talk. Put the phrases in each of these sentences into the correct order to find out what he is saying. The English translations are provided.

a. 你越越认真来。

你越越認真來。

nǐ yuè yuè rènzhēn lái.

You have become serious.

b. 你的身体强壮越来越。

你的身體强壯越來越。

nǐ de shēntǐ qiángzhuàng yuè lái yuè.

You are getting stronger and stronger.

c. 越你的技巧来越好。

越你的技巧來越好。

yuè nǐ de jìqiǎo lái yuè hǎo.

Your technique is getting better and better.

d. 快比赛的日子了要到。

快比賽的日子了要到。

kuài bǐsài de rìzi le yào dào.

The day of the race is coming up soon.

e. 你得跑三个小时每天。

你得跑三個小時每天。

nǐ děi pǎo sān gè xiǎoshí měitiān.

You must begin running three hours every day.

f. 你越跑越快跑得。

你越跑越快跑得。

nǐ yuè pǎo yuè kuài pǎo de.

The more you run the faster you will get.

⇨ 38.3

2 王小妹 **Wáng Xiǎomèi** is excited about all of the things that her new sister has learned to do. Translate her descriptions into Mandarin.

> Example: She can sing now. → 现在她会唱歌了。
> 现在她會唱歌了。
> **Xiànzài tā huì chàng gē le.**

a. She can walk now.

b. She can now say 'mama.'

c. She can now recognize her older brothers.

d. She likes to listen to music now.

e. She knows her own name.

⇨ 38.1

3 王小妹 **Wáng Xiǎomèi** made some new year's resolutions. Translate them into Mandarin.

> Example: I won't smoke anymore. → 我不再抽煙了。
> **Wǒ bù zài chōu yān le.**

a. I won't drink beer anymore.

b. I won't go to parties on Sunday nights anymore.

c. I will jog in the park every day. [跑步 **pǎo bù** jog]

d. I will call my parents once a week.

e. I will study Chinese every day.

f. I will not quarrel with my younger sister anymore. [吵架 **chǎo jià** quarrel]

⇨ 38.1

4 The following sentences describe changing situations. Express these changes in English.

a. 天气越来越冷了。
天氣越來越冷了。
Tiānqì yuè lái yuè lěng le.

b. 中文越来越有意思了。
中文越來越有意思了。
Zhōngwén yuè lái yuè yǒu yìsī le.

c. 中国人的生活越来越好了。
中國人的生活越來越好了。
Zhōngguó rén de shēnghuó yuè lái yuè hǎo le.

d. 我们越来越喜欢吃中国饭了。
我們越來越喜歡吃中國飯了。
Wǒmen yuè lái yuè xǐhuan chī Zhōngguó fàn le.

e. 我越吃越胖，越胖越想吃。
Wǒ yuè chī yuè pàng, yuè pàng yuè xiǎng chī.

f. 你越学越懂。

你越學越懂。

Nǐ yuè xué yuè dǒng.

g. 我越学越要学。

我越學越要學。

Wǒ yuè xué yuè yào xué.

h. 汉字越写越容易。

漢字越寫越容易。

Hàn zì yuè xiě yuè róngyì.

i. 这本书，我越看越觉得有意思。

這本書，我越看越覺得有意思。

Zhè běn shū, wǒ yuè kàn yuè juéde yǒu yìsī.

⇨ 38.3

5

Write a short paragraph in Mandarin using the pattern 越来越/越來越 **yuè lái yuè** in each sentence to describe a day in early spring.

> Example: weather: good → 天气越来越好了。
>
> 天氣越來越好了。
>
> **Tiānqì yuè lái yuè hǎo le.**

a. temperature: warmer

b. days: longer

c. flowers: more

d. sky: blue

e. people walking outside: more

⇨ 38.3.1

6

周莉 **Zhōu Lì** is writing a letter home describing her progress in Mandarin. Express her progress using 越⋯越 **yuè . . . yuè** for each situation.

> Example: study . . . interested → 我越读越有兴趣。
>
> 我越讀越有興趣。
>
> **Wǒ yuè dú yuè yǒu xìngqù.**

a. listen to Chinese . . . understand

b. write Chinese characters . . . pretty

c. talk . . . accurately

d. read . . . fast

⇨ 38.3.2

7 Complete these sentences by adding a Mandarin noun or verb that expresses change to best express the English translation.

a. 中国最近 _____ 很大。

中國最近 _____ 很大。

Zhōngguó zuì jìn _____ hěn dà.

China has recently changed a lot.

b. 他想将来 _____ 一个科学家。

他想將來 _____ 一個科學家。

Tā xiǎng jiānglái _____ yī gè kēxuéjiā.

He wants to become a scientist in the future.

c. 这个总统能 _____ 人民的生活吗？

這個總統能 _____ 人民的生活嗎？

Zhège zóngtǒng néng _____ rénmín de shēnghuó ma?

Can this president improve people's lives?

d. 天气热了。你回家 _____ 衣服吧！

天氣熱了。你回家 _____ 衣服吧！

Tiānqì rè le. Nǐ huí jiā _____ yīfu ba!

It's gotten hot. Go home and change your clothes!

e. 请你帮我 _____ 我中文作文里的错误。

請你幫我 _____ 我中文作文裏的錯誤。

Qǐng nǐ bāng wǒ _____ wǒ Zhōngwén zuòwén lǐ de cuòwù.

Please help me correct the mistakes in my Chinese essay.

f. 这篇文章我已经 _____ 了很多次了。

這篇文章我已經 _____ 了很多次了。

Zhè piān wénzhāng wǒ yǐjing _____ le hěn duō cì le.

I've already rewritten this essay many times.

g. 几年不见，他 _____ 了一个很有礼貌的孩子。

幾年不見，他 _____ 了一個很有禮貌的孩子。

Jǐ nián bù jiàn, tā _____ le yī gè hěn yǒu lǐmào de háizi.

I haven't seen him in a few years, and he has become a very polite child.

h. 几年不见，他 _____ 很有礼貌的学生。

幾年不見，他 _____ 很有禮貌的學生。

Jǐnián bù jiàn, tā _____ hěn yǒu lǐmào de xuésheng.

I haven't seen him in a few years, and he has become a very polite student.

i. 按照你的建议，他已经把文章里的错误 _____ 了。

按照你的建議，他已經把文章裏的錯誤 _____ 了。

Ànzhào nǐ de jiànyì, tā yǐjing bǎ wénzhāng lǐ de cuòwù _____ le.

Following your suggestions, he has already corrected the mistakes in his essay.

⇨ 38.4

8 周利 **Zhōu Lì** is writing a memo to his boss about his company's business prospects in China. Express his points in Mandarin.

a. The business climate in China has improved.

b. The economy is getting stronger and stronger.

c. There are more and more foreign businesses in China.

d. The more they invest, the more money they make.

e. Chinese people have more and more money.

f. The more money they have, the more things they buy.

g. I think our business in China will get better and better.

➪ 38.3, 38.4

9 You missed your 10-year school reunion last weekend. Your friend 小王 brought you a photo he took at the reunion and was telling you about how everyone has been doing. Fill in the blanks to complete 小王's narrative.

那天大家都来了。你看，小刘 (a)_____(became engaged)。 这是他的未婚妻 (fiancée)。
小高结婚得早，现在已经 (b)_____(has three children)。去年我们见到小李的时候
她还在工作，现在 (c)_____(not working anymore)，准备结婚。小周多年不见，
(d)_____(getting heavier and heavier)。小张 (e)_____(has changed the most)。以前跟女孩子说话
都会脸红 (blush)，现在竟然 (f)_____(became a celebrity)，到处演讲！对了，那天除了
你，就是小江没来。听说他毕了业就去了法国，已经在那儿住了快十年 (g)_____。

那天大家都來了。你看，小劉 (a)_____ (became engaged)。 這是他的未婚妻 (fiancée)。
小高結婚得早，現在已經 (b)_____ (has three children)。去年我們見到小李的時候她還
在工作，現在 (c)_____(not working anymore)，準備結婚。小周多年不見， (d)_____
(getting heavier and heavier)。小張 (e)_____ (has changed the most)。以前跟女孩子說話都會臉紅
(blush)，現在竟然 (f)_____(became a celebrity)，到處演講！對了，那天除了你，就是
小江沒來。聽說他畢了業就去了法國，已經在那兒住了快十年 (g)_____。

Nàtiān dàjiā dōu lái le. Nǐ kàn, Xiǎo Liú (a)_____(became engaged). Zhè shì
tā de wèihūnfù (fiancée). Xiǎo Gāo jiéhūn de zǎo, xiànzài yǐjīng
(b)_____ (has three children). Qùnián women jiàndào Xiǎo Lǐ de shíhòu tā hái zài
gōngzuò, xiànzài (c)_____(not working anymore) zhǔnbèi jiéhūn. Xiǎo Zhōu duōnián
bù jiàn, (d)_____(getting heavier and heavier). Xiǎo Zhāng (e)_____(has changed the most).
Yǐqián gēn nǚ háizi shuō huà dōu huì liǎnhóng (blush), xiànzài jìngrán
(f)_____(became a celebrity) dàochù yǎnjiǎng! Duìle, nàtiān chúle nǐ, jiù shì Xiǎo
Jiāng méi lái. Tīngshuō tā bì le yè jiù qù le Fǎguó, yǐjīng zài nàr zhù le
kuài shí nián (g)_____.

10 Have you ever attended a school reunion? Use the above paragraph as inspiration and write a few sentences about how your friends have changed.

_____

_____

_____

39
Talking about duration and frequency

Rewrite the following sentences, adding the duration phrase that follows in parentheses.

Example: 我今天晚上想看电视。（一个小时）

我今天晚上想看電視。（一個小時）

Wǒ jīntiān wǎnshang xiǎng kàn diànshì. (yī gè xiǎoshí)

→

我今天晚上想看一个小时的电视。

我今天晚上想看一個小時的電視。

Wǒ jīntiān wǎnshang xiǎng kàn yī gè xiǎoshí de diànshì.

a. 我打算在中国学中国话。（一年）

我打算在中國學中國話。（一年）

Wǒ dǎsuan zài Zhōngguó xué Zhōngguó huà. (yī nián)

I plan to study Chinese in China for a year.

b. 学生每天至少得学习。（三个钟头）

學生每天至少得學習。（三個鐘頭）

Xuésheng měitiān zhìshǎo děi xuéxí. (sān gè zhōngtóu)

The students should study at least three hours every day.

c. 我已经等了他了。（二十分钟）

我已經等了他了。（二十分鍾）

Wǒ yǐjing děng le tā le. (èrshí fēn zhōng)

I've already waited for him for twenty minutes.

d. 昨天晚上，我就睡觉了。（两个钟头）

昨天晚上，我就睡覺了。（兩個鐘頭）

Zuótiān wǎnshang wǒ jiù shuì jiào le. (liǎng gè zhōngtóu)

Last night I only slept for two hours.

e. 你每天晚上应该睡觉。（八个钟头）

你每天晚上應該睡覺。（八個鐘頭）

Nǐ měitiān wǎnshang yīnggāi shuì jiào. (bā gè zhōngtóu)

You should sleep eight hours every night.

f. 我每天看报。（一个半小时）

我每天看報。（一個半小時）

Wǒ měitiān kàn bào. (yī gè bàn xiǎoshí)

I read the newspaper for one and a half hours every day.

g. 我每天晚上听音乐。（一个钟头）

我每天晚上聽音樂。（一個鐘頭）

Wǒ měitiān wǎnshang tīng yīnyuè. (yī gè zhōngtou)

I listen to music for an hour every night.

⇨ 39.1

2

In complete Mandarin sentences, explain how long it has been that 王明 **Wáng Míng** has not done the following.

Example: Wang Ming has not eaten → 王明有一个月没吃中国饭。
Chinese food in a month.　　　 王明有一個月沒吃中國飯。

Wáng Míng yǒu yī gè yuè méi chī Zhōngguó fàn.

a. seen a movie – one month

b. gone home – one year

c. gone to class – five days

d. spoken – 45 minutes

e. slept – 36 hours

f. played ball – two weeks

⇨ 39.1.4

3

Rewrite these sentences so that the duration phrase is expressed with 有 **yǒu**.

Example: 她看电视已经看了两个小时了。 → 她看电视已经有两个小时了。
她看電視已經看了兩個小時了。　　 她看電視已經有兩個小時了。

Tā kàn diànshì yǐjing kàn le liǎng gè xiǎoshí le.　　**Tā kàn diànshì yǐjing yǒu liǎng gè xiǎoshí le.**

She's already been watching television for two hours.

a. 她写作文已经写了一个月了。

她寫作文已經寫了一個月了。

Tā xiě zuòwén yǐjing xiě le yī gè yuè le.

He's already been writing the essay for a month.

b. 他们打球打了三个小时。

他們打球打了三個小時。

Tāmen dǎ qiú dǎ le sān gè xiǎoshí.

They have been playing ball for three hours.

c. 他跟他的女朋友说话说了两个钟头了。

他跟他的女朋友說話說了兩個鐘頭了。

Tā gēn tā de nǚ péngyou shuō huà shuō le liǎng gè zhōngtóu le.

He spoke with his girlfriend for two hours.

d. 我等弟弟已经等了半个小时了。

我等弟弟已經等了半個小時了。

Wǒ děng dìdi yǐjing děng le bàn gè xiǎoshí le.

I've already been waiting for my younger brother for half an hour.

e. 他已经在中国住了两年了。

他已經在中國住了兩年了。

Tā yǐjing zài Zhōngguó zhù le liǎng nián le.

He has already lived in China for two years.

f. 他教书教了十年了。

他教書教了十年了。

Tā jiāo shū jiāo le shí nián le.

He has taught for ten years.

⇨ 39.1.2

4

The following sentences all indicate ongoing actions. Translate them into English.

a. 妈妈在做饭呢。

媽媽在做飯呢。

Māma zài zuò fàn ne.

b. 你看！公园里有很多人在跳舞呢。

你看！公園裏有很多人在跳舞呢。

Nǐ kàn! Gōngyuán lǐ yǒu hěn duō rén zài tiào wǔ ne.

c. 请你在这儿等着我。

請你在這兒等著我。

Qǐng nǐ zài zhèr děngzhe wǒ.

d. 你孩子还在美国学习吗？

你孩子還在美國學習嗎？

Nǐ háizi hái zài Měiguó xuéxí ma?

e. 她到现在还没有结婚呢。

她到現在還沒有結婚呢。

Tā dào xiànzài hái méi yǒu jiéhūn ne.

⇨ 17.2, 39.2.1

5 These sentences all describe situations in which an action occurs at the same time as a background event. Translate them into English.

a. 我们喜欢喝着茶谈话。
我們喜歡喝著茶談話。
Wǒmen xǐhuan hēzhe chá tán huà.

b. 学生喜欢听着音乐作功课。
學生喜歡聽著音樂作功課。
Xuésheng xǐhuan tīngzhe yīnyuè zuò gōngkè.

c. 你不可以吃着东西开车。
你不可以吃著東西開車。
Nǐ bù kéyǐ chīzhe dōngxi kāi chē.

d. 我不要你看着报吃早饭。
我不要你看著報吃早飯。
Wǒ bù yào nǐ kànzhe bào chī zǎofàn.

⇨ 17.2.4, 39.3

6 In complete Mandarin sentences, describe how often 王明 **Wáng Míng** has done each of the following activities.

Example: read that book – two times → 那本书她已经看过两次。
那本書她已經看過兩次。
Nà běn shū tā yǐjing kàn guò liǎng cì.

a. ridden in an airplane [坐飞机/坐飛機 **zuò fēijī**] – five times
b. eaten Japanese food [吃日本饭/吃日本飯 **chī Rìběnfàn**] – two times
c. gone to Paris [去巴黎 **qù Bālí**] – one time
d. sang karaoke [唱卡拉 OK **chàng kǎlā** OK] – three times
e. ridden on a motorcycle [骑摩托车/騎摩托車 **qí mótuōchē**] – four times
f. seen Chinese movies [看中国电影/看中國電影 **kàn Zhōngguó diànyǐng**] – six times

⇨ 39.4

7 家明 **Jiā Míng**'s parents have sent him to a strict boarding school this year. Today is the first time he has had the opportunity to hang out with his old friends. Use the following information to complete 家明 **Jiā Míng**'s complaints about the rigid schedule and rules in his new school.

Daily schedule:
6:30 wake up
6:40–7:00 morning run
8:00–5:00 classes (1 hour lunch break)
6:30–10:00 homework/study
10:00–10:30 free choice (5-minute shower time)
10:30 lights out/bed time

House Rules:
2 hours of television per week
2 outings per month

我们每天 (a)＿＿＿＿＿＿＿ 就得起床，先 (b)＿＿＿＿＿＿＿，从八点开始上课，要上 (c)＿＿＿＿。每天晚上要做 (d)＿＿＿＿＿＿(homework)，洗澡只可以 (e)＿＿＿＿＿＿。十点上床。不可以 (f)＿＿＿＿＿＿(sleep with the lights on)。老师都很严，如果忘了带东西，就 (g)＿＿＿＿＿(remain standing for the entire class)。一个星期只能 (h)＿＿＿＿＿(TV)，一个月只能 (i)＿＿＿＿＿＿。我没有自己的时间，已经 (j)＿＿＿＿＿＿(haven't played video games for 3 weeks: 打电动游戏)。

我們每天 (a)＿＿＿＿＿＿＿ 就得起床，先 (b)＿＿＿＿＿＿＿，從八點開始上課，要上 (c)＿＿＿＿。每天晚上要做 (d)＿＿＿＿＿＿(homework)，洗澡只可以 (e)＿＿＿＿＿＿。十點上床。不可以 (f)＿＿＿＿＿＿(sleep with the lights on)。老師都很嚴，如果忘了帶東西，就 (g)＿＿＿＿＿(remain standing for the entire class)。一個星期只能 (h)＿＿＿＿＿(TV)，一個月只能 (i)＿＿＿＿＿＿。我沒有自己的時間，已經 (j)＿＿＿＿＿＿(haven't played video games for 3 weeks: 打電動遊戲)。

Wǒmen měitiān (a)＿＿＿＿＿＿ jiù děi qǐchuáng, xiān (b)＿＿＿＿＿＿, cóng bā diǎn kāishǐ shàng kè, yào shàng (c)＿＿＿＿＿＿. Měitiān wǎnshang yào zuò (d)＿＿＿＿＿(homework), Xǐzǎo zhǐ kěyǐ (e)＿＿＿＿＿＿. Shí diǎn shàng chuáng. Bù kěyǐ (f)＿＿＿＿＿＿(sleep with the lights on). Lǎoshī dōu hěn yán, rúguǒ wàng le dài dōngxi, jiù (g)＿＿＿＿＿＿(remain standing for the entire class). Yī ge xīngqī zhǐ néng (h)＿＿＿＿＿(TV). Yī ge yuè zhǐ néng (i)＿＿＿＿＿＿, Wǒ méi yǒu zìjǐ de shíjiān, yǐjīng (j)＿＿＿＿＿＿(haven't played video games for 3 weeks: dǎ diàndòng yóuxì).

40

Expressing additional information

1

Insert 也 yě 'also' in the appropriate place in each of the following sentences and then translate the sentences into English.

Example: 她喜欢喝咖啡。她喜欢喝茶。

她喜歡喝咖啡。她喜歡喝茶。

Tā xǐhuan hē kāfēi. Tā xǐhuan hē chá.

→

她喜欢喝咖啡也喜欢喝茶。

她喜歡喝咖啡也喜歡喝茶。

Tā xǐhuan hē kāfēi yě xǐhuan hē chá.

She likes to drink coffee. She also likes to drink tea.

a. 我这学期选了中文选了日文。

我這學期選了中文選了日文。

Wǒ zhè xuéqī xuǎn le Zhōngwén xuǎn le Rìwén.

b. 他喜欢吃美国饭喜欢吃泰国饭。

他喜歡吃美國飯喜歡吃泰國飯。

Tā xǐhuan chī Měiguó fàn xǐhuan chī Tàiguó fàn.

c. 张小英很漂亮很聪明。

張小英很漂亮很聰明。

Zhāng Xiǎoyīng hěn piàoliang hěn cōngming.

d. 林伟学是学生。唐玫玲是学生。

林偉學是學生。唐玫玲是學生。

Lín Wěixué shì xuésheng. Táng Méilíng shì xuésheng.

e. 我给弟弟打了电话。我给妹妹打了电话。

我給弟弟打了電話。我給妹妹打了電話。

Wǒ gěi dìdi dǎ le diànhuà. Wǒ gěi mèimei dǎ le diànhuà.

f. 我喜欢喝咖啡，喜欢喝茶。

我喜歡喝咖啡，喜歡喝茶。

Wǒ xǐhuan hē kāfēi, xǐhuan hē chá.

⇨ 40.1

2 Rewrite each of the following sentences, adding the expression in parentheses. Translate your sentences into English.

a. 这本字典送给你。我有一本。（还）

這本字典送給你。我有一本。（還）

Zhè běn zìdiǎn sònggěi nǐ. Wǒ yǒu yīběn. (hái)

b. 你有什么事情要告诉我吗？（还）

你有甚麼事情要告訴我嗎？（還）

Nǐ yǒu shénme shìqing yào gàosu wǒ ma? (hái)

c. 对不起。我不懂你的意思。（还）

對不起。我不懂你的意思。（還）

Duìbuqǐ. Wǒ bù dǒng nǐ de yìsi. (hái)

d. 你有多少钱？（还）

你有多少錢？（還）

Nǐ yǒu duōshao qián? (hái)

e. 学中文有意思，可以找到好的工作。（不但…并且）

學中文有意思，可以找到好的工作。（不但…并且）

Xué Zhōngwén yǒu yìsi, kěyǐ zhǎodào hǎo de gōngzuò.

(bùdàn . . . bìngqiě)

f. 妹妹，我们都喜欢吃中国饭。（除了…以外）

妹妹，我們都喜歡吃中國飯。（除了…以外）

Mèimei, wǒmen dōu xǐhuan chī Zhōngguó fàn. (chúle . . . yǐwài)

g. 那个旅馆干净便宜。（又…又）[干净/乾淨 clean]

那個旅館乾淨便宜。（又…又）[便宜 cheap]

Nàge lǚguǎn gānjìng piányi. (yòu . . . yòu)

h. 妈妈上班，得照顾孩子。（不但…而且）[上班 go to work]

媽媽上班，得照顧孩子。（不但…而且）[照顾 take care of]

Māma shàng bān, děi zhàogù háizi. (bùdàn . . . érqiě)

⇨ 40

3 高蕾 Gāo Lěi has asked one of her professors to write her a letter of recommendation. Here are the professor's notes. Use them to write the letter in Mandarin. Incorporate the parenthesized expressions in each line.

a. smart and hardworking [又 yòu]

b. very reliable [并且 bìngqiě]

c. prepares course work carefully, does well on tests [功课/功課 gōngkè course work, 准备/準備 zhǔnbèi prepare, 仔细/仔細 zǐxì carefully] [不但 bùdàn . . . 而且 érqiě]

d. active in student organizations [学生组织/學生組織 xuéshēng zǔzhī student organizations, 积极分子/積極分子 jījí fēnzi activist] [还/還 hái]

e. good student, attends many extracurricular activities [课外活动/課外活動 **kè wài huódòng** extracurricular activities] [除了 **chúle** . . . 以外 **yǐwài**]

f. very willing to help others [而且 **érqiě**]

g. language ability strong, speaks English well [再说/再說 **zài shuō**]

⇨ 40

4

Millie is going away for six months and wants to sublet her apartment. Use her English notes to write an appealing advertisement in Mandarin incorporating these expressions.

又…又	不但…而且	除了…以外
yòu . . . yòu . . .	bùdàn . . . érqiě . . .	chúle . . . yǐwài . . .

Apartment for rent. 1 BR/1 bath. Big and clean. Furniture included (newly purchased). Close to subway station. Walking distance to restaurants and stores. $2000/mo. Water and utilities included, plus cable TV. Interested? Contact Millie (987) 654-3321 / millie1980@gmail.com

房屋出租。一房一厅，_____

_____

_____

意者请洽 Millie (987) 654-3321 / millie1980@gmail.com

房屋出租。一房一廳，_____

_____

_____

意者請洽 Millie (987) 654-3321 / millie1980@gmail.com

Fángwū chūzū. Yī fang yī tīng, _____

_____

_____

Yìzhě qǐng qià Millie (987) 654-3321 / millie1980@gmail.com

41

Expressing contrast

王丽丽/王麗麗 **Wáng Lìlì** is deciding whether or not to go out with 张伟/張偉 **Zhāng Wěi** and has made a list of his positive and negative qualities. Write up her list in complete Mandarin sentences using contrast connectors to link the pros and the cons.

Positive qualities	*Negative qualities*
a.	帅/帥 **shuài** [handsome]	不高 **bù gāo**
b.	聪明/聰明 **cōngming** [smart]	懒/懶 **lǎn** [lazy]
c.	有钱/有錢 **yǒu qián**	小气/小氣 **xiǎoqi** [stingy]
d.	跳舞跳得很好	唱歌唱得不好
	tiào wǔ tiào de hěn hǎo	**chàng gē chàng de bù hǎo**
	[跳舞 **tiào wǔ** to dance]	
e.	有车/有車	开车开得太快/開車開得太快
	yǒu chē	**kāi chē kāi de tài kuài**
f.	他很喜欢请客。	他喝酒喝得太多。
	他很喜歡請客。	他喝酒喝得太多。
	Tā hěn xǐhuan qǐng kè.	**Tā hē jiǔ hē de tài duō.**
g.	会说外语/會說外語	不喜欢旅游/不喜歡旅游
	huì shuō wàiyǔ	**bù xǐhuan lǚyóu**
		[旅游 **lǚyóu** to travel]
h.	大学毕业了/大學畢業了	没有工作
	dàxué bì yè le	**méi yǒu gōngzuò**
	[毕业/畢業 **bì yè** to graduate]	

⇨ | 41.1

2 张伟/張偉 **Zhāng Wěi** is giving a campus tour and is explaining some of the college rules. Translate them into Mandarin, using a contrast connector in each sentence.

Example: You can send email but not faxes.

→

你可以发电子邮件可是不可以发传真。

你可以發電子郵件可是不可以發傳真。

Nǐ kěyǐ fā diànzǐ yóujiàn kěshì bù kěyǐ fā chuánzhēn.

a.   You can eat in the dorm but you can't cook there.

b.   You can drink coffee in the study hall but you can't eat food there.

c.   You can have a party in the dorm but you can't drink alcohol.

d.   You can use a microwave in your room but you can't use a toaster oven.

e.   You can wear sneakers/trainers in the gym but you can't wear boots.

f.   You can use a calculator during a test but you can't use a computer.

g.   You can hang pictures on the bulletin board but not on the wall.

h.   You can borrow books from the library but you can't borrow dictionaries.

i.   You can practice language in the language lab but you can't read email.

j.   You can bring a cell phone to class but you must turn it off.

⇨ 41.1

3 Link each pair of clauses using 虽然/雖然 **suīrán** ... 可是 **kěshì** [or 虽然/雖然 **suīrán** ... 但是 **dànshì**] to make the contrast clear. Translate each sentence into English.

Example: 那个孩子还很小。他已经懂事了。

那個孩子還很小。他已經懂事了。

Nàge háizi hái hěn xiǎo. Tā yǐjing dǒng shì le.

→

那个孩子虽然还很小可是他已经懂事了。

那個孩子雖然還很小可是他已經懂事了。

Nàge háizi suīrán hái hěn xiǎo kěshì tā yǐjing dǒng shì le.

Although that child is still young he is already very sensible.

a.   中文很难学。很有用。

中文很難學。很有用。

Zhōngwén hěn nán xué. Hěn yǒu yòng.

b.   他是中国人。他没去过中国。

他是中國人。他沒去過中國。

Tā shì Zhōngguórén. Tā méi qùguo Zhōngguó.

c.   我想去。没时间。

我想去。沒時間。

Wǒ xiǎng qù. Méi shíjiān.

d. 今天没下雪。非常冷。

今天沒下雪。非常冷。

Jīntiān méi xià xuě. Fēicháng lěng.

e. 今天考试，同学们都到了。老师还没来。

今天考試，同學們都到了。老師還沒來。

Jīntiān kǎoshì, tóngxuémen dōu dào le. Lǎoshī hái méi lái.

f. 他嘴上不说。心里很不高兴。[嘴 zuǐ mouth]

他嘴上不說。心裏很不高興。

Tā zuǐ shàng bù shuō. Xīnlǐ hěn bù gāoxìng.

g. 她是中国人。她不喜欢吃中国饭。

她是中國人。她不喜歡吃中國飯。

Tā shì Zhōngguó rén. Tā bù xǐhuan chī Zhōngguó fàn.

h. 学中文很花时间。我很喜欢学。

學中文很花時間。我很喜歡學。

Xué Zhōngwén hěn huā shíjiān. Wǒ hěn xǐhuan xué.

⇨ 41.1

4 Add the contrast connector 却/卻 **què** to the sentences you created in (3).

⇨ 41.2.1

5 Add 反过来/反過來 **fǎnguòlái** or 反而 **fǎn'ér** to each sentence to best reflect the type of contrast involved.

a. 难的汉字写对了。容易的写错了。

難的漢字寫對了。容易的寫錯了。

Nán de Hàn zì xiěduì le. Róngyì de xiěcuò le.

The difficult Chinese characters are written correctly. The easy ones are written incorrectly.

b. 认真的学生大家都喜欢。不认真的学生大家都不喜欢。

認真的學生大家都喜歡。不認真的學生大家都不喜歡。

Rènzhēn de xuésheng dàjiā dōu xǐhuan. Bù rènzhēn de xuésheng dàjiā dōu bù xǐhuan.

Everyone likes conscientious students. No one likes students who are not conscientious.

c. 天气热人们穿的衣服就少。天气冷人们穿的衣服就多。

天氣熱人們穿的衣服就少。天氣冷人們穿的衣服就多。

Tiānqì rè rénmen chuān de yīfu jiù shǎo. Tiānqì lěng rénmen chuān de yīfu jiù duō.

When it is hot, people wear less clothing. When it is cold, people wear more clothing.

d. 下星期要交的报告他已经写好了。明天的考试忘了准备了。

下星期要交的報告他已經寫好了。明天的考試忘了準備了。

Xià xīngqī yào jiāo de bàogào tā yǐjing xiěhǎole. Míngtiān de kǎoshì wàng le zhǔnbèi le.

He has already finished writing the report he has to hand in next week.

He forgot to prepare for tomorrow's exam.

e. 中文不容易学。她学得很好。

中文不容易學。她學得很好。

Zhōngwén bù róngyì xué. Tā xué de hěn hǎo.

Chinese is not easy to learn. She is learning it well.

f. 容易的课选的学生多。难的课选的学生少。

容易的課選的學生多。難的課選的學生少。

Róngyì de kè xuǎn de xuésheng duō. Nán de kè xuǎn de xuésheng shǎo.

A lot of students select the easy classes. Few students select the hard classes.

⇨ 41.2.2

6

Your friend is telling you about her shopping experience. Use the pattern AV (adjectival verb) 是 **shì** AV or SV (stative verb) 是 **shì** SV to express her comments in complete Mandarin sentences.

Example: The movie was okay but it was too long.

→

那个电影好是好可是太长。

那個電影好是好可是太長。

Nàge diànyǐng hǎo shì hǎo kěshì tài cháng.

a. The shoes [鞋子 **xiézi**] were okay but they were too expensive.

b. The sweater [毛衣 **máoyī**] was pretty but it was too small.

c. The prices [价钱/價錢 **jiàqian**] were good but the goods [货/貨 **huò**] were inferior [差 **chà**].

d. The size is appropriate [大小 **dàxiǎo** – 合适/合適 **héshì**] but the color is too pale [颜色/顏色 **yánsè** – 淡 **dàn**].

e. The department store [百货公司/百貨公司 **bǎihuò gōngsī**] was big but there were too many people.

⇨ 41.3

7 Select the correct response in each conversation based on the context.

a. Two friends are shopping. 美美 is trying out a new skirt.

美美：你觉得这条裙子怎么样？

美美：你覺得這條裙子怎麼樣？

Měiměi: Nǐ juéde zhè tiáo qúnzi zěnmeyang?

玲玲：你本人很瘦，可是這条裙子的花色不好，反而让你看起来 _____。

玲玲：你本人很瘦，可是這條裙子的花色不好，反而讓你看起來 _____。

Línglíng: Nǐ běnrén hěn shòu, kěshì zhè tiáo qúnzi de huāsè bù hǎo, fǎn'ér rang nǐ kànqǐlái _____.

i. 更瘦 **gèng shòu**

ii. 有点胖/有點胖 **yǒu diǎn pàng**

iii. 特别矮 **tèbié ǎi**

b. Mrs. Wang is trying to talk her son 王杰 out of taking a part-time job.

王杰：这个工作薪水很高呢！

王傑：這個工作薪水很高呢！

Wáng Jié: Zhège gōngzuò xīnshuǐ hěn gāo ne!

王太太：薪水高是高，可是 _____。

Wáng Tàitai: Xīnshui gāo shì gāo, kěshì _____.

i. 我为你高兴 / 我為你高興 **wǒ wèi nǐ gāoxìng**

ii. 我觉得太危险了 / 我覺得太危險了 **wǒ juéde tài wéixiǎn le**

iii. 什么时候开始上班？/ 甚麼時候開始上班？ **shénme shíhou kāishǐ shàng bān?**

c. Mr. and Mrs. Hu are looking for a new apartment.

胡先生：我觉得这个房子有点小。

胡先生：我覺得這個房子有點小。

Hú xiānsheng: Wǒ juéde zhè ge fángzi yǒu diǎn xiǎo.

胡太太：的确是小了一点，不过 _____。

胡太太：的確是小了一點，不過 _____。

Hú tàitai: Díquè shì xiǎo le yī diǎn, bùguò, _____.

i. 我们应该找大一点的。/ 我們應該找大一點的。 **Wǒmen yīnggāi zhǎo dà yī diǎn de**

ii. 地点也不合适。/ 地點也不合適。 **dìdiǎn yě bù héshì**

iii. 价钱倒是很合理。/ 價錢倒是很合理。 **jiàqián dǎoshì hěn hélǐ**

42

Expressing sequence

1

Put the Mandarin phrases in the right order to describe each of the things that 小王 **Xiǎo Wáng** did before she went to class.

a. 她以前上课早饭吃了。
    她以前上課早飯吃了。
    tā yǐqián shàng kè zǎofàn chī le.
    Before she went to class she ate breakfast.

b. 以前她上课了看报纸。
    以前她上課了看報紙。
    yǐqián tā shàng kè le kàn bàozhǐ.
    Before she went to class she read the newspaper.

c. 她上课了复习中文以前。[复习/復習 **fùxí** to review]
    她上課了復習中文以前。
    tā shàng kè le fùxí Zhōngwén yǐqián.
    Before she went to class she reviewed Chinese.

d. 听了收音机她上课以前。[收音机/收音機 **shōuyīnjī** radio]
    聽了收音機她上課以前。
    tīng le shōuyīnjī tā shàng kè yǐqián.
    Before she went to class she listened to the radio.

e. 以前上课跑步了她在公园里。[跑步 **pǎo bù** to jog]
    以前上課跑步了她在公園裏。
    yǐqián shàng kè pǎo bù le tā zài gōngyuán lǐ.
    Before she went to class she jogged in the park.

⇨ 42.1

2

Write complete sentences using 以前 **yǐqián** 'before' to describe each of the things that 小王 **Xiǎo Wáng** does before she goes to sleep every night.

Example: brushes teeth → 小王睡觉以前刷牙。
                          小王睡覺以前刷牙。
                          Xiǎo Wáng shuì jiào yǐqián shuā yá.

Before going to sleep:

a. does homework

b. watches television

c. calls a friend on the phone

d. bathes

e. reads email

⇨ 42.1

3

Write complete Mandarin sentences using 以后/以後 **yǐhòu** and 了 **le** to describe what 小王 **Xiǎo Wáng** plans to do after taking her test.

> Example: eat icecream → 小王考了中文以后想吃冰淇淋。
>
> 小王考了中文以後想吃冰淇淋。
>
> **Xiǎo Wáng kǎo le Zhōngwén yǐhòu xiǎng chī bīngqilín.**

a. watch a movie

b. drink coffee

c. sleep

d. study with friends

e. play tennis [打网球/打網球 **dǎ wǎngqiú**]

⇨ 42.2

4

Write complete Mandarin sentences using 以后/以後 **yǐhòu**, 就 **jiù**, and 了 **le** to describe what each of the following people say they will do after they graduate.

> Example: 小王 **Xiǎo Wáng**: → 小王毕了业以后就学法文。
>
> study French 小王畢了業以後就學法文。
>
> **Xiǎo Wáng bì le yè yǐhòu jiù xué Fǎwén.**

a. 王鹏飞/王鵬飛 **Wáng Péngfēi**: travel

b. 张苹/張蘋 **Zhāng Píng**: look for a job

c. 陈玫玲/陳玫玲 **Chén Méilíng**: get married

d. 徐乃康 **Xú Nǎikāng**: attend graduate school

⇨ 42.2

5

Translate these sentences into English, capturing the meaning contributed by 才 **cái** in each sentence.

a. 我昨天晚上十一点半才睡觉。

我昨天晚上十一點半才睡覺。

Wǒ zuótiān wǎnshang shíyī diǎn bàn cái shuì jiào.

b. 考试开始以后他才来。

考試開始以後他才來。

Kǎoshì kāishǐ yǐhòu tā cái lái.

c.　我们第二学期才开始学写汉字。

　　我們第二學期才開始學寫漢字。

　　Wǒmen dì èr xuéqī cái kāishǐ xué xiě Hàn zì.

d.　昨天晚上他看完电影才作功课。

　　昨天晚上他看完電影才作功課。

　　Zuótiān wǎnshang tā kànwán diànyǐng cái zuò gōngkè.

e.　两点上课，可是老师两点十分才来。

　　兩點上課，可是老師兩點十分才來。

　　Liǎng diǎn shàng kè, kěshì lǎoshī liǎng diǎn shí fēn cái lái.

⇨ 42.2.2.2

6

Use 先 **xiān**...再 **zài** to describe 陈玫玲/陳玫玲 **Chén Méilíng**'s plan.

Example: get up...　　→　陈玫玲先起床再洗澡。

take a shower　　　　陳玫玲先起床再洗澡。

　　　　　　　　　　Chén Méilíng xiān qǐ chuáng zài xǐ zǎo.

a.　eat breakfast...read a newspaper

b.　read the newspaper...go to class

c.　return home...do homework

d.　do homework...practice tennis

e.　eat dinner...see friends

⇨ 42.3.1

7

For each sentence below, fill in the blank(s) with the correct word(s) (以前 **yǐqián** before, 以后/後 **yǐhòu** after, 先 **xiān**...再 **zài** first...then, 才 **cái** only then, or 就 **jiù** as soon as) so that the meaning of the Mandarin sentence corresponds to that of the English sentence.

a.　下课 _____，你要作什么？

　　下課 _____，你要作甚麼？

　　Xià kè _____, nǐ yào zuò shénme?

　　What are you going to do after class?

b.　我们看了电影 _____, _____ 去跳舞。

　　我們看了電影 _____, _____ 去跳舞。

　　Wǒmen kàn le diànyǐng _____, _____ qù tiào wǔ.

　　We are going to go dancing after we watch the movie.

c.　学生上课 _____ 得预备功课。

　　學生上課 _____ 得預備功課。

　　Xuéshēng shàng kè _____ děi yùbèi gōngkè.

　　Students have to prepare lessons before they go to class.

d. 我会说中文 _____ _____ 去中国旅游。

我會說中文 _____ _____ 去中國旅遊。

Wǒ huì shuō Zhōngwén _____ _____ **qù Zhōngguó lǚyóu.**

I will go to China to travel only after I can speak Chinese.

e. 你得 _____ 买票 _____ 上公共汽车。

你得 _____ 買票 _____ 上公共汽車。

Nǐ děi _____ **mǎi piào** _____ **shàng gōnggòng qìchē.**

You have to buy a ticket first before you get on the bus.

f. 我一会说中文 _____ 去中国旅游。

我一會說中文 _____ 去中國旅遊。

Wǒ yī huì shuō Zhōngwén _____ **qù Zhōngguó lǚyóu.**

As soon as I can speak Chinese, I will go to China to travel.

⇨ 42

8

The assignment for your Chinese class this week is to write instructions for making a Chinese dish. Mrs. Liu, your landlady, kindly offers to teach you how to prepare 西红柿炒鸡蛋/西紅柿炒雞蛋 **xīhóngshì chǎo jīdàn** (stir-fried tomatoes and eggs). As you watch Mrs. Liu cook you take the following notes. Write them up in paragraph form, using appropriate words and phrases to express the sequence of each step.

a.	洗手	洗手	**xǐ shǒu**	wash hands
b.	西红柿切片	西紅柿切片	**xīhóngshì qiē piàn**	slice tomatoes
c.	打蛋 (打到 起泡)	打蛋 (打到 起泡)	**dǎ dàn (dǎ dào qǐ pào)**	beat eggs (till they bubble)
d.	加热油锅	加熱油鍋	**jiā rè yóu guō**	heat wok
e.	倒油	倒油	**dào yóu**	pour oil
f.	把蛋倒进去	把蛋倒進去	**bǎ dàn dào jìnqù**	pour eggs
g.	翻炒	翻炒	**fān chǎo**	stir fry
h.	还没有全熟 就拿出来	還沒有全熟 就拿出來	**hái méi yǒu quán shóu jiù náchūlái**	take out before fully cooked
i.	炒西红柿	炒西紅柿	**chǎo xīhóngshì**	stir fry tomatoes
j.	加糖	加糖	**jiā táng**	add sugar
k.	把蛋倒回去	把蛋倒回去	**bǎ dàn dào huíqù**	put eggs back in
l.	加盐	加鹽	**jiā yán**	add salt
m.	起锅	起鍋	**qǐ guō**	take out

153

_____

_____

_____

_____

_____

_____

_____

_____

⇨ 42

43

Expressing simultaneous situations

1 My roommate 小李 **Xiǎo Lǐ** always does two things at a time. Use the verbs provided and the pattern 的时候/的時候 **de shíhou** to describe him.

> Example: 做功课/做功課 **zuò gōngkè** ... 听音乐/聽音樂 **tīng yīnyuè**
> →
> 小李做功课的时候，听音乐。
> 小李做功課的時候，聽音樂。
> **Xiǎo Lǐ zuò gōngkè de shíhòu, tīng yīnyuè.**

a. 上课/上課   跟同学说话/跟同學說話
    shàng kè   **gēn tóngxué shuō huà**

b. 走路   听中文录音/聽中文錄音
    zǒu lù   **tīng Zhōngwén lùyīn**

c. 开车/開車   听收音机/聽收音機
    kāi chē   **tīng shōuyīnjī**

d. 吃饭/吃飯   看电视/看電視
    chī fàn   **kàn diànshì**

e. 跟朋友聊天   喝酒
    gēn péngyou liáotiān **hē jiǔ**

f. 看电影/看電影   吃东西/吃東西
    kàn diànyǐng   **chī dōngxi**

g. 洗澡   唱歌
    xǐ zǎo   **chàng gē**

h. 跳舞   唱歌
    tiào wǔ   **chàng gē**

⇨ 43.1

2 Translate the following sentences into Mandarin using 的时候/的時候 **de shíhou**.

a. I did not like going to school when I was young.

b. It was already 11:00 p.m. when he came back last night.

c. It was raining when he left.

d. Students are not allowed to talk during the exam.

e. It's better not to use a cell phone while driving.

f. I was on the phone when you came in.

g. Please don't talk too loud when I am sleeping.

h. I came to know him when I was in Beijing last year.

⇨ 43.1

3

Describe 小李 **Xiǎo Lǐ** (in (1) above), using the pattern

(subject) 一边/邊 VP₁ 一边/邊 VP₂

(subject) **yībiān** VP₁ **yībiān** VP₂

> Example: 小李一边作功课，一边听音乐。
>
> 小李一遍作功課，一遍聽音樂。
>
> **Xiǎo Lǐ yībiān zuò gōngkè, yībiān tīng yīnyuè.**

⇨ 43.2

4

The following is a short passage about my friend. Everything about 小李 **Xiǎo Lǐ** is the opposite of my friend. After reading the passage, write another one describing 小李 **Xiǎo Lǐ** using the pattern 又 **yòu** verb₁ 又 **yòu** verb₂.

我的朋友又聪明，又用功。他说的中文又快又清楚。他写的汉字又好看，又整齐。他的宿舍又大又干净。他做的中国饭又好看又好吃。

我的朋友又聰明，又用功。他說的中文又快又清楚。他寫的漢字又好看，又整齊。他的宿舍又大又乾淨。他做的中國飯又好看又好吃。

Wǒ de péngyou yòu cōngming, yòu yònggōng. Tā shuō de Zhōngwén yòu kuài yòu qīngchu. Tā xiě de Hàn zì yòu hǎo kàn, yòu zhěngqí. Tā de sùshè yòu dà yòu gānjìng. Tā zuò de Zhōngguó fàn yòu hǎo kàn yòu hǎo chī.

⇨ 43.3, 43.4

5

Put the Mandarin phrases in the following sentences in the correct order to express the English meanings (a–g form a single narrative).

a. 今天又又刮风下雨外边

今天又又颮風下雨外邊

jīntiān yòu yòu guā fēng xià yǔ wàibian

Tonight it was windy and rainy outside.

b. 的时候我进宿舍同屋的我做在功课

的時候我進宿舍同屋的我做在功課

de shíhou wǒ jìn sùshè tóngwū de wǒ zuò zài gōngkè

When I entered the dorm my roommate was doing homework.

c. 他听音乐着功课做

他聽音樂著功課做

tā tīng yīnyuè zhe gōngkè zuò

He was listening to music while doing homework.

d. 正我进屋子他在打电话的时候
   正我進屋子他在打電話的時候
   zhèng wǒ jìn wūzi tā zài dǎ diànhuà de shíhou
   When I entered the room he was making a phone call.

e. 他一边一边打电话看电视
   他一邊一邊打電話看電視
   tā yībiān yībiān dǎ diànhuà kàn diànshì
   He was talking on the phone and watching television.

f. 在看电脑上电信还同时
   在看電腦上電信還同時
   zài kàn diànnǎo shàng diànxìn hái tóngshí
   At the same time, he was on the computer reading email.

g. 他打电话完了我等到已经睡着了
   他打電話完了我等到已經睡著了
   tā dǎ diànhuà wán le wǒ děngdào yǐjing shuìzháo le
   By the time he finished his phone call I was already asleep.

h. 一方面一方面那个国家要发展经济注重环保要
   一方面一方面那個國家要發展經濟注重環保要

   **yīfāngmiàn yīfāngmiàn nàge guójiā yào fāzhǎn jīngjì zhùzhòng
   huán bǎo yào**

   That country wants to develop its economy while emphasizing
   environmental protection.

⇨ 43

6

You are interviewing for a job in sales. Part of the interview is to see how
quickly you can come up with a line to sell each product you are given.
The key is to highlight the functionality or best features of each product.
Use the pattern in parentheses to complete each sentence.

a. bluetooth earphone:
   有了这个蓝芽耳机，你就可以 _____。（一边…一边…）
   有了這個藍芽手機，你就可以 _____。（一邊…一邊…）
   Yǒu le zhège lán yá shǒujī, nǐ jiù kěyǐ _____. (yībiān . . . yībiān . . .)

b. down jacket:
   这件羽绒夹克 _____（又…又…），最适合旅行的时候带。
   這件羽絨夾克 _____（又…又…），最適合旅行的時候帶。
   **Zhè jiàn yǔróng jiākè _____ (yòu . . . yòu . . .), zuì shìhé lǚxíng
   de shíhou dài.**

c. hybrid car [混合动力车/混合動力車 **hùnhé dònglì chē**]:

谁不想买混合动力车，这种车 ＿＿＿＿＿＿＿＿＿。（一方面…一方面…）

誰不想買混合動力車，這種車 ＿＿＿＿＿＿＿＿＿。（一方面…一方面…）

Shéi bù xiǎng mǎi hùnhé dònglì chē, zhèzhǒng chē ＿＿＿＿＿＿＿＿.

(yī fāngmiàn . . . yī fāngmiàn . . .)

d. Wii Sports:

这种电动游戏不但有趣，＿＿＿＿＿＿＿＿（同时），一举两得。

這種電動遊戲不但有趣，＿＿＿＿＿＿＿＿（同時），一舉兩得。

Zhè zhǒng diàndòng yóuxì bùdàn yǒuqù, ＿＿＿＿＿＿＿＿ **(tóngshí),**

yī jǔ liǎng dé.

e. motion sensor light

这种灯方便的设计让你半夜 ＿＿＿＿＿＿＿＿（…的时候）不会绊倒(trip over)。

這種燈方便的設計讓你半夜 ＿＿＿＿＿＿＿＿（…的時候）不會絆倒(trip over)。

Zhè zhǒng dēng fāngbiàn de shèjì ràng nǐ bàn yè ＿＿＿＿＿＿＿＿

(. . . de shíhou) bù huì bàndǎo.

44

Expressing cause and effect or reason and result

There is a cause and effect relationship between the two parts in each sentence below. Connect the parts using 因为/因爲 **yīnwéi** ... 所以 **suǒyǐ** to show the cause and effect relationship clearly.

Example: 我喜欢看电影。我每个周末都去看电影。

我喜歡看電影。我每個週末都去看電影。

Wǒ xǐhuan kàn diànyǐng. Wǒ měi gè zhōumò dōu qù kàn diànyǐng.

→

因为我喜欢看电影，所以每个周末都去看。

因爲我喜歡看電影，所以每個週末都去看。

Yīnwei wǒ xǐhuan kàn diànyǐng, suǒyǐ měi gè zhōumò dōuqù kàn.

a. 我喜欢中国文化，在学中文。

我喜歡中國文化，在學中文。

Wǒ xǐhuan Zhōngguó wénhuà, zài xué Zhōngwén.

I like Chinese culture so I am studying Chinese.

b. 我在学中文，找了一个中国同屋。

我在學中文，找了一個中國同屋。

Wǒ zài xué Zhōngwén, zhǎo le yī gè Zhōngguó tóngwū.

Because I am studying Chinese I looked for a Chinese roommate.

c. 我昨天病了，没去上课。

我昨天病了，沒去上課。

Wǒ zuótiān bìng le, méi qù shàng kè.

I was sick yesterday so I didn't go to class.

d. 我昨天没去上课，不知道今天有考试。

我昨天沒去上課，不知道今天有考試。

Wǒ zuótian méi qù shàng kè, bù zhīdào jīntiān yǒu kǎoshì.

Because I didn't go to class yesterday I didn't know there was a test today.

e.　我不知道今天有考试，没有准备。

　　我不知道今天有考試，沒有準備。

　　Wǒ bù zhīdào jīntiān yǒu kǎoshì, méi yǒu zhǔnbèi.

　　Because I didn't know there was a test today I didn't prepare.

f.　我没有准备，考得很不好。

　　我沒有準備，考得很不好。

　　Wǒ méi yǒu zhǔnbèi, kǎo de hěn bù hǎo.

　　Because I didn't prepare I didn't do well on the test.

g.　我考得很不好，很不高兴。

　　我考得很不好，很不高興。

　　Wǒ kǎo de hěn bù hǎo, hěn bù gāoxìng.

　　Because I didn't do well on the test I was very unhappy.

h.　我很不高兴，我的同屋今天晚上请我吃中国饭。

　　我很不高興，我的同屋今天晚上請我吃中國飯。

　　Wǒ hěn bù gāoxìng, wǒ de tóngwū jīntiān wǎnshang qǐng wǒ chī Zhōngguó fàn.

　　Because I was very unhappy, my roommate treated me to Chinese food tonight.

⇨　44.1

2　Translate the following sentences into English.

a.　因为生病的关系，他已经三天没来上课了。

　　因爲生病的關係，他已經三天沒來上課了。

　　Yīnwéi shēng bìng de guānxì, tā yǐjīng sān tiān méi lái shàng kè le.

b.　他之所以要去中国留学是因为他对中国流行歌曲非常感兴趣。

　　他之所以要去中國留學是因爲他對中國流行歌曲非常感興趣。

　　Tā zhī suǒyǐ yào qù Zhōngguó liúxué shì yīnwéi tā duì Zhōngguó liúxíng gēqū fēicháng gǎn xīngqù.

　　[留学/留學 **liúxué** study abroad, 流行歌曲 **liú xíng gē qū** popular songs]

c.　我之所以请你吃饭是因为我要给你介绍一个中国朋友。

　　我之所以請你吃飯是因爲我要給你介紹一個中國朋友。

　　Wǒ zhī suǒyǐ qǐng nǐ chī fàn shì yīnwéi wǒ yào gěi nǐ jièshào yī gè Zhōngguó péngyǒu.

d.　因为想家的关系，他一直吃不下饭，睡不着觉。

　　因爲想家的關係，他一直吃不下飯，睡不著覺。

　　Yīnwéi xiǎng jiā de guānxì, tā yīzhí chībuxià fàn, shuìbuzháo jiào.

e.　因为下大雪的关系，晚上的课都不上了。

　　因爲下大雪的關係，晚上的課都不上了。

　　Yīnwéi xià dà xuě de guānxì, wǎnshàng de kè dōu bù shàng le.

　　[雪 **xuě** snow]

f. 我之所以没来参加考试是因为我不知道有考试。

我之所以沒來參加考試是因爲我不知道有考試。

Wǒ zhī suǒyǐ méi lái cānjiā kǎoshì shì yīnwéi wǒ bù zhīdào yǒu kǎoshì.

g. 我之所以没写完报告是因为我的电脑坏了。

我之所以沒寫完報告是因爲我的電腦壞了。

Wǒ zhī suǒyǐ méi xiěwán bàogào shì yīnwéi wǒ de diànnǎo huài le.

[报告/報告 **bàogào** report, 电脑/電腦 **diànnǎo** computer]

h. 因为考试的关系，最近几天学生喝酒喝得少了。

因爲考試的關係，最近幾天學生喝酒喝得少了。

Yīnwéi kǎoshì de guānxì, zuì jìn jǐ tiān xuéshēng hē jiǔ hē de shǎo le.

⇨ 44.2

3

Rewrite the following sentences with the expression 是为了/是爲了 **shì wèile** to clearly indicate the reason for the action taken.

Example: 他去中国学中文。

他去中國學中文。

Tā qù Zhōngguó xué Zhōngwén.

He is going to China to study Chinese.

→

他去中国是为了学中文。

他去中國是爲了學中文。

Tā qù Zhōngguó shì wèile xué Zhōngwén.

a. 我去台湾旅游。

我去臺灣旅游。

Wǒ qù Táiwān lǚyóu.

I am going to Taiwan to travel.

b. 他去中国找工作。

他去中國找工作。

Tā qù Zhōngguó zhǎo gōngzuò.

He is going to China to look for a job.

c. 我们走路上学，锻炼身体。

我們走路上學，鍛煉身體。

Wǒmen zǒu lù shàng xué, duànliàn shēntǐ.

We walk to school to get exercise.

d. 她跟中国人说话，练习口语。

她跟中國人說話，練習口語。

Tā gēn Zhōngguó rén shuō huà, liànxí kóuyǔ.

She speaks with Chinese people to practice the spoken language.

e. 学生们每天听录音，提高听力。

学生們每天聽錄音，提高聽力。

Xuéshengmen měitiān tīng lùyīn, tígāo tīnglì.

The students listen to recordings every day to improve their listening skills.

f. 我的同屋去图书馆准备明天的考试。

我的同屋去圖書館準備明天的考試。

Wǒ de tóngwū qù túshūguǎn zhǔnbèi míngtiān de kǎoshì.

My roommate is going to the library to prepare for tomorrow's test.

g. 他们看中国电影，了解中国文化。

他們看中國電影，了解中國文化。

Tāmen kàn Zhōngguó diànyǐng, liáojiě Zhōngguó wénhuà.

They watch Chinese movies to understand Chinese culture.

h. 我找张老师请假。

我找張老師請假。

Wǒ zhǎo Zhāng lǎoshī qǐng jià.

I am looking for teacher Zhang to be excused from class.

⇨ 44.2

4

王明 **Wáng Míng** promised to meet 唐玫玲 **Táng Méilíng** at the coffee shop but he forgot. When he tried to apologize to her, 唐玫玲 **Táng Méilíng** was angry. Translate her sentences into English.

a. 你为什么来找我？

你爲甚麽來找我？

Nǐ wéi shénme lái zhǎo wǒ?

b. 你怎么没来咖啡店？

你怎麽沒來咖啡店？

Nǐ zěnme méi lái kāfēi diàn?

c. 你为什么没给我打电话？

你爲甚麽沒給我打電話？

Nǐ wèi shénme méi gěi wǒ dǎ diànhuà?

d. 你怎么能忘了？

你怎麽能忘了？

Nǐ zěnme néng wàng le?

⇨ 44.4

5

You are praising your colleagues for their cooperation [合作 hézuò] that has led to the successful completion of a task [成功 chénggōng]. Express this praise five different ways in Mandarin, using each of the following expressions.

a.   因为…的关系/因爲…的關係 yīnwéi . . . de guānxi

b.   之所以是因为/之所以是因爲 zhī suǒyǐ shì yīnwéi

c.   因为…所以/因爲…所以 yīnwéi . . . suǒyǐ

d.   由于/由于 yóuyú

⇨   44.1, 44.2

6

Three alumni were invited to share their experience at an event for students in the biology department. Here is their background information. Complete each of their answers using the structure provided in parentheses. You can add your own interpretation as long as it does not contradict the information in the table.

	REASON THEY CHOSE BIOLOGY	DURING COLLEGE YEARS	CAREER
Michael	wanted to be a doctor	worked hard to get straight As	physician
Wilson	always interested in science.	made lots of good friends	patent lawyer
Greg	parents wanted me to	skipped classes to explore options	school counselor

Question #1: 你为什么选择生物系?
　　　　　　　你為甚麼選擇生物系?
　　　　　　　Nǐ wèi shénme xuǎnzé shēngwùxì?

Michael: [之所以 zhī suǒyǐ] _____

_____

Wilson: [由于/由於 yóuyú] _____

_____

Greg: [因为/因為 yīnwèi] _____

_____

Question #2: 大学的时候你花最多的时间做什么？为什么？

大學的時候你花最多的時間做甚麼？為甚麼？

Dàxué de shíhou nǐ huā zuì duō de shíjiān zuò shénme? Wèi shénme?

Michael: [为了/為了 **wèi le**] _____

_____

Wilson: [所以 **suǒyǐ**] _____

_____

Greg: [之所以 **zhī suǒyǐ**] _____

_____

Question #3: 你现在的工作跟生物有关吗？你喜欢你的选择吗？

你現在的工作跟生物有關嗎？你喜歡你的選擇嗎？

Nǐ xiànzài de gōngzuò gēn shēngwù yǒuguān ma? Nǐ xǐhuān nǐ de xuǎnzé ma?

Michael: [因为/因為 **yīnwèi**] _____

_____

Wilson: [因为…的关系/因為…的關係 **yīnwèi . . . de guānxi**] _____

_____

Greg: [之所以 **zhī suǒyǐ**] _____

_____

7 All public places need safety regulations. Use your common sense to complete one safety rule for each place.

a. A swimming pool:

为了安全起见，_____。

為了安全起見，_____。

Wèi le ānquán qǐjiàn, _____.

b. A rollercoaster in an amusement park:

基于安全理由，_____。

基於安全理由，_____。

Jīyú ānquán lǐyóu, _____.

c. A small exhibition hall in a public library

因为场地的关系，_____。

因為場地的關係，_____。

Yīnwèi chǎngdì de guānxi _____.

45
Expressing conditions

1

Complete these sentences with one of the following words or expressions to best match the English meaning.

就是 **jiù shì**, 只要 **zhǐ yào**, 除非 **chúfēi**, 要不然/要不然 **yàobùrán**, 否则 **fǒuzé**

a. 你最好让你弟弟吃早饭，他就会饿得上不了课了。

你最好讓你弟弟吃早飯，他就會餓得上不了課了。

Nǐ zuì hǎo ràng nǐ dìdi chī zǎofàn, tā jiù huì è de shàngbuliǎo kè le.

You'd better make your younger brother eat breakfast. Otherwise he will be so hungry that he won't be able to go to class.

b. 你请你弟弟看电影，他就会高兴。

你請你弟弟看電影，他就會高興。

Nǐ qǐng nǐ dìdi kàn diànyǐng, tā jiù huì gāoxìng.

As long as you invite your little brother to see the movie he will be happy.

c. 你帮你弟弟做作业，他做不完。

你幫你弟弟做作業，他做不完。

Nǐ bāng nǐ dìdi zuò zuòyè, tā zuòbuwán.

Unless you help your brother do his homework he will not finish it.

d. 你最好帮你的弟弟做作业，他考不好。

你最好幫你的弟弟做作業，他考不好。

Nǐ zuìhǎo bāng nǐ de dìdì zuò zuòyè, tā kǎo bù hǎo.

You'd better help your brother do his homework. Otherwise, he will do poorly on the test.

e. 你用功，你一定考得上大学。

你用功，你一定考得上大學。

Nǐ yònggōng, nǐ yīdìng kǎodeshàng dàxué.

As long as you are hardworking, you will definitely get into college.

f. 你帮你的弟弟做作业，他也许还考得不好。

你幫你的弟弟做作業，他也許還考得不好。

Nǐ bāng nǐ de dìdi zuò zuòyè, tā yéxǔ hái kǎo de bù hǎo.

Even if you help your brother do his homework, he may still do poorly on the test.

g. 你帮你的弟弟作业，他还不懂。

你幫你的弟弟作作業，他還不懂。

Nǐ bāng nǐ de dìdi zuò zuòyè, tā hái bù dǒng.

Even if you help your brother do his homework, he will not understand it.

⇨ 45.2–45.5

2

I am discussing my dilemma with two friends. Here is my dilemma expressed in English. Translate it into Mandarin using 要是 **yàoshi** . . . 就 **jiù** . . . .

a. If I had money, I would not have to work in the library.

b. If I did not work, I would have more time to study.

c. If I had more time to study, my grades would be better.

d. If I had better grades, my parents would be very happy.

e. If my parents were happy, they would give me money.

f. If they gave me money, I would not have to work.

⇨ 45.1

3

After hearing my dilemma, my friend 小王 **Xiǎo Wáng** offers his opinion. Translate his opinion into Mandarin using 如果 **rúguǒ** . . . 就 **jiù** . . . .

a. If I were you, I would borrow some money from a friend first.

b. If I could borrow some money, I would not have to work.

c. If I did not work, I would have more time to study.

d. If I had more time to study, my grades would be better.

e. If I had better grades, my parents would be very happy.

f. If my parents were happy, they would give me money.

g. If they gave me money, I would return my friend's money.

⇨ 45.1

4

小张/小張 **Xiǎo Zhǎng** does not agree with 小王 **Xiǎo Wáng** because he does not think you should borrow money from friends. Here is his suggestion. Translate his suggestion into Mandarin using 倘若 **tǎngruò** . . . 就 **jiù** . . . .

a. If I were you, I would borrow some money from my parents first.

b. If they could loan me some money, I would not have to work.

c. If I did not work, I would study harder.

d. If I studied harder, my grades would be better.

e. If my grades were better, my parents would be very happy.

f. If my parents were happy, they would give me money.

g. If they gave me money, I would use it to pay them back.

⇨ 45.1

5

A few teachers are chatting in the faculty lounge about things that could make their lives a little easier. Imagine you are one of them and complete the sentences for them.

a. 如果教过的东西学生都能记住，＿＿＿＿＿＿＿＿＿＿＿＿＿＿＿＿。

如果教過的東西學生都能記住，＿＿＿＿＿＿＿＿＿＿＿＿＿＿＿＿。

Rúguǒ jiāoguo de dōngxi xuésheng dōu néng jìzhù, ＿＿＿＿＿＿＿.

b. 假使 ＿＿＿＿＿＿＿＿＿＿＿＿＿＿＿＿＿＿，我就可以早点回家。

假使 ＿＿＿＿＿＿＿＿＿＿＿＿＿＿＿＿＿＿，我就可以早點回家。

Jiǎshǐ ＿＿＿＿＿＿＿＿＿＿＿＿＿＿, **wǒ jiù kěyǐ zǎodiǎn huí jiā.**

c. 要是暑假可以长一点的话，＿＿＿＿＿＿＿＿＿＿＿＿＿＿＿。

要是暑假可以長一點的話，＿＿＿＿＿＿＿＿＿＿＿＿＿＿＿。

Yàoshì shǔjià kěyǐ cháng yī diǎn de huà, ＿＿＿＿＿＿＿＿.

6

At a recent Earth Day celebration, everyone wrote down their suggestions to improve the world and hung them on the branches of a big tree. Finish the following sentences to complete a few of these suggestions, and then write one yourself.

a. 只要我们 ＿＿＿＿＿＿＿＿＿＿＿＿＿＿＿＿，这个世界一定会更好。

只要我們 ＿＿＿＿＿＿＿＿＿＿＿＿＿＿＿＿，這個世界一定會更好。

Zhǐyào wǒmen ＿＿＿＿＿＿＿＿＿, **zhège shìjiè yīdìng huì gèng hǎo.**

b. 除非 ＿＿＿＿＿＿＿＿＿＿＿＿＿＿，要不然我们的地球会越来越糟糕。

除非 ＿＿＿＿＿＿＿＿＿＿＿＿＿＿，要不然我們的地球會越來越糟糕。

Chúfēi ＿＿＿＿＿＿, **yàobùrán wǒmen de dìqiú huì yuè lái yuè zāogāo.**

c. ＿＿＿＿＿＿＿＿＿＿＿＿＿＿＿＿＿＿＿＿＿＿＿＿＿＿

46

Expressing 'both,' 'all,' 'every,' 'any,' 'none,' 'not any,' and 'no matter how'

1 Rearrange the following sentences to match the English meanings.

a. 都　　我们　　　学中文　　　　喜欢。
　　都　　我們　　　學中文　　　　喜歡。
　　Dōu　wǒmen　xué Zhōngwén　xǐhuan.
　　We all like to study Chinese.

b. 我　买了　　都　　那些书。
　　我　買了　　都　　那些書。
　　Wǒ　mǎi le　dōu　nà xiē shū.
　　I bought all of those books.

c. 那些书　　　很贵　　都。
　　那些書　　　很貴　　都。
　　Nà xiē shū　hěn guì　dōu.
　　All those books are expensive.

d. 没　学生们　　　　去上课　　　都。
　　沒　學生們　　　　去上課　　　都。
　　Méi　xuéshengmen　qù shàng kè　dōu.
　　None of the students have gone to class.

e. 我　学　都　　中文日文。
　　我　學　都　　中文日文。
　　Wǒ　xué　dōu　Zhōngwén Rìwén.
　　I study both Chinese and Japanese.

f. 我　做完了　　都　　所有的功课。
　　我　做完了　　都　　所有的功課。
　　Wǒ　zuòwán le　dōu　suǒyǒu de gōngkè.
　　I have finished all the assignments.

g. 都　他　不　会　写　一个字。

　都　他　不　會　寫　一個字。

Dōu　tā　bù　huì　xiě　yī gè zì.

He does not know how to write a single character.

h. 那个老师　　都　　不喜欢　　我们。

　那個老師　　都　　不喜歡　　我們。

Nàge lǎoshī　dōu　bù xǐhuan　wǒmen.

None of us likes that teacher.

⇨ 46.1

2 Select a question word from the list below to best complete each of the following sentences to match the English translation.

Question words:　什么/甚麼 **shénme**

怎么/怎麼 **zěnme**

谁/誰 **shéi**

几/幾 **jǐ**

哪儿/哪兒 **nǎr?**

a. 你去图书馆了，可是我 _____ 都没去。

　你去圖書館了，可是我 _____ 都沒去。

Nǐ qù túshūguǎn le, kěshì wǒ _____ dōu méi qù.

You went to the library, but I did not go anywhere.

b. 你去图书馆了，可是我 _____ 地方都没去。

　你去圖書館了，可是我 _____ 地方都沒去。

Nǐ qù túshūguǎn le, kěshì wǒ _____ dìfang dōu méi qù.

You went to the library, but I did not go anywhere.

c. 你认识人，可是我 _____ 都不认识。

　你認識人，可是我 _____ 都不認識。

Nǐ rènshi rén, kěshì wǒ _____ dōu bù rènshi.

You know people, but I don't know anyone.

d. 你认识人，可是我 _____ 人都不认识。

　你認識人，可是我 _____ 人都不認識。

Nǐ rènshi rén, kěshì wǒ _____ rén dōu bù rènshi.

You know people, but I don't know anyone.

e. 你买书了，可是我 _____ 都没买。

　你買書了，可是我 _____ 都沒買。

Nǐ mǎi shū le, kěshì wǒ _____ dōu méi mǎi.

You bought books, but I didn't buy anything.

f. 他三点来，可是你 _____ 时候来都可以。

　他三點來，可是你 _____ 時候來都可以。

Tā sān diǎn lái, kěshì nǐ _____ shíhòu lái dōu kéyǐ.

He will come at 3:00, but you can come anytime.

g. 他三点来，你 _____ 点来都可以。

他三點來，你 _____ 點來都可以。

Tā sān diǎn lái, nǐ _____ diǎn lái dōu kéyǐ.

He will come at 3:00, but you can come anytime.

h. 他这样写，你 _____ 写都可以。

他這樣寫，你 _____ 寫都可以。

Tā zhè yàng xiě, nǐ _____ xiě dōu kéyǐ.

He writes this way, but you write any way you want.

⇨ 46.4

3

Answer the questions negatively using question words as in the example.
Translate your answers into English.

Example: A: 你想买什么？   B: 我什么都不想买。

你想買甚麼？   我甚麼都不想買。

Nǐ xiǎng mǎi shénme?   Wǒ shénme dōu bù xiǎng mǎi.

What do you want to buy?   I don't want to buy anything.

a. 你想看什么电影？

你想看甚麼電影？

Nǐ xiǎng kàn shénme diànyǐng?

Which movie do you want to watch?

b. 你想喝什么啤酒？

你想喝甚麼啤酒？

Nǐ xiǎng hē shénme píjiǔ?

What beer do you want to drink?

c. 你认识谁？

你認識誰？

Nǐ rènshi shéi?

Who do you know?

d. 这件事你想告诉谁？

這件事你想告訴誰？

Zhè jiàn shì nǐ xiǎng gàosu shéi?

Who do you want to inform about this matter?

e. 谁要把钱借给你？

誰要把錢借給你？

Shéi yào bǎ qián jiègěi nǐ?

Who wants to lend you money?

f. 你想跟我说什么？

你想跟我說甚麼？

Nǐ xiǎng gēn wǒ shuō shénme?

What do you want to tell me?

g. 你喜欢哪件毛衣？

你喜歡哪件毛衣？

Nǐ xǐhuan nǎ jiàn máoyī?

Which sweater do you like?

h. 你放假去什么地方？

你放假去甚麽地方？

Nǐ fang jià qù shénme dìfang?

Where do you want to go during the break?

⇨ 46.4.2

4 周利 Zhōu Lì had a bad experience with his last exam. Express his experience in Mandarin, using 怎么/怎麽 **zěnme** and the appropriate form of the bracketed resultative verb in each sentence.

Example: No matter how I review the lessons I do poorly on the tests.

→

我怎么复习功课也考不好。

我怎麽復習功課也考不好。

Wǒ zěnme fùxí gōngkè yě kǎo bù hǎo.

a. No matter how I studied, I couldn't master (the material). [学会/學會 **xuéhuì**]

b. No matter how I tried to memorize (things) I couldn't memorize (them). [记住/記住 **jìzhù**]

c. No matter how much I wrote, I couldn't finish writing. [写完/寫完 **xiěwán**]

d. No matter how I tried to guess, I couldn't guess. [猜着/猜著 **cāizhāo**]

e. No matter how I read (it), I couldn't understand (it). [看懂 **kàndǒng**]

f. No matter how I thought, I couldn't think of the answers. [想起来 **xiǎngqǐlai**, 答案 **dá'àn** answer]

⇨ 32.1, 32.2, 46.4.3

5 小李 Xiǎo Lǐ finds his roommate difficult to live with. Describe his roommate's behavior in Mandarin using the parenthesized words.

Example: He doesn't go anywhere. → 他哪儿都不去。

(哪儿/哪兒 **nǎr**)   他哪兒都不去。

Tā nǎr dōu bù qù.

a. He doesn't like anyone. [谁/誰 **shéi**]

b. He is not willing to do anything. [什么/甚麽 **shénme**]

c. No matter how much you speak with him, he doesn't listen. [怎么/怎麽 **zěnme**]

d. His things are all over the room. (In the room, his things are everywhere.) [哪儿/哪兒 **nǎr**]

e. No matter how dirty his clothing is, he won't wash it. [多么/多麽 **duóme**]

f. In the evening, he is always watching television. [什么时候/甚麽時候 **shénme shíhòu**]

g. No matter how you ask, he won't turn it off. [怎么/怎麼 **zěnme**]

h. In the morning, no matter how you call him, he won't wake up.
   [怎么/怎麼 **zěnme**]

⇨ 46.4

6

Mrs. Zhao is worried about her son, Jason, who has been depressed since his girlfriend of five years left him. Mrs. Zhao is on the phone with her best friend, Mrs. Guo. Mrs. Zhao complains that her son does not want to see anyone, does not do anything, does not go anywhere, does not eat anything either. Mrs. Guo tells her that everyone needs time to think about things. Use this information to complete their conversation in Mandarin.

赵太太：他已经把自己关在房间里三天了，_____

_____ 我担心死了。

赵太太：他已經把自己關在房間裡三天了，_____

_____ 我擔心死了。

Zhào tàitai: Tā yǐjīng bǎ zìjǐ guānzài fángjiān lǐ sāntiān le, _____

_____ **Wǒ dānxīn sǐ le.**

郭太太：我知道你很担心，可是，遇到这种事，_____。

郭太太：我知道你很擔心，可是，遇到這種事，_____。

Guō tàitai: Wǒ zhīdào nǐ hěn dānxīn, kěshì, yùdào zhè zhǒng shì, _____

_____.

7

Miranda got a job house sitting for the Jensens, who are going on vacation for three weeks. Today Miranda meets with Mrs. Jensen to go over the tasks she will be expected to perform as the house sitter. Translate them into Mandarin.

a. Walk the dog every day: once in the morning, once in the evening.
   [遛狗 **liù gǒu**]

b. Water the plants every two days. [浇花/澆花 **jiāo huā**]

c. Pick up the mail every week. [拿信 **nà xìn**]

47
Expressing location and distance

Here is a map of my hometown. Everything in the box is inside of the city, and everything outside of the box is outside of the city. Answer the questions in complete Mandarin sentences based on the map [城 **chéng** city].

中学/中學 **zhōngxué** middle school	书店/書店 **shūdiàn** bookstore	宿舍 **sùshè** dormitory	
		图书馆/圖書館 **túshūguǎn** library	银行/銀行 **yínháng** bank
医院/醫院 **yīyuàn** hospital		火车站/火車站 **huǒchēzhàn** train station	体育馆/體育館 **tǐyùguǎn** gymnasium

湖 **hú** lake

公园/公園 **gōngyuán** park

N
W — E
S

Answer these questions using compass directions.

> Example: Where is the lake? → 湖在公园的西边。
> 湖在公園的西邊。
> **Hú zài gōngyuán de xībian.**

a. Where is the hospital?

b. Where is the middle school?

c. Where is the train station?

d. Where is the bank?

Answer these questions in complete Mandarin sentences.

e. Is the park to the left of the lake or to the right of the lake?

f. Is the park inside the city or outside the city?

g. Is the bank north of the gymnasium or south of the gymnasium?

h. Is the bookstore east of the middle school or west of the middle school?

i. What is between the dorm and the middle school?

j. What is next to the park?

⇨ 47.1

2 Here is the seating arrangement in today's Chinese class. Answer the questions in complete Mandarin sentences based on the seating arrangement.

王鹏飞/王鵬飛 Wáng Péngfēi	陈玫玲/陳玫玲 Chén Méilíng	徐乃康 Xú Nǎikāng	唐新花 Táng Xīnhuā
高蕾 Gāo Lěi	饶兴荣/饒興榮 Ráo Xīngróng	马嘉美/馬嘉美 Mǎ Jiāměi	林道余/林道餘 Lín Dàoyú

Example: 马嘉美在林道余的哪边？

馬嘉美在林道餘的哪邊？

Mǎ Jiāměi zài Lín Dàoyú de nǎbiān?

→

马嘉美在林道余的左边。

馬嘉美在林道餘的左邊。

Mǎ Jiāměi zài Lín Dàoyú de zuǒbian.

a. 高蕾的右边是谁？

高蕾的右邊是誰？

Gāo Lěi de yòubian shì shéi?

b. 林道余的后头是谁？

林道餘的後頭是誰？

Lín Dàoyú de hòutou shì shéi?

c. 谁在陈玫玲跟唐新花的中间？

誰在陳玫玲跟唐新花的中間？

Shéi zài Chén Méilíng gēn Táng Xīnhuā de zhōngjiān?

d. Who is to Chen Meiling's left?

e. Who is in front of Xu Naikang?

f. Who is to the right of Wang Pengfei?

g. Who is beside Lin Daoyu?

⇨ 47.1

3 Translate the following expressions into Mandarin.

a. in front of the house

b. between the two cars

c. to the left of the house

d. in front of the person

e. the books on the table

f.   the house on the right

g.   the train station behind the school

h.   the person who is in front

i.   The cat is on top of the table. [猫/貓 **māo** cat]

j.   The dog is behind the house. [狗 **gǒu** dog]

k.   There are flowers in the park.

l.   There is no one in the house.

m.   There are students in the library.

n.   There are no cats in the dormitory.

⇨   47.1, 47.2, 47.3

4   When I leave my home and travel east on Main Street I pass these destinations. Here are their distances from my home.

公园/公園	火车站/火車站	大学/大學	飞机场/飛機場
gōngyuán	**huǒchēzhàn**	**dàxué**	**fēijī chǎng**
park	train station	university	airport
2 km	5 km	12 km	25 km

I consider 1–3 kilometers to be a short distance, 4–15 kilometers to be far, and anything over 15 kilometers to be very far. Based on this information, answer the following questions in complete Mandarin sentences.

Example: 我家离公园有多远？　→　你家离公园有两公里。
我家離公園有多遠？　　　你家離公園有兩公里。
Wǒ jiā lí gōngyuán　　**Nǐ jiā lí gōngyuán yǒu**
yǒu duō yuǎn?　　　　**liǎng gōnglǐ.**

a.   我家离大学远吗？
我家離大學遠嗎？
Wǒ jiā lí dàxué yuǎn ma?

b.   我家离公园远不远？
我家離公園遠不遠？
Wǒ jiā lí gōngyuán yuǎn bù yuǎn?

c.   Is my house far from the train station?

d.   Is the park far from the university?

e.   Is my house far from the airport?

f.   我家离大学有多远？
我家離大學有多遠？
Wǒ jiā lí dàxué yǒu duō yuǎn?

g.   How far is it from my house to the train station?

h.   How far is it from the park to the airport?

i.   How far is it from the university to the airport?

j.   How far is it from my house to the airport?

⇨   47.4, 47.5

175

48

Talking about movement, directions, and means of transportation

1 Translate these questions into Mandarin.

a. Where is the university?

b. How do you get to the university?

c. How do you get to the university from here?

d. How do you get from the dormitory to the bookstore?

e. Do you turn left?

f. Do you turn left or right?

g. Is the library on the left or the right?

h. Do you know where the bookstore is?

⇨ 48.1, 48.2

2 Complete these sentences by filling in the blanks with the appropriate Mandarin expressions to correspond to the English sentences.

a. 请问，(1)_____ 这儿 (2)_____ 中国大使馆 (3)_____ 走？

請問，(1)_____ 這兒 (2)_____ 中國大使館 (3)_____ 走？

Qǐng wèn, (1)_____ zhèr (2)_____ Zhōngguó dàshǐguǎn

(3)_____ **zǒu?**

May I ask, how do you get to the Chinese embassy from here?

b. 对 (1)_____，我 (2)_____。

對 (1)_____，我 (2)_____。

Duì (1)_____, wǒ (2)_____.

Sorry, I don't know.

c. 劳驾，你 (1)_____ 到中国大使馆 (2)_____ 走吗？

勞駕，你 (1)_____ 到中國大使館 (2)_____ 走嗎？

Láojià, nǐ (1)_____ dào Zhōngguó dàshǐguǎn (2)_____ zǒu ma?

Excuse me, do you know how to get to the Chinese embassy from here?

d. 知道。你 (1)_____ 这儿一直 (2)_____ 前走 (3)_____ 两个红绿灯往右 (4)_____，再 (5)_____ 几分钟，(6)_____ 边的一个大房子就是了。

知道。你 (1)_____ 這兒一直 (2)_____ 前走 (3)_____ 兩個紅綠燈往右 (4)_____，再 (5)_____ 幾分鐘，(6)_____ 邊的一個大房子就是了。

Zhīdào. Nǐ (1)_____ **zhè ér yīzhí** (2)_____ **qián zǒu** (3)_____ **liǎng gè hónglǜ dēng wǎng yòu** (4)_____, **zài** (5)_____ **jǐ fēn zhōng,** (6)_____ **biān de yī gè dà fángzi jiù shì le.**

Yes, I do. Go straight ahead, pass two traffic lights, turn right, then walk a few minutes. It will be the big building on your left.

⇨ 48.1, 48.2

3 Translate the directions from my house to the park into Mandarin.

a. Walk east.

b. Walk east on Zhongshan Road. [中山路 **Zhōngshān lù**]

c. Cross one intersection.

d. Cross Park Avenue. [公园路/公園路 **gōngyuán lù**]

e. Continue (going) east.

f. Turn right on Library Road.

g. Keep going straight ahead.

h. Cross two intersections.

i. At the third intersection, turn left.

j. That will be White Lake Road.

k. The park is on your right.

⇨ 48.1, 48.2, 48.3

4 Put these words in the correct order to correspond to the English translations.

a. 开去我们了进。
开去我們了進。
kāi qù wǒmen le jìn.
We drove in.

b. 了爬山去我们上。
了爬山去我們上。
le pá shān qù wǒmen shàng.
We hiked up the mountain.

c. 来她了过跑。
來她了過跑。
lái tā le guò pǎo.
She ran over here.

d. 都他们了出走去。

都他們了出走去。

dōu tāmen le chū zǒu qù.

They all walked out.

e. 拿回我书了来把。

拿回我書了來把。

ná huí wǒ shū le lái bǎ.

I carried the books back here.

⇨ 48.8

5

In complete sentences, say how each of the following people got to school today. Use the 是…的 **shì . . . de** pattern to focus on the means of transportation.

Example: 小毛 **Xiǎo Máo**: → 我是坐船来的。

I came by boat. 我是坐船來的。

Wǒ shì zuò chuán lái de.

a. 周利 **Zhōu Lì**: I came by bus.

b. 高蕾 **Gāo Lěi**: I came by car.

c. 王明 **Wáng Míng**: I came by bicycle.

d. 王小妹 **Wáng Xiǎomèi**: I came on foot.

e. 珠莉 **Zhū Lì**: I came by motorcycle.

f. 张苹/張苹 **Zhāng Píng**: I came by subway.

⇨ 48.5.2, 57.2.4

6

Your are on the phone with your little sister, who is away at college. She is telling you all about the neighborhood she lives in to prepare you for your visit next week. Identify each building with the correct letter based on her description.

我的宿舍旁边有一个咖啡馆。图书馆在宿舍和公园的中间。我的宿舍在东边，公园在西边。从我的宿舍到学校，先往北走，到路口往左拐，再往西走，一会儿就到了。学校在右边。银行在学校的后边。银行的左边有一个小书店。

我的宿舍旁邊有一個咖啡館。圖書館在宿舍和公園的中間。我的宿舍在東邊，公園在西邊。從我的宿舍到學校，先往北走，到路口往左拐，再往西走，一會兒就到了。學校在右邊。銀行在學校的後邊。銀行的左邊有一個小書店。

Wǒ de sùshè pángbiān yǒu yī gè kāfēiguǎn. Túshūguǎn zài sùshè hé gōngyuán de zhōngjiān. Wǒ de sùshè zài dōngbian, gōngyuán zài xībiān. Cóng wǒ de sùshè dào xuéxiào xiān wǎng běi zǒu, dào lùkǒu wǎng zuǒ guǎi, zài wǎng xī zǒu, yīhuìr jiù dàole. Xuéxiào zài yòubian. Yínháng zài xuéxiào de hòubian. Yínháng de zuǒbian yǒu yī gè xiǎo shūdiàn.

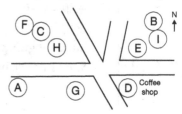

Talking about movement, directions, and means of transportation

a.   dorm: _____

b.   library: _____

c.   park: _____

d.   school: _____

e.   bank: _____

f.   bookstore: _____

49
Talking about clock time and calendar time

1 Rewrite the Chinese time expressions in English and the English time expressions in Chinese.

a. 11:30

b. 一点三刻/一點三刻 **yī diǎn sān kè**

c. 6:50 (use 差 **chà**)

d. 三点一刻/三點一刻 **sān diǎn yī kè**

e. 7:40

f. 两点二十/兩點二十 **liǎng diǎn èrshí**

g. 8:01 (use 过/過 **guò**)

h. 九点过二十五分/九點過二十五分
    jiǔdiǎn guò èrshíwǔ fēn

i   5:55 (use 差 **chà**)

j. 12:12 (use 过/過 **guò**)

⇨ 49.1

2 Translate these expressions into Mandarin.

a. 2 weeks   f. 2^1/$_2$ weeks

b. 2 days   g. 2^1/$_2$ days

c. 2 hours   h. 2^1/$_2$ minutes

d. 2 semesters   i. 2^1/$_2$ months

e. 2 minutes   j. 2^1/$_2$ years

⇨ 6.6.4, 49.1

3 Translate the English dates into Mandarin and the Mandarin dates into English.

a. July 1, 1993

b. 一八八四年二月十六日
    yī bā bā sì nián èr yuè shíliù rì

c. May 23, 2003

d. 二零零五年三月二十七日
    èr líng líng wǔ nián sān yuè èrshíqī rì

e. October 5, 1998

f. 二零零八年八月二十二号
二零零八年八月二十二號
èr líng líng bā nián bā yuè èrshí'èr hào

g. January 1, 2002

h. 一九一六年九月十九号
一九一六年九月十九號
yī jiǔ yī liù nián jiǔyuè shíjiǔ hào

⇨ 49.2

4

Here is 王小妹 **Wáng Xiǎomèi**'s appointment book. Reply to each question in a complete Mandarin sentence based on this information, using the example sentence as your model.

	Sun	Mon	Tues	Wed	Thurs	Fri	Sat
last week		A			B		
this week	C			TODAY			D
next week	E		F			G	

A. 买飞机票/買飛機票 **mǎi fēijī piào** buy an airline ticket

B. 游泳 **yóuyǒng** swim

C. 回家 **huí jiā** go home

D. 考中文 **kǎo Zhōngwén** take a Chinese test

E. 看电影/看電影 **kàn diànyǐng** see movies

F. 听音乐会/聽音樂會 **tīng yīnyuè huì** attend a music concert

G. 看朋友 **kàn péngyou** see friends

Example: 王小妹什么时候看朋友？
王小妹甚麼時候看朋友？
Wáng Xiǎomèi shénme shíhòu kàn péngyou?
→
王小妹下星期五看朋友。
Wáng Xiǎomèi xià xīngqīwǔ kàn péngyou.

a. 王小妹什么时候买飞机票了？
王小妹甚麼時候買飛機票了？
Wáng Xiǎomèi shénme shíhòu mǎi fēijī piào le?

b. 王小妹什么时候游泳了？
王小妹甚麼時候游泳了？
Wáng Xiǎomèi shénme shíhòu yóuyǒng le?

c. 王小妹什么时候回家了？
王小妹甚麼時候回家了？
Wáng Xiǎomèi shénme shíhòu huí jiā le?

d. 王小妹什么时候考中文？
王小妹甚麼時候考中文？
Wáng Xiǎomèi shénme shíhòu kǎo Zhōngwén?

e. 王小妹什么时候看电影？
王小妹甚麼時候看電影？
Wáng Xiǎomèi shénme shíhòu kàn diànyǐng?

f. 王小妹什么时候听音乐会？
王小妹甚麼時候聽音樂會？
Wáng Xiǎomèi shénme shíhòu tīng yīnyuèhuì?

g. 王小妹什么时候看朋友？
王小妹甚麼時候看朋友？
Wáng Xiǎomèi shénme shíhòu kàn péngyou?

⇨ 4.5, 49.2.3.2, 49.2.4.2

5 Name the date in relation to 'today'.

a. March 12   大前天 **dàqiántiān** three days ago
b. March 13
c. March 14
d. March 15   今天 **jīntiān** today
e. March 16
f. March 17
g. March 18

⇨ 49.2.4.3

6 The following are typical announcements that you might hear in an airport in China. Read the announcements and answer the questions in Mandarin.

Announcement 1

各位旅客请注意。原定六点钟从上海飞往青岛的405号班机因天气的关系，
延迟一个半小时起飞。

各位旅客請注意。原定六點鐘從上海飛往青島的405號班機因天氣的關係，
延遲一個半小時起飛。

Gèwèi lǚkè qǐng zhùyì. Yuándìng liù diǎn zhōng cóng Shànghǎi fēiwǎng Qīngdǎo de 405 hào bānjī yīn tiānqì de guānxi, yánchí yī gè bàn xiǎoshí qǐfēi.

Questions

a. What time was the flight to Qingdao originally scheduled to depart?
b. How late will the flight be?
c. What is the reason for the delay?

Announcement 2

各位旅客请注意。从上海飞往东京的337号班机还有一刻钟就要起飞了。请还没有
登机的旅客，马上登机。

各位旅客請注意。從上海飛往東京的337號班機還有一刻鐘就要起飛了。請還沒有
登機的旅客，馬上登機。

**Gèwèi lǚkè qǐng zhùyì. Cóng Shànghǎi fēiwǎng Dōngjīng de 337 hào bānjī hái
yǒu yī kè zhōng jiù yào qǐfēi le. Qǐng hái méi yǒu dēngjī de lǚkè, mǎshàng dēngjī.**

Questions

d. What is the flight number from Shanghai to Tokyo?

e. When will the flight to Tokyo depart?

f. What is the purpose of this announcement?

Announcement 3

原定在10号登机门登机，晚7点45分飞往伦敦的231号班机因故取消。请乘客到
服务台办理换机手续。

原定在10號登機門登機，晚7點45分飛往倫敦的231號班機因故取消。請乘客到
服務台辦理換機手續。

**Yuándìng zài 10 hào dēng jī mén dēngjī, wǎn 7 diǎn 45 fēn fēiwǎng Lúndūn de
231 hào bānjī yīn gù qǔxiāo. Qǐng chéngkè dào fúwùtái bànlǐ huànjī shǒuxù.**

Questions

g. What time was flight 231 originally scheduled to depart?

h. Is there any specific reason given for the cancellation?

i. What are the passengers asked to do?

Announcement 4

从芝加哥到上海的飞机原定飞行时间十二个半小时。因为风向的关系，延迟一个
小时到达。到达时间为晚九点。

從芝加哥到上海的飛機原定飛行時間十二個半小時。因爲風向的關係，延遲一個
小時到達。到達時間爲晚九點。

**Cóng Zhījiāgē dào Shànghǎi de fēijī yuándìng fēixíng shíjiān shí'èr gè bàn
xiǎoshí. Yīnwei fēng xiàng de guānxi, yánchí yī gè xiǎoshí dàodá. Dàodá
shíjiān wéi wǎn jiǔ diǎn.**

Questions

j. How long will the flight be from Chicago to Shanghai?

k. What time was the flight from Chicago originally scheduled to arrive in Shanghai?

l. How late will the flight be?

Announcement 5

原定从香港起飞8点到达的666号班机已经到达。请迎接旅客的人到领取行李处接客。

原定從香港起飛8點到達的666號班機已經到達。請迎接旅客的人到領取行李處接客。

**Yuándìng cóng Xiānggǎng qǐfēi 8 diǎn dàodá de 666 hào bānjī yǐjing
dàodá. Qǐng yíngjiē lǚkè de rén dào lǐngqǔ xíngli chù jiē kè.**

Questions

m.   What is the status of flight 666?

n.   Where are those people meeting passengers on flight 666 asked to go?

Announcement 6

本飞机场设有指定的吸烟区。请吸烟的旅客到指定的吸烟区吸烟。

本飛機場設有指定的吸煙區。請吸煙的旅客到指定的吸煙區吸煙。

Běn fēijīchǎng shèyǒu zhǐdìng de xī yān qū. Qǐng xī yān de lǚkè dào zhǐdìng de xīyān qū xī yān.

Question

o.   Are you allowed to smoke in the airport?

⇨   48, 49, 50.1, 50.2, 51.2

7

You are a professional wedding planner. Today you are meeting with the future Mr. and Mrs. Mo to discuss their wedding plans. They plan to get married next July 4th, which gives them a year to plan the wedding. Here's a list of things they need to include in their planning schedule. Using this information, write a plan for Mr. and Mrs. Mo. For example: 明年三月买戒指/明年三月買戒指/ **míngnián sānyuè mǎi jièzhǐ.**

This Year	
July–Sept.	Book photographer, florist, makeup 订摄影师、花店、化妆师/訂攝影師、花店、化妝師 **dìng shèyǐng shī, huādiàn, huàzhuāngshī**
Sept/Oct.	Prepare guest list 决定请客名单/決定請客名單 **juédìng qǐngkè míngdān**
Oct.	Reserve location 订场地/訂場地 **dìng chǎngdì**
Nov.	Book hotel 订饭店/訂飯店 **dìng fàndiàn** Buy dress 买礼服/買禮服 **mǎi lǐfú**
Dec.	Design invitation 设计请帖/設計請帖 **shèjì qǐngtiě**
Next Year	
Jan.	Registry 注册礼物/註冊禮物 **zhùcè lǐwù**
Feb.	Confirm all reservations 确认所有预约项目/確認所有預約項目 **quèrèn suǒyǒu yùyuē xiàngmù**
Mar	Buy rings 买戒指/買戒指 **mǎi jièzhǐ**
June	Make seating chart 决定座位/決定座位 **juédìng zuòwèi** Finalize ceremony schedule 确定典礼流程/確定典禮流程 **quèdìng diǎnlǐ liúchéng**

50
Expressing obligations and prohibitions

1

Mom is dropping 小明 **Xiǎo Míng** off at college. This is 小明 **Xiǎo Míng**'s first semester and Mom is anxious. The following is what she says to 小明 **Xiǎo Míng**. Translate it into Mandarin.

a. We have to go now.

b. Since you are alone at school, you have to take care of yourself.

c. You have to go to bed early and get up early.

d. Don't go to bed too late.

e. Also, you have to go to class and turn in your assignments on time.

f. Don't be nervous when taking exams.

g. If you have any problems, you should talk to your teacher.

h. If you do not feel comfortable, you should go to the hospital immediately.

i. Also, you have to call us every day.

⇨ 50.1, 50.2

2

For each of the following signs, identify the word or phrase that indicates the prohibition and translate it into English. Indicate the action that is being prohibited and translate it into English.

a. 禁止随地吐痰。   *Prohibition:*
禁止隨地吐痰。   *Prohibited activity:*
Jìnzhǐ suídì tǔtán.

b. 请勿停车。   *Prohibition:*
請勿停車。   *Prohibited activity:*
Qǐng wù tíng chē.

c. 闲人免进。   *Prohibition:*
閑人免進。   *Prohibited activity:*
Xián rén miǎn jìn.

d. 禁止拍照。   *Prohibition:*
Jìnzhǐ pāi zhào.   *Prohibited activity:*

e. 严禁酒后开车。   *Prohibition:*
  严禁酒後開車。   *Prohibited activity:*
  Yán jìn jiǔ hòu kāi chē.

f. 请勿吸烟。   *Prohibition:*
  請勿吸煙。   *Prohibited activity:*
  Qǐng wù xī yān.

⇨ 50.2.3

3 Rephrase the warnings and prohibitions in (2) in colloquial form.

⇨ 50.2

4 You are helping an international student, **Yao Qiang**, to find an apartment near campus. Today he is about to sign the lease. Help him understand the lease by translating these highlights of the agreement into Mandarin with the words provided.

Terms: Landlord [房东/房東 **fángdōng**]; Resident [房客 **fángkè**]

a. Rent: $1200 <u>should</u> be paid by the 5th of the month. [应当/應當 **yīngdāng**]

b. Utilities: Resident <u>must</u> pay for cable themselves but <u>does not have to</u> pay for water/electricity bills. [必须 **bìxū**; 不必 **bùbì**]

c. Pets: No pets allowed. [不许/不許 **bùxǔ**]

d. House rules: No smoking. No noise after 12:00 a.m. [禁止 **jìnzhǐ**]

e. Guests: Guests staying over 15 days <u>must have</u> the consent of the landlord. Guests staying fewer than 15 days <u>do not need</u> permission. [必须 **bìxū**; 无须/無須 **wú xū**]

5 Based on your own experience, give **Yao Qiang** more tips on the Dos and Don'ts of being a good tenant.

NOTE | For additional exercises involving obligations and prohibitions, see Chapter 51.

51

Expressing commands and permission

1 Rewrite these expressions of permission as commands.

    Example: 你可以骑自行车去。   →   骑自行车去吧！

              你可以騎自行車去。   騎自行車去吧！

              Nǐ kěyǐ qí zìxíngchē qù.   **Qí zìxíngchē qù ba!**

              You can go by bicycle.   Go by bicycle!

a.   你可以看电视。

     你可以看電視。

     Nǐ kěyǐ kàn diànshì.

     You can watch television.

b.   你可以给你的弟弟打电话。

     你可以給你的弟弟打電話。

     Nǐ kěyǐ gěi nǐ de dìdi dǎ diànhuà.

     You can call your younger brother.

c.   你可以吃饭。

     你可以吃飯。

     Nǐ kěyǐ chī fàn.

     You can eat.

d.   你可以去看奶奶。

     Nǐ kěyǐ qù kàn nǎinai.

     You can go to see grandma.

e.   你可以说话。

     你可以說話。

     Nǐ kěyǐ shuō huà.

     You can speak.

f.   你可以睡觉。

     你可以睡覺。

     Nǐ kěyǐ shuì jiào.

     You can go to sleep.

g. 你可以回家。

Nǐ kěyǐ huí jiā.

You can go home.

h. 你可以洗澡。

Nǐ kěyǐ xǐ zǎo.

You can take a bath.

⇨ 51.1.1, 51.2.1

2 Here is a list of the rules in 周利 **Zhōu Lì**'s dorm. Rewrite the list in complete sentences in Mandarin.

Permissible activities

a. smoking in common room [公用的房间/公用的房間 **gōngyòng de fángjiān** common room]

b. cooking in common room

c. watching television in room

d. inviting friends to room

Impermissible activities

e. smoking in room

f. drinking alcohol in the dorm

g. playing loud music

h. cooking in room

Required activities

i. dispose of your trash every day [垃圾 **lājī** trash, 扔掉 **rēngdiào** throw away]

j. return to the dorm by 10 p.m.

k. turn your lights out by 11:30 p.m. [关灯/關燈 **guān dēng** turn out lights]

⇨ 50.2.1, 51.1.1, 51.2.1

3 This is the first day of Chinese language class. The teacher tells the students the following rules. Translate them into Mandarin.

a. Don't come to class late.

b. No eating in class.

c. No drinking in class.

d. Before class begins, turn off your cell phone.

e. Students are not allowed to send text messages during class.

f. Students are not allowed to turn in assignments late.

[交作业/交作業 **jiāo zuòyè** hand in homework]

g. Before coming to class, review the lesson.

h. Raise your hand if you have a question. [举手/舉手 **jǔshǒu** raise one's hand]

⇨ 50.2, 51.1, 51.2

4　小毛 **Xiǎo Máo** missed his first Chinese language class. 小王 **Xiǎo Wáng** tells him the rules. Write down what 小王 **Xiǎo Wáng** says. For rules a–f, begin each sentence with the following expression:

老师不让我们…

老師不讓我們…

Lǎoshī bù ràng women . . .

The teacher won't let us . . .

Express rules g and h as strong obligations with 得 **děi**, 必得 **bìděi**, or 必须/必須 **bìxū** 'must.'

⇨　50.2, 51.1, 51.2.2

5　Detective Johnson is interrogating a suspect who only speaks Chinese. You are the translator on this case. Help Detective Johnson with the process by translating for both parties.

	English	Mandarin
Detective	Sit!	
Detective	You are **Jiāng Sōng**, right? （江松）	
Detective	Say it, who told you to steal that vase? [花瓶 **huāpíng** vase]	
Suspect		没人让我偷。我可以抽烟吗？ 沒人讓我偷。我可以抽煙嗎？ **Méirén rang wǒ tōu.** **Wǒ kěyǐ chōu yān ma?**
Detective	No smoking here. But you can have a glass of water. Hold it!	

Later

	English	Mandarin
Detective	Are you ready to write your confession? [自白 **zìbái** confession] Write!	

52
Expressing ability and possibility

1 张小姐/張小姐 **Zhāng xiǎojie** is making a list of her credentials in preparation for a job search. Describe her abilities in Mandarin, using the modal verb 会/會 **huì** in your answers.

> Example: drive a car → 我会开车。   我不会开车。
>   我會開車。   我不會開車。
>   **Wǒ huì kāi chē.** **Wǒ bù huì kāi chē.**
>   I can drive.   I can't drive.

       I can   *I am not able to*

a. speak Japanese   e. speak Chinese

b. sing (very well)   f. drive

c. dance   g. use a computer

d. play basketball

⇨ 52.1

2 Rearrange the phrases in the following sentences to correspond to the English sentences.

a. 能　　汉字　　你一天　　多少　　学?
　　能　　漢字　　你一天　　多少　　學?
　　néng Hàn zì nǐ yītiān duōshao xué?
　　How many Chinese characters can you learn in a day?

b. 考好　　这次　　我能　　一定。
　　考好　　這次　　我能　　一定。
　　kǎo hǎo zhècì wǒ néng yīdìng.
　　I can definitely do well on the test today.

c. 同屋　　我的　　不能　　病了　　去上课。
　　同屋　　我的　　不能　　病了　　去上課。
　　tóngwū wǒ de bù néng bìng le qù shàng kè.
　　My roommate is sick and can't go to class.

d. 没事　　　去看电影　　　我晚上　　　　能跟你们。

没事　　　去看電影　　　我晚上　　　　能跟你們。

méi shì　qù kàn diànyǐng　wǒ wǎnshang　néng gēn nǐmen.

I am free this evening, (I) can go to the movie with you.

➪ 52.1

3

Here is a short conversation between two students waiting for a friend. Translate the conversation into English.

A:　你觉得他今天晚上会来吗？

你覺得他今天晚上會來嗎？

Nǐ juéde tā jīntiān wǎnshang huì lái ma?

B:　我想他一定会来。

我想他一定會來。

Wǒ xiǎng tā yīdìng huì lái de.

A:　但是天气预报说今天晚上会下大雪。

但是天氣預報說今天晚上會下大雪。

Dànshì tiānqì yùbào shuō jīntiān wǎnshang huì xià dà xuě.

B:　如果下大雪他就不会来了。

如果下大雪他就不會來了。

Rúguǒ xià dà xuě tā jiù bù huì lái le.

➪ 52.1, 52.2

4

Read this passage and answer the following questions in complete sentences in Mandarin.

老王向来很能喝酒。可是最近身体不好，大夫说他不能再喝酒了。他只可以喝
可乐，汽水，茶，什么的，就是不能喝酒。老王想他病一好就可以喝酒了。
没想到，前两天他喝了一点酒就觉得很不舒服。后来，朋友请他喝酒，他就说
'我能喝酒可是我不可以喝酒了。'

老王向來很能喝酒。可是最近身體不好，大夫說他不能再喝酒了。他只可以喝
可樂，汽水，茶，甚麼的，就是不能喝酒。老王想他病一好就可以喝酒了。
沒想到，前兩天他喝了一點酒就覺得很不舒服。後來，朋友請他喝酒，他就說
'我能喝酒可是我不可以喝酒了。'

**Lǎo Wáng xiànglái hěn néng hē jiǔ. Kěshì zuì jìn shēntǐ bù hǎo, dàifu
shuō tā bù néng zài hē jiǔ le. Tā zhǐ kěyǐ hē kělè, qìshuǐ, chá, shénmede,
jiù shì bù néng hē jiǔ. Lǎo Wáng xiǎng tā bìng yī hǎo jiù kěyǐ hē jiǔ le.
Méi xiǎngdào, qián liǎng tiān tā hē le yīdiǎn jiǔ jiù juéde hěn bù shūfú.
Hòulái, péngyou qǐng tā hē jiǔ, tā jiù shuō 'wǒ néng hē jiǔ kěshì wǒ bù
kěyǐ hē jiǔ le.'**

a. 老王向来可以喝很多酒，对不对？

老王向來可以喝很多酒，對不對？

Lǎo Wáng xiànglái kěyǐ hē hěn duō jiǔ, duì bù duì?

b. 大夫为什么不让老王喝酒了？

大夫爲甚麼不讓老王喝酒了？

Dàifu wéi shénme bù ràng Lǎo Wáng hē jiǔ le?

c. 老王可以喝什么？

老王可以喝甚麼？

Lǎo Wáng kěyǐ hē shénme?

d. 老王认为他什么时候可以再喝酒？

老王認爲他甚麼時候可以再喝酒？

Lǎo Wáng rènwéi tā shénme shíhòu kěyǐ zài hē jiǔ?

e. 前两天他喝了酒以后觉得怎么样？

前兩天他喝了酒以後覺得怎麼樣？

Qián liǎng tiān tā hē le jiǔ yǐhòu juéde zěnmeyàng?

f. 后来朋友请他喝酒时他说什么？

後來朋友請他喝酒時他說甚麼？

Hòulái péngyou qǐng tā hē jiǔ tā shuō shénme?

⇨ 52

5

You are working in a bakery that makes fortune cookies. Your task is to write some new, interesting fortunes. You've just written a–d. Translate them into Mandarin and then write two more.

a. Tonight you will meet a beautiful girl. She will give you her phone number.

b. Do you speak Chinese? After you learn Chinese, you can go work in China.

c. This Saturday someone will buy you dinner.

d. There's a little shop next to the restaurant. After dinner, go there and buy a lottery ticket [乐透券/樂透券 **lètòuquàn**]. You will win! [中奖/中獎 **zhòngjiǎng**]

e. (Create your own) _____

f. (Create your own) _____

53
Expressing desires, needs, preferences, and willingness

1 Complete these sentences by adding 希望 **xīwàng**, 要 **yào**, 愿意/願意 **yuànyì**, 宁可/寧可 **nìngkě**, 偏爱/偏愛 **piān'ài**, or 情愿/情願 **qíngyuàn** as appropriate.

a.　我毕业以后一定 _____ 工作。

　　我畢業以後一定 _____ 工作。

　　Wǒ bìyè yǐhòu yīdìng _____ gōngzuò.

b.　我 _____ 能在政府工作。

　　Wǒ _____ néng zài zhèngfǔ gōngzuò.

c.　我 _____ 作一个翻译。

　　我 _____ 作一個翻譯。

　　Wǒ _____ zuò yī gè fānyì yuán.

d.　要是他们 _____ 给我这个工作我就高兴极了。

　　要是他們 _____ 給我這個工作我就高興極了。

　　Yàoshi tāmen _____ gěi wǒ zhège gōngzuò wǒ jiù gāoxìngjíle.

e.　要是他们不要给我这个工作我 _____ 不在政府做事了。

　　要是他們不要給我這個工作我 _____ 不在政府做事了。

　　Yàoshi tāmen bù yào gěi wǒ zhège gōngzuò wǒ _____ bù zài zhèngfǔ zuòshì le.

f.　我 _____ 少赚钱也希望能在政府部门工作。

　　我 _____ 少賺錢也希望能在政府部門工作。

　　Wǒ _____ shǎo zhuànqián yě xīwàng néng zài zhèngfǔ bùmén gōngzuò.

g.　农村生活虽然艰苦，但我 _____ 到农村去工作。

　　農村生活雖然艱苦，但我 _____ 到農村去工作。

　　Nóngcūn shēnghuó suīrán jiānkǔ, dàn wǒ _____ dào nóngcūn qù gōngzuò.

⇨　53

2

You are interviewing four college seniors about their post-graduation plans. Write up the interview in Mandarin.

a. You: Ask the students what they want to do after they graduate.

b. 王明 **Wáng Míng** says that he plans to go to China to look for a job.

c. 唐玫玲 **Táng Méilíng** says that she hopes to have the opportunity to study for a Ph.D.

d. 周利 **Zhōu Lì** says that he needs to find a job. He says he prefers to work in his own country [国内/國內 **guónèi**] and that he is not willing to work abroad [国外/國外 **guówài**].

⇨ 53

3

You and a friend have gone to a restaurant for dinner. Complete your part of the conversation in Mandarin according to the cues. Translate the server's responses into English.

a. You: Request seats in the non-smoking section.

b. 服务员：对不起，我们没有无烟的座位。你愿意坐在那边吗？
服務員：對不起，我們沒有無煙的座位。你願意坐在那邊嗎？
Fúwùyuán: Duìbuqǐ, wǒmen méi yǒu wúyān de zuòwèi. Nǐ yuànyi zuò zài nàbiān ma?

c. You: Say that you hope that the people in that area won't smoke. Say that you'd prefer to sit upstairs.

d. 服务员：没问题。楼上有座位。
服務員：沒問題。樓上有座位。
Fúwùyuán: Méi wèntí. Lóushàng yǒu zuòwèi.

e. 服务员：你们要什么菜？
服務員：你們要甚麼菜？
Fúwùyuán: Nǐmen yào shénme cài?

f. Say that you would like two dishes and a soup. Say that you hope that they don't add too much m.s.g. [味精 **wèijīng** monosodium glutamate, m.s.g.]

g. 服务员：你们还需要一点什么？
服務員：你們還需要一點甚麼？
Fúwùyuán: Nǐmen hái xūyào yīdiǎn shénme?

h. You: Say that you also want a bottle of beer and that you don't want anything else.

⇨ 53

4

The Zhuang family is doing some spring cleaning and Mrs. Zhuang has assigned tasks to each of her five children, as indicated in Table A. The children swap assignments based on their preferences, and their final assignments are listed in Table B. Complete their discussion based on the information in these tables.

Table A: Original assignments

老大	老二	老三	老四	老五
扫地	洗床单	擦窗户	洗碗	收拾房间
掃地	洗床單	擦窗戶	洗碗	收拾房間
sǎo dì	xǐ chuángdān	cā chuānghù	xǐ wǎn	shōushí fángjiān
sweep	wash the sheets	clean the windows	wash the dishes	clean up the rooms

Table B: Assignments after the swap

老大	老二	老三	老四	老五
擦窗户	扫地	洗床单	Will pay 老五	洗碗+收拾房间
擦窗戶	掃地	洗床單	$5.00	洗碗+收拾房間
cā chuānghù	sǎodì	xǐ chuángdān		xǐ wǎn + shōushí fángjiān

老大： 我 ＿＿＿＿＿＿ 也不要 ＿＿＿＿＿＿。（宁可）

我 ＿＿＿＿＿＿ 也不要 ＿＿＿＿＿＿。（寧可）

lǎo dà: Wǒ ＿＿＿＿＿＿ yě bùyào ＿＿＿＿＿＿. (nìngkě)

老二： 我 ＿＿＿＿＿＿，＿＿＿＿＿＿ 跟我交换？（愿意）

我 ＿＿＿＿＿＿，＿＿＿＿＿＿ 跟我交換？（願意）

lǎo èr: Wǒ ＿＿＿＿＿＿，＿＿＿＿＿＿ gēn wǒ jiāohuàn? (yuànyì)

老三： 我 ＿＿＿＿＿＿ 也不要 ＿＿＿＿＿＿。（情愿）

我 ＿＿＿＿＿＿ 也不要 ＿＿＿＿＿＿。（情願）

lǎo sān: Wǒ ＿＿＿＿＿＿ yě bùyào ＿＿＿＿＿＿. (qíngyuàn)

老四： 有没有人要帮我做？我今天 ＿＿＿＿＿＿，哪儿有时间洗碗！（得）

有沒有人要幫我做？我今天 ＿＿＿＿＿＿，哪兒有時間洗碗！（得）

lǎo sì: Yǒu méi yǒu rén yào bāng wǒ zuò? Wǒ jīntiān ＿＿＿＿＿＿,

nǎr yǒu shíjiān xǐwǎn! (děi)

老五： 妈妈总是 ＿＿＿＿＿＿，老四的工作比较容易！（偏爱）

媽媽總是 ＿＿＿＿＿＿，老四的工作比較容易！（偏爱）

lǎo wǔ: Māma zǒngshì ＿＿＿＿＿＿. Lǎosì de gōngzuò bǐjiào róngyì!

(piān'ài)

54

Expressing knowledge, advice, and opinions

1 Translate the following sentences into Mandarin using 会/會 **huì**, 认识/認識 **rènshi**, or 知道 **zhīdao** as appropriate.

a. I can speak a little Japanese.

b. I know where the library is.

c. I know that person.

d. Don't worry. I know the road, and I am able to find it.

e. I know of him, but I don't know him (personally).

f. I know this character, but I don't know how to write it.

g. I know why he is not coming.

➪ 54.1

2 Choose the appropriate word from the following list to complete each sentence: 想 **xiǎng**, 认为/認爲 **rènwéi**, 以为/以爲 **yǐwéi**, 看 **kàn**.

a. 下雨了。我 _____ 我们别出去吃饭了吧。

下雨了。我 _____ 我們別出去吃飯了吧。

Xià yǔ le. Wǒ _____ wǒmen bié chūqu chī fàn le ba.

It's raining. I think we shouldn't go out to eat.

b. 听说你病了，我 _____ 你不来上课了。怎么来了？

聽說你病了，我 _____ 你不來上課了。怎麼來了？

Tīngshuō nǐ bìng le, wǒ _____ nǐ bù lái shàng kè le. Zěnme lái le?

I heard you were sick, and I thought you would not come to class. Why did you come?

c. 你 _____ 过他今天会来吗？

你 _____ 過他今天會來嗎？

Nǐ _____ guò tā jīntiān huì lái?

Did you ever think he would come today?

d. 我不 _____ 这个老师很好。

我不 _____ 這個老師很好。

Wǒ bù _____ zhège lǎoshī hěn hǎo.

I don't think this teacher is very good.

e. 不要让学生 _____ 写字比说话重要。

不要讓學生 _____ 寫字比說話重要。

Bù yào ràng xuésheng _____ xiě zì bǐ shuō huà zhòngyào.

Don't let the students think that writing characters is more important than speaking.

f. 我个人 _____ 我们不应该这样做。

我個人 _____ 我們不應該這樣做。

Wǒ gèrén _____ wǒmen bù yīnggāi zhèyàng zuò.

I personally think that we should not do it this way.

g. 你 _____ 只有你一个人认识这个字吗？

你 _____ 只有你一個人認識這個字嗎？

Nǐ _____ zhǐ yǒu nǐ yī gè rén rènshi zhège zì ma?

Do you think you are the only one who recognizes this character?

⇨ 54.2

Your friend is asking for your advice. Tell your friend to do as he/she pleases as in the following example.

Example: 你想我应该喝什么？ → 你想喝什么就喝什么。

你想我應該喝甚麼？ 你想喝甚麼就喝甚麼。

Nǐ xiǎng wǒ yīnggāi **Nǐ xiǎng hē shénme jiù**

hē shénme? **hē shénme.**

What do you think I should drink? Drink whatever you want.

a. 你想我应该问谁？

你想我應該問誰？

Nǐ xiǎng wǒ yīnggāi wèn shéi?

Who do you think I should ask?

b. 你想我应该去哪儿？

你想我應該去哪兒？

Nǐ xiǎng wǒ yīnggāi qù nǎr?

Where do you think I should go?

c. 你想我应该买哪个？

你想我應該買哪個？

Nǐ xiǎng wǒ yīnggāi mǎi nǎge?

Which one do you think I should buy?

d. 你想我应该吃什么？

你想我應該吃甚麼？

Nǐ xiǎng wǒ yīnggāi chī shénme?

What do you think I should eat?

e. 你想我应该借多少?

你想我應該借多少?

Nǐ xiǎng wǒ yīnggāi jiè duōshǎo?

How much do you think I should borrow?

f. 你想我应该怎么去?

你想我應該怎麼去?

Nǐ xiǎng wǒ yīnggāi zěnme qù?

How do you think I should go?

g. 你想我应该选哪门课?

你想我應該選哪門課?

Nǐ xiǎng wǒ yīnggāi xuǎn nǎ mén kè?

Which class do you think I should take?

h. 你想我应该看哪个电影?

你想我應該看哪個電影?

Nǐ xiǎng wǒ yīnggāi kàn nǎge diànyǐng?

Which movie do you think I should see?

⇨ 54.2.4

4 Read the following passage and answer the questions in complete sentences in Mandarin.

我认为现在中国的私人汽车太多了。我认识的人都有车 。他们说因为交通不方便，只好买车。我觉得他们不应该买车。因为第一，我看他们不太会开车，第二，没有停车的地方。我以为汽油的价钱高了人就不买车了。没想到，他们不以为然，还认为有车才有面子。

我認爲現在中國的私人汽車太多了。我認識的人都有車 。他們說因爲交通不方便，只好買車。我覺得他們不應該買車。因爲第一，我看他們不太會開車，第二，沒有停車的地方。我以爲汽油的價錢高了人就不買車了。沒想到，他們不以爲然，還認爲有車才有面子。

Wǒ rènwéi xiànzài Zhōngguó de sīrén qìchē tài duō le. Wǒ rènshi de rén dōu yǒu chē. Tāmen shuō yīnwéi jiāotōng bù fāngbiàn, zhǐ hǎo mǎi chē. Wǒ juéde tāmen bù yīnggāi mǎi chē. Yīnwéi dì yī, wǒ kàn tāmen bù tài huì kāi chē, dì èr, méi yǒu tíng chē de dìfang. Wǒ yǐwéi qìyóu de jiàqian gāo le rén jiù bù mǎi chē le. Méi xiǎngdào, tāmen bùyǐwéirán, hái rènwéi yǒu chē cái yǒu miànzi.

a. In the narrator's opinion, what is the main reason why people should not buy cars?

b. What reason do people give for buying their own cars?

c. In the narrator's opinion, what is the main reason why people want their own cars?

d. Do you think that the narrator owns a car? Why or why not?

e. What is the narrator surprised about?

f. What advice do you think the narrator would give to a friend who wanted to buy a car?

⇨ 54.2

5

What do you say in these situations? Express your opinions, advice or inquiries with the words provided.

a. Your roommate asked if her outfit is appropriate for her job interview today. Tell her with honesty: wearing this outfit, people would <u>think</u> she was already 40 years old. Tell her she <u>should</u> wear that white one. [以为/**yǐwéi**; 应该/應該 **yīnggāi**]

b. Tell your friend it <u>looks like</u> you will have to cancel your date for dinner tomorrow because you can't finish your work in time. [我看··· **wǒ kàn** ...]

c. You are a journalist writing a piece about Chinese history. You are calling a Chinese history professor because you have some questions about Chinese history that you would like to ask her about. [请教/請教 **qǐngjiào**]

d. Your friend turns to you for advice: her parents want her to major in biology but she has always been interested in visual arts. [最好 **zuì hǎo**]

e. Your little brother keeps bothering you with unimportant questions all morning while you are trying to study for a mid-term tomorrow. Finally, when he walks into your room and asks what you two should eat for lunch, you lose your patience and tell him that he can eat whatever he wants to. It doesn't matter to you. [什么···就什么···/甚麼···就甚麼··· **shénme** ... **jiù shénme** ...]

55
Expressing fear, worry, and anxiety

1 Your friend 小李 **Xiǎo Lǐ**, little Li, is afraid of, or worried about, everything. You have to constantly tell 小李 **Xiǎo Lǐ** not to be afraid. When 小李 **Xiǎo Lǐ** says the following to you, what do you say?

> Example: 我怕狗。 → 别(不要)怕狗。
>
> **Wǒ pà gǒu.** **Bié (bù yào) pà gǒu.**
>
> I am afraid of dogs. Don't be afraid of dogs.

a. 我怕冷。

Wǒ pà lěng.

I'm afraid of the cold.

b. 我怕那个老师。

我怕那個老師。

Wǒ pà nàge lǎoshī.

I'm afraid of that teacher.

c. 我怕开车。

我怕開車。

Wǒ pà kāi chē.

I'm afraid to drive.

d. 我怕没有人来。

我怕沒有人來。

Wǒ pà méi rén lái.

I'm afraid no one will show up.

e. 我怕我学不会。

我怕我學不會。

Wǒ pà wǒ xuébuhuì.

I'm afraid I won't be able to learn (it).

f. 我怕黑天一个人走路。

我怕黑天一個人走路。

Wǒ pà hēitiān yī gè rén zǒu lù.

I'm afraid of walking alone in the dark.

g.   我很害怕考试。

我很害怕考試。

Wǒ hěn hàipà kǎoshì.

I'm very afraid of exams.

h.   考试的时候我很紧张。

考試的時候我很緊張。

Kǎoshì de shíhou wǒ hěn jǐnzhāng.

When I take tests I am very nervous.

➪   55.1

2

Select the appropriate expression from among the following to fill in the blanks and complete the passage: 怕 **pà**, 恐怕 **kǒngpà**, 害怕 **hàipà**, 可怕 **kěpà**, 恐怖 **kǒngbù**, 吓/嚇 **xià**, 怕死 **pàsǐ**, 紧张/緊張 **jǐnzhāng**, 着急 **zháojí**, 恐惧/恐懼 **kǒngjù**.

我认为 (a)_____ 鬼的人最可笑。世界上本来没有鬼。他们 (b)_____
这个世界不乱。一定要找一个没有的东西来 (c)_____ 自己。把鬼说得多么
(d)_____, 一听见'鬼'这个字, 就 (e)_____, 就 (f)_____,
就 (g)_____ 得不得了。

我認爲 (a)_____ 鬼的人最可笑。世界上本來没有鬼。他們 (b)_____
這個世界不亂。一定要找一個没有的東西來 (c)_____ 自己。把鬼說得多麼
(d)_____, 一聽見'鬼'這個字, 就 (e)_____, 就 (f)_____,
就 (g)_____ 得不得了。

Wǒ rènwéi (a)_____ **guǐ de rén zuì kěxiào. Shìjiè shàng běnlái méi yǒu
guǐ. Tāmen** (b)_____ **zhège shìjiè bù luàn. Yīdìng yào zhǎo yī gè méi yǒu
de dōngxi lái** (c)_____ **zìjǐ. Bǎ guǐ shuō de duōme** (d)_____, **yī tīngjiàn
'guǐ' zhège zì, jiù** (e)_____, **jiù** (f)_____, **jiù** (g)_____ **de bùdeliǎo.**

➪   55.1–55.5

3

You are a therapist working with an anxiety support group. Today is the first meeting, and participants are taking turns expressing their anxieties. Complete their sentences by adding the appropriate expressions.

Participant 1:   我 _____ 跟人说话。(afraid of)

我 _____ 跟人說話。

Wǒ _____ gēn rén shuō huà.

Participant 2:   一想到要去人多的地方, 我心里就 _____。(filled with fear)

一想到要去人多的地方, 我心裏就 _____。

Yī xiǎng dào yào qù rén duō de dìfang, wǒ xīnlǐ jiù _____.

Participant 3:   我常常 _____ 别人在看我。(worry about)

Wǒ chángcháng _____ biérén zài kàn wǒ

Participant 4: 我觉得人多的地方很 _____。(scary)

我覺得人多的地方很 _____。

Wǒ juéde rén duō de dìfang hěn _____.

Participant 5: 不管我要参加什么活动，一两个星期以前我就开始 _____。
(nervous)

不管我要参加甚麼活動，一兩個星期以前我就開始 _____。

Bù guǎn wǒ yào cānjiā shénme huódòng, yī liǎng ge xīngqī yǐqián wǒ jiù kāishǐ _____.

56
Expressing speaker attitudes and perspectives

1 Add an appropriate interjection to each sentence.

a. ＿＿＿＿＿，他们怎么还没来啊？

＿＿＿＿＿，他們怎麼還沒來啊？

＿＿＿＿＿，**tāmen zěnme hái méi lái a?**

How come they are still not here?

b. ＿＿＿＿＿，你真的不去啦！

＿＿＿＿＿，**nǐ zhēnde bù qù la!**

It's true that you are not going!

c. ＿＿＿＿＿，还是得听我的吧！

＿＿＿＿＿，還是得聽我的吧！

＿＿＿＿＿，**háishi děi tīng wǒ de ba!**

In the end you have to listen to me!

d. ＿＿＿＿＿，电影就要开始了。我们得进去了。

＿＿＿＿＿，電影就要開始了。我們得進去了。

＿＿＿＿＿，**diànyǐng jiù yào kāishǐ le. Wǒmen děi jìnqu le.**

The movie is about to start. We have to go in.

e. ＿＿＿＿＿，你可来了。都把我想死了。

＿＿＿＿＿，你可來了。都把我想死了。

＿＿＿＿＿，**nǐ kě lái le. Dōu bǎ wǒ xiǎngsǐ le.**

You have finally come. I miss you so much.

f. ＿＿＿＿＿，跟你说了多少回了。你怎么就记不住呢？

＿＿＿＿＿，跟你說了多少回了。你怎麼就記不住呢？

＿＿＿＿＿，**gēn nǐ shuō le duōshǎo huí le. Nǐ zěnme jiù jìbuzhù ne?**

I have told you so many times. How come you can't remember?

g. ＿＿＿＿＿，原来你们以前见过。

＿＿＿＿＿，原來你們以前見過。

＿＿＿＿＿，**yuánlái nǐmen yǐqián jiànguò.**

As a matter of fact, you have met before.

h. _____，我的手机找不着了。

_____，我的手机找不著了。

_____, **wǒ de shǒujī zhǎobuzháo le.**

I can't find my cell phone.

⇨ 56.1

2 Add an appropriate sentence final particle to each sentence.

a. 考试前当然要认真准备 _____。

考試前當然要認真準備 _____。

Kǎoshì qián dāngrán yào rènzhēn zhǔnbèi _____.

Of course you have to prepare carefully before the exam.

b. 请你不要再麻烦我 _____！

請你不要再麻煩我 _____！

Qǐng nǐ bù yào zài máfan wǒ _____!

Please don't bother me anymore!

c. 你要早一点儿睡觉 _____！

你要早一點兒睡覺 _____！

Nǐ yào zǎo yīdiǎr shuì jiào _____!

You need to go to sleep a little earlier!

d. 你别再喝 _____！

Nǐ bié zài hē _____!

You shouldn't drink anymore!

⇨ 56.2

57

Topic, focus, and emphasis

1

Rewrite the following sentences to emphasize, or topicalize, the underlined phrase.

Example: 我不喜欢<u>外国电影</u>。　　→　<u>外国电影</u>，我不喜欢。

我不喜歡<u>外國電影</u>。　　　　<u>外國電影</u>，我不喜歡。

Wǒ bù xǐhuan　　　　　　**Wàiguó diànyǐng, wǒ bù**

<u>**wàiguó diànyǐng**</u>**.**　　　**xǐhuan.**

I don't like <u>foreign films</u>.　Foreign films, I don't like them.

a. 我不喜欢<u>那个饭馆</u>。

我不喜歡<u>那個飯館</u>。

Wǒ bù xǐhuan <u>nàge fànguǎn</u>.

I do not like <u>that restaurant</u>.

b. 我觉得<u>中文课</u>很有意思。

我覺得<u>中文課</u>很有意思。

Wǒ juéde <u>Zhōngwén kè</u> hěn yǒu yìsī.

I think <u>Chinese class</u> is very interesting.

c. 我没看过<u>那个电影</u>。

我沒看過<u>那個電影</u>。

Wǒ méi kànguò <u>nàge diànyǐng</u>.

I have not seen <u>that movie</u>.

d. 听说<u>这次考试</u>很容易。

聽說<u>這次考試</u>很容易。

Tīngshuō <u>zhè cì kǎoshì</u> hěn róngyì.

I've heard that <u>the exam this time</u> is very easy.

e. 我没吃过<u>日本饭</u>。

我沒吃過<u>日本飯</u>。

Wǒ méi chīguò <u>Rìběn fàn</u>.

I have not eaten <u>Japanese food</u> before.

f. 我每天都写<u>汉字</u>。

我每天都寫<u>漢字</u>。

Wǒ měitiān dōu xiě <u>Hàn zì</u>.

I write <u>Chinese characters</u> every day.

g. 我不太清楚<u>中国的经济情况</u>。

我不太清楚<u>中國的經濟情况</u>。

Wǒ bù tài qīngchu <u>Zhōngguó de jīngjì qíngkuàng</u>.

I'm not quite clear about <u>the economic situation in China</u>.

h. 请你不要管<u>别人的事</u>。

請你不要管<u>別人的事</u>。

Qǐng nǐ bù yào guǎn <u>biéren de shì</u>.

Please don't pay attention to <u>other people's business</u>.

⇨ 57.1

2

张苹/張苹 **Zhāng Píng** is organizing a Chinese New Year Party and is giving instructions to her friends. She uses 把 **bǎ** in all of her sentences. Write her instructions in Mandarin.

a. First we'll carry all of the chairs out of the classroom.

b. Then we'll move the desks to the back of the classroom.

c. 小陈/小陳 **Xiǎo Chén**, put the food and drink on the desks.

d. 小王 **Xiǎo Wáng**, sweep the floor clean. [扫干净/掃乾淨 **sǎo gānjìng** sweep clean]

e. 小李 **Xiǎo Lǐ**, wipe the blackboard clean (erase the blackboard). [擦干净/擦乾淨 **cā gānjìng** wipe clean]

f. 小毛 **Xiǎo Máo**, prepare the music. [准备音乐/準備音樂 **zhǔnbèi yīnyuè** prepare music]

g. You two write '春节好/春節好 **chūnjié hǎo**' on the blackboard. [春节好/春節好 **chūnjié hǎo** happy new year]

h. You three hang these two Chinese paintings on the wall. [挂/掛 **guà** to hang]

⇨ 18, 19, 20, 32.1, 57.2.1

3

Rewrite the following sentences using 除了 **chúle** . . . 以外 **yǐwài** to correspond to the English translations. Include either 都 **dōu**, 也 **yě**, or 还/還 **hái** as appropriate.

Example: 我哥哥喜欢看美国电影。他不喜欢看别的电影。

我哥哥喜歡看美國電影。他不喜歡看別的電影。

Wǒ gēge xǐhuan kàn Měiguó diànyǐng. Tā bù xǐhuan kàn bié de diànyǐng.

Except for American movies, my older brother doesn't like to watch movies.

→

除了美国电影以外，我哥哥不喜欢看别的电影。

除了美國電影以外，我哥哥不喜歡看別的電影。

Chúle Měiguó diànyǐng yǐwài, wǒ gēge bù xǐhuan kàn biéde diànyǐng.

a. 我不喜欢上中文课。别的同学喜欢上中文课。

    我不喜歡上中文課。別的同學喜歡上中文課。

    Wǒ bù xǐhuan shàng Zhōngwén kè. Bié de tóngxué xǐhuan shàng Zhōngwén kè.

    Except for me, all of the other students like to go to Chinese class.

b. 我去看电影了。他们去看电影了。

    我去看電影了。他們去看電影了。

    Wǒ qù kàn diànyǐng le. Tāmen qù kàn diànyǐng le.

    In addition to me, they also went to see a movie.

c. 我和我的同学都去过中国。

    我和我的同學都去過中國。

    Wǒ hé wǒ de tóngxué dōu qùguò Zhōngguó.

    In addition to me, my classmates have also all been to China.

d. 我学中文，也学中国文学和中国历史。

    我學中文，也學中國文學和中國歷史。

    Wǒ xué Zhōngwén, yě xué Zhōngguó wénxué hé Zhōngguó lìshǐ.

    Besides Chinese language, I also study Chinese literature and Chinese history.

e. 他星期一到星期六都工作。只有星期日不工作。

    Tā xīngqīyī dào xīngqīliù dōu gōngzuò. Zhǐ yǒu xīngqīrì bù gōngzuò.

    He works every day except Sunday.

f. 我的同屋就喜欢足球。别的运动他不喜欢。

    我的同屋就喜歡足球。別的運動他不喜歡。

    Wǒ de tóngwū jiù xǐhuan zúqiú. Biéde yùndòng tā bù xǐhuan.

    Except for football, my roommate doesn't like any sports.

g. 我每天都练习写汉字，也听录音，复习语法并且念课文。

    我每天都練習寫漢字，也聽錄音，復習語法並且念課文。

    Wǒ měitiān dōu liànxí xiě Hàn zì, yě tīng lùyīn, fùxí yǔfǎ bìngqiě niàn kèwén.

    In addition to practicing writing characters every day, I also listen to recordings, review grammar, and read the lesson aloud.

h. 这个学校，就是餐厅的饭不太好吃，别的都很好。

    這個學校，就是餐廳的飯不太好吃，別的都很好。

    Zhège xuéxiào, jiùshì cāntīng de fàn bù tài hǎo chī, bié de dōu hěn hǎo.

    At this school, except for the cafeteria food, everything is very good.

⇨ 46, 57.2.2

4

Rewrite the following sentences with 连/連 **lián** to match the English translations, including either 都 **dōu** or 也 **yě** as appropriate. The phrase that should follow 连/連 **lián** and receive focus is underlined.

Example: 我哥哥不喜欢看电影。他不喜欢看<u>美国电影</u>。

我哥哥不喜歡看電影。他不喜歡看<u>美國電影</u>。

Wǒ gēge bù xǐhuan kàn diànyǐng. Tā bù xǐhuan kàn <u>Měiguó diànyǐng</u>.

My older brother doesn't like to watch movies. He doesn't like to watch American movies.

→

他连<u>美国电影</u>都 [or 也] 不喜欢看。

他連<u>美國電影</u>都 [or 也] 不喜歡看。

Tā lián <u>Měiguó diànyǐng</u> dōu [or yě] bù xǐhuan kàn.

He doesn't even like to watch <u>American</u> movies.

a. 这个字一定很难。<u>老师</u>不认识。

這個字一定很難。<u>老師</u>不認識。

Zhège zì yīdìng hěn nán. <u>Lǎoshī</u> bù rènshí.

This character must be very hard. Even <u>the teacher</u> doesn't recognize it.

b. 这个字很容易。<u>一年级的学生</u>认识。

這個字很容易。<u>一年級的學生</u>認識。

Zhège zì hěn róngyì. <u>Yīniánjí de xuésheng</u> rènshi.

This character is very easy. Even <u>the first year students</u> know it.

c. 我没有<u>一个中国朋友</u>。

我沒有<u>一個中國朋友</u>。

Wǒ méi yǒu <u>yī gè Zhōngguó péngyou</u>.

I don't have even <u>one Chinese friend</u>.

d. 他不念书。他没去过<u>图书馆</u>。

他不念書。他沒去過<u>圖書館</u>。

Tā bù niàn shū. Tā méi qùguò <u>túshūguǎn</u>.

He doesn't study. He hasn't even been to the library.

e. 他不会写字。他不会写<u>他自己的名字</u>。

他不會寫字。他不會寫<u>他自己的名字</u>。

Tā bù huì xiě zì. Tā bù huì xiě <u>tā zìjǐ de míngzi</u>.

He can't write characters. He can't even write <u>his own name</u>.

f. 小王不喜欢美国饭。他不喜欢<u>汉堡包</u>。

小王不喜歡美國飯。他不喜歡<u>漢堡包</u>。

Xiǎo Wáng bù xǐhuan Měiguó fàn. Tā bù xǐhuan <u>hànbǎobāo</u>.

Xiao Wang doesn't like American food. He doesn't even like <u>hamburgers</u>.

g.　我不会做饭。我不会炒<u>鸡蛋</u>。

　　我不會做飯。我不會炒<u>鷄蛋</u>。

　　Wǒ bù huì zuò fàn. Wǒ bù huì chǎo jīdàn.

　　I can't cook. I can't even fry <u>an egg</u>.

h.　他每天都工作。<u>星期天</u>工作。

　　Tā měitiān dōu gōngzuò. Xīngqītiān gōngzuò.

　　He works every day. He even works on <u>Sunday</u>.

⇨ 57.2.3

5

This is the first day of a Chinese class. Each student is asked to say a few words about him/herself in Mandarin. 王明 **Wáng Míng** provides the following information. Write his self-introduction in Mandarin, using 是 **shì** . . . 的 **de** in every sentence to emphasize the underlined phrase.

Example: I was born <u>in Boston</u>.　→　我是<u>在波士顿</u>生的。

　　　　　　　　　　　　　　　　　我是<u>在波士頓</u>生的。

　　　　　　　　　　　　　　　　　Wǒ shì zài Bōshìdùn shēng de.

a.　I grew up <u>in Boston</u>.

b.　It is only <u>last night</u> that I came back to school.

c.　I came back <u>with my roommate</u>.

d.　We came <u>by car</u>.

e.　My roommate came <u>from China</u>.

f.　He came <u>two years ago</u>.

g.　He came <u>by plane</u>.

h.　It was <u>at a party</u> where we met each other.

i.　It was <u>he</u> who told me to learn Chinese.

j.　It was last night that I drove from Boston back to school with my roommate.

k.　It was two years ago that he came to America from China.

l.　It was two years ago that he came to America from China by plane.

⇨ 57.2.4

6

Lauren is getting married! At her bridal shower, her friends want to know all about her fiancé and their plans. Complete the following questions and answers.

Ask <u>questions</u> in Mandarin to learn about –

a.　How they met:

　　i.　When: _____

　　ii.　Where: _____

　　iii.　Who introduced them: _____

b.　About the proposal [求婚 **qiúhūn**]:

　　i.　Where did he purchase the ring? [戒指 **jièzhǐ**]

　　　_____

　　ii.　How did he propose?

　　　_____

Laura provides additional information. Help her express it by completing these sentences in Mandarin.

c. Wedding guests: family and 50 friends are invited.

除了 _____

Chúle _____

d. Future timeline: Get married this December; buy a house next year; have a baby the year after.

关于未来，我们打算 _____

關於未來，我們打算 _____

Guānyú wèilái, wǒmen dǎsuàn _____

58
Guest and host

1 Your guests have just arrived. Using Mandarin:

a.   Welcome the guests at the door.

b.   Ask the guests to come in.

c.   Invite the guests to sit down.

d.   Offer the guests something to drink (the choices are tea and coffee).

e.   At the end of their visit, ask the guests to come back again when they
     have time.

f.   At the door, tell the guests not to hurry off.

⇨ | 58.1–58.4

2 These are expressions commonly used at a dinner party. Decide whether they
are spoken by the host or a guest.

a.   欢迎、欢迎 / 歡迎、歡迎 huānyíng, huānyíng

b.   这是一点小礼物送给你们/這是一點小禮物送給你們 Zhè shì yī diǎn xiǎo
     lǐwù sònggěi nǐmen

c.   请进。/ 請進。Qǐng jìn.

d.   请坐，喝点什么？茶还是咖啡？
     請坐，喝點甚麼？茶還是咖啡？
     Qǐng zuò, hē diǎn shénme? Chá háishì kāfēi?

e.   哪里哪里，这房子很旧了。
     哪裏哪裏，這房子很舊了。
     Nǎlǐ, nǎlǐ, zhè fángzi hěn jiù le.

f.   多吃点，别客气。/ 多吃點，別客氣。Duō chī diǎn, bié kèqì.

g.   太好吃了，我从来没吃过这么好吃的菜。
     太好吃了，我從來沒吃過這麼好吃的菜。
     Tài hǎo chī le, wǒ cónglái méi chīguò zhème hǎo chī de cài.

h.   你家布置得真漂亮。/ 你家佈置得真漂亮。Nǐ jiā bùzhì de zhēn piàoliang.

i.   谢谢你的邀请 / 謝謝你的邀請 Xièxie nǐ de yāoqǐng.

j.   请留步 / 請留步 Qǐng liú bù.

k.   慢走，有空再来。/ 慢走，有空再來。Màn zǒu, yǒu kòng zài lái.

59
Giving and responding to compliments

1

Give an appropriate response to each of the following compliments. There may be more than one appropriate response.

a.　你的中文说得很好。

你的中文說得很好。

Nǐ de Zhōngwén shuō de hěn hǎo.

You speak Chinese very well.

b.　您做的饭太好吃了。

您做的飯太好吃了。

Nín zuò de fàn tài hǎo chī le.

The food you cooked is so delicious.

c.　你的毛衣很漂亮。

Nǐ de máoyī hěn piàoliang.

Your sweater is beautiful.

d.　你的歌儿唱得真是好听极了。

你的歌兒唱得真是好聽極了。

Nǐ de gēr chàng de zhēn shì hǎo tīngjíle.

You sing extremely well.

e.　这是你画的吗？真漂亮。

這是你畫的嗎？真漂亮。

Zhè shì nǐ huà de ma? Zhēn piàoliang.

Did you paint that? It is so beautiful.

f.　你今天穿的裙子真好看！

Nǐ jīntiān chuān de qúnzi zhēn hǎo kàn!

The skirt you are wearing today is very pretty.

g.　您今天讲得非常精采。

您今天講得非常精采。

Nín jīntiān jiǎng de fēicháng jīngcǎi.

Your talk today was outstanding.

h. 这么多菜！太丰盛了！

這麽多菜！太豐盛了！

Zhème duō cài! Tài fēngshèng le!

So many dishes! Such a sumptuous feast!

⇨ 59.2, 59.3

2 高蕾 **Gāo Lěi** has made a presentation in class and 王明 **Wáng Míng** wants to praise her. Express the conversation in Mandarin.

a. 王明 **Wáng Míng** tells 高蕾 **Gāo Lěi** that he has read her essay and thinks it is terrific.

b. 高蕾 **Gāo Lěi** deflects the praise and says she can learn a lot from him.

c. 王明 **Wáng Míng** tells 高蕾 **Gāo Lěi** that he thinks her presentation [描述 **miáoshù**] was brilliant [高明 **gāomíng**].

d. 高蕾 **Gāo Lěi** says that he is being excessive in his praise and that her presentation was just ordinary.

e. 王明 **Wáng Míng** says that her examples and explanations [实例说明/實例說明 **shílì shuōmíng**] were particularly good and that he thinks she is really talented. [有才气/有才氣 **yǒu cáiqì** have talent, ability]

f. 高蕾 **Gāo Lěi** says that they were so-so, certainly nothing special.

⇨ 59.1, 59.2, 59.3

3 What do they say in the following situations?

A. After a recent piano recital, 刘太太/劉太太 Mrs. Liu and 张太太/張太太 Mrs. Zhang praised each other's children. Complete their sentences with the appropriate compliments and responses.

Vocabulary: 钢琴/鋼琴 **gāngqín** piano; 弹琴/彈琴 **tán qín** play a stringed instrument; play the piano

刘太太： 你儿子弹琴弹得 (a)_____！

劉太太： 你兒子彈琴彈得 (a)_____！

Liú tàitai: **Nǐ érzi tán qín tán de** (a)_____！

Mrs. Liu: Your son plays piano _____！

张太太： (b)_____, 你儿子弹得才好呢！

張太太： (b)_____, 你兒子彈得才好呢！

Zhāng tàitai: (b)_____, **nǐ érzi tán de cái hǎo ne!**

Mrs. Zhang: _____, your son plays the best.

刘太太： (c)_____, 是老师教得好。

劉太太： (c)_____, 是老師教得好。

Liú tàitai: (c)_____, **shì lǎoshī jiāo de hǎo.**

Mrs. Liu: _____, it is that the teacher taught well.

B. At the company's end-of-year dinner party, 赵先生/趙先生 Mr. Zhao is declared salesman of the year. He credits his success to his manager, 白先生 Mr. Bai, for his mentoring. 白先生 Mr. Bai politely deflects the compliment.

赵先生：	我能够有今天的成就，都是白经理的功劳。
趙先生：	我能夠有今天的成就，都是白經理的功勞。
Zhào xiānsheng:	**Wǒ nénggòu yǒu jīntiān de chéngjiù, dōu shì Bái jīnglǐ de gōngláo.**
Mr. Zhao:	My accomplishments today are all made possible by manager Bai's hard work.
白先生：	(a)_____，这是他自己的努力。
白先生：	(a)_____，這是他自己的努力。
Bái xiānsheng:	(a)_____, **zhè shì tā zìjǐ de nǔlì.**
Mr. Bai:	_____, this is all due to his own efforts.

60
Expressing satisfaction and dissatisfaction

1

Respond to each question indicating your degree of satisfaction. '10' indicates the highest degree of satisfaction. '1' indicates the lowest degree of satisfaction. Refer to *Modern Mandarin Chinese Grammar*, Chapter 60, for words used to indicate the degree of satisfaction in Mandarin.

a. 你们学校怎么样？喜欢吗？ (3)

  你們學校怎麼樣？喜歡嗎？

  Nǐmen xuéxiào zěnmeyàng? Xǐhuan ma?

  How is your school? Do you like it?

b. 这里的菜味道还好吧？ (10)

  這裏的菜味道還好吧？

  Zhèlǐ de cài wèidao hái hǎo ba?

  The (flavor of the) food here is good, right?

c. 那个饭馆的服务怎么样？ (5)

  那個飯館的服務怎麼樣？

  Nàge fànguǎn de fúwù zěnmeyàng?

  How is the service at that restaurant?

d. 这门课怎么样？ (8)

  這門課怎麼樣？

  Zhè mén kè zěnmeyàng?

  How is this class?

e. 你住的地方还可以吗？ (1)

  你住的地方還可以嗎？

  Nǐ zhù de dìfāng hái kěyǐ ma?

  Is the place where you are living okay?

f. 那个电影怎么样？ (3)

  那個電影怎麼樣？

  Nàge diànyǐng zěnme yàng?

  How is that movie?

⇨ 60.1

2

Respond to each question indicating your degree of dissatisfaction. '10' indicates that you are greatly dissatisfied. '1' indicates that you are a little dissatisfied. Translate the questions into English. Refer to *Modern Mandarin Chinese Grammar*, Chapter 60, for words used to indicate the degree of dissatisfaction in Mandarin.

a. 这个饭馆的饭怎么样？(10)

這個飯館的飯怎麼樣？

Zhège fànguǎn de fàn zěnmeyàng?

b. 那个城市的治安好不好？(3) [治安 zhì'ān the public security]

那個城市的治安好不好？

Nàge chéngshì de zhì'ān hǎo bù hǎo?

c. 最近的天气怎么样？(5)

最近的天氣怎麼樣？

Zuì jìn de tiānqì zěnmeyàng?

d. 那本书怎么样？(7)

那本書怎麼樣？

Nà běn shū zěnmeyàng?

e. 那个医院怎么样？(4)

那個醫院怎麼樣？

Nàge yīyuàn zěnmeyàng?

f. 你的车子怎么样？(1)

你的車子怎麼樣？

Nǐ de chēzi zěnmeyàng?

⇨ | 60.2

3

One of your friends is asking you how you are adjusting to life in China. Translate her questions into English and express your answers in Mandarin.

a. Friend: 你的宿舍怎么样？

你的宿舍怎麼樣？

Nǐ de sùshè zěnmeyàng?

b. You: It's okay.

c. Friend: 卫生间干净不干净？

衛生間乾淨不乾淨？

Wèishēngjiān gānjìng bù gānjìng?

d. You: It's all right in the morning. By night-time it is not too clean anymore.

e. Friend: 你习惯了吗？

你習慣了嗎？

Nǐ xíguàn le ma?

f. You: Yes. After a while you get used to things.

g. Friend: 食堂的饭怎么样？

食堂的飯怎麼樣？

Shítáng de fàn zěnmeyàng?

h. You: It's okay. It's so-so.

i. Friend: 食堂的服务好不好？

食堂的服務好不好？

Shítáng de fúwù hǎo bù hǎo?

j. You: Nothing special.

➪ 60.1, 60.2

4 The newly opened Chinese restaurant *Furong Garden* is giving away $25 gift cards to selected patrons who fill out their satisfaction survey form [意见表/ 意見表 **yìjiàn biǎo**] after their dinner. Help translate the survey into Mandarin.

Thank you for filling out the survey for us. Your feedback will help us provide a better service and dining experience [用餐经验/用餐經驗 **yòngcān jīngyàn**]. To show our appreciation, each week we will give a $25 gift card to five selected patrons who fill out the survey.

_____

_____

_____

_____

Please tell us what you think:

_____

	Excellent	Good	Acceptable	Inferior	Unacceptable
Dining Environment					
Food					
Service					
Overall Experience					

Would you recommend our restaurant to a friend? ☐ Yes ☐ No

_____

Additional comments:

_____:

Contact information:

Name _____ / email: _____

61

Expressing gratitude and responding to expressions of gratitude

1 Provide an appropriate response to each of the following expressions of gratitude. More than one response may be appropriate.

a. 非常感谢你的帮助。
   非常感謝你的幫助。
   Fēicháng gǎnxiè nǐ de bāngzhù.
   I really appreciate your help.

b. 太麻烦你了。
   太麻煩你了。
   Tài máfan nǐ le.
   This caused you too much trouble.

c. 真不好意思。
   Zhēn bù hǎoyìsi.
   I am really embarrassed.

d. 谢谢您给我们的建议。
   謝謝您給我們的建議。
   Xièxie nín gěi wǒmen de jiànyì.
   Thank you very much for your suggestions.

e. 我代表全体同学向您表示感谢。
   我代表全體同學向您表示感謝。
   Wǒ dàibiǎo quántǐ tóngxué xiàng nín biǎoshì gǎnxiè.
   I represent all the students in expressing our thanks to you.

f. 我代表学校向你道谢。
   我代表學校向你道謝。
   Wǒ dàibiǎo xuéxiào xiàng nǐ dàoxiè.
   I represent the school in expressing our thanks to you.

⇨ | 61.1, 61.2

2 You are preparing a graduation speech in which you will convey your gratitude to your teachers, classmates, and family members. Express the following in Mandarin.

a. First, thank your parents for their ongoing support. [支持 **zhīchí** support]

b. Say that you appreciate the sacrifices they have made to give you a good education. [良好的教育 **liánghǎo de jiàoyù** good education, 牺牲/犧牲 **xīshēng** sacrifice]

c. At the same time, thank your teachers for their guidance and instruction. [指导和教诲/指導和教誨 **zhídǎo hé jiàohuì** guidance and instruction]

d. Say that not only did they give you knowledge, but more importantly, they taught you to be an honest person. [知识/知識 **zhīshi** knowledge, 正直的人 **zhèngzhí de rén** honest person]

e. Finally, thank your classmates and friends for their companionship and help. [友情 **yǒuqíng** friendship/companionship]

f. Say that it is very hard to imagine how you could have survived the college years without them. [想像 **xiǎngxiàng** to imagine, 渡过/渡過 **dùguò** to get through, 大学时光/大學時光 **dàxué shíguāng** college years]

g. Say that college graduation is the beginning of a new life. You will work and study even harder, and you will not let your audience down ('I won't let you down'). [辜负/辜負 **gūfù** to let down/to disappoint someone]

⇨ 25.11, 61.1

3 Fill in the blanks with appropriate expressions of gratitude and responses to complete each mini-dialogue.

a. The assistant gives the manager the minutes of a meeting as the manager has requested.

Assistant: 这是您要的会议记录。/ 這是您要的會議記錄。
　　　　　Zhè shì nín yào de huìyì jìlù.

Manager: 谢谢/謝謝, _____ 你了。
　　　　　Xièxie, _____ nǐ le.

b. The security guard helps Ms. Guān to bring her grocery bags upstairs.

Ms. Guān:　太感谢你了，每次都 (i)_____ 你，真 (ii)_____。
　　　　　太感謝你了，每次都 (i)_____ 你，真 (ii)_____。
　　　　　Tài gǎnxiè nǐ le, měi cì dōu (i)_____ **nǐ, zhēn** (ii)_____.

Security guard: (iii)_____! 这是我应该做的。
　　　　　(iii)_____! 這是我應該做的。
　　　　　(iii)_____! **Zhè shì wǒ yīnggāi zuò de.**

c. Mr. Jiang visits his old boss, Mr. Wu, to seek advice. He has brought a gift to give to Mr. Wu.

Mr Jiang: 感谢您百忙之中跟我见面。这点小礼物请 (i)_____。

感謝您百忙之中跟我見面。這點小禮物請 (i)_____。

Gǎnxiè nín bǎimáng zhīzhōng gēn wǒ jiànmiàn. Zhè diǎn xiǎo lǐwù qǐng (i)_____.

Mr. Wu: 你太 (ii)_____ 了，怎么还带东西来呢？

你太 (ii)_____ 了，怎麼還帶東西來呢？

Nǐ tài (ii)_____ **le, zěnme hái dài dōngxi lái ne?**

62
Invitations, requests, and refusals

1 Accept each of the following invitations. More than one answer may be possible.

a. 周末我请你看电影，好吗？
   周末我請你看電影，好嗎？
   Zhōumò wǒ qǐng nǐ kàn diànyǐng, hǎo ma?
   I invite you to see a movie this weekend, okay?

b. 一起喝杯咖啡，怎么样？
   一起喝杯咖啡，怎麼樣？
   Yīqǐ hē bēi kāfēi, zěnmeyàng?
   Let's have a cup of coffee together, okay?

c. 一块儿吃个便饭吧，我请客。
   一塊兒吃個便飯吧，我請客。
   Yīkuàr chī gè biànfàn ba, wǒ qǐng kè.
   Let's have a bite to eat, my treat.

d. 晚上跟我去听音乐会吧，我有两张票。
   晚上跟我去聽音樂會吧，我有兩張票。
   Wǎnshang gēn wǒ qù tīng yīnyuèhuì ba, wǒ yǒu liǎng zhāng piào.
   Come with me to hear a concert tonight. I have two tickets.

e. 下星期我请你看足球赛，好吗？
   下星期我請你看足球賽，好嗎？
   Xià xīngqī wǒ qǐng nǐ kàn zúqiú sài, hǎo ma?
   I'm inviting you to watch the football game with me next week, okay?

⇨ 62.1.2

2 Give a 'face-saving' refusal for each of the following invitations and requests based on the cue that follows each invitation.

a. 周末我请你看电影，好吗？ (the inviter needn't be so polite)
   週末我請你看電影，好嗎？
   Zhōumò wǒ qǐng nǐ kàn diànyǐng, hǎo ma?
   I invite you to see a movie this weekend, okay?

b. 一起喝杯咖啡，怎么样？ (the inviter needn't be so polite)

一起喝杯咖啡，怎麼樣？

Yīqǐ hē bēi kāfēi, zěnmeyàng?

Let's have a cup of coffee together, okay?

c. 你能帮我买书吗？ (promise to try)

你能幫我買書嗎？

Nǐ néng bāng wǒ mǎi shū ma?

Can you help me buy a book?

d. 请你送我去飞机场，可以吗？ (plead a time conflict)

請你送我去飛機場，可以嗎？

Qǐng nǐ sòng wǒ qù fēijīchǎng, kěyǐ ma?

Please can you take me to the airport?

e. 我有几个问题，要向您请教。 (plead a time conflict right at the moment)

我有幾個問題，要向您請教。

Wǒ yǒu jǐ gè wèntí, yào xiàng nín qǐngjiào.

I have a few questions that I'd like to ask you.

f. 你能不能帮我找工作？ (plead inability to help)

你能不能幫我找工作？

Nǐ néng bu néng bāng wǒ zhǎo gōngzuò?

Can you help me find a job?

⇨ 62.3

3

Refuse each of the following requests with an explanation according to the parenthesized cues.

a. 你能帮我买书吗？ (inability – not going to bookstore)

你能幫我買書嗎？

Nǐ néng bāng wǒ mǎi shū ma?

Can you help me buy a book?

b. 请你送我去飞机场，可以吗？ (time conflict – have other plans)

請你送我去飛機場，可以嗎？

Qǐng nǐ sòng wǒ qù fēijīchǎng, kěyǐ ma?

Can you please take me to the airport?

c. 带我去图书馆，行吗？ (time conflict – have to go to class)

帶我去圖書館，行嗎？

Dài wǒ qù túshūguǎn, xíng ma?

Take me to the library with you, okay?

d. 你能不能帮我买两张电影票？ (inability – don't have time to go to the ticket office)

你能不能幫我買兩張電影票？

Nǐ néng bu néng bāng wǒ mǎi liǎng zhāng diànyǐng piào?

Can you help me buy two movie tickets?

e. 我有几个问题，要向您请教。 (time conflict – have to attend a meeting)

我有幾個問題，要向您請教。

Wǒ yǒu jǐ gè wèntí, yào xiàng nín qǐngjiào.

I have a few questions that I'd like to ask you.

f. 我可以借用一下您的电话吗？ (inability – phone is broken)

我可以借用一下您的電話嗎？

Wǒ kěyǐ jièyòng yīxià nín de diànhuà ma?

Can I borrow your phone for a minute?

⇨ 62.3

Kelly is having coffee with her girlfriends when she receives a text message from a man she met the other day asking her to dinner at a Thai restaurant next week. She does not want to go and she is asking her friends for advice on how to turn him down. Translate her girlfriends' suggestions:

Abby: Tell him you don't like Thai food.

_____

Cathy: Just say you've been very busy lately so you are afraid you don't have time.

_____

Emily: Say you'll think about it and that it's a little inconvenient to talk right now.

_____

Imagine you are one of Kelly's girlfriends. What suggestion would you give her?

_____

63

Expressing apologies, regrets, sympathy, and bad news

1 Here are some short exchanges. Complete them by adding the appropriate apology.

a. A: _____。我来晚了。
    _____。我來晚了。
    _____. **Wǒ lái wán le.**
    _____. I got here late.

   B: 没关系。
      沒關係。
      Méi guānxi.
      It's not important.

b. A: _____。我没听懂。请再说一次。
    _____。我沒聽懂。請再說一次。
    _____. **Wǒ méi tīngdǒng. Qǐng zài shuō yīcì.**
    _____. I didn't understand. Please say it again.

   B: 没关系。我可以再说一次。
      沒關係。我可以再說一次。
      Méi guānxi. Wǒ kéyǐ zàishuō yīcì.
      No problem. I can say it again.

c. A: _____。我听不见。请大点声。
    _____。我聽不見。請大點聲。
    _____. **Wǒ tīngbujiàn. Qǐng dà diǎn shēng.**
    _____. I can't hear. Please say it a little louder.

   B: 好。
      Hǎo.
      Okay.

d. A: 让您久等了。_____。
    讓您久等了。_____。
    Ràng nín jiǔ děng le. _____.
    I've made you wait a long time. _____

   B: 没事。
      Méi shì.
      It's not important.

e. A: _____。是我没说清楚。

_____。是我沒說清楚。

_____. **Shì wǒ méi shuō qīngchu.**

_____. It is I who didn't speak clearly.

B: 没关系。慢慢说。

沒關係。慢慢說。

Méi guānxi. Mànmàn shuō.

It's all right. Take your time.

⇨ 63.1.1–63.1.3

2 Provide an expression of sympathy to comfort your friend when he tells you his bad news.

a. 我昨天刚买的字典，今天就丢了。

我昨天剛買的字典，今天就丢了。

Wǒ zuótiān gāng mǎi de zìdiǎn, jīntiān jiù diū le.

The dictionary that I bought only yesterday, I lost it today.

(Today I lost the dictionary that I just bought yesterday.)

b. 我住了十几天医院，昨天刚出院。

我住了十幾天醫院，昨天剛出院。

Wǒ zhù le shí jǐ tiān yīyuàn, zuótiān gāng chūyuàn.

I was hospitalized for more than ten days and was only released yesterday.

c. 我这次考试考得很不好。

我這次考試考得很不好。

Wǒ zhè cì kǎoshì kǎo de hěn bù hǎo.

I did really poorly on this exam.

d. 这个实验很不成功。

這個實驗很不成功。

Zhège shíyàn hěn bù chénggōng.

This experiment has not been successful.

e. 听说老王的孩子没有考上大学。

聽說老王的孩子沒有考上大學。

Tīngshuō lǎo Wáng de háizi méi yǒu kǎoshàng dàxué.

I've heard that Lao Wang's child did not pass the college entrance examination.

f. 我最近太忙。身体也不太舒服。

我最近太忙。身體也不太舒服。

Wǒ zuì jìn tài máng. Shēntǐ yě bù tài shūfu.

I have been really busy lately, and my health has not been too good.

⇨ 63.2

3

Select the correct response to complete each mini-dialogue.

A. Michael apologized to James for the delay in their project. James said that it was okay.

Michael: ＿＿＿＿＿＿，是我耽误了大家 / ＿＿＿＿＿＿，是我耽誤了大家。
＿＿＿＿＿＿，shì wǒ dānwù le dàjiā.

James: 没关系，我们还有时间 / 沒關係，我們還有時間。
Méi guānxi, wǒmen hái yǒu shíjiān.

a　百岁 / 百歲 Bǎisuì
b.　真可惜 Zhēn kěxí
c.　抱歉 Bàoqiàn

B. Ben is visiting his friend Neal in the hospital.

Ben: 我给你带了一些水果。＿＿＿＿＿＿。/ 我給你帶了一些水果。＿＿＿＿＿＿。
Wǒ gěi nǐ dài le yī xiē shuǐguǒ. ＿＿＿＿＿＿.

Neal: 怎么这么客气，谢谢你。/ 怎麼這麼客氣？謝謝你。
Zěnme zhème kèqì? Xièxie nǐ.

a.　希望你早日康复 / 希望你早日康復 xīwàng nǐ zǎorì kāngfù
b.　真可惜 zhēn kěxí
c.　请原谅我 / 請原諒我 qǐng yuánliàng wǒ

C. James is telling his boss that the project has been delayed and that they need more time.

James: 对不起，这个计划 ＿＿＿＿＿＿ 不能如期完成。
對不起，這個計劃 ＿＿＿＿＿＿ 不能如期完成。
Duìbuqǐ, zhège jìhuà ＿＿＿＿＿＿ bù néng rúqī wánchéng.

Boss: 那，你还需要多少时间？那，你還需要多少時間？
Nà, nǐ hái xūyào duōshǎo shíjiān?

a.　可怕 kěpà
b.　恐怕 kǒngpà
c.　抱歉 bàoqiàn

D. Debbie is inviting Linda to go to the movies with her and some co-workers after work today.

Debbie: 今天下班以后要不要一起去看电影？
今天下班以後要不要一起去看電影？
Jīntiān xià bān yǐhòu yào bù yào yīqǐ qù kàn diànyǐng?

Linda: ＿＿＿＿＿＿，今天晚上我有事，你们自己去吧。
＿＿＿＿＿＿，今天晚上我有事，你們自己去吧。
＿＿＿＿＿＿，jīntiān wǎnshang wǒ yǒu shì, nǐmen zìjǐ qù ba.

a.　不要紧 / 不要緊 Bù yàojǐn
b.　不好意思 Bùhǎo yìsi
c.　请原谅我 / 請原諒我 Qǐng yuánliàng wǒ

64

Expressing congratulations and good wishes

1 Provide the appropriate expression of congratulation and good wishes for each of the following situations.

a.   You run into a colleague on Christmas day.

b.   You see a neighbor on New Year's day.

c.   You see an old friend during Spring Festival.

d.   Your friends have just gotten married.

e.   Your friend has just opened a restaurant.

f.   Your cousin has just turned 15 years old.

g.   Your grandfather has just turned 70 years old.

h.   Your nephew has just graduated from college/university.

i.   Your aunt and uncle are celebrating their wedding anniversary.

⇨   64.1, 64.2

2 You are writing a note of congratulation to friends on their marriage. Which of the following expressions are appropriate for that occasion? Indicate 'yes' or 'no' for each phrase.

a.   祝生意兴隆！
     祝生意興隆！
     Zhù shēngyi xīnglóng!

b.   庆祝结婚纪念。
     慶祝結婚紀念。
     Qìngzhù jiéhūn jìniàn.

c.   天作之合！
     Tiān zuò zhī hé!

d.   寿比南山
     壽比南山
     Shòu bǐ nánshān

e.   百年好合！
     Bǎi nián hǎo hé!

f.   恭贺新禧
     恭賀新禧
     Gōnghè xīnxǐ

g.   福如东海
     福如東海
     Fú rú dōng hǎi

h.   祝贺毕业！
     祝賀畢業！
     Zhùhé bì yè.

i.   鹏程万里。
     鵬程萬里。
     Péngchéng wànlǐ.

j.   庆祝新婚。
     慶祝新婚。
     Qìngzhù xīn hūn.

k.　长命百岁！
　　長命百歲！
　　Cháng mìng bǎi suì!

l.　恭喜！
　　Gōngxǐ!

m.　前途无量
　　前途無量
　　Qiántú wú liàng

n.　高风亮节！
　　高風亮節！
　　Gāo fēng liàng jié!

o.　白头偕老！
　　白頭偕老！
　　Bái tóu xié lǎo!

p.　恭喜发财！
　　恭喜發財！
　　Gōngxǐ fācái!

⇨　64.1, 64.2

3

This exercise contains additional expressions that can be used to convey congratulations and good wishes. Read the situations below and decide which expressions are appropriate for the occasion described. You may need to consult a dictionary for this exercise.

A. Jamie is attending her college roommate's wedding. Which of the following expressions should **NOT** appear in her card:

　a.　天赐良缘/天賜良緣 **tiān cì liángyuán** A match made in heaven
　b.　永结同心/永結同心 **yǒngjié tóngxīn** Be of one mind forever
　c.　作育英才 **zuòyù yīngcái** Cultivate the talented mind.

B. To thank Dr. Yan's outstanding skill that saved his wife's life, Mr. Li commissioned a scroll that reads:

　a.　近悦远来/近悅遠來 **jìnyuè yuǎnlái** Doing one's best to satisfy people near and far
　b.　妙手回春 **miàoshǒu huíchūn** You have effected a miraculous cure
　c.　琴瑟和鸣/琴瑟和鳴 **qínsè hémíng** Wishing you a harmonious marriage

C. To congratulate the grand opening of Mr. Wang's business, Mr. Zhou had a flower stand arrangement delivered with a card that reads:

　a.　鸿图大展/鴻圖大展 **hóngtú dàzhǎn** May your business prosper
　b.　金榜题名/金榜題名 **jīnbǎng tímíng** Wishing you academic success
　c.　松柏长春/松柏長春 **sōngbǎi chángchūn** Pine trees and cypress trees are forever green (Wishes for continued long life)

D. Mr. Huang, a famous calligrapher, is asked to write something for an art gallery opening. Which of the following expressions is most likely to be chosen:

　a.　步步高升 **bùbù gāoshēng** Rise up step by step
　b.　财源广进/財源廣進 **cáiyuán guǎngjìn** Wishing you abundant wealth
　c.　巧夺天工/巧奪天工 **qiǎo duó tiāngōng** Craftmanship surpassing nature itself

Answer key

A Structures

1 Overview of pronunciation and Pinyin romanization

1 a. **xiān** b. **bié** c. **xuǎn** d. **yuè** e. **tóu** f. **huài** g. **chuī** h. **zǎo**

2 a. **Xiáo Lǐ** b. **wú bá yǐzi** c. **Ní yóu gǒu ma?** d. **Wó hén hǎo.** e. **Tā yé xiáng mái bǐ.** f. **Wó xiáng mǎi shū.** g. **Tā yóu jiǔ gè péngyou.** h. **wǔshíwú běn shū**

3 a. **kuai** b. **wan** c. **pengyou** d. **qian** e. **duo** f. **yue** g. **xuesheng** h. **zhongguo** i. **xiao** j. **yao**

2 Syllable, meaning, and word

1 a. **yì tiáo lù** b. **bú tài guì** c. **yí kuài qián** d. **yì mén kè** e. **yì suǒ fángzi** f. **yí gè rén** g. **yí shù huār** h. **yì háng** i. **yí bù diànyǐng** j. **bú cuò**

3 The Chinese writing system: an overview

1 a. 女 b. 亻 c. 言 d. 艹 e. 糸 f. 金 g. 辶 h. 氵 i. 彳

2 a. 辶 b. 户 c. 门 d. 忄 e. 攵 f. 寸 g. 木 h. 耳 i. 氵

3 a. 门 b. 车 c. 纟 d. 饣 e. 马 f. 贝 g. 钅 h. 鱼

4 a. D b. F c. G d. C e. B f. E g. H h. A

5 a. 講 → 讲 b. 塊 → 块 c. 樣 → 样 d. 蘭 → 兰 e. 連 → 连 f. 歐 → 欧 g. 學 → 学 h. 認 → 认 i. 聽 → 听 j. 曆 → 历

6

Group 1 ba	Group 2 zhan	Group 3 gang	Group 4 dong	Group 5 cheng
爸 吧 把	站 占 战	綱 剛 鋼	東 棟 凍	城 誠 成

7 a. 4 b. 7 c. 5 d. 11 e. 7 f. 15 g. 5

4 Phrase order in the Mandarin sentence

1

a. [我]昨天跟朋友吃[午饭]了。
[我]昨天跟朋友吃[午飯]了。
[Wǒ] zuótiān gēn péngyou chī [wǔfàn] le.
Yesterday [I] ate [lunch] with friends.

b. 我的[弟弟]每天看[电视]。
我的[弟弟]每天看[電視]。
Wǒ de [dìdi] měitiān kàn [diànshì].
My [younger brother] watches [television] every day.

c. 中国的[大学生]也上[网]吗？
中國的[大學生]也上[網]嗎？
Zhōngguó de [dàxuéshēng] yě shàng [wǎng] ma?
Do Chinese [university students] also surf the web?

d. 城里的[书店]有很多[外国书]。
城裏的[書店]有很多[外國書]。
Chéng lǐ de [shūdiàn] yǒu hěn duō [wàiguó shū].
The [bookstore] in the city has a lot of [foreign books].

e. [我]今天下午在公园的[门口]等[你]。
[我]今天下午在公園的[門口]等[你]。
[Wǒ] jīntiān xiàwǔ zài gōngyuán de [ménkǒu] děng [nǐ].
[I] will wait for [you] at the park [gate] this afternoon.

2

a. 我给奶奶写信了。
我給奶奶寫信了。
Wǒ gěi nǎinai xiě xìn le.
I wrote a letter to my grandma.

b. 我对心理学很有兴趣。
我對心理學很有興趣。
Wǒ duì xīnlǐxué hěn yǒu xìngqù.
I am very interested in psychology.

c. 我很喜欢跟朋友去玩。
我很喜歡跟朋友去玩。
Wǒ hěn xǐhuan gēn péngyou qù wán.
I really like to go out with my friends.

d. 要是你忙，我可以替你作这件事。
要是你忙，我可以替你作這件事。
Yàoshi nǐ máng, wǒ kěyǐ tì nǐ zuò zhè jiàn shì.
If you are busy I can do that for you.

e. 你什么时候到我家来？
你甚麼時候到我家來？
Nǐ shénme shíhòu dào wǒ jiā lái?
When are you coming to my house?

3

a. 我去年在中国学中文了。
我去年在中國學中文了。
Wǒ qùnián zài Zhōngguó xué Zhōngwén le.

b. 我每天都在学生中心碰到他。
我每天都在學生中心碰到他。
Wǒ měitiān dōu zài xuésheng zhōngxīn pèngdào tā.

c. 你想将来跟什么样的人结婚？
你想將來跟甚麼樣的人結婚？
Nǐ xiǎng jiānglái gēn shénme yàng de rén jiéhūn?

d. 他昨天晚上给我打电话了。
他昨天晚上給我打電話了。
Tā zuótiān wǎnshang gěi wǒ dǎ diànhuà le.

e. 他请我礼拜六跟他去看电影。
他請我禮拜六跟他去看電影。
Tā qǐng wǒ lǐbài liù gēn tā qù kàn diànyǐng.

4

a. 我在日本住了五年。
Wǒ zài Rìběn zhùle wǔ nián.

b. 我也喜欢看电影。
我也喜歡看電影。
Wǒ yě xǐhuān kàn diànyǐng.

c. 我每个周末都回家。
我每個週末都回家。
Wǒ měi gè zhōumò dōu huí jiā.

d. 我在图书馆工作。
我在圖書館工作。
Wǒ zài túshūguǎn gōngzuò.

e. 你要不要跟我去看电影？
你要不要跟我去看電影？
Nǐ yào bù yào gēn wǒ qù kàn diànyǐng?

f. 我对外国电影没有兴趣。
我對外國電影沒有興趣。
Wǒ duì wàiguó diànyǐng méi yǒu xìngqù.

5

a. 我不喜欢吃臭豆腐。
我不喜歡吃臭豆腐。
Wǒ bù xǐhuān chī chòu dòufu.

b. 我们不想跟你一起去看电影。
我們不想跟你一起去看電影。
Wǒmen bù xiǎng gēn nǐ yīqǐ qù kàn diànyǐng.

c. 他不在餐厅工作，他在宿舍工作。
他不在餐廳工作，他在宿舍工作。
Tā bù zài cāntīng gōngzuò, tā zài sùshè gōngzuò.

d. 他没给我打电话。
   他沒給我打電話。
   Tā méi gěi wǒ dǎ diànhuà.
e. 他不在法国念书，他在德国念书。
   他不在法國唸書，他在德國唸書。
   Tā bù zài Fǎguó niànshū, tā zài Déguó niànshū.

5 Nouns

1 a. 我们/我們 wǒmen *or* 咱们/咱們 zánmen b. 我们/我們 wǒmen _____ 你 nǐ *or* 你们/你們 nǐmen c. 他们/他們 tāmen *or* 她们/她們 tāmen d. 我 wǒ _____ 他们/他們 tāmen *or* 她们/她們 tāmen e. 我 wǒ _____ 他 tā _____ 她 tā

2 a. 她的 tā de b. 我的 wǒ de c. 我的 wǒ de *or* 我 wǒ d. 你的 nǐ de; 我们的/我們的 wǒmen de e. 你的 nǐ de

3
a. 他们/他們 tāmen, 我 wǒ, 我们/我們 wǒmen
b. 她 tā, 她 tā, 我 wǒ, 她 tā, 你 nǐ
c. 我 wǒ, 你 nǐ, 我 wǒ / 我 wǒ, 自己 zìjǐ

6 Numbers

1 a. 六 liù b. 十五 shíwǔ c. 十一 shíyī d. 三十六 sānshíliù e. 二十三 èrshísān f. 八十四 bāshísì g. 五十五 wǔshíwǔ h. 九十七 jiǔshíqī

2 a. 六五零五七八二三 liù wǔ líng wǔ qī bā èr sān b. 七八一二八三二一九一 qī bā yī èr bā sān èr yī jiǔ yī c. 九一一 jiǔ yī yī (jiǔ yāo yāo) d. 零三二四五七七六三九 líng sān èr sì wǔ qī qī liù sān jiǔ e. 八五二二六零九五四九八 bā wǔ èr èr liù líng jiǔ wǔ sì jiǔ bā f. 八五二九六六八八 bā wǔ èr jiǔ liù liù bā bā

3 a. 两/兩 liǎng b. 二 èr c. 二 èr d. 两/兩 liǎng e. 两/兩 liǎng f. 两/兩 liǎng g. 两/兩 liǎng h. 两/兩 liǎng i. 二 èr j. 二 èr *or* 两/兩 liǎng

4

	Arabic numeral	Chinese number
a.	1,276	一千二百七十六
		yī qiān èr bǎi qīshí liù
b.	35,634	三万五千六百三十四
		三萬五千六百三十四
		sānwàn wǔqiān liùbǎi sānshísì
c.	256,758	二十五万六千七百五十八
		二十五萬六千七百五十八
		èrshí wǔ wàn liù qiān qī bǎi wǔshí bā

		Arabic numeral	Chinese number
	d.	9,600,000	九百六十万
			九百六十萬
			jiǔbǎi liù shí wàn
	e.	1,893,683	一百八十九万三千六百八十三
			一百八十九萬三千六百八十三
			yī bǎi bāshí jiǔ wàn sān qiān liù bǎi bāshísān
	f.	3,027	三千零二十七
			sān qiān líng èrshí qī
	g.	370,035	三十七万零三十五
			三十七萬零三十五
			sānshí qī wàn líng sānshí wǔ
	h.	279,005	二十七万九千零五
			二十七萬九千零五
			èrshí qī wàn jiǔ qiān líng wǔ
	i.	3,079,001	三百零七万九千零一
			三百零七萬九千零一
			sānbǎi líng qī wàn jiǔqiān líng yī
	j.	66,209,380	六千六百二十万九千三百八十
			六千六百二十萬九千三百八十
			liùqiān liùbǎi èrshí wàn jiǔqiān sānbǎi bāshí

5

		English ordinal	Mandarin ordinal
	a.	20th	第二十 dì èrshí
	b.	9th	第九 dì jiǔ
	c.	3rd	第三 dì sān
	d.	17th	第十七 dì shíqī
	e.	1st	第一 dì yī
	f.	12th	第十二 dì shí'èr
	g.	48th	第四十八 dì sìshí bā
	h.	36th	第三十六 dì sānshíliù

6

		English	Mandarin
	a.	50 more or less	五十左右
			wǔshí zuǒyòu
	b.	less than two hundred	两百以下
			兩百以下
			liǎng bǎi yǐxià
	c.	almost 100	差不多一百
			chàbuduō yī bǎi

English	Mandarin
d. two or three students	两三个学生 兩三個學生 **liǎng sān gè xuésheng**
e. nine or ten students	九个十个学生 九個十個學生 **jiǔ gè shí gè xuésheng**
f. less than 10	十以下 **shí yǐxià**
g. more than 50	五十以上 **wǔshí yǐshàng**
h. more than a month	一个多月/一個多月 **yī gè duō yuè**

7

English	Mandarin
a. 5/8	八分之五 **bā fēn zhī wǔ**
b. 1/3	三分之一 **sān fēn zhīyī**
c. 0.75	零点七五/零點七五 **líng diǎn qī wǔ**
d. 30%	百分之三十 **bǎi fēn zhī sānshí**
e. 8.33	八点三三/八點三三 **bā diǎn sān sān**
f. 0.003	零点零零三/零點零零三 **líng diǎn líng líng sān**
g. 4/5	五分之四 **wǔ fēn zhī sì**
h. 1/7	七分之一 **qī fēn zhī yī**

8

a. 9½ hours	九个半钟头/九個半鐘頭 **jiǔ gè bàn zhōngtóu**
b. 1½ cups of coffee	一杯半咖啡/一盃半咖啡 **yī bēi bàn kāfēi**
c. ½ month	半个月/半個月 **bàn gè yuè**
d. 1½ months	一个半月/一個半月 **yī gè bàn yuè**
e. ½ year	半年 **bàn nián**
f. 3½ years	三年半 **sān nián bàn**

g. ½ book   半本书/半本書
bàn běn shū

h. 2½ semesters   两个半学期/兩個半學期
liǎng gè bàn xuéqī

i. 3½ bowls of rice   三碗半饭/三碗半飯
sān wǎn bàn fàn

j. ½ glass of beer   半杯啤酒/半盃啤酒
bàn bēi píjiǔ

9   a. 打七折 **dǎ qīzhé** b. 打九折 **dǎ jiǔzhé** c. 打五折 **dǎ wǔzhé**
d. 打七点五折/打七點五折 **dǎ qī diǎn wǔzhé**

10   a. 27 元 **yuán** b. 128 元 **yuán** c. 40 元 **yuán** d. 100 元 **yuán** e. 750 元 **yuán**
f. 14400 元 **yuán**

7   Specifiers and demonstratives

1   a. 这/這 **zhè**, 那 **nà** b. 哪儿/哪兒 **nǎr** or 哪里/哪裏 **nǎli** c. 哪儿/哪兒 **nǎr** or 哪里/哪裏 **nǎli** d. 这/這 **zhè** e. 哪儿/哪兒 **nǎr** or 哪里/哪裏 **nǎli** f. 那儿/那兒 **nàr** or 那里/那裏 **nàlǐ** g. 这儿/這兒 **zhèr** or 这里/這裏 **zhèlǐ** h. 这/這 **zhè**, 这儿/這兒 **zhèr** or 这里/這裏 **zhèlǐ** i. 那儿/那兒 **nàr** or 那里/那裏 **nàlǐ**, 这儿/這兒 **zhèr** or 这里/這裏 **zhèlǐ**, 那儿/那兒 **nàr** or 那里/那裏 **nàlǐ** j. 哪儿/哪兒 **nǎr** or 哪里/哪裏 **nǎli**, 这儿/這兒 **zhèr** or 这里/這裏 **zhèlǐ**

2   a. 哪儿/哪兒 **nǎr** or 哪里/哪裏 **nǎli**, b. 这儿/這兒 **zhèr** or 这里/這裏 **zhèlǐ**, c. 那儿/那兒 **nàr** or 那里/那裏 **nàlǐ**, d. 那 **nà**, e. 哪儿/哪兒 **nǎr** or 哪里/哪裏 **nǎli**, f. 这儿/這兒 **zhèr** or 这里/這裏 **zhèlǐ**, g. 那 **nà**, h. 这/這 **zhè**, i. 那儿/那兒 **nàr** or 那里/那裏 **nàlǐ**, j. 这儿/這兒 **zhèr** or 这里/這裏 **zhèlǐ**, k. 那 **nà**, l. 哪 **nǎ**, m. 那 **nà**

8   Classifiers

1   a.   这两张桌子
這兩張桌子
zhè liǎng zhāng zhuōzi

b.   这三位教授
這三位教授
zhè sān wèi jiàoshòu

c.   那两双鞋子
那兩雙鞋子
nà liǎng shuāng xiézi

d.   那四瓶啤酒
nà sì píng píjiǔ

e. 那三本中文书
那三本中文書
nà sān běn Zhōngwén shū

f. 这两件毛衣
這兩件毛衣
zhè liǎng jiàn máoyī

g. 这两个英国学生
這兩個英國學生
zhè liǎng gè Yīngguó xuésheng

h. 那四门文学课
那四門文學課
nà sì mén wénxué kè

2

a. 那十个学生/那十個學生 **nà shí gè xuésheng**

b. 这三天/這三天 **zhè sān tiān**

c. 那个手机/那個手機 **nàge shǒujī**

d. 那五张照片/那五張照片 **nà wǔ zhāng zhàopiàn**

e. 这杯咖啡/這杯咖啡 **zhè bēi kāfēi**

f. 那张纸/那張紙 **nà zhāng zhǐ**

3

Scenario 1

A. a. 枝 **zhī** b. 本 **běn** c. 个/個 **gè** d. 件 **jiàn** e. 条/條 **tiáo** f. 张/張 **zhāng**

B. Translation:

Kevin: The semester is about to begin. I'm going to buy some things for school. Look, the things in this store are really cheap: I bought ten pencils, two dictionaries, a backpack, two pieces of clothing, a pair of slacks, and altogether it was only $30. Their paper is even cheaper, 500 sheets are only $4.50.

Scenario 2

A. a. 条/條 **tiáo** b. 瓶 **píng** c. 个/個 **gè** d. 张/張 **zhāng** e. 把 **bǎ**
f. 张/張 **zhāng** g. 瓶 **píng** h. 条/條 **tiáo** i. 件 **jiàn**

B. Translation:

Tina: Are the tables and chairs all set up? I've bought the five loaves of bread and four bottles of wine that you wanted.

Lily: There are altogether ten people. We might not all be able to fit at the table. We still need another table. Also, bring over three more chairs. In addition, we need to put a vase of flowers on each table.

Tina: Okay. What are you wearing tonight? I want to wear my red skirt.

Lily: I'm planning to wear the new skirt that I bought. It looks really good with that white jacket.

4

a. 一万三千四百五十九块
一萬三千四百五十九塊
yī wàn sān qiān sì bǎi wǔshí jiǔ kuài

b. 两千八百五十块
两千八百五十塊
liǎng qiān bā bǎi wǔshí kuài

c. 七毛五（分）
qī máo wǔ (fēn)

d. 四百五十块零二分
四百五十塊零二分
sì bǎi wǔshí kuài líng èr fēn

e. 一千二百二十二块
一千二百二十二塊
yī qiān èr bǎi èrshí'èr kuài

f. 九万六千四百五十七块四毛五（分）
九萬六千四百五十七塊四毛五（分）
jiǔ wàn liù qiān sì bǎi wǔ shí qī kuài sì máo wǔ (fēn)

5　a. \$93.81 b. \$45.03 c. \$8.1 d. \$2,703 e. \$6.09 f. \$0.66

9　Noun phrases

1
a. 的 de cannot be included in this noun phrase

b. 五本很有意思的小说
五本很有意思的小說
wǔ běn hěn yǒu yìsī de xiǎoshuō

c. 五张很便宜的飞机票
五張很便宜的飛機票
wǔ zhāng hěn piányi de fēijī piào

d. 那条蓝色的裤子
那條藍色的褲子
nà tiáo lánsè de kùzi

e. 那门中文（的）课
那門中文（的）課
nà mén Zhōngwén (de) kè

f. 那六把很漂亮的椅子
nà liù bǎ hěn piàoliang de yǐzi

g. 一瓶五十块钱的葡萄酒
一瓶五十塊錢的葡萄酒
yī píng wǔshí kuài qián de pútao jiǔ

2
a. 我的五枝铅笔
我的五枝鉛筆
wǒ de wǔ zhī qiānbǐ

b. 我的一个朋友
   我的一個朋友
   wǒ de yī gè péngyou

c. 他的两个同学
   他的兩個同學
   tā de liǎng gè tóngxué

d. 我们的三位老师
   我們的三位老師
   wǒmen de sān wèi lǎoshī

e. 我的四本书
   我的四本書
   wǒ de sì běn shū

f. 他的那把椅子
   tā de nà bǎ yǐzi

g. 喜欢旅游的女孩子
   喜歡旅游的女孩子
   xǐhuan lǚyóu de nǚháizi

h. 两张很贵的飞机票
   兩張很貴的飛機票
   liǎng zhāng hěn guì de fēijī piào

i. 那位很高的德文老师
   那位很高的德文老師
   nà wèi hěn gāo de Déwén lǎoshī

j. 我的很好的朋友
   wǒ de hěn hǎo de péngyou

k. 一件黄颜色的毛衣
   一件黄顏色的毛衣
   yī jiàn huáng yánsè de máoyī

l. 一块钱的中国地图
   一塊錢的中國地圖
   yī kuài qián de Zhōngguó dìtú

3 a. Whose Chinese book? b. A Chinese book written by whom? c. A Chinese book that you bought when? d. A Chinese book that you bought where? e. Which book written by Professor Ma? f. Which book that you like? g. A book that costs how much money?

4 a. 这三本书
   這三本書
   zhè sān běn shū

b. 那两个学生
   那兩個學生
   nà liǎng gè xuésheng

c. 那五枝笔
    那五枝筆
    nà wǔ zhī bǐ

d. 这十个本子 *or* 这十本本子
    這十個本子 *or* 這十本本子
    zhè shí gè běnzi *or* **zhè shí běn běnzi**

e. 这张纸
    這張紙
    zhè zhāng zhǐ

f. 这些报纸
    這些報紙
    zhè xiē bàozhǐ

g. 这条裤子
    這條褲子
    zhè tiáo kùzi

h. 这三把椅子
    這三把椅子
    zhè sān bǎ yǐzi

i. 那五张桌子
    那五張桌子
    nà wǔ zhāng zhuōzi

j. 那个人
    那個人
    nàge rén

5

a. 三个学中文的人
    三個學中文的人
    sān gè xué Zhōngwén de rén

b. 我昨天看的电影
    我昨天看的電影
    wǒ zuótiān kàn de diànyǐng

c. 我会写的汉字
    我會寫的漢字
    wǒ huì xiě de Hàn zì

d. 跟你谈话的那位先生
    跟你談話的那位先生
    gēn nǐ tánhuà de nà wèi xiānsheng

e. 今天早上跟你谈话的那位先生
    今天早上跟你談話的那位先生
    jīntiān zǎoshang gēn nǐ tánhuà de nà wèi xiānsheng

f. 今天早上在餐厅跟你谈话的那位先生
    今天早上在餐廳跟你談話的那位先生
    jīntiān zǎoshang zài cāntīng gēn nǐ tánhuà de nà wèi xiānsheng

g. 我买的鞋子

我買的鞋子

wǒ mǎi de xiézi

h. 我在意大利买的鞋子

我在意大利買的鞋子

wǒ zài Yìdàlì mǎi de xiézi

6

a. '图书馆'是看书借书的地方。'圖書館'是看書借書的地方。'Túshūguǎn' **shì kàn shū jiè shū de dìfang.**

b. '同屋'是跟你一起住的人。'Tóngwū' **shì gēn nǐ yīqǐ zhù de rén.**

c. '厨师'是做菜的人。'廚師'是做菜的人。'Chúshī' **shì zuò cài de rén.**

d. '医生'是看病的人。'醫生'是看病的人。'Yīshēng' **shì kàn bìng de rén.**

e. '学校'是跟同学学习的地方。'學校'是跟同學學習的地方。'Xuéxiào' **shì gēn tóngxué xuéxí de dìfang.**

10 Adjectival verbs

1

a. 他忙不忙？   or   他忙吗？

他忙嗎？

Tā máng bù máng?   **Tā máng ma?**

b. 那本书有意思没有？   or   那本书有意思吗？

那本書有意思沒有？   那本書有意思嗎？

Nà běn shū yǒu yìsi méi yǒu?   **Nà běn shū yǒu yìsi ma?**

c. 飞机票贵不贵？   or   飞机票贵吗？

飛機票貴不貴？   飛機票貴嗎？

Fēijī piào guì bù guì?   **Fēijī piào guì ma?**

d. 那件事情复杂不复杂？   or   那件事情复杂吗？

那件事情複雜不複雜？   那件事情複雜嗎？

Nà jiàn shìqing fùzá bù fùzá?   **Nà jiàn shìqing fùzá ma?**

e. 她的男朋友好看不好看？   or   她的男朋友好看吗？

她的男朋友好看嗎？

Tā de nán péngyou hǎo kàn   **Tā de nán péngyou hǎo kàn ma?**
bù hǎo kàn?

f. 他们用功不用功？   or   他们用功吗？

他們用功不用功？   他們用功嗎？

Tāmen yònggōng bù yònggōng?   **Tāmen yònggōng ma?**

g. 他有钱没有？   or   他有钱吗？

他有錢沒有？   他有錢嗎？

Tā yǒu qián méi yǒu?   **Tā yǒu qián ma?**

h. 那辆车快不快？   or   那辆车快吗？

那輛車快不快？   那輛車快嗎？

Nà liàng chē kuài bù kuài?   **Nà liàng chē kuài ma?**

2

a. 他不忙。
Tā bù máng.

b. 那本书没有意思。
那本書沒有意思。
Nà běn shū méi yǒu yìsi.

c. 飞机票不贵。
飛機票不貴。
Fēijī piào bù guì.

d. 那件事情不复杂。
那件事情不複雜。
Nà jiàn shìqing bù fùzá.

e. 她的男朋友不好看。
Tā de nán péngyou bù hǎokàn.

f. 他们不用功。
他們不用功。
Tāmen bù yònggōng.

g. 他没有钱。
他沒有錢。
Tā méi yǒu qián.

h. 那辆车不快。
那輛車不快。
Nà liàng chē bù kuài.

3

a. 他很高。
Tā hěn gāo.

b. 他非常帅。
他非常帥。
Tā fēicháng shuài.

c. 他相当聪明。
他相當聰明。
Tā xiāngdāng cōngming.

d. 他太胖。
Tā tài pàng.

e. 他很客气。
他很客氣。
Tā hěn kèqi.

f. 他真有意思。
Tā zhēn yǒu yìsi.

4

a. 王明很聪明。周利更聪明。
王明很聰明。周利更聰明。
Wáng Míng hěn cōngming. Zhōu Lì gèng cōngming.

b. 王明有本事。周利更有本事。
   Wáng Míng yǒu běnshi. Zhōu Lì gèng yǒu běnshi.

c. 王明很帅。周利更帅。
   王明很帥。周利更帥。
   Wáng Míng hěn shuài. Zhōu Lì gèng shuài.

d. 王明很和气。周利更和气。
   王明很和氣。周利更和氣。
   Wáng Míng hěn héqi. Zhōu Lì gèng héqi.

5

a. 一样/一样 yīyàng

b. 更 gèng

c. 远/远 yuǎn

d. 小 xiǎo

e. 李家同的房间和张天一的房间/李家同的房间和张天一的房间 Lǐ Jiātóng de fángjiān hé Zhāng Tiānyī de fángjiān

11 Stative verbs

1

a. 他不想吃中国饭。
   他不想吃中國飯。
   Tā bù xiǎng chī Zhōngguó fàn.

b. 他不怕陌生人。
   Tā bù pà mòshēng rén.

c. 我不懂他的意思。
   Wǒ bù dǒng tā de yìsi.

d. 我不爱他。我不愿意嫁给他。
   我不愛他。我不願意嫁給他。
   Wǒ bù ài tā. Wǒ bù yuànyi jià gěi tā.

e. 他不像他爷爷。
   他不像他爺爺。
   Tā bù xiàng tā yéye.

2

a. 她姓张。
   她姓張。
   Tā xìng Zhāng.

b. 她叫小春。
   Tā jiào Xiǎo Chūn.

c. 她今年十八岁。
   她今年十八歲。
   Tā jīnnián shíbā suì.

d. 她是大学生。
   她是大學生。
   Tā shì dàxuéshēng.

e. 她没有汽车。她有一只猫。
她沒有汽車。她有一隻貓。
Tā meí yǒu qìchē. Tā yǒu yī zhī māo.

f. 她很喜欢历史。
她很喜歡歷史。
Tā hěn xǐhuan lìshǐ.

g. 她怕狗。
Tā pà gǒu.

h. 她非常想去中国。
她非常想去中國。
Tā fēicháng xiǎng qù Zhōngguó.

3 a. 在 zài b. 有 yǒu c. 姓 xìng d. 是 shì e. 在 zài f. 有 yǒu g. 是 shì . . .
有 yǒu

4 a. 养狗，对吗？你的房子就在学校的旁边。还有，你很喜欢化学和历史。
養狗，對嗎？你的房子就在學校的旁邊。還有，你很喜歡化學和歷史。
yǎng gǒu, duì ma? Nǐ de fángzi jiù zài xuéxiào de pángbiān. Hái yǒu,
nǐ hěn xǐhuān huàxué hé lìshǐ.

b. 最怕开车。/ 最怕開車。zuì pà kāi chē.

c. 不怕了。bù pà le.

12 Modal verbs

1 a. 会/會 huì b. 会/會 huì c. 能 néng d. 会/會 huì, 能 néng, *or* 可以 kěyǐ
e. 能 néng *or* 可以 kěyǐ f. 能 néng *or* 可以 kěyǐ g. 可以 kěyǐ h. 会/會 huì,
能 néng, *or* 可以 kěyǐ

2 a. 不必 bù bì b. 应该/應該 yīnggāi or 应当/應當 yīngdāng c. 不应该/不應該
bù yīnggāi d. 必须/必須 bìxū or 得 děi e. 必须/必須 bìxū or 得 děi f. 不必 bù bì
g. 不许/不許 bù xǔ h. 不许/不許 bù xǔ

3 a. 你应该对老师客气。
你應該對老師客氣。
Nǐ yīnggāi duì lǎoshī kèqi.

b. 你必得每天上课。
你必得每天上課。
Nǐ bìděi měitiān shàng kè.

c. 你应该每天晚上学中文。
你應該每天晚上學中文。
Nǐ yīnggāi měitiān wǎnshang xué Zhōngwén.

d. 你必须买一本中文字典。
你必須買一本中文字典。
Nǐ bìxū mǎi yī běn Zhōngwén zìdiǎn.

e. 你不必看那个电影。
你不必看那個電影。
Nǐ bù bì kàn nàge diànyǐng.

4　a. 你应该每天早上吃早饭。
你應該每天早上吃早飯。
Nǐ yīnggāi měitiān zǎoshang chī zǎofàn.

b. 你得锁门。
你得鎖門。
Nǐ děi suǒ mén.

c. 你不应该喝太多咖啡。
你不應該喝太多咖啡。
Nǐ bù yīnggāi hē tài duō kāfēi.

d. 你不应该看别人的信。
你不應該看別人的信。
Nǐ bù yīnggāi kàn biéren de xìn.

e. 你不必等我。
Nǐ bù bì děng wǒ.

f. 你(必)得找工作。
Nǐ (bì) děi zhǎo gōngzuò.

g. 你不必早回家。
Nǐ bù bì zǎo huí jiā.

h. 你不许在医院里抽烟。
你不許在醫院裏抽煙。
Nǐ bù xǔ zài yīyuàn lǐ chōu yān.

5　a. 得 **děi**

b. 不许/不許 **bùxǔ**

c. 别 **bié**

d. 不可以 **bù kěyǐ**

e. 可以 **kěyǐ**

f. 会/會 **huì**

6　a. 不能 **bù néng** b. 不应该/不應該 **bù yīnggāi** c. 不让/不讓 **bù ràng**

13　Action verbs

1　a. 过/過 **guo** . . . 过/過 **guo** b. 过/過 **guo** c. 了 **le** d. 过/過 **guo** e. 了 **le**
f. 过/過 **guo** g. 了 **le**

2　a. 他没吃早饭。
他沒吃早飯。
Tā méi chī zǎofàn.

b. 他上课了。
他上課了。
Tā shàng kè le.

c. 他在图书馆学习了。
他在圖書館學習了。
Tā zài túshūguǎn xuéxí le.

d. 他吃中饭了。
他吃中飯了。
Tā chī zhōngfàn le.

e. 他没看他的女朋友。
他沒看他的女朋友。
Tā méi kàn tā de nǚ péngyou.

f. 他看了一个电影。
他看了一個電影。
Tā kàn le yī gè diànyǐng.

g. 他去书店了。
他去書店了。
Tā qù shūdiàn le.

h. 他没买书。
他沒買書。
Tā méi mǎi shū.

3

a. 我看书了。
我看書了。
Wǒ kàn shū le.

b. 我跟朋友唱歌儿了。
我跟朋友唱歌兒了。
Wǒ gēn péngyou chàng gēr le.

c. 我在图书馆念书了。（我在图书馆学习了。）
我在圖書館念書了。（我在圖書館學習了。）
Wǒ zài túshūguǎn niàn shū le. (Wǒ zài túshūguǎn xuéxí le.)

d. 我画了两张画儿。
我畫了兩張畫兒。
Wǒ huàle liǎng zhāng huàr.

e. 我看电视看了两个钟头。
我看電視看了兩個鐘頭。
Wǒ kàn diànshì kànle liǎng gè zhōngtóu.

4 (Free response.)

5 Amy 站着吃饭。
Amy 站著吃飯。
Amy zhàn zhe chī fàn.

Beth 开着门睡觉。
Beth 開著門睡覺。
Beth kāizhe mén shuì jiào.

Carmen 卧室的墙上挂着一件长大衣。
Carmen 臥室的牆上掛著一件長大衣。
Carmen Wòshì de qiáng shang guàzhe yī jiàn cháng dàyī.

Derek 的书桌上放／摆着十二个石狮子。
Derek 的書桌上放／擺著十二個石獅子。
Derek de shūzhuō shàng fàng/bǎi zhe shí'èr ge shí shīzi.

Emily 只能坐着唱歌。
Emily 只能坐著唱歌。
Emily zhǐ néng zuòzhe chàng gē.

Frank 只穿着睡衣去学校。
Frank 只穿著睡衣去學校。
Frank zhǐ chuānzhe shuìyī qù xuéxiào.

14 Prepositions and prepositional phrases

1   a. 替 tì b. 往 wǎng c. 对/對 duì d. 跟 gēn e. 对/對 duì f. 在 zài _____ 到 dào g. 跟 gēn *or* 对/對 duì h. 往 wǎng

2

a. 我给我的朋友打电话了。
我給我的朋友打電話了。
Wǒ gěi wǒ de péngyou dǎ diànhuà le.

b. 她请我到她家来吃饭。
她請我到她家來吃飯。
Tā qǐng wǒ dào tā jiā lái chī fàn.

c. 我在图书馆念书了。
我在圖書館念書了。
Wǒ zài túshūguǎn niàn shū le.

d. 我从图书馆到她家去了。
我從圖書館到她家去了。
Wǒ cóng túshūguǎn dào tā jiā qù le.

e. 我给他买了糖。
我給她買了糖。
Wǒ gěi tā mǎi le táng.

f. 她给我介绍她的父母。
她給我介紹她的父母。
Tā gěi wǒ jièshào tā de fùmǔ.

g. 后来，我跟她看电影了。
後來，我跟她看電影了。
Hòulái, wǒ gēn tā kàn diànyǐng le.

h. 我们在书房(里)看电影了。
我們在書房(裏)看電影了。
Wǒmen zài shūfáng (lǐ) kàn diànyǐng le.

3

a. 这位是我们新来的老师。
這位是我們新來的老師。
Zhè wèi shì wǒmen xīn lái de lǎoshī.

b. 我给你们介绍介绍。
我給你們介紹介紹。
Wǒ gěi nǐmen jièshào jièshào.

c. 他刚从美国来。
他剛從美國來。
Tā gāng cóng Měiguó lái.

d. 他今年在我们学校教英文。
他今年在我們學校教英文。
Tā jīnnián zài wǒmen xuéxiào jiào Yīngwén.

e. 他对中国文化很有兴趣。
他對中國文化很有興趣。
Tā duì Zhōngguó wénhuà hěn yǒu xìngqù.

f. 他希望到各地去旅行。
Tā xīwàng dào gè dì qù lǚxíng.

g. 也希望多跟中国人来往。
也希望多跟中國人來往。
Yě xīwàng duō gēn Zhōngguó rén láiwǎng.

4

a. 下课以后我不给你打电话。
下課以後我不給你打電話。
Xià kè yǐhòu wǒ bù gěi nǐ dǎ diànhuà.

b. 我不把书还给图书馆。
我不把書還給圖書館。
Wǒ bù bǎ shū hái gěi túshūguǎn.

c. 我不跟老师说你病了。
我不跟老師說你病了。
Wǒ bù gēn lǎoshī shuō nǐ bìng le.

d. 我不在餐厅等你。
我不在餐廳等你。
Wǒ bù zài cāntīng děng nǐ.

e. 我不把我的书拿走。
我不把我的書拿走。
Wǒ bù bǎ wǒ de shū názǒu.

f. 我不给你买午饭。
我不給你買午飯。
Wǒ bù gěi nǐ mǎi wǔfàn.

15   Adverbs

1 a. 也 yě b. 还/還 hái c. 只 zhǐ [就 jiù] d. 都 dōu e. 也 yě f. 只 zhǐ g. 只 zhǐ
h. 就 jiù i. 才 cái j. 都 dōu

2 小李 Xiǎo Lǐ's responses:

a.   我学英文，也学日文。
     我學英文，也學日文。
     Wǒ xué Yīngwén, yě xué Rìwén.

b.   我只[就][才]十六岁。
     我只[就][才]十六歲。
     Wǒ zhǐ [jiù] [cái] shíliù suì.

c.   还没有。我还没出过国。
     還沒有。我還沒出過國。
     Hái méi yǒu. Wǒ hái méi chūguo guó.

d.   想。我毕业了以后才有机会出国。
     想。我畢業了以後才有機會出國。
     Xiǎng. Wǒ bìyè le yǐhòu cái yǒu jīhuì chū guó.

e.   我想去英国，也想去美国。
     我想去英國，也想去美國。
     Wǒ xiǎng qù Yīngguó, yě xiǎng qù Měiguó.

f.   我去了英国，美国以后就想去日本。
     我去了英國，美國以後就想去日本。
     Wǒ qù le Yīngguó, Měiguó yǐhòu jiù xiǎng qù Rìběn.

The interviewer's questions:

a.   你学哪个外语？（你学什么外语？）
     你學哪個外語？（你學甚麼外語？）
     Nǐ xué nǎge wàiyǔ? (Nǐ xué shénme wàiyǔ?)

b.   你多大年纪？
     你多大年紀？
     Nǐ duō dà niánjì?

c.   你去过外国吗？（你出过国没有？）
     你去過外國嗎？（你出過國沒有？）
     Nǐ qùguo wàiguó ma? (Nǐ chūguo guó méiyou?)

d.   你想出国吗？
     你想出國嗎？
     Nǐ xiǎng chū guó ma?

e.   你想去哪儿[哪里]？（你想到哪儿去？）
     你想去哪兒[哪裏]？（你想到哪兒去？）
     Nǐ xiǎng qù nǎr [nǎli]? (Nǐ xiǎng dào nǎr qù?)

f.   你也想去日本吗？
     你也想去日本嗎？
     Nǐ yě xiǎng qù Rìběn ma?

3

A: 昨天<u>刚</u>开学，明天中文课<u>就</u>有小考，<u>真</u>让人受不了。

昨天<u>剛</u>開學，明天中文課<u>就</u>有小考，<u>真</u>讓人受不了。

Zuótiān <u>gāng</u> kāi xué, míngtiān Zhōngwén kè <u>jiù</u> yǒu xiǎokǎo, <u>zhēn</u> ràng rén shòubùliǎo.

B: 刚开学你<u>就</u>受不了了，你<u>还</u>学不学了？

剛開學你<u>就</u>受不了了，你<u>還</u>學不學了？

Gāng kāi xué nǐ <u>jiù</u> shòubùliǎo le, nǐ <u>hái</u> xué bù xué le?

A: <u>学还</u>要学，我<u>只</u>抱怨一下<u>而已</u>。

<u>學還</u>要學，我<u>只</u>抱怨一下<u>而已</u>。

Xué <u>hái</u> yào xué, wǒ <u>zhǐ</u> bàoyuàn yīxià <u>éryǐ</u>.

B: 抱怨有什么用，<u>只</u>能让你自己不高兴。

抱怨有甚麼用，<u>只</u>能讓你自己不高興。

Bàoyuàn yǒu shénme yòng, <u>zhǐ</u> néng ràng nǐ zìjǐ bù gāoxìng.

A: 你<u>也</u>常常抱怨呀。

Nǐ yě chángcháng bàoyuàn ya.

B: 我<u>只</u>抱怨你抱怨得<u>太</u>多。

Wǒ zhǐ bàoyuàn nǐ bàoyuàn de tài dūo.

16　Conjunctions

1

a. 和 hé/跟 gēn b. 还是/還是 háishi c. 或者 huòzhě d. 还是/還是 háishi
e. 和 hé/跟 gēn f. 和 hé/跟 gēn g. 和 hé/跟 gēn h. 或者 huòzhě

2

小李：我不知道选中文课好还是选中国历史课好。

我不知道選中文課好還是選中國歷史課好。

Wǒ bù zhīdào xuǎn Zhōngwén kè hǎo háishi xuǎn Zhōngguó lìshǐ kè hǎo.

小王：中文课和中国历史课你更喜欢哪个？

中文課和中國歷史課你更喜歡哪個？

Zhōngwén kè hé Zhōngguó lìshǐ kè nǐ gèng xǐhuān nǎ ge?

小李：中文课和中国历史课我都喜欢。

中文課和中國歷史課我都喜歡。

Zhōngwén kè hé Zhōngguó lìshǐ kè wǒ dōu xǐhuān.

小王：那你就选中文课和中国历史课。

那你就選中文課和中國歷史課。

Nà nǐ jiù xuǎn Zhōngwén kè hé Zhōngguó lìshǐ kè.

小李：我没有那么多时间。

我沒有那麼多時間。

Wǒ méi yǒu nàme duō shíjiān.

小王：那你就选中文课或者中国历史课。

那你就選中文課或者中國歷史課。

Nà nǐ jiù xuǎn Zhōngwén kè huòzhě Zhōngguó lìshǐ kè.

小李：你也不知道我应该选中文课还是选中国历史课。
你也不知道我應該選中文課還是選中國歷史課。
Nǐ yě bù zhīdào wǒ yīnggāi xuǎn Zhōngwén kè háishi Zhōngguó lìshǐ kè.

小王：我当然不知道，因为跟我没关系。
我當然不知道，因為跟我沒關係。
Wǒ dāngrán bù zhīdào, yīnwèi gēn wǒ méi guānxi.

小李：多谢！
多謝！
Duō xiè!

17 Aspect

1

a. 小李昨天看了两本书。
小李昨天看了兩本書。
Xiǎo Lǐ zuótiān kànle liǎng běn shū.

b. 小李昨天和朋友喝咖啡了。
Xiǎo Lǐ zuótiān hé péngyou hē kāfēi le.

c. 小李昨天看电视看了一个钟头。
小李昨天看電視看了一個鐘頭。
Xiǎo Lǐ zuótiān kàn diànshì kànle yī ge zhōngtou.
小李昨天看了一个钟头的电视。
小李昨天看了一個鐘頭的電視。
Xiǎo Lǐ zuótiān kàn le yī ge zhōngtou de diànshì.

d. 小李昨天和同屋去买东西了。
小李昨天和同屋去買東西了。
Xiǎo Lǐ zuótiān hé tóngwū qù mǎi dōngxi le.

e. 小李昨天买了一双很贵的运动鞋。
小李昨天買了一雙很貴的運動鞋。
Xiǎo Lǐ zuótiān mǎile yī shuāng hěn guì de yùndòng xié.

2

a. 学校没开学。
學校沒開學。
Xuéxiào méi kāi xué.
School has not started.

b. 我没买课本。
我沒買課本。
Wǒ méi mǎi kèběn.
I did not buy textbooks.

c. 我没买中文书。
我沒買中文書。
Wǒ méi mǎi Zhōngwén shū.
I didn't buy Chinese books.

d. 我没做功课。

我沒做功課。

Wǒ méi zuò gōngkè.

I didn't do my homework.

e. 我的同屋白天不睡觉。

我的同屋白天不睡覺。

Wǒ de tóngwū báitiān bù shuì jiào.

My roommate doesn't sleep during the day.

f. 我没学过中文。

我沒學過中文。

Wǒ méi xuéguo Zhōngwén.

I have not studied Chinese before.

g. 我没在中国学过中文。

我沒在中國學過中文。

Wǒ méi zài Zhōngguó xuéguo Zhōngwén.

I haven't studied Chinese in China.

h. 我妹妹不学中文。

我妹妹不學中文。

Wǒ mèimei bù xué Zhōngwén.

My younger sister does not study Chinese.

i. 我没跟朋友去买东西。

我沒跟朋友去買東西。

Wǒ méi gēn péngyou qù mǎi dōngxi.

I did not go shopping with my friends.

3 a. 你这个星期看了电影[吗/没有]？

你這個星期看了電影[嗎/沒有]？

Nǐ zhège xīngqī kànle diànyǐng [ma/méi yǒu]?

b. 你星期五晚上和爸爸妈妈吃晚饭了[吗/没有]？

你星期五晚上和爸爸媽媽吃晚飯了[嗎/沒有]？

Nǐ xīngqīwǔ wǎnshang hé bàba māma chī wǎnfàn le [ma/méi yǒu]?

c. 你去了那个新的咖啡馆[吗/没有]？

你去了那個新的咖啡館[嗎/沒有]？

Nǐ qùle nàge xīn de kāfēiguǎn [ma/méi yǒu]?

d. 你买了新的外套[吗/没有]？

你買了新的外套[嗎/沒有]？

Nǐ mǎile xīn de wàitào [ma/méi yǒu]?

e. 你看完了那本历史书[吗/没有]？

你看完了那本歷史書[嗎/沒有]？

Nǐ kànwánle nà běn lìshǐ shū [ma/méi yǒu]?

4 a. 小李在做功课呢。

小李在做功課呢。

Xiǎo Lǐ zài zuò gōngkè ne.

b.　小李在穿衣服呢。
　　小李在穿衣服呢。
　　Xiǎo Lǐ zài chuān yīfú ne.

c.　小李正在收拾屋子呢。
　　小李正在收拾屋子呢。
　　Xiǎo Lǐ zhèngzài shōushi wūzi ne.

d.　小李在开(着)车呢。
　　小李在開(著)車呢。
　　Xiǎo Lǐ zài kāi(zhe) chē ne.

e.　小李在吃(着)饭呢。
　　小李在吃(著)飯呢。
　　Xiǎo Lǐ zài chī(zhe) fàn ne.

5

a.　了 **le**
b.　了 **le**
c.　着/著 **zhe**
d.　在 **zài**
e.　了 **le**
f.　了 **le**
g.　了 **le**
h.　了 **le**
i.　了 **le**
j.　了 **le**
k.　了 **le**
l.　着/著 **zhe**

6

Sample answer:

Tommy 没登过长城。他也没去过圆明园。饺子他吃过很多次，可是他没吃过北京烤鸭。他没看过京剧，可是他说他没有兴趣看。他逛过胡同，可是他说他还想再去一次。

Tommy 沒登過長城。他也沒去過圓明園。餃子他吃過很多次，可是他沒吃過北京烤鴨。他沒看過京劇，可是他說他沒有興趣看。他逛過胡同，可是他說他還想再去一次。

Tommy méi dēngguo Chángchéng. Tā yě méi qùguo Yuánmíngyuán. Jiǎozi tā chīguo hěn duō cì, kěshì tā méi chīguo Běijīng Kǎoyā. Tā méi kànguo Jīngjù, kěshì tā shuō ta méi yǒu xìngqù kàn. Tā guàngguo hútòng, kěshì tā shuō tā hái xiǎng zài qù yī cì.

7

Sample answer:

对不起，王先生正在开会，不能接电话。他开完会就给你打电话。
對不起，王先生正在開會，不能接電話。他開完會就給你打電話。
Duìbuqǐ, Wáng xiānsheng zhèngzài kāi huì, bù néng jiē diànhuà. Tā kāiwán huì jiù gěi nǐ dǎ diànhuà.

8

Sample answer:

我家门上挂着一个花圈，门口放着一盆花。

我家門上掛著一個花圈，門口放著一盆花。

Wǒ jiā mén shàng guàzhe yī ge huāquān, ménkǒu fàngzhe yī pén huā.

9

Sample answer:

不好意思我今天晚上不去了。我累死了，今天写了五页汉字，洗了很多碗，还整理了三个书架。

不好意思我今天晚上不去了。我累死了，今天寫了五頁漢字，洗了很多碗，還整理了三個書架。

Bùhǎoyìsi, wǒ jīntiān wǎnshang bù qù le. Wǒ lèisǐle. Jīntiān xiěle wǔ gè Hànzì, xǐle hěn duō wǎn, hái zhěnglǐ le sān gè shūjià.

18 Resultative verbs

1
a. 我听懂了。/ 我聽懂了。Wǒ tīngdǒng le.
b. 功课做完了。/ 功課做完了。Gōngkè zuòwán le.
c. 那本书我找到 / 着了。/ 那本書我找到 / 著了。
   Nà běn shū wǒ zhǎodào/zháo le.
d. 那本书我还没有看完。/ 那本書我還沒有看完。Nà běn shū wǒ hái méi kànwán.
e. 现在我能看懂中国电影了。/ 現在我能看懂中國電影了。
   Xiànzài wǒ néng kàndǒng Zhōngguó diànyǐng le.
f. 我的手机在路上丢掉了。真麻烦。/ 我的手機在路上丢掉了。真麻煩。
   Wǒ de shǒujī zài lùshang diūdiào le. Zhēn máfan.
g. 饭做好了，可以吃了。/ 飯做好了，可以吃了。Fàn zuòhǎo le, kěyǐ chī le.
h. 他每个字都写错了。/ 他每個字都寫錯了。Tā měi gè zì dōu xiěcuò le.

2
a. 我记不住他的名字。/ 我記不住他的名字。
   Wǒ jìbuzhù tā de míngzi.
b. 我们已经做完了今天的功课。我們已經做完了今天的功課。
   Wǒmen yǐjing zuòwánle jīntiān de gōngkè.
c. 今天的功课，你一个钟头做得完做不完？
   今天的功课，你一個鐘頭做得完做不完？
   Jīntiān de gōngkè, nǐ yī ge zhōngtou zuòde wán zuò bù wán?
d. 一个钟头做不完。一個鐘頭做不完。Yīge zhōngtou zuòbuwán.
e. 我打不开窗户。你打得开吗？
   我打不開窗戶。你打得開嗎？
   Wǒ dǎbukāi chuānghu. Nǐ dǎdekāi ma?
f. 我还没洗完衣服。（我还没把衣服洗完。）
   我還沒洗完衣服。（我還沒把衣服洗完。）
   Wǒ hái méi xǐwán yīfu. (Wǒ hái méi bǎ yīfu xǐwán.)

g. 这件衬衫很脏。你想你洗得干净吗？

這件襯衫很髒。你想你洗得乾淨嗎？

Zhè jiàn chènshān hěn zāng. Nǐ xiǎng nǐ xǐde gānjìng ma?

h. 你刚说的话我没有听清楚。

你剛說的話我沒有聽清楚。

Nǐ gāng shuō de huà wǒ méi yǒu tīng qīngchu.

i. 我听不懂老师说的话。

我聽不懂老師說的話。

Wǒ tīngbudǒng lǎoshī shuō de huà.

j. 倪买得起买不起飞机票？

你買得起買不起飛機票？

Nǐ mǎideqǐ mǎibuqǐ fēijīpiào?

3 a. 你来得及来不及？ / 你來得及來不及？ **Nǐ láidejí láibují?**

b. 这些书你拿得动拿不动？ / 這些書你拿得動拿不動？ **Zhè xiē shū nǐ nádedòng nábudòng?**

c. 你找到了工作没有？ / 你找到了工作沒有？ **Nǐ zhǎodào le gōngzuò méi yǒu?**

d. 你看得见看不见？ / 你看得見看不見？ **Nǐ kàndejiàn kànbujiàn?**

4 a. 找不到 **zhǎobudào**

b. 吃完 **chīwán**

c. 吃完 **chīwán**

d. 买不到/買不到 **mǎibùdào**; 卖完/賣完 **màiwán**

5 a. 会/會 **huì**

b. 完 **wán**

c. 饱/飽 **bǎo**

d. 住 **zhù**

e. 掉 **diào**

f. 到 **dào**

6 a. 他吃不了东西。 / 他吃不了東西。 **Tā chībuliǎo dōngxi.**

b. 他每天要做的事情都记不住。他每天要做的事情都記不住。

Tā měitiān yào zuò de shìqing dōu jìbuzhù.

c. 他看不清楚。他看不清楚。 **Tā kànbùqīngchu.**

d. 他找不到手机。他找不到手機。 **Tā zhǎobudào shǒujī.**

e. 别人说的话他听不懂。別人說的話他聽不懂。 **Biéren shuō de huà tā tīngbudǒng.**

7 a. 我找到鞋子就来。我找到鞋子就來。 **Wǒ zhǎodào xiézi jiù lái.**

b. 我洗了澡就来。我洗了澡就來。 **Wǒ xǐ le zǎo jiù lái.**

c. 我买到书就来。我買到書就來。 **Wǒ mǎidàoshū jiù lái.**

d. 我扔掉衣服就来。我扔掉衣服就來。 **Wǒ rēngdiào yīfu jiù lái.**

e. 我把闹钟修好就来。我把鬧鐘修好就來。 **Wǒ bǎ nàozhōng xiūhǎo jiù lái.**

19 Directional verbs

1
a. Stand up (站)起来/(站)起來 (zhàn) qǐlái
b. Go in 进去/進去 jìnqù
c. Come out 出来/出來 chūlái
d. Lie down 躺下 tǎngxià
e. Lie down on your stomach 趴下 pāxià
f. Jump over (jump past) it 跳过去/跳過去 tiào guòqù
g. Come here (come towards me) 过来/過來 guòlái

2
a. Don't lie down! 不可以躺下 bù kěyǐ tǎngxià
b. Don't run out! 不可以跑出去 bù kěyǐ pǎo chūqù
c. Don't climb up! 不可以爬上去 bù kěyǐ pá shàngqù
d. Don't jump down! 不可以跳下来/不可以跳下來 bù kěyǐ tiào xiàlái

3
a. 起来/起來 qǐlái
b. 起来/起來 qǐlái
c. 下去 xiàqù
d. 下去 xiàqù
e. 起来/起來 qǐlái; 起来/起來 qǐlái
f. 起来/起來 qǐlái

4
a. 起来/起來 qǐlái
b. 出来/出來 chūlái
c. 下去 xiàqù
d. 起来/起來 qǐlái
e. 起来/起來 qǐlái
f. 起来/起來 qǐlái
g. 上去 shàngqù
h. 下去 xiàqù
i. 出来/出來 chūlái
j. 起来/起來 qǐlái *or* 下来/下來 xiàlái

5
a. 我跑回学校来。
   我跑回學校來。
   Wǒ pǎohuí xuéxiào lái.
   I will run back to school.
b. 我跑回家来。
   我跑回家來。
   Wǒ pǎohuí jiā lái.
   I will run back home.
c. 我跑下楼来。
   我跑下樓來。
   Wǒ pǎo xià lóu lái.
   I will run downstairs.

d. 我跑上山来。
   我跑上山來。
   Wǒ pǎoshàng shān lái.
   I will run up the hill.

e. 我跑出图书馆来。
   我跑出圖書館來。
   Wǒ pǎochū túshūguǎn lái.
   I will run out of the library.

f. 我跑回宿舍来。
   我跑回宿舍來。
   Wǒ pǎohuí sùshè lái.
   I will run back to the dorm.

g. 我跑进教室来。
   我跑進教室來。
   Wǒ pǎojìn jiàoshì lái.
   I will run into the classroom.

h. 我跑过马路来。
   我跑過馬路來。
   Wǒ pǎoguò mǎlù lái.
   I will run across the street.

20 把 bǎ sentences

1

a. 小王把书还给图书馆了。
   小王把書還給圖書館了。
   Xiǎo Wàng bǎ shū huán gěi túshūguǎn le.
   Xiao Wang returned the book to the library.

b. 大伟把车开回家了。
   大偉把車開回家了。
   Dà Wěi bǎ chē kāi huí jiā le.
   David drove the car home.

c. 小李把衣服洗干净了。
   小李把衣服洗乾淨了。
   Xiǎo Lǐ bǎ yīfu xǐ gānjing le.
   Xiao Li washed the clothes clean.

d. 老师把窗户开开了。
   老師把窗戶開開了。
   Lǎoshī bǎ chuānghu kāikāi le.
   The teacher opened the window.

e. 我把课本买到了。
   我把課本買到了
   Wǒ bǎ kèběn mǎidào le.
   I was successful in buying the textbook.

f. 弟弟把功课做完了。
    弟弟把功課做完了。
    Dìdi bǎ gōngkè zuòwán le.
    Younger brother finished doing his homework.

g. 张明把我的电脑用坏了。
    張明把我的電腦用壞了。
    Zhāng Míng bǎ wǒ de diànnǎo yòng huài le.
    Zhang Ming used my computer until it was broken.

h. 他把他的汽车卖了。
    他把他的汽車賣了。
    Ta bǎ tā de qìchē mài le.
    He sold his car.

2

a. 小王没把书还给图书馆。
    小王沒把書還給圖書館。
    Xiǎo Wàng méi bǎ shū huán gěi túshūguǎn.
    Xiao Wang did not return the book to the library.

b. 大伟没把车开回家。
    大偉沒把車開回家。
    Dà Wěi méi bǎ chē kāi huí jiā.
    David did not drive the car home.

c. 小李没把衣服洗干净。
    小李沒把衣服洗乾淨。
    Xiǎo Lǐ méi bǎ yīfu xǐ gānjing.
    Xiao Li did not wash the clothes clean.

d. 老师没把窗户开开。
    老師沒把窗戶開開。
    Lǎoshī méi bǎ chuānghu kāikāi.
    The teacher did not open the window.

e. 我没把课本买到。
    我沒把課本買到。
    Wǒ méi bǎ kèběn mǎidào.
    I was not successful in buying the textbook.

f. 弟弟没把功课做完了。
    弟弟沒把功課做完了。
    Dìdi méi bǎ gōngkè zuòwán.
    Younger brother did not finish doing his homework.

g. 张明没把我的电脑用坏。
    張明沒把我的電腦用壞。
    Zhāng Míng méi bǎ wǒ de diànnǎo yòng huài le.
    Zhang Ming did not break my computer while using it.

h. 他没把他的汽车卖了。
    他沒把他的汽車賣了。
    Ta méi bǎ tā de qìchē mài le.
    He did not sell his car.

3

a. 他把我的书借走了。
他把我的書借走了。
Tā bǎ wǒ de shū jièzǒu le.
He borrowed (away) my book.

b. 他把饺子吃完了。
他把餃子吃完了。
Tā bǎ jiǎozi, chīwán le.
He ate all the dumplings.

c. 我把手机忘在教室了。
我把手機忘在教室了。
Wǒ bǎ shǒujī wàngzài jiāoshì le.
I forgot my cell phone in the classroom.

d. 我把电脑带来了。
我把電腦帶來了。
Wǒ bǎ diànnǎo dàilái le.
I brought the computer over.

e. 学生们把电影看完了。
學生們把電影看完了。
Xuéshēngmen bǎ diànyǐng kànwán le.
The students finished watching the movie.

f. 我的同屋把宿舍整理好了。
我的同屋把宿舍整理好了。
Wǒ de tóngwū bǎ sùshè zhěnglǐhǎo le.
My roommate tidied up our dorm.

g. 妈妈把我的衣服给洗干净了。
媽媽把我的衣服給洗乾淨了。
Māma bǎ wǒde yīfú gěi xǐgānjìng le.
My mom washed my clothes clean.

h. 我把你的椅子给搬到门外边去了。
我把你的椅子給搬到門外邊去了。
Wǒ bǎ nǐde yǐzi gěi bāndào mén wàibiān qù le.
I moved your chair outside of the door.

4

a. 不可以把这里的书拿走。
不可以把這裡的書拿走。
Bù kěyǐ bǎ zhèlǐ de shū ná zǒu.
You can't take the books from here away.

b. 他们都把外套穿好了。
他們都把外套穿好了。
Tāmen dōu bǎ wàitào chuān hǎo le.
They all put on their coats.

c. 我把所有的功课都写好了。

我把所有的功課都寫好了。

Wǒ bǎ suǒyǒu de gōngkè dōu xiě hǎo le.

I finish all the homework.

d. 不要把水果吃光。

Bù yào bǎ shuǐguǒ chī guāng.

Don't eat all the fruit.

e. 明天得把雨伞带着。

明天得把雨傘帶著。

Míngtiān děi bǎ yǔsǎn dàizhe.

Tomorrow (you) have to bring an umbrella.

5 把床单<u>洗一洗</u>，把垃圾<u>丢掉/拿出去</u>。把冬天的衣服<u>收起来</u>，把鞋子都<u>放回鞋柜去</u>，顺便把鞋柜<u>整理整理/整理一下</u>。再把晚餐的材料<u>准备好</u>。对了，如果你有时间，可以帮我把裙子<u>改短一点</u>吗？我把裙子<u>放在床上</u>了。你走之前，别忘了把钥匙<u>留下</u>。

把床單<u>洗一洗</u>，把垃圾<u>丢掉/拿出去</u>。把冬天的衣服<u>收起來</u>，把鞋子都<u>放回鞋櫃去</u>，順便把鞋櫃<u>整理整理/整理一下</u>。再把晚餐的材料<u>準備好</u>。對了，如果你有時間，可以幫我把裙子<u>改短一點</u>嗎？我把裙子<u>放在床上</u>了。你走之前，別忘了把鑰匙<u>留下</u>。

Bǎ chuángdān <u>xǐ yī xǐ</u>, bǎ lājī <u>diūdiào/náchūqù</u>. Bǎ dōngtiān de yīfu <u>shōu qǐlái</u>, bǎ xiézi dōu <u>fàng huí xiéguì qù</u>, shùnbiàn bǎ xiéguì <u>zhěnglǐ zhěnglǐ/ zhěnglǐ yīxià</u>. Zài bǎ wǎncān de cáiliào <u>zhǔnbèi hǎo</u>. Duì le, rúguǒ nǐ yǒu shíjiān, kěyǐ bāng wǒ bǎ qúnzi <u>gǎi duǎn yīdiǎn</u> ma? Wǒ bǎ qúnzi <u>fàng zài chuángshàng</u> le. Nǐ zǒu zhīqián, bié wàngle bǎ yàoshi <u>liúxia</u>.

6 a. 他把我最喜欢的花瓶打破了。

他把我最喜歡的花瓶打破了。

Tā bǎ wǒ zuì xǐhuān de huāpíng dǎpò le.

b. 他把我的功课放进洗衣机里了。

他把我的功課放進洗衣機裡了。

Tā bǎ wǒ de gōngkè fang jìn xǐyījī lǐ le.

c. 他把我的饼干都吃掉/吃光了。

他把我的餅乾都吃掉/吃光了。

Tā bǎ wǒ de bǐnggān dōu chīdiào/chīguāng le.

21 The passive

1 a. 台灯被他的同屋打破了。

臺燈被他的同屋打破了。

Táidēng bèi tā de tóngwū dǎpò le.

The desk lamp was broken by his roommate.

b. 他的电脑被小偷偷走了。

他的電腦被小偷偷走了。

Tā de diànnǎo bèi xiǎotōu tōuzǒu le.

His computer was stolen by a thief.

c. 他的钥匙让他的朋友弄丢了。
    他的鑰匙讓他的朋友弄丟了。
    Tā de yàoshi ràng tā de péngyou nòngdiū le.
    His keys were lost by his friend.

d. 他的三明治让他的狗吃掉了。
    他的三明治讓他的狗吃掉了。
    Tā de sānmíngzhì ràng tā de gǒu chīdiào le.
    His sandwich was eaten by his dog.

e. 字典被他用坏了。
    字典被他用壞了。
    Zìdiǎn bèi tā yònghuài le.
    His dictionary fell apart on him. (. . . was used by him until it fell apart)

f. 他的自行车让人家碰坏了。
    他的自行車讓人家碰壞了。
    Tā de zìxíngchē ràng rénjiā pènghuài le.
    His bike was hit and destroyed by someone.

g. 他让他的教练骂了。
    他讓他的教練罵了。
    Tā ràng tā de jiàoliàn mà le.
    He was scolded by his coach.

h. 他的衣服让猫撕破了。
    他的衣服讓貓撕破了。
    Tā de yīfu ràng māo sīpò le.
    His clothing was torn by the cat.

2 a. 他的同屋把台灯打破了。
    他的同屋把臺燈打破了。
    Tā de tóngwū bǎ táidēng dǎpò le.
    His roommate broke his desk lamp.

b. 小偷把他的电脑偷走了。
    小偷把他的電腦偷走了。
    Xiǎotōu bǎ tā de diànnǎo tōuzǒu le.
    A thief stole his computer.

c. 他的朋友把他的钥匙弄丢了。
    他的朋友把他的鑰匙弄丟了。
    Tā de péngyou bǎ tā de yàoshi nòngdiū le.
    His friend lost his keys.

d. 他的狗把他的三明治吃掉了。
    Tā de gǒu bǎ tā de sānmíngzhì chīdiào le.
    His dog ate his sandwich.

e. 他把字典用坏了。
    他把字典用壞了。
    Tā bǎ zìdiǎn yònghuài le.
    He destroyed the dictionary through use.

f. 人家把他的自行车碰坏了。
人家把他的自行車碰壞了。
Rénjiā bǎ tā de zìxíngchē pènghuài le.
Someone hit and destroyed his bike.

g. 他的教练把他骂了。
他的教練把他罵了。
Tā de jiàoliàn bǎ tā mà le.
His coach scolded him.

h. 猫把他的衣服撕破了。
貓把他的衣服撕破了。
Māo bǎ tā de yīfu sīpò le.
The cat tore his clothing.

3

a. 我被解雇了。
Wǒ bèi jiěgù le.

b. 我的房子被火烧了。
我的房子被火燒了。
Wǒ de fángzi bèi huǒ shāo le.

c. 我的窗户被打破了。
Wǒ de chuānghù bèi dǎ pò le.

d. 我来的时候被抢了。
我來的時候被搶了。
Wǒ lái de shíhou bèi qiǎng le.

B Situations and functions

22 Names, kinship terms, titles, and terms of address

1

a. (i) 赵先生/趙先生 Zhào xiānsheng
(ii) 赵小姐/趙小姐 Zhào xiǎojie
(iii) 赵太太/趙太太 Zhào tàitai

b. 老赵/老趙 Lǎo Zhào

c. 西杰 Xījié

d. (i) 姐姐 jiějie
(ii) 哥哥 gēge

e. 我家有六口人，爸爸，妈妈，哥哥，妹妹，弟弟和我。我爸爸 45 岁。
妈妈 43 岁。哥哥 20 岁。妹妹 16 岁。弟弟 14 岁。我 18 岁。
我家有六口人，爸爸，媽媽，哥哥，妹妹，弟弟和我。我爸爸 45 歲。
媽媽 43 歲。哥哥 20 歲。妹妹 16 歲。弟弟 14 歲。我 18 歲。
Wǒ jiā yǒu liù kǒu rén, bàba, māma, gēge, mèimei, dìdi hé wǒ.
Wǒ bàba 45 suì. Māma 43 suì. Gēge 20 suì. Mèimei 16 suì.
Dìdi 14 suì. Wǒ 18 suì.

f. 我有一个哥哥，一个姐姐和一个弟弟。我哥哥 20 岁，他叫赵明智。

姐姐 18 岁，她叫赵西杰。弟弟 14 岁，他叫赵明义。

我有一個哥哥，一個姐姐和一個弟弟。我哥哥 20 歲，他叫趙明智。

姐姐 18 歲，她叫趙西杰。弟弟 14 歲，他叫趙明義。

Wǒ yǒu yī gè gēgē, yīgè jiějie hé yī gè dìdi. Wǒ gēgē 20 suì, tā jiào Zhào Míngzhì. Jiějie 18 suì, tā jiào Zhào Xījié. Dìdi 14 suì, tā jiào Zhào Míngyì.

g. 我有一个哥哥，两个姐姐。哥哥 20 岁，他叫赵明智。大姐 18 岁，

她叫赵西杰。二姐 16 岁，她叫赵西清。我 14 岁，我叫赵明义。

我有一個哥哥，兩個姐姐。哥哥 20 歲，他叫趙明智。大姐 18 歲，

她叫趙西杰。二姐 16 歲，她叫趙西清。我 14 歲，我叫趙明義。

Wǒ yǒu yī gè gēgē, liǎng gè jiějie. Gēgē 20 suì, tā jiào Zhào Míngzhì. Dàjie 18 suì, tā jiào Zhào Xījié. Èrjiě 16 suì, tā jiào Zhào Xīqīng. Wǒ 14 suì, wǒ jiào Zhào Míngyì.

h. 叔叔是爸爸的弟弟。

Shūshu shì bàbà de dìdi. Male, same generation as your father.

i. 奶奶是爸爸的妈妈。

Nǎinai shì bàba de māma. Female, same generation as the child's grandmother.

j. (i)   请问，您贵姓？

请問，您貴姓？

Qǐng wèn, nín guìxìng?

(ii) 我姓赵。

我姓趙。

Wǒ xìng Zhào.

(iii) 你叫什么名字？

你叫甚麼名字？

Nǐ jiào shénme míngzì?

(iv) 我应该怎么称呼你？

我應該怎麼稱呼你？

Wǒ yīnggāi zěnme chēnghu nǐ?

2 a. Guo Mingzhi b. 010-65666557（手机：13196118888）c. Gold Mountain International Garden d. 010-6566555

23   Introductions

1

你：   周利，这位是王明，我的同学。他是学经济的。他会说英文。王明，

这位是周利，也是学生。他是我的堂弟，是学语言学的。他会说日文。

你：   周利，這位是王明，我的同學。他是學經濟的。他會說英文。王明，

這位是周利，也是學生。他是我的堂弟，是學語言學的。他會說日文。

Nǐ: **Zhōu Lì, zhè wèi shì Wáng Míng, wǒ de tóngxué. Tā shì xué jīngjì de. Tā huì shuō Yīngwén. Wáng Míng, zhè wèi shì Zhōu Lì, yě shì xuésheng. Tā shì wǒ de tángdì, shì xué yǔyánxué de. Tā huì shuō Rìwén.**

王 Wáng: 你好。Nǐ hǎo.

周 Zhōu: 你好。Nǐ hǎo.

2

你：　　　　　　我给你们介绍介绍。这位是林教授。这位是张医生。
你：　　　　　　我給你們介紹介紹。這位是林教授。這位是張醫生。
Nǐ:　　　　　　Wǒ gěi nǐmen jièshào jièshào. Zhè wèi shì Lín jiàoshòu.
　　　　　　　　Zhè wèi shì Zhāng yīshēng.
林教授：　　　久闻大名。
林教授：　　　久聞大名。
Lín jiàoshòu:　Jiǔ wén dà míng.
张医生：　　　彼此，彼此。
張醫生：　　　彼此，彼此。
Zhāng yīshēng: Bícǐ, bícǐ.

3

a. 你好。我是周利，是山东人。
　　你好。我是周利，是山東人。
　　Nǐ hǎo. Wǒ shì Zhōu Lì, shì Shāndōng rén.

b. 我很高兴认识你。希望我们今年能合作，互相帮助。
　　我很高興認識你。希望我們今年能合作，互相幫助。
　　Wǒ hěn gāoxìng rènshi nǐ. Xīwàng wǒmen jīnnián néng hézuò,
　　hùxiāng bāngzhù.

c. 我是学化学的。
　　我是學化學的。
　　Wǒ shì xué huàxué de.

d. 真巧!
　　Zhēn qiǎo!

24 Greetings and goodbyes

1

a. 4 b. 7 c. 5 d. 2 e. 1 f. 6 g. 3

2

a. 再见。/再見。Zài jiàn. b. 一会儿见。/一會兒見。Yīhuìr jiàn.
c. 回头见。/回頭見。Huí tóu jiàn. d. 明天见。/明天見。Míngtiān jiàn.
e. 下星期见。/下星期見。Xià xīngqī jiàn.

3

a. *Greeting:*　　伟强兄如晤：
　　　　　　　　偉强兄如晤：
　　　　　　　　Wěiqiáng xiōng rúwù:
　Goodbye:　　新年快乐。弟，绪武。
　　　　　　　　新年快樂。弟，緒武。
　　　　　　　　Xīnnián kuàilè. Dì, Xùwǔ.

b. *Greeting:*　　唐老师惠鉴：
　　　　　　　　唐老師惠鑒：
　　　　　　　　Táng lǎoshī huìjiàn:
　Goodbye:　　敬颂夏安。学生张晓春谨禀。
　　　　　　　　敬頌夏安。學生張曉春謹禀。
　　　　　　　　Jìngsòng xià ān. Xuésheng Zhāng Xiǎochūn jǐnbǐng.

4

a. 我找王明。

Wǒ zhǎo Wáng Míng.

b. 王明，好久不见。你最近忙什么呢？

王明，好久不見。你最近忙甚麼呢？

Wáng Míng, hǎo jiǔ bù jiàn. Nǐ zuì jìn máng shénme ne?

c. 你去澳大利亚吗？一路顺风。

你去澳大利亞嗎？一路順風。

Nǐ qù Aòdàlìyà ma? Yī lù shùn fēng.

d. 回来再见。

回來再見。

Huí lai zài jiàn.

25 Basic strategies for communication

1

a. 4 b. 6 c. 8 d. 1 e. 7 f. 9 g. 3 h. 2 i. 5

2

a. 司机，麻烦你。王府井离这儿远吗？

司機，麻煩你。王府井離這兒遠嗎？

Sījī, máfan nǐ. Wángfǔjǐng lí zhèr yuǎn ma?

b. 对不起，我不懂。请你再说。

對不起，我不懂。請你再說。

Duìbuqǐ, wǒ bù dǒng. Qǐng nǐ zài shuō.

c. 真对不起。请你说慢一点。

真對不起。請你說慢一點。

Zhēn duìbuqǐ. Qǐng nǐ shuō màn yīdiǎn.

d. 懂了，懂了。谢谢你。

懂了，懂了。謝謝你。

Dǒng le, dǒng le. Xièxie nǐ.

3

a. 弟 b. 氵 c. 李 d. 章 e. 陈/陳 f. 王

4

首先；还有；比方说；至于；总而言之

首先；還有；比方說；至於；總而言之

shǒuxiān; háiyǒu; bǐfāngshuō; zhìyú; zǒngéryánzhī

5

(Free response.)

26 Telecommunications and e-communications: telephones, the internet, and faxes

1

a. 六二一九一〇七四

liù èr yī jiǔ yī líng qī sì

b. 一三六五一二八一一八〇

yī sān liù wǔ yī èr bā yī yī bā líng

c. 六七一七九四六九

liù qī yī qī jiǔ sì liù jiǔ

2

Conversation A

You: 我找王明。Wǒ zhǎo Wáng Míng.

You: 请他给我回电话。我的手机号码是一三五〇一三二七八〇六。

請他給我回電話。我的手機號碼是一三五〇一三二七八〇六。

Qǐng tā gěi wǒ huí diànhuà. Wǒ de shǒujī hàomǎ shì yī sān wǔ líng yī sān èr qī bā líng liù.

Conversation B

You: 王明在吗？/ 王明在嗎？Wáng Míng zài ma?

You: 请他给我发电子信（电子邮件）。

請他給我發電子信（電子郵件）。

Qǐng tā gěi wǒ fā diànzǐ xìn (diànzǐ yóujiàn).

Conversation C

You: 请王明讲话。/ 請王明講話。Qǐng Wáng Míng jiǎng huà.

You: 好，我会给他发个短信。

好，我會給他發個短信。

Hǎo, wǒ huì gěi tā fā gè duǎnxìn.

3

a. 请你再拨一次。

請你再撥一次。

Qǐng nǐ zài bō yī cì.

b. 请你留言。

請你留言。

Qǐng nǐ liú yán.

c. 去网吧上网。

去網吧上網。

Qù wǎngbā shàng wǎng.

d. 给我发个短信。

給我發個短信。

Gěi wǒ fā gè duǎnxìn.

e. 请打他的手机。

請打他的手機。

Qǐng dǎ tā de shǒujī.

f. 打开附加件。

打開附加件。

Dǎkāi fùjiājiàn.

g. 进行视频通话。

進行視頻通話。

Jìnxíng shìpín tōnghuà.

4   发/發 fā, 打 dǎ, 发/發 fā

5   附加件 fùjiā jiàn, 在 zài, 留话/留話 liú huà, 发/發 fā, 输入/輸入 shūrù

27   Negating information

1   a.   我不要跟他们吃饭。
我不要跟他們吃飯。
Wǒ bù yào gēn tāmen chī fàn.

b.   我听不懂他的话。
我聽不懂他的話。
Wǒ tīngbùdǒng tā de huà.

c.   我不愿意跟他结婚。
我不願意跟他結婚。
Wǒ bù yuànyi gēn tā jiéhūn.

d.   我还没决定买什么。
我還沒決定買甚麼。
Wǒ hái méi juédìng mǎi shénme.

e.   我不常来这里。
我不常來這裏。
Wǒ bù cháng lái zhèlǐ.

f.   我根本没有钱。
我根本沒有錢。
Wǒ gēnběn méi yǒu qián.

g.   我不在餐厅吃饭。
我不在餐廳吃飯。
Wǒ bù zài cāntīng chī fàn.

h.   我们都不会说广东话。
我們都不會說廣東話。
Wǒmen dōu bù huì shuō Guǎngdōng huà.

i.   我没听懂他的话。
我沒聽懂他的話。
Wǒ méi tīngdǒng tā de huà.

2   a.   我不喜欢面条。
我不喜歡麵條。
Wǒ bù xǐhuan miàntiáo.

b.   我没有朋友。
Wǒ méi yǒu péngyou.

c.   我没做功课。
我沒做功課。
Wǒ méi zuò gōngkè.

d. 我不高。
   Wǒ bù gāo.
e. 我昨天不忙。
   Wǒ zuótiān bù máng.
f. 我从来没听过那首歌。
   我從來沒聽過那首歌。
   Wǒ cónglái méi tīngguo nà shǒu gē.
g. 家里没人。
   家裏沒人。
   Jiāli méi rén.
h. 昨天没下雨。
   Zuótiān méi xià yǔ.
i. 我不会开车。
   我不會開車。
   Wǒ bù huì kāi chē.
j. 我大学还没毕业。
   我大學還沒畢業。
   Wǒ dàxué hái méi bìyè.

3 a. 3 b. 4 c. 5 d. 1 e. 2 f. 7 g. 6

4

Tom: 我没有女朋友。我不认识任何女孩子。
          我沒有女朋友。我不認識任何女孩子。
          Wǒ méi yǒu nǚ péngyou. Wǒ bù rènshi rènhé nǚ háizi.

Collins: 我从来没去过 / 参加过舞会。
          我從來沒去過 / 參加過舞會。
          Wǒ cónglái méi qùguò / cānjiāguò wǔhuì.

Jackie: 我今年三十五岁，可是我不会开车。
          我今年三十五歲，可是我不會開車。
          Wǒ jīnnián sānshíwǔ suì, kěshì wǒ bù huì kāi chē.

Abby: 我已经学中文学了两年了，可是我根本听不懂老师说什么。
          我已經學中文學了兩年了，可是我根本聽不懂老師說甚麼。
          Wǒ yǐjīng xué Zhōngwén xuéle liǎng nián le, kěshì wǒ gēnběn tīngbùdǒng lǎoshī shuō shénme.

Dennis: 我没钱了。毫无疑问，我应该得到那个布朗尼。
          我沒錢了。毫無疑問，我應該得到那個布朗尼。
          Wǒ méi qián le. Háowú yíwèn, wǒ yīnggāi dédào nà ge bùlǎngní.

Sophia: 我四十二岁，没有工作，还跟父母住在一起。无论如何我都应该得到那个布朗尼。
          我四十二歲，沒有工作，還跟父母住在一起。無論如何我都應該得到那個布朗尼。
          Wǒ sìshí'èr suì, méi yǒu gōngzuò, hái gēn fùmǔ zhù zài yīqǐ.
          Wúlùn rúhé wǒ dōu yīnggāi dédào nàge bùlǎngní.

YOU:

28 Asking questions and replying to questions

1

a. 你想去中国吗？
你想去中國嗎？
Nǐ xiǎng qù Zhōngguó ma?
Do you want to go to China?

b. 她有男朋友吗？
Tā yǒu nán péngyou ma?
Does she have a boyfriend?

c. 你吃过生鱼片吗？
你吃過生魚片嗎？
Nǐ chīguò shēngyúpiàn ma?
Have you eaten sashimi (raw fish slices) before?

d. 他们会说中国话吗？
他們會說中國話嗎？
Tāmen huì shuō Zhōngguó huà ma?
Can they speak Chinese?

e. 他是英国人吗？
他是英國人嗎？
Tā shì Yīngguó rén ma?
Is he English?

f. 你喜欢旅行吗？
你喜歡旅行嗎？
Nǐ xǐhuan lǚxíng ma?
Do you like to travel?

g. 中国人爱唱歌儿吗？
中國人愛唱歌兒嗎？
Zhōngguó rén ài chàng gēr ma?
Do Chinese people love to sing?

h. 他每天在公园跑步吗？
他每天在公園跑步嗎？
Tā měitiān zài gōngyuán pǎo bù ma?
Does he jog in the park every day?

2

a. 你想不想去中国？
你想不想去中國？
Nǐ xiǎng bù xiǎng qù Zhōngguó?

b. 她有没有男朋友？
Tā yǒu méi yǒu nán péngyou?

c. 你吃过没吃过生鱼片？
你吃過沒吃過生魚片？
Nǐ chīguò méi chīguò shēngyúpiàn?

d. 他们会不会说中国话？
他們會不會說中國話？
Tāmen huì bù huì shuō Zhōngguó huà?

e. 他是不是英国人？
他是不是英國人？
Tā shì bù shì Yīngguó rén?

f. 你喜欢不喜欢旅行？
你喜歡不喜歡旅行？
Nǐ xǐhuan bù xǐhuan lǚxíng?

g. 中国人爱不爱唱歌儿？
中國人愛不愛唱歌兒？
Zhōngguó rén ài bù ài chàng gēr?

h. 他每天在不在公园跑步？
他每天在不在公園跑步？
Tā měitiān zài bù zài gōngyuán pǎo bù? (Is this where he jogs?)
or
他每天在公园跑不跑步？
他每天在公園跑不跑步？
Tā měitiān zài gōngyuán pǎo bù pǎo bù? (Is this what he does in the park?)

3

a. 你是否想去中国？
你是否想去中國？
Nǐ shìfǒu xiǎng qù Zhōngguó?

b. 她是否有男朋友？
Tā shìfǒu yǒu nán péngyou?

c. 你是否吃过生鱼片？
你是否吃過生魚片？
Nǐ shìfǒu chīguò shēngyúpiàn?

d. 他们是否会说中国话？
他們是否會說中國話？
Tāmen shìfǒu huì shuō Zhōngguó huà?

e. 他是否是英国人？
他是否是英國人？
Tā shìfǒu shì Yīngguó rén?

f. 你是否喜欢旅行？
你是否喜歡旅行？
Nǐ shìfǒu xǐhuan lǚxíng?

g. 中国人是否爱唱歌儿？
中國人是否愛唱歌兒？
Zhōngguó rén shìfǒu ài chàng gēr?

h. 他每天是否在公园跑步？
他每天是否在公園跑步？
Tā měitiān shìfǒu zài gōngyuán pǎo bù?

4

a. 是。我是学生。
是。我是學生。
Shì. Wǒ shì xuésheng.
Yes. I am a student.

b. 会。我会开车。
會。我會開車。
Huì. Wǒ huì kāi chē.
Yes. I can drive a car.

c. 喝过。我喝过中国茶。
喝過。我喝過中國茶。
Hēguò. Wǒ hēguò Zhōngguó chá.
Yes. I have drunk Chinese tea before.

d. 吃过。我吃过北京烤鸭。
吃過。我吃過北京烤鴨。
Chīguò. Wǒ chīguò Běijīng kǎoyā.
Yes. I have eaten Beijing roast duck (Peking duck) before.

e. 喜欢。我喜欢看电影。
喜歡。我喜歡看電影。
Xǐhuan. Wǒ xǐhuan kàn diànyǐng.
Yes. I like to watch movies.

f. 有。台北有地铁。
有。臺北有地鐵。
Yǒu. Táiběi yǒu dìtiě.
Yes. Taipei has a subway.

g. 漂亮。桂林的山水很漂亮。
Piàoliang. Guìlín de shānshuǐ hěn piàoliang.
Yes. Guilin's scenery is pretty.

h. 用。我用筷子吃饭。
用。我用筷子吃飯。
Yòng. Wǒ yòng kuàizi chī fàn.
Yes. I use chopsticks to eat.

5

a. 不是。我不是学生。
不是。我不是學生。
Bù shì. Wǒ bù shì xuésheng.
No. I am not a student.

b. 不会。我不会开车。
不會。我不會開車。
Bù huì. Wǒ bù huì kāi chē.
No. I can't drive a car.

c. 没喝过。我没喝过中国茶。
沒喝過。我沒喝過中國茶。
Méi hēguò. Wǒ méi hēguò Zhōngguó chá.
No. I haven't drunk Chinese tea before.

d. 没吃过。我没吃过北京烤鸭。

没吃過。我沒吃過北京烤鴨。

Méi chīguò. Wǒ méi chīguò Běijīng kǎoyā.

No. I have not eaten Beijing roast duck (Peking duck) before.

e. 不喜欢。我不喜欢看电影。

不喜歡。我不喜歡看電影。

Bù xǐhuan. Wǒ bù xǐhuan kàn diànyǐng.

No. I do not like to watch movies.

f. 没有。台北没有地铁。

沒有。臺北沒有地鐵。

Méi yǒu. Táiběi méi yǒu dìtiě.

No. Taipei does not have a subway.

g. 不漂亮。桂林的山水不漂亮。

Bù piàoliang. Guìlín de shānshuǐ bù piàoliang.

No. Guilin's scenery is not pretty.

h. 不用。我不用筷子吃饭。

不用。我不用筷子吃飯。

Bù yòng. Wǒ bù yòng kuàizi chī fàn.

No. I do not use chopsticks to eat.

6

a. 你喜欢吃中餐还是西餐？

你喜歡吃中餐還是西餐？

Nǐ xǐhuan chī Zhōngcān háishi xīcān?

Do you like to eat Chinese food or Western food?

b. 你是学生还是老师？

你是學生還是老師？

Nǐ shì xuésheng háishi lǎoshī?

Are you a student or a teacher?

c. 你学中国文学还是学英国文学？

你學中國文學還是學英國文學？

Nǐ xué Zhōngguó wénxué háishi xué Yīngguó wénxué?

Do you study Chinese literature or English literature?

d. 你是二十一岁还是二十二岁？

你是二十一歲還是二十二歲？

Nǐ shì èrshíyī suì háishi èrshíèr suì?

Are you 21 years old or 22?

e. 你喜欢看电视还是喜欢听收音机？

你喜歡看電視還是喜歡聽收音機？

Nǐ xǐhuan kàn diànshì háishi xǐhuan tīng shōuyīnjī?

Do you like to watch TV or listen to radio?

f. 你上高中还是上大学？

你上高中還是上大學？

Nǐ shàng gāozhōng háishi shàng dàxué?

Are you in high school or in college?

7

a. 我喜欢吃西餐。你喜欢吃西餐吗？
　　我喜歡吃西餐。你喜歡吃西餐嗎？
　　Wǒ xǐhuan chī xīcān. Nǐ xǐhuan chī xīcān ma?

b. 我是学生。你是学生吗？
　　我是學生。你是學生嗎？
　　Wǒ shì xuésheng. Nǐ shì xuésheng ma?

c. 我学中国文学。你学中国文学吗？
　　我學中國文學。你學中國文學嗎？
　　Wǒ xué Zhōngguó wénxué. Nǐ xué Zhōngguó wénxué ma?

d. 我喜欢看电视。你喜欢看电视吗？
　　我喜歡看電視。你喜歡看電視嗎？
　　Wǒ xǐhuan kàn diànshì. Nǐ xǐhuan kàn diànshì ma?

e. 我上大学。你上大学吗？
　　我上大學。你上大學嗎？
　　Wǒ shàng dàxué. Nǐ shàng dàxué ma?

f. 我爱看中国电影。你爱看中国电影吗？
　　我愛看中國電影。你愛看中國電影嗎？
　　Wǒ ài kàn Zhōngguó diànyǐng. Nǐ ài kàn Zhōngguó diànyǐng ma?

g. 我不抽烟。你抽烟吗？
　　我不抽煙。你抽煙嗎？
　　Wǒ bù chōu yān. Nǐ chōu yān ma?

h. 我去过中国。你去过中国吗？
　　我去過中國。你去過中國嗎？
　　Wǒ qùguò Zhōngguó. Nǐ qùguò Zhōngguó ma?

8

a. 地铁票多少钱？
　　地鐵票多少錢？
　　Dìtiě piào duōshao qián?
　　How much is a subway ticket?

b. 哥哥特别喜欢吃什么？
　　哥哥特別喜歡吃甚麼？
　　Gēgē tèbié xǐhuan chī shénme?
　　What does older brother particularly like to eat?

c. 现在几点钟？
　　現在幾點鐘？
　　Xiànzài jǐdiǎn zhōng?
　　What time is it now?

d. 他在美国住了多久？
　　他在美國住了多久？
　　Tā zài Měiguó zhù le duō jiǔ?
　　How long did he live in America?

e. 她是哪国人？
她是哪國人？
Tā shì nǎguó rén?
Which country does she come from?

f. 北海公园在哪儿？
北海公園在哪兒？
Běihǎi gōngyuán zài nǎr?
Where is Beihai Park?

g. 你有几个同屋？
你有幾個同屋？
Nǐ yǒu jǐge tóngwū?
How many roommates do you have?

h. 你跟谁一起租一个房子？
你跟誰一起租一個房子？
Nǐ gēn shéi yīqǐ zū yīgè fángzi?
With whom are you renting a house?

9

a. 你为什么不愿意穿高跟鞋？
你爲甚麼不願意穿高跟鞋？
Nǐ wèishénme bù yuànyì chuān gāogēnxié?

b. 你昨天晚上几点钟回家的？
你昨天晚上幾點鐘回家的？
Nǐ zuótiān wǎnshang jǐdiǎn zhōng huí jiā de?

c. 你在哪儿上大学？
你在哪兒上大學？
Nǐ zài nǎr shàng dàxué?

d. 你的中文班有多少学生？
你的中文班有多少學生？
Nǐ de Zhōngwén bān yǒu duōshao xuésheng?

e. 你每天在什么地方停车？
你每天在甚麼地方停車？
Nǐ měitiān zài shénme dìfang tíng chē?

f. 巴黎离伦敦有多远？
巴黎離倫敦有多遠？
Bālí lí Lúndūn yǒu duō yuǎn?

g. 这个车能坐几个人？
這個車能坐幾個人？
Zhège chē néng zuò jǐ gè rén?

h. 今天是几月几号？
今天是幾月幾號？
Jīntiān shì jǐ yuè jǐ hào?

10

a. 你在哪儿学中文？
你在哪兒學中文？
Nǐ zài nǎr xué Zhōngwén?

b. 你什么时候吃晚饭？
你甚麼時候吃晚飯？
Nǐ shènme shíhòu chī wǎnfàn?

c. 这个商店几点开门？
這個商店幾點開門？
Zhège shāngdiàn jǐdiǎn kāi mén?

d. 你学了多长时间的中文了？ *or* 你学中文学了多长时间？
你學了多長時間的中文了？ *or* 你學中文學了多長時間？
Nǐ xué le duō cháng shíjiān de Zhōngwén le? *or*
Nǐ xué Zhōngwén xuéle duō cháng shíjiān?

e. 你请了几个人吃晚饭？
你請了幾個人吃晚飯？
Nǐ qǐng le jǐ ge rén chī wǎnfàn?

f. 你认识谁？
你認識誰？
Nǐ rènshi shéi?

g. 你为什么想看那个电影？
你爲甚麼想看那個電影？
Nǐ wéishénme xiǎng kàn nàge diànyǐng?

h. 他们有几个孩子？
他們有幾個孩子？
Tāmen yǒu jǐ ge háizi?

11

a. 你要在上海待多久？ **Nǐ yào zài Shànghǎi dāi duōjiǔ?**

b. 你来过中国吗？ / 你來過中國嗎？ **Nǐ lái guo Zhōngguó ma?**

c. 中文难学吗？为什么？ / 中文難學嗎？為什麼？ **Zhōngwén nán xué ma? Wèishénme?**

d. 你最想吃什么中国菜？ / 你最想吃什麼中國菜？ **Nǐ zuì xiǎng chī shénme Zhōngguó cài?**

e. 你能不能多告诉我们一点关于这个角色的事情？ / 你能不能多告訴我們一點關於這個角色的事情？ **Nǐ néng bù néng duō gàosu wǒmen yī diǎn guānyú zhège juésè de shìqing?**

29 Expressing identification, possession, and existence

1

a. 在 **zài** b. 有 **yǒu** c. 是 **shì** d. 在 **zài** e. 是 **shì** f. 在 **zài** g. 有 **yǒu** h. 是 **shì** i. 有 **yǒu** j. 在 **zài**

2

a. my older brother's girlfriend b. your new car c. our foreign language teacher d. the child's mom e. my younger brother's roommate's friend f. my friend's roommate's younger brother g. teacher Zhang's younger sister's student h. teacher Zhang's student's younger sister

3

a. 她的很漂亮的女孩子
tā de hěn piàoliang de nǚ háizi

b. 我的中文课本
我的中文課本
wǒ de Zhōngwén kèběn

c. 你的外国朋友
你的外國朋友
nǐ de wàiguó péngyou

d. 我城里的房子
我城裏的房子
wǒ chénglǐ de fángzi

e. 她的和气的朋友
她的和氣的朋友
tā de héqì de péngyou

f. 我的很舒服的鞋子
wǒ de hěn shūfu de xiézi

4 在 zài; 有 yǒu; 有 yǒu; 是 shì; 在 zài; 在 zài; 有 yǒu; 是 shì

5 (Free response.)

30 Describing people, places, and things

1

a. 王明十八岁。
王明十八歲。
Wáng Míng shíbā suì.

b. 王明是学生。
王明是學生。
Wáng Míng shì xuésheng.

c. 王明很聪明。
王明很聰明。
Wáng Míng hěn cōngming.

d. 王明很高。
Wáng Míng hěn gāo.

e. 王明是加拿大人。
Wáng Míng shì Jiānádà rén.

2

a. 他多大？
Tā duō dà?

b. 他说哪国话？
他說哪國話？
Tā shuō nǎguó huà?

c. 他是哪国人？
他是哪國人？
Tā shì nǎguó rén?

d. 他喜欢什么电影？
他喜歡甚麼電影？
Tā xǐhuan shénme diànyǐng?

e. 他的生日是几月几号？
他的生日是幾月幾號？
Tā de shēngri shì jǐ yuè jǐ hào?

f. 他有几个弟弟？
他有幾個弟弟？
Tā yǒu jǐ gè dìdi?

g. 他每年去哪儿？
他每年去哪兒？
Tā měinián qù nǎr?

h. 他买了一本什么字典？
他買了一本甚麼字典？
Tā mǎi le yī běn shénme zìdiǎn?

3

a. 书是用纸做的。
書是用紙做的。
Shū shì yòng zhǐ zuò de.

b. 糖果是用糖做的。
Tángguǒ shì yòng táng zuò de.

c. 馒头是用面粉做的。
饅頭是用麪粉做的。
Mántou shì yòng miànfěn zuò de.

d. 冰块是用水做的。
冰塊是用水做的。
Bīngkuài shì yòng shuǐ zuò de.

e. 房子是用木头做的。
房子是用木頭做的。
Fángzi shì yòng mùtou zuò de.

4

a. 纽约冷，下雪，气温华氏15度。
紐約冷，下雪，氣溫華氏15度。
Niǔyuē lěng, xià xuě, qìwēn huáshì 15 dù.

b. 北京多云，刮风，气温摄氏零下2度。
北京多雲，颳風，氣溫攝氏零下2度。
Běijīng duō yún, guā fēng, qìwēn shèshì língxià 2 dù.

c. 台北晴，潮湿，气温摄氏30度。
臺北晴，潮濕，氣溫攝氏30度。
Táiběi qíng, cháoshī, qìwēn shèshì 30 dù.

5

你：	医生，我不舒服。咳嗽，头很疼，也流鼻涕。
你：	醫生，我不舒服。咳嗽，頭很疼，也流鼻涕。
Nǐ:	Yīshēng, wǒ bù shūfu. Késou, tóu hěn téng, yě liú bíti.
医生：	你发不发烧？
醫生：	你發不發燒？
Yīshēng:	Nǐ fā bù fā shāo?
你：	不发烧。
你：	不發燒。
Nǐ:	Bù fā shāo.
医生：	你拉稀吗？
醫生：	你拉稀嗎？
Yīshēng:	Nǐ lā xī ma?
你：	拉稀。
Nǐ:	Lā xī.
医生：	你的肚子疼不疼？
醫生：	你的肚子疼不疼？
Yīshēng:	Nǐ de dùzi téng bù téng?
你：	不疼。
Nǐ:	Bù téng.
医生：	你感冒了。我给你开一个药方，每四个钟头吃一次。多睡觉，多喝水，最好不要吃辣的。过几天你就会好了。
醫生：	你感冒了。我給你開一個藥方，每四個鐘頭吃一次。多睡覺，多喝水，最好不吃辣的。過幾天你就會好了。
Yīshēng:	Nǐ gǎnmào le. Wǒ gěi nǐ kāi yī gè yàofāng, měi sì gè zhōngtóu chī yī cì. Duō shuì jiào, duō hē shuǐ, zuì hǎo bù yào chī là de. Guò jǐtiān nǐ jiù huì hǎo le.

31 Describing how actions are performed

1

a. 唐玫玲说得很慢。
唐玫玲說得很慢。
Táng Méilíng shuō de hěn màn.

b. 唐玫玲写得很清楚。
唐玫玲寫得很清楚。
Táng Méilíng xiě de hěn qīngchu.

c. 唐玫玲吃得很多。
Táng Méilíng chī de hěn duō.

d. 唐玫玲（开车）开得太快。
唐玫玲（開車）開得太快。
Táng Méilíng (kāi chē) kāi de tài kuài.

e. 唐玫玲学得太少。
   唐玫玲學得太少。
   Táng Méilíng xué de tài shǎo.

f. 唐玫玲(跑步)跑得很快。
   Táng Méilíng (pǎo bù) pǎo de hěn kuài.

g. 唐玫玲做饭做得很好。
   唐玫玲做飯做得很好。
   Táng Méilíng zuò fàn zuò de hěn hǎo.

h. 唐玫玲(唱歌)唱得很多。
   Táng Méilíng (chàng gē) chàng de hěn duō.

2

a. 唐玫玲说日本话说得很慢。
   唐玫玲說日本話說得很慢。
   Táng Méilíng shuō Rìběn huà shuō de hěn màn.

b. 唐玫玲写汉字写得很清楚。
   唐玫玲寫漢字寫得很清楚。
   Táng Méilíng xiě Hàn zì xiě de hěn qīngchu.

c. 唐玫玲喝茶喝得很多。
   Táng Méilíng hē chá hē de hěn duō.

d. 唐玫玲开车开得太快。
   唐玫玲開車開得太快。
   Táng Měilíng kāi chē kāi de tài kuài.

e. 唐玫玲学中文学得太少。
   唐玫玲學中文學得太少。
   Táng Méilíng xué Zhōngwén xué de tài shǎo.

f. 唐玫玲打网球打得很多。
   唐玫玲打網球打得很多。
   Táng Méilíng dǎ wǎngqiú dǎ de hěn duō.

g. 唐玫玲做中国饭做得很好。
   唐玫玲做中國飯做得很好。
   Táng Méilíng zuò Zhōngguó fàn zuò de hěn hǎo.

h. 唐玫玲唱卡拉OK唱得很多。
   Táng Méilíng chàng kǎ lā OK chàng de hěn duō.

3

a. How are her studies? b. How does she cook? c. How does she drive?
d. How does she sing? e. How does she dance? f. How does she speak English?

4

a. 她学得很好。
   她學得很好。
   Tā xué de hěn hǎo.

b. 她做菜做得非常好。
   Tā zuò cài zuò de fēicháng hǎo.

c. 她开车开得有一点慢。
   她開車開得有一點慢。
   Tā kāi chē kāi de yǒu yīdiǎn màn.

d. 她唱歌儿唱得不错。
    她唱歌兒唱得不錯。
    Tā chàng gēr chàng de bù cuò.
e. 她跳舞跳得不太好。
    Tā tiào wǔ tiào dé bù tài hǎo.
f. 她说英国话说得特别准。
    她說英國話說得特別准。
    Tā shuō Yīngguó huà shuō de tèbié zhǔn.

5 a. 唐玫玲慢慢地把门开开了。
        唐玫玲慢慢地把門開開了。
        Táng Méilíng mànmàn de bǎ mén kāikai le.
    b. 唐玫玲快快地吃完了晚饭。
        唐玫玲快快地吃完了晚飯。
        Táng Méilíng kuàikuài de chīwán le wǎnfàn.
    c. 唐玫玲偷偷地把同屋的光碟借走了。
        Táng Méilíng tōutōu de bǎ tóngwū de guāngdié jièzǒu le.
    d. 唐玫玲自愿地帮助了妹妹。
        唐玫玲自願地幫助了妹妹。
        Táng Méilíng zìyuàn de bāngzhù le mèimei.
    e. 唐玫玲匆忙地洗了盘子。
        唐玫玲匆忙地洗了盤子。
        Táng Méilíng cōngmáng de xǐ le pánzi.
    f. 唐玫玲大声地叫了朋友。
        唐玫玲大聲地叫了朋友。
        Táng Méilíng dàshēng de jiào le péngyou.
    g. 唐玫玲用心地写了论文。
        唐玫玲用心地寫了論文。
        Táng Méilíng yòngxīn de xiě le lùnwén.
    h. 唐玫玲认真地听了报告。
        唐玫玲認真地聽了報告。
        Táng Méilíng rènzhēn de tīng le bàogào.

6 a. 他说中文说得很好。法文也说得不错。/ 他說中文說得很好。法文也說得
        不錯。**Tā shuō Zhōngwén shuō de hěn hǎo, Fǎwén yě shuō de bù cuò.**
    b. 他开车开得很好。/ 他開車開得很好。**Tā kāi chē kāi de hěn hǎo.**
    c. 他跳舞跳得很好。/ 他跳舞跳得很好。**Tā tiào wǔ tiào de hěn hǎo.**
    d. 他弹钢琴弹得不错。/ 他彈鋼琴彈得不錯。 **Tā tán gāngqín tán de bù cuò.**

7 a. 他跑步跑得快不快？/ 他跑步跑得快不快？**Tā pǎo bù pǎo de kuài bù kuài?**
    b. 他写字写得漂亮吗？/ 他寫字寫得漂亮嗎？**Tā xiě zì xiě de piàoliang ma?**
    c. 他唱歌唱得怎么样？/ 他唱歌唱得怎麼樣？**Tā chàng gē chàng de zěnmeyàng?**
    d. 他说话说得清楚不清楚？/ 他說話說得清楚不清楚？**Tā shuō huà shuō de
        qīngchu bù qīngchu?**

8

安安静静地/安安靜靜地 ān'ān jìngjing de
大声地/大聲地 dàshēng de
认真地/認真地 rènzhēn de
悄悄地 qiǎoqiǎo de
急急忙忙地 jíjí mángmáng de

32　Indicating result, conclusion, potential, and extent

1

a. 饱/飽 bǎo b. 够 gòu c. 完 wán d. 完 wán e. 到 dào *or* 着/著 zháo f. 住 zhù
g. 见/見 jiàn h. 错/錯 cuò

2

a. 这课我学会了。
　　這課我學會了。
　　Zhè kè wǒ xuéhuì le.
b. 这些字我记不住。
　　這些字我記不住。
　　Zhè xiē zì wǒ jìbuzhù.
c. 我没听见。
　　我沒聽見。
　　Wǒ méi tīngjian.
d. 那本书我买不到。
　　那本書我買不到。
　　Nà běn shū wǒ mǎibudào.
e. 字典我买到了。
　　字典我買到了。
　　Zìdiǎn wǒ mǎidào le.
f. 我听得懂中文。
　　我聽得懂中文。
　　Wǒ tīngdedǒng Zhōngwén.
g. 我没听懂。
　　我沒聽懂。
　　Wǒ méi tīngdǒng.
h. 我吃不完。
　　Wǒ chībùwán.

3

a. 我买错了书。
　　我買錯了書。
　　Wǒ mǎicuò le shū.
b. 你看得见地铁站吗？
　　你看得見地鐵站嗎？
　　Nǐ kàndejiàn dìtiě zhàn ma?

c. 那本书你买到了吗？
那本書你買到了嗎？
Nà běn shū nǐ mǎidào le ma?

d. 我买到了。
我買到了。
Wǒ mǎidào le.

e. 你看完了吗？
Nǐ kànwán le ma?

f. 没有，我还没看完呢。
沒有，我還沒看完呢。
Méi yǒu, wǒ hái méi kànwán ne.

g. 你看得懂吗？
你看得懂嗎？
Nǐ kàndedǒng ma?

h. 我看得懂。
Wǒ kàndedǒng.

4

a. It is snowing. We can't go now. b. My car is broken. I can't drive it.
c. So much food. Are you able to eat it? d. He says that his hand hurts. He is
unable to write. e. All your flowers are frozen to death. They can't survive.
f. Are you able to come tomorrow? g. Listen to me and you can't go wrong.
h. I am busy today and am unable to attend your evening party.

5

a. 考不上 **kǎobushàng** b. 买不起/買不起 **mǎibuqǐ** c. 忘不了 **wàngbuliǎo**
d. 来不及/來不及 **láibují** e. 做完 **zuòwán** f. 做不了 **zuòbuliǎo**
g. 进不去/進不去 **jìnbuqù** h. 对不起/對不起 **duìbuqǐ**

6

a. 吃不完 **chībuwán** b. 学不会/學不會 **xuébuhuì** c. 看不懂 **kànbudǒng**
d. 做不对/做不對 **zuòbuduì** e. 做不了 **zuòbuliǎo** f. 找不着/找不著 **zhǎobuzháo**

7

a. 他高兴得唱起歌儿来了。
他高興得唱起歌兒來了。
Tā gāoxìng de chàng qǐ gēr lái le.

b. 我累得睡了两天。
我累得睡了兩天。
Wǒ lèi de shuì le liǎng tiān.

c. 他们忙得把吃饭都忘了。
他們忙得把吃飯都忘了。
Tāmen máng de bǎ chī fàn dōu wàng le.

d. 他饿得把饺子都吃完了。
他餓得把餃子都吃完了。
Tā è de bǎ jiǎozi dōu chīwán le.

e. 他唱得嗓子都疼了。
Tā chàng de sǎngzi dōu téng le.

f. 他走得腿都肿了。
    他走得腿都腫了。
    Tā zǒu de tuǐ dōu zhǒng le.

g. 他吃得都走不動了。
    他吃得都走不动了。
    Tā chī de dōu zǒubudòng le.

h. 这本书有意思得我简直都放不下。
    這本書有意思得我簡直都放不下。
    Zhè běn shū yǒu yì sī de wǒ jiǎnzhí dōu fàngbùxià.

8

a. 我数学已经复习完了。
    我數學已經復習完了。
    Wǒ shùxué yǐjing fùxí wán le.

b. 我化学还没学完。
    我化學還沒學完。
    Wǒ huàxué hái méi xuéwán.

c. 化学公式，我怎么记也记不住。
    化學公式，我怎麼記也記不住。
    Huàxué gōngshì, wǒ zěnme jì yě jìbuzhù.

d. 英文诗我看不懂。
    英文詩我看不懂。
    Yīngwén shī wǒ kànbudǒng.

e. 我已经把英文词汇都学会了。
    我已經把英文詞彙都學會了。
    Wǒ yǐjing bǎ Yīngwén cíhuì dōu xuéhuì le.

f. 我紧张得睡不着也吃不下。
    我緊張得睡不著也吃不下。
    Wǒ jǐnzhāng de shuìbuzháo yě chībuxià.

g. 我怎么睡也睡不着。
    我怎麼睡也睡不著。
    Wǒ zěnme shuì yě shuì bùzháo.

h. 我累得都学不了了。
    我累得都學不了了。
    Wǒ lèi de dōu xuébuliǎo le.

9

a. Homework
b. Bath
c. Dinner
d. 10 French sentences: Check the sentences. If there are errors, Lao da needs to rewrite them.
e. Dictionary: Look for the dictionary for Lao'er. If the nanny can't find it, purchase one online.
f. T-shirt: Hand wash it first. If it doesn't get clean, throw the T-shirt into the washer.

g. Soup: If there is leftover soup, put it in the refrigerator.

h. Phone call: Call Mrs. Peng if anything comes up. If Mrs. Peng does not answer the phone, leave a message.

33   Making comparisons

1

a. 王明跟周利一样高。
王明跟周利一樣高。
Wáng Míng gēn Zhōu Lì yīyàng gāo.

b. 王明比周利聪明。
王明比周利聰明。
Wáng Míng bǐ Zhōu Lì cōngming.

c. 周利没有王明快。
Zhōu Lì méi yǒu Wáng Míng kuài.

d. 王明比周利帅。
王明比周利帥。
Wáng Míng bǐ Zhōu Lì shuài.

e. 周利没有王明用功。
Zhōu Lì méi yǒu Wáng Míng yònggōng.

f. 王明跟周利一样有意思。
王明跟周利一樣有意思。
Wáng Míng gēn Zhōu Lì yīyàng yǒu yìsi.

g. 王明比周利懒。
王明比周利懶。
Wáng Míng bǐ Zhōu Lì lǎn.

h. 周利没有王明和气。
周利没有王明和氣。
Zhōu Lì méi yǒu Wáng Míng héqì.

i. 王明比周利瘦。
Wáng Míng bǐ Zhōu Lì shòu.

j. 王明跟周利一样高兴。
王明跟周利一樣高興。
Wáng Míng gēn Zhōu Lì yīyàng gāoxìng.

2

a. 王明跟周利一样聪明吗？
王明跟周利一樣聰明嗎？
Wáng Míng gēn Zhōu Lì yīyàng cōngming ma?

b. 周利比王明高吗？
周利比王明高嗎？
Zhōu Lì bǐ Wáng Míng gāo ma?

c. 王明比周利懒吗？
王明比周利懶嗎？
Wáng Míng bǐ Zhōu Lì lǎn ma?

d. 王明跟周利一样有意思吗？

王明跟周利一樣有意思嗎？

Wáng Míng gēn Zhōu Lì yīyàng yǒu yìsī ma?

e. 王明比周利帅吗？

王明比周利帥嗎？

Wáng Míng bǐ Zhōu Lì shuài ma?

3

a. 王明比周利唱歌唱得好。

Wáng Míng bǐ Zhōu Lì chàng gē chàng de hǎo.

b. 王明比周利写汉字写得好。

王明比周利寫漢字寫得好。

Wáng Míng bǐ Zhōu Lì xiě Hàn zì xiě de hǎo.

c. 王明比周利做事做得快。

Wáng Míng bǐ Zhōu Lì zuò shì zuò de kuài.

d. 王明比周利做菜做得好。

Wáng Míng bǐ Zhōu Lì zuò cài zuò de hǎo.

e. 王明比周利说英国话说得好。

王明比周利說英國話說得好。

Wáng Míng bǐ Zhōu Lì shuō Yīngguó huà shuō de hǎo.

f. 王明比周利跳舞跳得好。

Wáng Míng bǐ Zhōu Lì tiào wǔ tiào de hǎo.

g. 王明比周利学得多。

王明比周利學得多。

Wáng Míng bǐ Zhōu Lì xué de duō.

h. 王明比周利看书看得多。

王明比周利看書看得多。

Wáng Míng bǐ Zhōu Lì kàn shū kàn de duō.

i. 王明比周利看电影看得多。

王明比周利看電影看得多。

Wáng Míng bǐ Zhōu Lì kàn diànyǐng kàn de duō.

j. 王明比周利打球打得好。

Wáng Míng bǐ Zhōu Lì dǎ qiú dǎ de hǎo.

4

a. 周利没有王明唱歌唱得好。

Zhōu Lì méi yǒu Wáng Míng chàng gē chàng de hǎo.

b. 周利没有王明写汉字写得好。

周利沒有王明寫漢字寫得好。

Zhōu Lì méi yǒu Wáng Míng xiě Hàn zì xiě de hǎo.

c. 周利没有王明做事做得快。

Zhōu Lì méi yǒu Wáng Míng zuò shì zuò de kuài.

d. 周利没有王明做菜做得好。

Zhōu Lì méi yǒu Wáng Míng zuò cài zuò de hǎo.

e. 周利没有王明说英国话说得好。
周利沒有王明說英國話說得好。
Zhōu Lì méi yǒu Wáng Míng shuō Yīngguó huà shuō de hǎo.

f. 周利没有王明跳舞跳得好。
Zhōu Lì méi yǒu Wáng Míng tiào wǔ tiào de hǎo.

g. 周利没有王明学得多。
周利沒有王明學得多。
Zhōu Lì méi yǒu Wáng Míng xué de duō.

h. 周利没有王明看书看得多。
周利沒有王明看書看得多。
Zhōu Lì méi yǒu Wáng Míng kàn shū kàn de duō.

i. 周利没有王明看电影看得多。
周利沒有王明看電影看得多。
Zhōu Lì méi yǒu Wáng Míng kàn diànyǐng kàn de duō.

j. 周利没有王明打球打得好。
Zhōu Lì méi yǒu Wáng Míng dǎ qiú dǎ de hǎo.

5 a. 王明跟周利唱歌唱得一样好。
王明跟周利唱歌唱得一樣好。
Wáng Míng gēn Zhōu Lì chàng gē chàng de yīyàng hǎo.

b. 王明跟周利写汉字写得一样好。
王明跟周利寫漢字寫得一樣好。
Wáng Míng gēn Zhōu Lì xiě Hàn zì xiě de yīyàng hǎo.

c. 王明跟周利做事做得一样快。
王明跟周利做事做得一樣快。
Wáng Míng gēn Zhōu Lì zuò shì zuò de yīyàng kuài.

d. 王明跟周利做菜做得一样好。
王明跟周利做菜做得一樣好。
Wáng Míng gēn Zhōu Lì zuò cài zuò de yīyàng hǎo.

e. 王明跟周利说英文说得一样好。
王明跟周利說英文說得一樣好。
Wáng Míng gēn Zhōu Lì shuō Yīngwén shuō de yīyàng hǎo.

f. 王明跟周利跳舞跳得一样好。
王明跟周利跳舞跳得一樣好。
Wáng Míng gēn Zhōu Lì tiàowǔ tiào de yīyàng hǎo.

g. 王明跟周利学得一样好。
王明跟周利學得一樣好。
Wáng Míng gēn Zhōu Lì xué de yīyàng hǎo.

h. 王明跟周利看书看得一样多。
王明跟周利看書看得一樣多。
Wáng Míng gēn Zhōu Lì kàn shū kàn de yīyàng duō.

i. 王明跟周利看电影看得一样多。
王明跟周利看電影看得一樣多。
Wáng Míng gēn Zhōu Lì kàn diànyǐng kàn de yīyàng duō.

j. 王明跟周利打球打得一样好。
王明跟周利打球打得一樣好。
Wáng Míng gēn Zhōu Lì dǎ qiú dǎ de yīyàng hǎo.

6

a. 周利的薪水比王明的薪水多一倍。
Zhōu Lì de xīnshui bǐ Wáng Míng de xīnshui duō yībèi.

b. 周利的朋友比王明的朋友多得多。
Zhōu Lì de péngyou bǐ Wáng Míng de péngyou duō de duō.

c. 周利比王明高一点。
周利比王明高一點。
Zhōu Lì bǐ Wáng Míng gāo yīdiǎn.

d. 林伟学比周利更高。
林偉學比周利更高。
Lín Wěixué bǐ Zhōu Lì gèng gāo.

e. 王明写汉字写得最漂亮。
王明寫漢字寫得最漂亮。
Wáng Míng xiě Hàn zì xiě de zuì piàoliang.

7

a. Zhou Li is two years older than Wang Ming. b. Zhou Li's car is (worth) $5,000 more than Wang Ming's. c. Zhou Li's car is a little bigger than Wang Ming's. d. Lin Weixue's car is even bigger. e. This book is much more expensive than that one. f. Zhou Li eats much more than Wang Ming does. g. Lin Weixue eats the most. h. Wang Ming does not write characters as nice looking as Zhou Li does.

8

a. 我弟弟做事比我做得快。
我弟弟做事比我做得快。
Wǒ dìdi zuò shì bǐ wǒ zuò de kuài.

b. 我弟弟吃饭比我吃得多得多。
我弟弟吃飯比我吃得多得多。
Wǒ dìdi chī fàn bǐ wǒ chī de duō de duō.

c. 我弟弟赚钱赚得比我少。
我弟弟賺錢賺得比我少。
Wǒ dìdi zhuàn qián zhuàn de bǐ wǒ shǎo.

d. 我赚的钱比他多得多。
我賺的錢比他多得多。
Wǒ zhuàn de qián bǐ tā duō de duō.

e. 我比我弟弟大十一岁。
我比我弟弟大十一歲。
Wǒ bǐ wǒ dìdi dà shíyī suì.

f. 这个电影没有那个电影有意思。
這個電影沒有那個電影有意思。
Zhège diànyǐng méi yǒu nèige diànyǐng yǒu yìsi.

g. 我最喜欢那个电影。
   我最喜歡那個電影。
   Wǒ zuì xǐhuan nèige diànyǐng.

h. 这本书比那本贵一倍。
   這本書比那本貴一倍。
   Zhè běn shū bǐ nà běn guì yī bèi.

9 a. There are quite a lot of new words in this lesson. b. All the courses I am taking this semester are relatively easy. c. Learning Japanese is not as good as learning Chinese. d. This kind of dictionary is relatively difficult to buy. e. He thinks no one is better than he. f. That student studies rather hard.

10 a. 中国的房子多少钱？
         中國的房子多少錢？
         Zhōngguó de fángzi duōshǎo qián?

b. (i)   城外头的房子没有城里头的房子贵。
         城外頭的房子沒有城裏頭的房子貴。
         Chéng wàitou de fángzi méi yǒu chéng lǐtou de fángzi guì.

   (ii) 城外头的房子也比城里头的房子大。
         城外頭的房子也比城裏頭的房子大。
         Chéng wàitou de fángzi yě bǐ chéng lǐtou de fángzi dà.

   (iii) 不过，住在城外头没有住在城里头那么方便。
         不過，住在城外頭沒有住在城裏頭那麼方便。
         Bùguò, zhù zài chéng wàitou méi yǒu zhù zài chéng lǐtou nàme fāngbiàn.

c. 要是我买城里的房子，哪种房子是最便宜的？
   要是我買城裏的房子，哪種房子是最便宜的？
   Yàoshi wǒ mǎi chéng lǐ de fángzi, nǎ zhǒng fángzi shì zuì piányi de?

d. (i)   朝南的房子比朝北的房子贵。
         朝南的房子比朝北的房子貴。
         Cháo nán de fángzi bǐ cháo běi de fángzi guì.

   (ii) 朝东的房子比朝西的房子便宜一点。
         朝東的房子比朝西的房子便宜一點。
         Cháo dōng de fángzi bǐ cháo xī de fángzi piányi yīdiǎn.

11 a. 美如 Měirú; 美芸/美藝 Měiyún; 三岁/三歲 sān suì

b. 美如和美芸一样高。/ 美如和美藝一樣高。/ Měirú hé Měiyún yīyang gāo.

c. 美如开车开得比美芸好多了 / 美如開車開得比美藝好多了 / Měirú kāi chē kāi de bǐ Měiyún hǎo duō le.

d. 美如的成绩没有美芸好 / 美如的成績沒有美藝好 / Měirú de chéngjì méi yǒu Měiyún hǎo.

e. 美芸不象妈妈，跟爸爸比较象。/ 美藝不像媽媽，跟爸爸比較像。/ Měiyún bù xiàng māma, gēn bàba bǐjiào xiàng.

12 (Free response.)

34 Talking about the present

1

a. 王明今年学中文。
王明今年學中文。
Wáng Míng jīnnián xué Zhōngwén.
Wang Ming is studying Chinese this year.

b. 王明这个月放假。
王明這個月放假。
Wáng Míng zhège yuè fang jià.
Wang Ming has vacation this month.

c. 王明这个星期在意大利旅行。
王明這個星期在意大利旅行。
Wáng Míng zhège xīngqī zài Yìdàlì lǚxíng.
Wang Ming is traveling in Italy this week.

d. 王明现在跟朋友吃饭。
王明現在跟朋友吃飯。
Wáng Míng xiànzài gēn péng yǒu chī fàn.
Wang Ming is eating with his friends now.

e. 王明现在在洗澡。
王明現在在洗澡。
Wáng Míng xiànzài zài xǐ zǎo.
Wang Ming is bathing (now).

2

a. 王明在看电视。
王明在看電視。
Wáng Míng zài kàn diànshì.

b. 周利在唱歌。
Zhōu Lì zài chàng gē.

c. 林伟学在打球。
林偉學在打球。
Lín Wěixué zài dǎ qiú.

d. 唐玫玲在写信。
唐玫玲在寫信。
Táng Méilíng zài xiě xìn.

3

a. There is a person standing outside of the door. b. There are a lot of books placed on the desk. c. The child is lying in bed. d. There are many patients waiting in the hospital. e. There are many students sitting in the classroom.

4

a. 王明已经吃了三十个饺子了。
王明已經吃了三十個餃子了。
Wáng Míng yǐjing chī le sānshí gè jiǎozi le.

b. 王明已经走了五里路了。
王明已經走了五里路了。
Wáng Míng yǐjing zǒu le wǔ lǐ lù le.

c. 王明已经学了一百个汉字了。
王明已經學了一百個漢字了。
Wáng Míng yǐjing xué le yībǎi gè Hàn zì le.

d. 王明已经唱了三首歌了。
王明已經唱了三首歌了。
Wáng Míng yǐjing chàng le sān shǒu gē le.

e. 王明已经睡了十个小时了。
王明已經睡了十個小時了。
Wáng Míng yǐjing shuì le shí gè xiǎoshí le.

5

a. I am a senior in college. b. I am presently writing my senior thesis on the economic conditions of modern China. c. I am applying to the economics department at your university for admission to your graduate program in economics. d. I am particularly interested in economics and would like to study for a doctoral degree. e. At present, I am in the process of conducting market research for my thesis. f. At the same time, I am preparing to take the TOEFL exam. g. Please let me know what credentials you expect to find in your successful applicants. h. Also, please inform me of any financial assistance that may be available for foreign graduate students.

6

a. 廖先生在纽约住了三十年了。他自己是一个有名的画家。现在是纽约三个画廊的老板。
廖先生在紐約住了三十年了。他自己是一個有名的畫家。現在是紐約三個畫廊的老闆。
Liào xiānsheng zài Niǔyuē zhù le sānshí nián le. Tā zìjǐ shì yī ge yǒumíng de huàjiā. Xiànzài shì Niǔyuē sān ge huàláng de lǎobǎn.

b. Yamaguchi 教授教中国文学已经教了二十多年了。目前在纽约大学教书。
他写了五本关于中国文学和历史的书，现在正在写第六本。
Yamaguchi 教授教中國文學已經教了二十多年了。目前在紐約大學教書。
他寫了五本關於中國文學和歷史的書，現在正在寫第六本。
Yamaguchi jiàoshòu jiāo Zhōngguó wénxué yǐjīng jiāo le èrshíduō nián le. Mùqián zài Niǔyuē Dàxué jiāoshū. Tā xiě le wǔ běn guānyú Zhōngguó wénxué hé lìshǐ de shū, xiànzài zhèngzài xiě dì liù běn.

c. Simon 小姐学了七年多的中文了。目前正在纽约大学学习艺术史。
Simon 小姐學了七年多的中文了。目前正在紐約大學學習藝術史。
Simon xiǎojie xué le qī nián duō Zhōngwén le. Mùqián zhèngzài Niǔyuē Dàxué xuéxí yìshù shǐ.

35 Talking about habitual actions

1

a. 我常常早上跑步。
Wǒ chángcháng zǎoshang pǎo bù.

b. 他们经常吃中国饭。
他們經常吃中國飯。
Tāmen jīngcháng chī Zhōngguó fàn.

c. 我平常七点钟吃晚饭。
我平常七點鐘吃晚飯。
Wǒ píngcháng qīdiǎn zhōng chī wǎnfàn.

d. 以前我们总是去法国旅行。
以前我們總是去法國旅行。
Yǐqián wǒmen zǒngshì qù Fǎguó lǚxíng.

e. 我总是早上喝咖啡。
我總是早上喝咖啡。
Wǒ zǒngshì zǎoshang hē kāfēi.

f. 我们常常下班以后打网球。
我們常常下班以後打網球。
Wǒmen chángcháng xià bān yǐhòu dǎ wǎngqiú.

g. 你常常在那个饭馆吃饭吗？
你常常在那個飯館吃飯嗎？
Nǐ chángcháng zài nàge fànguǎn chī fàn ma?

h. 我经常看那个电视节目。
我經常看那個電視節目。
Wǒ jīngcháng kàn nàge diànshì jiémù.

i. 我老晚上遛狗。
Wǒ lǎo wǎnshang liù gǒu.

j. 我每星期都看电影。
我每星期都看電影。
Wǒ měi xīngqī dōu kàn diànyǐng.

2   a. 除了周末以外我每天都上课。
除了週末以外我每天都上課。
Chúle zhōumò yǐwài wǒ měitiān dōu shàng kè.

b. 每天早晨八点半上课。
每天早晨八點半上課。
Měitiān zǎochén bādiǎn bàn shàng kè.

c. 我们平常下午四点下课，可是星期五一点就下课。
我們平常下午四點下課，可是星期五一點就下課。
Wǒmen píngcháng xiàwǔ sìdiǎn xià kè, kěshì xīngqī wǔ yīdiǎn jiù xià kè.

d. 每个星期五下午我在医院里工作。
每個星期五下午我在醫院裏工作。
Měi gè xīngqīwǔ xiàwǔ wǒ zài yīyuàn lǐ gōngzuò.

e. 星期六下午天气好的时候，我经常在公园里散步。
星期六下午天氣好的時候，我經常在公園裏散步。
Xīngqī liù xiàwǔ tiānqì hǎo de shíhou, wǒ jīngcháng zài gōngyuán lǐ sàn bù.

f. 星期六晚上我都跟朋友去看电影。
星期六晚上我都跟朋友去看電影。
Xīngqī liù wǎnshang wǒ dōu gēn péngyou qù kàn diànyǐng.

g. 我星期天一向跟家里人到饭馆去吃饭。
我星期天一向跟家裏人到飯館去吃飯。
Wǒ xīngqī tiān yīxiàng gēn jiālǐ rén dào fànguǎn qù chī fàn.

h. 星期日我常常留在宿舍作功课。
星期日我常常留在宿舍作功課。
Xīngqīrì wǒ chángcháng liú zài sùshè zuò gōngkè.

3

a. 他每天早上七点半出门。
他每天早上七點半出門。
Tā měitiān zǎoshang qīdiǎn bàn chū mén.

b. 他总是先在公共汽车站旁边的店买一杯咖啡。
他總是先在公共汽車站旁邊的店買一杯咖啡。
Tā zǒngshì zài gōnggòng qìchē zhàn pángbiān de diàn mǎi yī bēi kāfēi.

c. 他常常中午去健身房。
他常常中午去健身房。
Tā chángcháng zhōngwǔ qù jiànshēnfáng.

d. 他下班以后总是直接回家，从来不跟同事去吃饭。
他下班以後總是直接回家，從來不跟同事去吃飯。
Tā xià bān yǐhòu zǒngshì zhíjiē huí jiā, cónglái bù gēn tóngshì qù chī fàn.

e. 他每个星期天都去一家书店打工。
他每個星期天都去一家書店打工。
Tā měi ge xīngqītiān dōu qù yī jiā shūdiàn dǎ gōng.

4

a. (Free response.)

b. 总是/一向/向来/都；从来没
總是/一向/向來/都；從來沒
zǒngshì/yīxiàng/xiànglái/dōu; cónglái méi

c. 老/一向/向来/都
老/一向/向來/都
lǎo/yīxiàng/xiànglái/dōu

d. 经常/时常
經常/時常
jīngcháng/shícháng

e. (Free response.)

36 Talking about the future

1

a. 你今天要去哪儿跳舞？
你今天要去哪兒跳舞？
Nǐ jīntiān yào qù nǎr tiào wǔ?
Where are you going to go to dance today?

b. 他将来一定会有很多钱。

他將來一定會有很多錢。

Tā jiānglái yīdìng huì yǒu hěn duō qián.

He will definitely have a lot of money in the future.

c. 我明天晚上请你去看电影。

我明天晚上請你去看電影。

Wǒ míngtiān wǎnshang qǐng nǐ qù kàn diànyǐng.

I invite you to watch a movie tomorrow evening.

d. 谁明年去中国学习？

誰明年去中國學習？

Shéi míngnián qù Zhōngguó xuéxí?

Who is going to study in China next year?

e. 我们下个星期放假。

我們下個星期放假。

Wǒmen xià gè xīngqī fàng jià.

We have vacation next week.

f. 我们打算下个月去意大利旅行。

我們打算下個月去意大利旅行。

Wǒmen dǎsuan xià gè yuè qù Yìdàlì lǚxíng.

We are planning to travel in Italy next month.

g. 天气预报说后天会下雪。

天氣預報說後天會下雪。

Tiānqì yùbào shuō hòutiān huì xià xuě.

The weather forecast says that it will snow the day after tomorrow.

h. 我想明天早上给奶奶打电话。

我想明天早上給奶奶打電話。

Wǒ xiǎng míngtiān zǎoshang gěi nǎinai dǎ diànhuà.

I want to call my grandmother tomorrow morning.

2 a. 快 kuài b. 再 zài c. 可能 kěnéng d. 可能 kěnéng e. 愿意/願意 yuànyì
f. 打算 dǎsuan g. 想 xiǎng h. 再 zài

3 a. 我今天下午要跟我的同屋借钱。

我今天下午要跟我的同屋借錢。

Wǒ jīntiān xiàwǔ yào gēn wǒ de tóngwū jiè qián.

b. 明天早上我要给我的女朋友买生日礼物。

明天早上我要給我的女朋友買生日禮物。

Míngtiān zǎoshang wǒ yào gěi wǒ de nǚ péngyou mǎi shēngri lǐwù.

c. 后天我要在饭馆定位子。

後天我要在飯館定位子。

Hòutiān wǒ yào zài fànguǎn dìng wèizi.

d. 下星期我要还同屋的钱。

下星期我要還同屋的錢。

Xià xīngqī wǒ yào huán tóngwū de qián.

e. 我下星期二要再跟同屋借钱。
   我下星期二要再跟同屋借錢。
   Wǒ xià xīngqī'èr yào zài gēn tóngwū jiè qián.

f. 我下个月一定得找工作。
   我下個月一定得找工作。
   Wǒ xià gè yuè yīdìng děi zhǎo gōngzuò.

4

a. 今天下午两点半/今天下午兩點半 jīntiān xiàwǔ liǎngdiǎn bàn
b. 又 yòu
c. 打算 dǎsuàn
d. 跟陈先生吃午饭。/跟陳先生吃午飯。Gēn Chén xiānsheng chī wǔfàn.
e. 下午两点半/下午兩點半 xiàwǔ liǎng diǎn bàn
f. 可能 kěnéng
g. 愿意不愿意/願意不願意 yuànyì bù yuànyì
h. 后天/後天 hòutiān
i. 后天下午一点半/後天下午一點半 hòutiān xiàwǔ yī diǎn bàn
j. 上午 shàngwǔ
k. 下午四点/下午四點 xiàwǔ sìdiǎn
l. 准备/準備 zhǔnbèi
m. 要 yào

37 Indicating completion and talking about the past

1

a. 我哥哥上个月买了一栋房子。
   我哥哥上個月買了一棟房子。
   Wǒ gēgē shàng gè yuè mǎi le yī dòng fángzi.

b. 上个星期他请了一些朋友来他家吃晚饭。
   上個星期他請了一些朋友來他家吃晚飯。
   Shàng gè xīngqī tā qǐng le yī xiē péngyou lái tā jiā chī wǎnfàn.

c. 他做了五个菜。
   他做了五個菜。
   Tā zuò le wǔ gè cài.

d. 他也做了一个汤。
   他也做了一個湯。
   Tā yě zuò le yī gè tāng.

e. 他的朋友送给他一瓶酒。
   Tā de péngyou sòng gěi tā yī píng jiǔ.

f. 他们把饭吃了，把酒喝了。
   他們把飯吃了，把酒喝了。
   Tāmen bǎ fàn chī le, bǎ jiǔ hē le.

2

a. 客人到了以后，我哥哥就请他们喝茶。
客人到了以後，我哥哥就請他們喝茶。
Kèren dào le yǐhòu, wǒ gēgē jiù qǐng tāmen hē chá.

b. 他们喝了茶以后，我哥哥就请他们吃晚饭。
他們喝了茶以後，我哥哥就請他們吃晚飯。
Tāmen hē le chá yǐhòu, wǒ gēgē jiù qǐng tāmen chī wǎnfàn.

c. 吃了晚饭以后，他们都唱了一些歌。
吃了晚飯以後，他們都唱了一些歌。
Chī le wǎnfàn yǐhòu, tāmen dōu chàng le yī xiē gē.

d. 唱了歌以后，他们就回家了。
唱了歌以後，他們就回家了。
Chàng le gē yǐhòu, tāmen jiù huí jiā le.

e. 他们离开了以后，哥哥就开始洗盘子。
他們離開了以後，哥哥就開始洗盤子。
Tāmen líkāi le yǐhòu, gēgē jiù kāishǐ xǐ pánzi.

f. 洗了盘子以后，他就去睡觉了。
洗了盤子以後，他就去睡覺了。
Xǐ le pánzi yǐhòu, tā jiù qù shuì jiào le.

3

a. 王明已经选课了。
王明已經選課了。
Wáng Míng yǐjing xuǎn kè le.

b. 王明已经买练习本了。
王明已經買練習本了。
Wáng Míng yǐjing mǎi liànxíběn le.

c. 王明已经付学费了。
王明已經付學費了。
Wáng Míng yǐjing fù xuéfèi le.

d. 王明还没买课本呢。
王明還沒買課本呢。
Wáng Míng hái méi mǎi kèběn ne.

e. 王明还没复习汉字呢。
王明還沒復習漢字呢。
Wáng Míng hái méi fùxí Hàn zì ne.

f. 王明还没找教室呢。
王明還沒找教室呢。
Wáng Míng hái méi zhǎo jiàoshì ne.

4

a. 你收拾屋子了吗？
你收拾屋子了嗎？
Nǐ shōushi wūzi le ma?

b. 你做作业了吗？
你做作業了嗎？
Nǐ zuò zuòyè le ma?

c. 你写完作文了吗？
你寫完作文了嗎？
Nǐ xiě wán zuòwén le ma?

d. 你找工作了吗？
你找工作了嗎？
Nǐ zhǎo gōngzuò le ma?

e. 你选课了吗？
你選課了嗎？
Nǐ xuǎn kè le ma?

f. 你买课本了吗？
你買課本了嗎？
Nǐ mǎi kèběn le ma?

5 a. 我父母又去日本了。
Wǒ fùmǔ yòu qù Rìběn le.
My parents went to Japan again.

b. 你又出错误了。
你又出錯誤了。
Nǐ yòu chū cuòwù le.
You made a mistake again.

c. 我又给了他二十块钱。
我又給了他二十塊錢。
Wǒ yòu gěi le tā èrshí kuài qián.
I gave him another $20.

d. 我又跟朋友看了那个电影。
我又跟朋友看了那個電影。
Wǒ yòu gēn péngyou kàn le nàge diànyǐng.
I saw the movie with friends again.

e. 我又打篮球了。
我又打籃球了。
Wǒ yòu dǎ lánqiú le.
I played basketball again.

f. 我又给她打电话了。
我又給她打電話了。
Wǒ yòu gěi tā dǎ diànhuà le.
I gave her another phone call. (I called her on the phone again.)

6 a. 我没有看过中国电影。
我沒有看過中國電影。
Wǒ méi yǒu kànguò Zhōngguó diànyǐng.

b. 我今年没有检查过身体。
我今年沒有檢查過身體。
Wǒ jīnnián méi yǒu jiǎncháguò shēntǐ.

c. （我）学过（英文）。

（我）學過（英文）。

(Wǒ) xuéguò (Yīngwén).

d. 我也从来没吃过这个菜。

我也從來沒吃過這個菜。

Wǒ yě cónglái méi chīguò zhège cài.

e. 我没有看过这本书。

我沒有看過這本書。

Wǒ méi yǒu kànguo zhè běn shū.

f. 我学过经济学。

我學過經濟學。

Wǒ xuéguò jīngjìxué.

g. 我还没唱过卡拉 OK。

我還沒唱過卡拉 OK。

Wǒ hái méi chàngguo kǎlā OK.

h. 我吃过日本饭。

我吃過日本飯。

Wǒ chīguò Rìběn fàn.

7 a. 过/過 guo or 了 le b. 过/過 guo, 了 le c. 过/過 guo d. 了 le [过了/過了 guo le], 了 le e. 过/過 guo

8 a. 他以前（从前/從前）是我的男朋友。

Tā yǐqián (cóngqián) shì wǒ de nán péngyou.

b. 我以前（从前/從前）每天早上都喝咖啡。

Wǒ yǐqián (cóngqián) měitiān zǎoshang dōu hē kāfēi.

c. 我小的时候很喜欢说话。

我小的時候很喜歡說話。

Wǒ xiǎo de shíhou hěn xǐhuan shuō huà.

d. 一九六二年的时候，汽油一毛九一加仑。

一九六二年的時候，汽油一毛九一加侖。

Yī jiǔ liù èr nián de shíhou, qìyóu yī máo jiǔ yī jiālún.

e. 以前（从前）这里是公园。

以前（從前）這裏是公園。

Yǐqián (cóngqián) zhèli shì gōngyuán.

f. 以前（从前）我对中国不感兴趣。

以前（從前）我對中國不感興趣。

Yǐqián (cóngqián) wǒ duì Zhōngguó bù gǎn xìngqù.

9 a. 他们是一九七零年结的婚。

他們是一九七零年結的婚。

Tāmen shì yī jiǔ qī líng nián jié de hūn.

b. 我们是在中国认识的。

我們是在中國認識的。

Wǒmen shì zài Zhōngguó rènshi de.

c.　弟弟是一九九八年毕业的。
　　弟弟是一九九八年畢業的。
　　Dìdi shì yī jiǔ jiǔ bā nián bìyè de.

d.　这件毛衣是我父母给我买的。
　　這件毛衣是我父母給我買的。
　　Zhè jiàn máoyī shì wǒ fùmǔ gěi wǒ mǎi de.

e.　那本书是王老师写的。
　　那本書是王老師寫的。
　　Nà běn shū shì Wáng lǎoshī xiě de.

f.　这本字典是在书店买的。
　　這本字典是在書店買的。
　　Zhè běn zìdiǎn shì zài shūdiàn mǎi de.

g.　是他告訴我的。
　　Shì tā gàosu wǒ de.

h.　我是坐公共汽车去的。
　　我是坐公共汽車去的。
　　Wǒ shì zuò gōnggòng qìchē qù de.

10　a.　我去过北京。/ 我去過北京。**Wǒ qù guò Běijīng.**

b.　是什么时候去的/是甚麼時候去的 **shì shénme shíhou qù de**

c.　我是2004年跟我妈妈去的/我是2004年跟我媽媽去的 **Wǒ shì 2004 nián gēn wǒ māma qù de**

d.　去了什么地方/去了甚麼地方 **qù le shénme dìfāng**

e.　了 **le**; 了 **le**; 了 **le**

f.　住了多久 **zhù le duō jiǔ**

g.　去了上海 **qù le Shànghǎi**

h.　是怎么去的/是怎麼去的 **shì zěnme qù de**

i.　坐了多久 **zuò le duō jiǔ**

j.　没去过中国/沒去過中國 **méi qùguò Zhōngguó**

k.　又去了(一次)中国/又去了(一次)中國 **yòu qù le yī cì Zhōngguó**

38　Talking about change, new situations, and changing situations

1　a.　你越来越认真。
　　你越來越認真。
　　Nǐ yuè lái yuè rènzhēn.

b.　你的身体越来越强壮。
　　你的身體越來越强壯。
　　Nǐ de shēntǐ yuè lái yuè qiángzhuàng.

c.　你的技巧越来越好。
　　你的技巧越來越好。
　　Nǐ de jìqiǎo yuè lái yuè hǎo.

d. 比赛的日子快要到了。
   比賽的日子快要到了。
   Bǐsài de rìzi kuài yào dào le.

e. 你每天得跑三个小时。
   你每天得跑三個小時。
   Nǐ měitiān děi pǎo sān gè xiǎoshí.

f. 你越跑，越跑得快。
   Nǐ yuè pǎo, yuè pǎo de kuài.

2

a. 现在她会走路了。
   現在她會走路了。
   Xiànzài tā huì zǒu lù le.

b. 现在她会叫'妈妈'了。
   現在她會叫'媽媽'了。
   Xiànzài tā huì jiào māma le.

c. 现在她可以认出他的哥哥了。
   現在她可以認出他的哥哥了。
   Xiànzài tā kěyǐ rènchū tā de gēgē le.

d. 现在她喜欢听音乐了。
   現在她喜歡聽音樂了。
   Xiànzài tā xǐhuan tīng yīnyuè le.

e. 现在她知道她自己的名字了。
   現在她知道她自己的名字了。
   Xiànzài tā zhīdao tā zìjǐ de míngzì le.

3

a. 我不再喝啤酒了。
   Wǒ bù zài hē píjiǔ le.

b. 我星期日晚上不再去参加晚会了。
   我星期日晚上不再去參加晚會了。
   Wǒ xīngqīrì wǎnshàng bù zài qù cānjiā wǎnhuì le.

c. 我每天都要在公园跑步。
   我每天都要在公園跑步。
   Wǒ měitiān dōu yào zài gōngyuán pǎo bù.

d. 我每个星期都要给我的父母打一次电话。
   我每個星期都要給我的父母打一次電話。
   Wǒ měi gè xīngqī dōu yào gěi wǒ de fùmǔ dǎ yī cì diànhuà.

e. 我每天都要学中文。
   我每天都要學中文。
   Wǒ měitiān dōu yào xué Zhōngwén.

f. 我不再跟我的妹妹吵架了。
   Wǒ bù zài gēn wǒ de mèimei chǎo jià le.

4 a. The weather is getting colder and colder. b. Chinese is becoming more and more interesting. c. Chinese people's lives are getting better and better. d. We like to eat Chinese food more and more. e. The more I eat, the fatter I get. The fatter I get, the more I want to eat. f. The more you study, the more you understand. g. The more I study, the more I want to study. h. The more you write Chinese characters, the easier they become. i. The more I read this book, the more interesting I think it is.

5 a. 春天到了。天气越来越暖和，
春天到了。天氣越來越暖和，
Chūntiān dào le. Tiānqì yuè lái yuè nuǎnhuo,

　b. 白天越来越长，
白天越來越長，
báitiān yuè lái yuè cháng,

　c. 花越来越多，
花越來越多，
huā yuè lái yuè duō,

　d. 天空越来越蓝，
天空越來越藍，
tiānkōng yuè lái yuè lán,

　e. 在外边散步的人越来越多。
在外邊散步的人越來越多。
zài wàibian sànbù de rén yuè lái yuè duō.

6 a. 中文我越听越懂。
中文我越聽越懂。
Zhōngwén wǒ yuè tīng yuè dǒng.

　b. 汉字我越写越好看。
漢字我越寫越好看。
Hàn zì wǒ yuè xiě yuè hǎo kàn.

　c. 我越说越准，
我越說越準，
Wǒ yuè shuō yuè zhǔn,

　d. 我越读越快。
我越讀越快。
Wǒ yuè dú yuè kuài.

7 a. 变化/變化 **biànhuà** b. 成为/成爲 **chéngwéi** c. 改善 **gǎishàn** d. 换/換 **huàn** e. 改 **gǎi** f. 改写/改寫 **gǎi xiě** g. 变成/變成 **biànchéng** h. 变成/變成 **biànchéng** i. 改正 **gǎizhèng**

8 a. 中国的商业环境有所改进。
中國的商業環境有所改進。
Zhōngguó de shāngyè huánjìng yǒu suǒ gǎijìn.

b. 经济越来越强大。

經濟越來越強大。

Jīngjì yuè lái yuè qiángdà.

c. 在中国的外国企业越来越多。

在中國的外國企業越來越多。

Zài Zhōngguó de wàiguó qǐyè yuè lái yuè duō.

d. 投资越多，赚的钱就越多。

投資越多，賺的錢就越多。

Tóuzī yuè duō, zhuàn de qián jiù yuè duō.

e. 中国人越来越有钱。

中國人越來越有錢。

Zhōngguórén yuè lái yuè yǒu qián.

f. 他们钱越多，买的东西越多。

他們錢越多，買的東西越多。

Tāmen qián yuè duō, mǎi de dōngxī yuè duō.

g. 我认为我们在中国的生意会越来越好。

我認爲我們在中國的生意會越來越好。

Wǒ rènwéi wǒmen zài Zhōngguó de shēngyì huì yuè lái yuè hǎo.

9

a. 订婚了/訂婚了 **dìnghūn le**

b. 有三个孩子了/有三個孩子了 **yǒu sān gè háizi le**

c. 不工作了/不工作了 **bù gōngzuò le**

d. 越来越胖/越來越胖 **yuè lái yuè pàng**

e. 变化最大/變化最大 **biànhuà zuì dà**

f. 成了名人 **chéng le míngrén**

g. 了 **le**

10

(Free response.)

39 Talking about duration and frequency

1

a. 我打算在中国学一年的中国话。

我打算在中國學一年的中國話。

Wǒ dǎsuan zài Zhōngguó xué yī nián de Zhōngguóhuà.

b. 学生每天至少得学习三个钟头。

學生每天至少得學習三個鐘頭。

Xuésheng měitiān zhìshǎo děi xuéxí sān gè zhōngtóu.

c. 我已经等了他二十分钟了。

我已經等了他二十分鐘了。

Wǒ yǐjing děng le tā èrshí fēn zhōng le.

d. 昨天晚上，我就睡了两个钟头的觉。

昨天晚上，我就睡了兩個鐘頭的覺。

Zuótiān wǎnshang, wǒ jiù shuì le liǎng gè zhōngtóu de jiào.

Answer key

e. 你每天晚上应该睡八个钟头的觉。
   你每天晚上應該睡八個鐘頭的覺。
   Nǐ měitiān wǎnshang yīnggāi shuì bā gè zhōngtóu de jiào.
f. 我每天看一个半小时的报。
   我每天看一個半小時的報。
   Wǒ měitiān kàn yī gè bàn xiǎoshí de bào.
g. 我每天晚上听一个钟头的音乐。
   我每天晚上聽一個鐘頭的音樂。
   Wǒ měitiān wǎnshang tīng yī ge zhōngtou de yīnyuè.

2 a. 王明有一个月没看电影。
      王明有一個月沒看電影。
      Wáng Míng yǒu yī gè yuè méi kàn diànyǐng.
   b. 王明有一年没回家。
      Wáng Míng yǒu yī nián méi huí jiā.
   c. 王明有五天没上课。
      王明有五天沒上課。
      Wáng Míng yǒu wǔ tiān méi shàng kè.
   d. 王明有四十五分钟没说话。
      王明有四十五分鐘沒說話。
      Wáng Míng yǒu sìshíwǔ fēn zhōng méi shuō huà.
   e. 王明有三十六个小时没睡觉。
      王明有三十六個小時沒睡覺。
      Wáng Míng yǒu sānshíliù gè xiǎoshí méi shuì jiào.
   f. 王明有两个星期没打球。
      王明有兩個星期沒打球。
      Wáng Míng yǒu liǎng gè xīngqī méi dǎ qiú.

3 a. 她写作文已经写了有一个月了。
      她寫作文已經寫了有一個月了。
      Tā xiě zuòwén yǐjing xiě le yǒu yī gè yuè le.
   b. 他们打球打了有三个小时。
      他們打球打了有三個小時。
      Tāmen dǎ qiú dǎ le yǒu sān gè xiǎoshí.
   c. 他跟他的女朋友说话说了有两个钟头了。
      他跟他的女朋友說話說了有兩個鐘頭了。
      Tā gēn tā de nǚ péngyǒu shuō huà shuō le yǒu liǎng gè zhōngtóu le.
   d. 我等弟弟已经等了有半个小时了。
      我等弟弟已經等了有半個小時了。
      Wǒ děng dìdi yǐjing děng le yǒu bàn gè xiǎoshí le.
   e. 他已经在中国住了有两年了。
      他已經在中國住了有兩年了。
      Tā yǐjing zài Zhōngguó zhù le yǒu liǎng nián le.

f. 他教书教了有十年了。
他教書教了有十年了。
Tā jiāo shū jiāo le yǒu shí nián le.

4 a. Mom is cooking. b. Look! There are a lot of people dancing in the park. c. Please wait for me here. d. Is your child still studying in the U.S.? e. She has not gotten married yet.

5 a. We like to drink tea while talking. b. Students like to listen to music while doing homework. c. You can't eat while driving. d. I don't want you to read the newspaper while eating breakfast.

6 a. 王明坐过五次飞机。
王明坐過五次飛機。
Wáng Míng zuò guò wǔ cì fēijī.

b. 王明吃过两次日本饭。
王明吃過兩次日本飯。
Wáng Míng chī guò liǎng cì Rìběn fàn.

c. 王明去过一次巴黎。
Wáng Míng qù guò yī cì Bālí.

d. 王明唱过三次卡拉 OK。
Wáng Míng chàng guò sān cì kǎlā OK.

e. 王明骑过四次摩托车。
王明騎過四次摩托車。
Wáng Míng qí guò sì cì mótuōchē.

f. 王明看过六次中国电影。
王明看過六次中國電影。
Wáng Míng kàn guò liù cì Zhōngguó diànyǐng.

7 a. 早上六点半/早上六點半 zǎoshang liù diǎn bàn
b. 跑步跑二十分钟/跑步跑二十分鐘 pǎobù pǎo èrshí fēn zhōng
c. 八个钟头/八個鐘頭 bā ge zhōngtou
d. 三个半小时的功课/三個半小時的功課 sān ge bàn xiǎoshí de gōngkè
e. 洗五分钟/洗五分鐘 xǐ wǔ fēn zhōng
f. 开着灯睡觉/開著燈睡覺 kāi zhe dēng shuì jiào
g. 站着上课/站著上課 zhàn zhe shàng kè
h. 看两个小时的电视/看兩個小時的電視 kàn liǎng gè xiǎoshí de diànshì
i. 出去两次/出去兩次 chūqù liǎng cì
j. 三个星期没有打电动游戏了/三個星期沒有打電動遊戲了 sān gè xīngqī méi yǒu dǎ diàndòng yóuxì le

40 Expressing additional information

1

a. 我这学期选了中文，也选了日文。
我這學期選了中文，也選了日文。
Wǒ zhè xuéqī xuǎn le Zhōngwén, yě xuǎn le Rìwén.
This semester I am taking Chinese and I am also taking Japanese.
(lit. I selected Chinese and I also selected Japanese.)

b. 他喜欢吃美国饭，也喜欢吃泰国饭。
他喜歡吃美國飯，也喜歡吃泰國飯。
Tā xǐhuan chī Měiguó fàn, yě xǐhuan chī Tàiguó fàn.
He likes to eat American food and he also likes Thai food.

c. 张小英很漂亮，也很聪明。
張小英很漂亮，也很聰明。
Zhāng Xiǎoyīng hěn piàoliang, yě hěn cōngming.
Zhang Xiaoying is very pretty and also very smart.

d. 林伟学是学生。唐玫玲也是学生。
林偉學是學生。唐玫玲也是學生。
Lín Wěixué shì xuésheng. Táng Méilíng yě shì xuésheng.
Lin Weixue is a student. Tang Meiling is also a student.

e. 我给弟弟打了电话。我也给妹妹打了电话。
我給弟弟打了電話。我也給妹妹打了電話。
Wǒ gěi dìdi dǎ le diànhuà. Wǒ yě gěi mèimei dǎ le diànhuà.
I called my younger brother. I also called my younger sister.

f. 我喜欢喝咖啡，也喜欢喝茶。
我喜歡喝咖啡，也喜歡喝茶。
Wǒ xǐhuan hē kāfēi, yě xǐhuan hē chá.
I like to drink coffee and I also like to drink tea.

2

a. 这本字典送给你。我还有一本。
這本字典送給你。我還有一本。
Zhè běn zìdiǎn sònggěi nǐ. Wǒ hái yǒu yīběn.
I am giving this dictionary to you. I still have one.

b. 你还有什么事情要告诉我吗？
你還有甚麼事情要告訴我嗎？
Nǐ hái yǒu shénme shìqing yào gàosu wǒ ma?
Do you have anything else you want to tell me?

c. 对不起。我还不懂你的意思。
對不起。我還不懂你的意思。
Duìbuqǐ. Wǒ hái bù dǒng nǐ de yìsi.
Sorry. I still do not understand what you mean.

d. 你还有多少钱？
你還有多少錢？
Nǐ hái yǒu duōshao qián?
How much money do you have left?

ANSWER KEY

e. 学中文不但有意思，并且可以找到好的工作。
學中文不但有意思，并且可以找到好的工作。
Xué Zhōngwén bùdàn yǒu yìsi, bìngqiě kěyǐ zhǎodào hǎo de gōngzuò.
Learning Chinese is not only interesting; it can also (help) in finding a good job.

f. 除了妹妹以外，我们都喜欢吃中国饭。
除了妹妹以外，我們都喜歡吃中國飯。
Chúle mèimei yǐwài, wǒmen dōu xǐhuan chī Zhōngguó fàn.
Except for [besides] my younger sister, we all like Chinese food.

g. 那个旅馆又干净又便宜。
那個旅館又乾淨又便宜。
Nàge lǚguǎn yòu gānjìng yòu piányi.
That hotel is both clean and inexpensive.

h. 妈妈不但上班，而且得照顾孩子。
媽媽不但上班，而且得照顧孩子。
Māma bùdàn shàng bān, érqiě děi zhàogù háizi.
Not only does Mom work, she also has to take care of the children.

3

a. 高蕾又聪明又用功。
高蕾又聰明又用功。
Gāo Lěi yòu cōngming yòu yònggōng.

b. 并且很可靠。
并且很可靠。
Bìngqiě hěn kěkào.

c. 不但功课准备得很仔细，而且考试考得好。
不但功課準備得很仔細，而且考試考得好。
Bùdàn gōngkè zhǔnbèi de hěn zǐxì, érqiě kǎoshì kǎo de hǎo.

d. 她还是学生组织的积极分子。
她還是學生組織的積極分子。
Tā hái shì xuéshēng zǔzhī de jījí fēnzi.

e. 除了是一个好学生以外，她还参加很多课外活动。
除了是一個好學生以外，她還參加很多課外活動。
Chúle shì yī gè hǎo xuéshēng yǐwài, tā hái cānjiā hěn duō kèwài huódòng.

f. 而且她很愿意帮助别人。
而且她很願意幫助別人。
Érqiě tā hěn yuànyì bāngzhù bié rén.

g. 再说，她的语言能力很强。英文，说得写得都很好。
再說，她的語言能力很强。英文，說得寫得都很好。
Zài shuō, tā de yǔyán nénglì hěn qiáng. Yīngwén, shuō de xiě de dōu hěn hǎo.

4

Sample answer:

房屋出租。一房一厅，又大又干净。不但附家具而且家具都是新的。离地铁站还有很多餐厅、商店都很近。一个月两千块。除了水电以外，也包括有线电视。意者请洽 Millie (987) 654-3321/millie1980@gmail.com

房屋出租。一房一廳，又大又乾淨。不但附傢具而且傢具都是新的。離地鐵站還有很多餐廳、商店都很近。一個月兩千塊。除了水電以外，也包括有線電視。意者請洽 Millie (987) 654-3321/millie1980@gmail.com

Fángwū chūzū. Yī fang yī tīng, yòu dà yòu gānjìng. Bùdàn fù jiājù érqiě jiājù dōu shì xīn de. Lí dìtiě zhàn hái yǒu hěn duō cāntīng, shāngdiàn dōu hěn jìn. Yī ge yuè liǎng qiān kuài. Chúle shuǐ diàn yǐwài, yě bāokuò yǒuxiàn diànshì. Yìzhě qǐng qià Millie (987) 654-3321/millie1980@gmail.com

41 Expressing contrast

1

a. 张伟虽然很帅，但是不高。
张偉雖然很帥，但是不高。
Zhāng Wěi suīrán hěn shuài, dànshì bù gāo.

b. 张伟虽然很聪明，但是很懒。
張偉雖然很聰明，但是很懶。
Zhāng Wěi suīrán hěn cōngming, dànshì hěn lǎn.

c. 张伟虽然很有钱，但是很小气。
張偉雖然很有錢，但是很小氣。
Zhāng Wěi suīrán hěn yǒu qián, dànshì hěn xiǎoqi.

d. 张伟虽然跳舞跳得很好，但是唱歌唱得不好。
張偉雖然跳舞跳得很好，但是唱歌唱得不好。
Zhāng Wěi suīrán tiào wǔ tiào de hěn hǎo, dànshì chàng gē chàng de bù hǎo.

e. 张伟虽然有车，但是开车开得太快。
張偉雖然有車，但是開車開得太快。
Zhāng Wěi suīrán yǒu chē, dànshì kāi chē kāi de tài kuài.

f. 张伟虽然喜欢请客，但是他喝酒喝得太多。
張偉雖然喜歡請客，但是他喝酒喝得太多。
Zhāng Wěi suīrán xǐhuan qǐng kè, dànshì tā hē jiǔ hē de tài duō.

g. 张伟虽然会说外语，但是他不喜欢旅游。
張偉雖然會說外語，但是他不喜歡旅游。
Zhāng Wěi suīrán huì shuō wàiyǔ, dànshì tā bù xǐhuan lǚyóu.

h. 张伟虽然大学毕业了，但是没有工作。
張偉雖然大學畢業了，但是沒有工作。
Zhāng Wěi suīrán dàxué bì yè le, dànshì méi yǒu gōngzuò.

2

a. 你可以在宿舍吃饭，但是不可以在那里做饭。
你可以在宿舍吃飯，但是不可以在那裏做飯。
Nǐ kěyǐ zài sùshè chīfàn, dànshì bù kěyǐ zài nàli zuò fàn.

b. 你可以在阅览室喝咖啡，但是不能在那里吃东西。
你可以在閱覽室喝咖啡，但是不能在那裏吃東西。
Nǐ kěyǐ zài yuèlǎn shì hē kāfēi, dànshì bù néng zài nàli chī dōngxi.

c. 你可以在宿舍举行晚会，但是不可以喝酒。
你可以在宿舍舉行晚會，但是不可以喝酒。
Nǐ kěyǐ zài sùshè jǔxíng wǎnhuì, dànshì bù kěyǐ hē jiǔ.

d. 你可以在你的屋子里用微波炉，但是不可以用面包炉。
你可以在你的屋子裏用微波爐，但是不可以用麵包爐。
Nǐ kěyǐ zài nǐ de wūzi lǐ yòng wēibōlú, dànshì bù kěyǐ yòng miànbāolú.

e. 在体育馆里可以穿球鞋，不可以穿靴子。
在體育館裏可以穿球鞋，不可以穿靴子。
Zài tǐyùguǎn lǐ kěyǐ chuān qiúxié, bù kěyǐ chuān xuēzi.

f. 考试的时候可以用计算器，可是不可以用计算机。
考試的時候可以用計算器，可是不可以用計算機。
Kǎoshì de shíhou kěyǐ yòng jìsuànqì, kěshì bù kěyǐ yòng jìsuànjī.

g. 你可以在布告栏上放相片，但是不能在墙上。
你可以在布告欄上放相片，但是不能在墙上。
Nǐ kěyǐ zài bùgào lán shàng fàng xiàngpiàn, dànshì bù néng zài qiángshàng.

h. 你可以在图书馆借书，但是不可以借字典。
你可以在圖書館借書，但是不可以借字典。
Nǐ kěyǐ zài túshūguǎn jièshū, dànshì bù kěyǐ jiè zìdiǎn.

i. 你可以在语言实验室练习语言，但是不可以看电子邮件。
你可以在語言實驗室練習語言，但是不可以看電子郵件。
Nǐ kěyǐ zài yǔyán shíyànshì liànxí yǔyán, dànshì bù kěyǐ kàn diànzi yóujiàn.

j. 你可以把手机带进教室，但是一定得关机。
你可以把手機帶進教室，但是一定得關機。
Nǐ kěyǐ bǎ shǒujī dài jìn jiàoshì, dànshì yīdìng děi guān jī.

3

a. 中文虽然很难学，可是很有用。
中文雖然很難學，可是很有用。
Zhōngwén suīrán hěn nán xué, kěshì hěn yǒu yòng.
Chinese is difficult to learn, but it is very useful.

b. 他虽然是中国人，可是没去过中国。
他雖然是中國人，可是沒去過中國。
Tā suīrán shì Zhōngguórén, kěshì méi qùguo Zhōngguó.
Although he is Chinese, he has never been to China.

c. 我虽然想去，可是没时间。
我雖然想去，可是沒時間。
Wǒ suīrán xiǎng qù, kěshì méi shíjiān.
I want to go but I have no time.

d. 今天虽然没下雪，可是非常冷。
今天雖然沒下雪，可是非常冷。
Jīntiān suīrán méi xià xuě, kěshì fēicháng lěng.
It didn't snow today, but it is extremely cold.

e. 今天考试，同学们虽然都到了，可是老师还没来。
今天考試，同學們雖然都到了，可是老師還沒來。
Jīntiān kǎoshì, tóngxuémen suīrán dōu dào le, kěshì lǎoshī hái méi lái.
For today's test, the students have all arrived but the teacher hasn't arrived yet.

f. 他虽然嘴上不说，可是心里很不高兴。
他雖然嘴上不說，可是心裏很不高興。
Tā suīrán zuǐ shang bù shuō, kěshì xīnlǐ hěn bù gāoxìng.
He hasn't said anything, but in his heart he is very unhappy.

g. 虽然她是中国人，可是她不喜欢吃中国饭。
雖然她是中國人，可是她不喜歡吃中國飯。
Suīrán tā shì Zhōngguórén, kěshì tā bù xǐhuan chī Zhōngguó fàn.
Although she is Chinese, she doesn't like Chinese food.

h. 学中文虽然很花时间，可是我很喜欢学。
學中文雖然很花時間，可是我很喜歡學。
Xué Zhōngwén suīrán hěn huā shíjiān, kěshì wǒ hěn xǐhuan xué.
Although studying Chinese takes a lot of time, I like to study it.

4

a. 中文虽然很难学，可是却很有用。
中文雖然很難學，可是卻很有用。
Zhōngwén suīrán hěn nán xué, kěshì què hěn yǒu yòng.

b. 他虽然是中国人，可是却没去过中国。
他雖然是中國人，可是卻沒去過中國。
Tā suīrán shì Zhōngguórén, kěshì què méi qùguo Zhōngguó.

c. 我虽然想去，可是却没时间。
我雖然想去，可是卻沒時間。
Wǒ suīrán xiǎng qù, kěshì què méi shíjiān.

d. 今天虽然没下雪，可是却非常冷。
今天雖然沒下雪，可是卻非常冷。
Jīntiān suīrán méi xià xuě, kěshì què fēicháng lěng.

e. 今天考试，同学们虽然都到了，可是老师却还没来。
今天考試，同學們雖然都到了，可是老師卻還沒來。
Jīntiān kǎoshì, tóngxuémen suīrán dōu dào le, kěshì lǎoshī què hái méi lái.

f. 他虽然嘴上不说，可是心里却很不高兴。
他雖然嘴上不說，可是心裏卻很不高興。
Tā suīrán zuǐ shang bù shuō, kěshì xīnlǐ què hěn bù gāoxìng.

g. 虽然她是中国人，可是她却不喜欢吃中国饭。
雖然她是中國人，可是她卻不喜歡吃中國飯。
Suīrán tā shì Zhōngguórén, kěshì tā què bù xǐhuan chī Zhōngguó fàn.

h. 学中文虽然很花时间，可是我却很喜欢学。
   學中文雖然很花時間，可是我卻很喜歡學。
   Xué Zhōngwén suīrán hěn huā shíjiān, kěshì wǒ què hěn xǐhuan xué.

5

a. 难的汉字写对了，容易的反而写错了。
   難的漢字寫對了，容易的反而寫錯了。
   Nán de Hàn zì xiěduì le, róngyì de fǎn'ér xiěcuò le.

b. 认真的学生大家都喜欢，反过来，不认真的学生大家都不喜欢。
   認真的學生大家都喜歡，反過來，不認真的學生大家都不喜歡。
   Rènzhēn de xuésheng dàjiā dōu xǐhuan, fǎnguòlái, bù rènzhēn de xuésheng dàjiā dōu bù xǐhuan.

c. 天气热人们穿的衣服就少，反过来，天气冷人们穿的衣服就多。
   天氣熱人們穿的衣服就少，反過來，天氣冷人們穿的衣服就多。
   Tiānqì rè rénmen chuān de yīfu jiù shǎo, fǎnguòlái, tiānqì lěng rénmen chuān de yīfu jiù duō.

d. 下星期要交的报告他已经写好了，明天的考试反而忘了准备了。
   下星期要交的報告他已經寫好了，明天的考試反而忘了準備了。
   Xià xīngqī yào jiāo de bàogào tā yǐjing xiěhǎole, míngtiān de kǎoshì fǎn'ér wàng le zhǔnbèi le.

e. 中文不容易学，她反而学得很好。
   中文不容易學，她反而學得很好。
   Zhōngwén bù róngyì xué, tā fǎn'ér xué de hěn hǎo.

f. 容易的课选的学生多，反过来，难的课选的学生少。
   容易的課選的學生多，反過來，難的課選的學生少。
   Róngyì de kè xuǎn de xuésheng duō, fǎnguòlái, nán de kè xuǎn de xuésheng shǎo.

6

a. 鞋子好是好，但是太贵了。
   鞋子好是好，但是太貴了。
   Xiézi hǎo shì hǎo, dànshì tài guì le.

b. 毛衣好看是好看，但是太小了。
   Máoyī hǎo kàn shì hǎo kàn, dànshì tài xiǎo le.

c. 价钱好是好，但是货太差了。
   價錢好是好，但是貨太差了。
   Jiàqian hǎo shì hǎo, dànshì huò tài chà le.

d. 大小合适是合适，但是颜色太淡了。
   大小合適是合適，但是顏色太淡了。
   Dà xiǎo héshì shì héshì, dànshì yánsè tài dàn le.

e. 百货公司大是大，但是人太多了。
   百貨公司大是大，但是人太多了。
   Bǎihuò gōngsī dà shì dà, dànshì rén tài duō le.

7

a. ii b. ii c. iii

42 Expressing sequence

1

a. 她上课以前，吃早饭了。
她上課以前，吃早飯了。
Tā shàng kè yǐqián, chī zǎofàn le.

b. 她上课以前，看报纸了。
她上課以前，看報紙了。
Tā shàng kè yǐqián, kàn bàozhǐ le.

c. 她上课以前，复习中文了。
她上課以前，復習中文了。
Tā shàng kè yǐqián, fùxí Zhōngwén le.

d. 她上课以前，听收音机了。
她上課以前，聽收音機了。
Tā shàng kè yǐqián, tīng shōuyīnjī le.

e. 上课以前，她在公园里跑步了。
上課以前，她在公園裏跑步了。
Shàng kè yǐqián, tā zài gōngyuán lǐ pǎo bù le.

2

a. 小王睡觉以前，作功课。
小王睡覺以前，作功課。
Xiǎo Wáng shuì jiào yǐqián zuò gōngkè.

b. 小王睡觉以前，看电视。
小王睡覺以前，看電視。
Xiǎo Wáng shuì jiào yǐqián kàn diànshì.

c. 小王睡觉以前，给朋友打电话。
小王睡覺以前，給朋友打電話。
Xiǎo Wáng shuì jiào yǐqián gěi péngyou dǎ diànhuà.

d. 小王睡觉以前，洗澡。
小王睡覺以前，洗澡。
Xiǎo Wáng shuì jiào yǐqián xǐ zǎo.

e. 小王睡觉以前，看电子邮件。
小王睡覺以前，看電子郵件。
Xiǎo Wáng shuì jiào yǐqián kàn diànzi yóujiàn.

3

a. 小王考了试以后，想去看电影。
小王考了試以後，想去看電影。
Xiǎo Wáng kǎo (le) shì yǐhòu, xiǎng qù kàn diànyǐng.

b. 小王考了试以后，想去喝咖啡。
小王考了試以後，想去喝咖啡。
Xiǎo Wáng kǎo le shì yǐhòu, xiǎng qù hē kāfēi.

c. 小王考（了）试以后，想睡觉。
小王考（了）試以後，想睡覺。
Xiǎo Wáng kǎo (le) shì yǐhòu, xiǎng qù shuì jiào.

d. 小王考（了）试以后，想跟朋友一起学习。
小王考（了）試以後，想跟朋友一起學習。
Xiǎo Wáng kǎo (le) shì yǐhòu, xiǎng gēn péngyou yīqǐ xuéxí.

e. 小王考（了）试以后，想去打网球。
小王考（了）試以後，想去打網球。
Xiǎo Wáng kǎo (le) shì yǐhòu, xiǎng qù dǎ wǎngqiú.

4

a. 王鹏飞毕了业以后，就去旅行。
王鵬飛畢了業以後，就去旅行。
Wáng Péngfēi bì le yè yǐhòu, jiù qù lǚxíng.

b. 张苹毕了业以后，就找工作。
張苹畢了業以後，就找工作。
Zhāng Píng bì le yè yǐhòu, jiù zhǎo gōngzuò.

c. 陈玫玲毕了业以后，就结婚。
陳玫玲畢了業以後，就結婚。
Chén Méilíng bì le yè yǐhòu, jiù jiéhūn.

d. 徐乃康毕了业以后，就读研究所。
徐乃康畢了業以後，就讀研究所。
Xú Nǎikāng bì le yè yǐhòu, jiù dú yánjiūsuǒ.

5

a. I did not go to bed until 11:30 p.m. last night. b. He did not show up until after the exam had started. c. We did not start learning to write Chinese characters until second semester. d. He did not do his homework last night until he had finished watching the movie. e. We went to class at 2:00, but the teacher did not come until 2:10.

6

a. 陈玫玲先吃早饭再看报纸。
陳玫玲先吃早飯再看報紙。
Chén Méilíng xiān chī zǎofàn zài kàn bàozhǐ.

b. 陈玫玲先看报纸再去上课。
陳玫玲先看報紙再去上課。
Chén Méilíng xiān kàn bàozhǐ zài qù shàng kè.

c. 陈玫玲先回家再作功课。
陳玫玲先回家再作功課。
Chén Méilíng xiān huí jiā zài zuò gōngkè.

d. 陈玫玲先作功课再练习打网球。
陳玫玲先作功課再練習打網球。
Chén Méilíng xiān zuò gōngkè zài liànxí dǎ wǎngqiú.

e. 陈玫玲先吃饭再看朋友。
陳玫玲先吃飯再看朋友。
Chén Méilíng xiān chī fàn zài kàn péngyou.

7

a. 以后/後 *yǐhòu* b. 以后/後 *yǐhòu*, 就 *jiù* c. 以前 *yǐqián* d. 以后/後 *yǐhòu*, 才 *cái* e. 先 *xiān* . . . 再 *zài* f. 就 *jiù*

8 Sample reponse:

先洗手，再把西红柿切片，打蛋。打起泡以后，加热油锅，倒油，再把蛋倒进去，翻炒。还没有全熟就拿出来，炒西红柿。加糖，再把蛋倒回去，加盐。翻炒一分钟，再起锅。

先洗手，再把西紅柿切片，打蛋。打起泡以後，加熱油鍋，倒油，再把蛋倒進去，翻炒。還沒有全熟就拿出來，炒西紅柿。加糖，再把蛋倒回去，加鹽。翻炒一分鐘，再起鍋。

Xiān xǐ shǒu, zài bǎ xīhóngshì qiēpiàn, dǎ dàn. Dǎqǐ pào yǐhòu, jiārè yóuguō, dǎo yóu, zài bǎ dàn dàojìn qù, fānchǎo. Hái méi yǒu quán shóu jiù náchūlái, chǎo xīhóngshì. Jiā táng, zài bǎ dàn dǎohuíqu, jiā yán. Fānchǎo yī fēn zhōng, zài qǐ guō.

43 Expressing simultaneous situations

1
a. 小李上课的时候，跟同学说话。
小李上課的時候，跟同學說話。
Xiǎo Lǐ shàng kè de shíhou, gēn tóngxué shuō huà.
b. 小李走路的时候，听中文录音。
小李走路的時候，聽中文錄音。
Xiǎo Lǐ zǒu lù de shíhou, tīng Zhōngwén lùyīn.
c. 小李开车的时候，听收音机。
小李開車的時候，聽收音機。
Xiǎo Lǐ kāi chē de shíhou, tīng shōuyīnjī.
d. 小李吃饭的时候，看电视。
小李吃飯的時候，看電視。
Xiǎo Lǐ chī fàn de shíhou, kàn diànshì.
e. 小李跟朋友聊天的时候，喝酒。
小李跟朋友聊天的時候，喝酒。
Xiǎo Lǐ gēn péngyou liáotiān de shíhou, hē jiǔ.
f. 小李看电影的时候，吃东西。
小李看電影的時候，吃東西。
Xiǎo Lǐ kàn diànyǐng de shíhou, chī dōngxi.
g. 小李洗澡的时候，唱歌。
小李洗澡的時候，唱歌。
Xiǎo Lǐ xǐ zǎo de shíhou, chàng gē.
h. 小李跳舞的时候，唱歌。
小李跳舞的時候，唱歌。
Xiǎo Lǐ tiào wǔ de shíhou, chàng gē.

2
a. 我小的时候，不喜欢上学。
我小的時候，不喜歡上學。
Wǒ xiǎo de shíhou, bù xǐhuan shàng xué.

b. 他昨天晚上回来的时候，已经十一点了。
他昨天晚上回來的時候，已經十一點了。
Tā zuótiān wǎnshang huí lai de shíhou, yǐjing shíyī diǎn le.

c. 他走的时候，下雨了。
他走的時候，下雨了。
Tā zǒu de shíhou, xià yǔ le.

d. 考试的时候，学生不许讲话。
考試的時候，學生不許講話。
Kǎo shì de shíhou, xuésheng bù xǔ jiǎng huà.

e. 开车的时候，最好不要用手机。
開車的時候，最好不要用手機。
Kāi chē de shíhou, zuì hǎo bù yào yòng shǒujī.

f. 你进来的时候，我在打电话。
你進來的時候，我在打電話。
Nǐ jìnlai de shíhou, wǒ zài dǎ diànhuà.

g. 我睡觉的时候，请不要大声说话。
我睡覺的時候，請不要大聲說話。
Wǒ shuì jiào de shíhou, qǐng bù yào dà shēng shuō huà.

h. 我去年在北京的时候认识他的。
我去年在北京的時候認識他的。
Wǒ qùnián zài Běijīng de shíhou rènshi tā de.

3

a. 小李一边上课，一边跟同学说话。
小李一邊上課，一邊跟同學說話。
Xiǎo Lǐ yībiān shàng kè, yībiān gēn tóngxué shuō huà.

b. 小李一边走路，一边听中文录音。
小李一邊走路，一邊聽中文錄音。
Xiǎo Lǐ yībiān zǒu lù, yībiān tīng Zhōngwén lùyīn.

c. 小李一边开车，一边听收音机。
小李一邊開車，一邊聽收音機。
Xiǎo Lǐ yībiān kāi chē, yībiān tīng shōuyīnjī.

d. 小李一边吃饭，一边看电视。
小李一邊吃飯，一邊看電視。
Xiǎo Lǐ yībiān chī fàn, yībiān kàn diànshì.

e. 小李一边跟朋友聊天，一边喝酒。
小李一邊跟朋友聊天，一邊喝酒。
Xiǎo Lǐ yībiān gēn péngyou liáotiān, yībiān hē jiǔ.

f. 小李一边看电影，一边吃东西。
小李一邊看電影，一邊吃東西。
Xiǎo Lǐ yībiān kàn diànyǐng, yībiān chī dōngxi.

g. 小李一边洗澡，一边唱歌。
小李一邊洗澡，一邊唱歌。
Xiǎo Lǐ yībiān xǐ zǎo, yībiān chàng gē.

h. 小李一边跳舞，一边唱歌。

小李一邊跳舞，一邊唱歌。

Xiǎo Lǐ yībiān tiào wǔ, yībiān chàng gē.

4　小李又笨又懒。他说的中文又慢又不清楚。他写的汉字又不好看，又不整齐。他的宿舍又小又不干净。他做的中国饭又不好看又不好吃。

小李又笨又懶。他說的中文又慢又不清楚。他寫的漢字又不好看，又不整齊。他的宿舍又小又不乾淨。他做的中國飯又不好看又不好吃。

Xiǎo Li yòu bèn yòu lǎn. Tā shuō de Zhōngwén yòu màn yòu bù qīngchu. Tā xiě de Hàn zì yòu bù hǎo kàn, yòu bù zhěngqí. Tā de sùshè yòu xiǎo yòu bù gānjìng. Tā zuò de zhōngguó fàn yòu bù hǎo kàn yòu bù hǎo chī.

5　a. 今天外边又刮风又下雨。

今天外邊又颱風又下雨。

Jīntiān wàibian yòu guā fēng yòu xià yǔ.

b. 我进宿舍的时候我的同屋在做功课。

我進宿舍的時候我的同屋在做功課。

Wǒ jìn sùshè de shíhou wǒ de tóngwū zài zuò gōngkè.

c. 他听着音乐做功课。

他聽著音樂做功課。

Tā tīngzhe yīnyuè zuò gōngkè.

d. 我进屋子的时候他正在打电话。

我進屋子的時候他正在打電話。

Wǒ jìn wūzi de shíhou tā zhèngzài dǎ diànhuà.

e. 他一边打电话一边看电视。

他一遍打電話一邊看電視。

Tā yībiān dǎ diànhuà yībiān kàn diànshì.

f. 同时，还在电脑上看电信。

同時，還在電腦上看電信。

Tóngshí, hái zài diànnǎo shàng kàn diànxìn.

g. 等到他打完了电话我已经睡着了。

等到他打完了電話我已經睡著了。

Děngdào tā dǎ wán le diànhuà wǒ yǐjing shuìzháo le.

h. 那个国家一方面要发展经济，一方面要注重环保。

那個國家一方面要發展經濟，一方面要注重環保。

Nàge guójiā yīfāngmiàn yào fāzhǎn jīngjì, yīfāngmiàn yào zhùzhòng huán bǎo.

6　(Free response.)

44 Expressing cause and effect or reason and result

1

a. 因为我喜欢中国文化，所以在学中文。
因爲我喜歡中國文化，所以在學中文。
Yīnwei wǒ xǐhuan Zhōngguó wénhuà, suǒyǐ zài xué Zhōngwén.

b. 因为我在学中文，所以找了一个中国同屋。
因爲我在學中文，所以找了一個中國同屋。
Yīnwei wǒ zài xué Zhōngwén, suǒyǐ zhǎo le yī gè Zhōngguó tóngwū.

c. 因为我昨天病了，所以没去上课。
因爲我昨天病了，所以沒去上課。
Yīnwei wǒ zuótiān bìng le, suǒyǐ méi qù shàng kè.

d. 因为我昨天没去上课，所以不知道今天有考试。
因爲我昨天沒去上課，所以不知道今天有考試。
Yīnwei wǒ zuótiān méi qù shàng kè, suǒyǐ bù zhīdào jīntiān yǒu kǎoshì.

e. 因为我不知道今天有考试，所以没有准备。
因爲我不知道今天有考試，所以沒有準備。
Yīnwei wǒ bù zhīdào jīntiān yǒu kǎoshì, suǒyǐ méi yǒu zhǔnbèi.

f. 因为我没有准备，所以考得很不好。
因爲我沒有準備，所以考得很不好。
Yīnwei wǒ méi yǒu zhǔnbèi, suǒyǐ kǎo de hěn bù hǎo.

g. 因为我考得很不好，所以很不高兴。
因爲我考得很不好，所以很不高興。
Yīnwei wǒ kǎo de hěn bù hǎo, suǒyǐ hěn bù gāoxīng.

h. 因为我很不高兴，所以我的同屋今天晚上请我吃中国饭。
因爲我很不高興，所以我的同屋今天晚上請我吃中國飯。
Yīnwei wǒ hěn bù gāoxīng, suǒyǐ wǒ de tóngwū jīntiān wǎnshang qǐng wǒ chī Zhōngguó fàn.

2

a. Because he was sick, he has not come to class for three days. b. The reason why he wants to study in China is that he is very interested in Chinese pop music. c. The reason why I am inviting you to dinner is that I want to introduce you to a Chinese friend. d. Because he is homesick, he can't eat or sleep. e. Because of the heavy snow, I am not going to any of my evening classes. f. The reason why I did not come to the exam was that I did not know there was an exam. g. The reason why I did not finish writing my report was that my computer is broken. h. Because of exams, students recently have been drinking less.

3

a. 我去台湾是为了旅游。
我去臺灣是爲了旅游。
Wǒ qù Táiwān shì wèile lǚyóu.

b. 他去中国是为了找工作。
他去中國是爲了找工作。
Tā qù Zhōngguó shì wèile zhǎo gōngzuò.

c. 我们走路上学是为了锻炼身体。
　　我們走路上學是爲了鍛煉身體。
　　Wǒmen zǒu lù shàng xué shì wèile duànliàn shēntǐ.

d. 她跟中国人说话是为了练习口语。
　　她跟中國人說話是爲了練習口語。
　　Tā gēn Zhōngguórén shuō huà shì wèile liànxí kǒuyǔ.

e. 学生们每天听录音是为了提高听力。
　　學生們每天聽錄音是爲了提高聽力。
　　Xuéshēngmen měitiān tīng lùyīn shì wèile tígāo tīnglì.

f. 我的同屋去图书馆是为了准备明天的考试。
　　我的同屋去圖書館是爲了準備明天的考試。
　　Wǒ de tóngwū qù túshūguǎn shì wèile zhǔnbèi míngtiān de kǎoshì.

g. 他们看中国电影是为了了解中国文化。
　　他們看中國電影是爲了瞭解中國文化。
　　Tāmen kàn Zhōngguó diànyǐng shì wèile liáojiě Zhōngguó wénhuà.

h. 我找张老师是为了请假。
　　我找張老師是爲了請假。
　　Wǒ zhǎo Zhāng lǎoshī shì wèile qǐng jià.

4 a. Why have you come to look for me? b. Why didn't you go to the coffee shop? c. Why didn't you call me? d. How could you forget?

5 a. 因为大家合作的关系，我们成功了。
　　因爲大家合作的關係，我們成功了。
　　Yīnwéi dàjiā hézuò de guānxi, wǒmen chénggōng le.

b. 我们之所以成功是因为大家的合作。
　　我們之所以成功是因爲大家的合作。
　　Wǒmen zhī suǒyǐ chénggōng shì yīnwéi dàjiā de hézuò.

c. 因为大家的合作，所以我们成功了。
　　因爲大家的合作，所以我們成功了。
　　Yīnwéi dàjiā de hézuò, suǒyǐ wǒmen chénggōng le.

d. 由于大家的合作，我们成功了。
　　由于大家的合作，我們成功了。
　　Yóuyú dàjiā de hézuò, wǒmen chénggōng le.

6 (Free response.)

7 (Free response.)

45 Expressing conditions

1

a. 你最好让你弟弟吃早饭，否则他就会饿得上不了课。

你最好讓你弟弟吃早飯，否則他就會餓得上不了課。

Nǐ zuì hǎo ràng nǐ dìdi chī zǎofàn, fǒuzé tā jiù huì è de shàngbùliǎo kè.

b. 只要你请你弟弟看电影，他就会高兴。

只要你請你弟弟看電影，他就會高興。

Zhǐ yào nǐ qǐng nǐ dìdi kàn diànyǐng, tā jiù huì gāoxìng.

c. 除非你帮你弟弟做作业，要不然他做不完。

除非你幫你弟弟做作業，要不然他做不完。

Chúfēi nǐ bāng nǐ dìdi zuò zuòyè, yàobùrán tā zuòbuwán.

d. 你最好帮你的弟弟做作业，要不然他考不好。

你最好幫你的弟弟做作業，要不然他考不好。

Nǐ zuìhǎo bāng nǐ de dìdi zuò zuòyè, yàobùrán tā kǎo bù hǎo.

e. 只要你用功，你一定考得上大学。

只要你用功，你一定考得上大學。

Zhǐ yào nǐ yònggōng, nǐ yīdìng kǎodeshàng dàxué.

f. 就是你帮你的弟弟做作业，他也许还考得不好。

就是你幫你的弟弟做作業，他也許還考得不好。

Jiù shì nǐ bāng nǐ de dìdi zuò zuòyè, tā yéxǔ hái kǎo de bù hǎo.

g. 就是你帮你的弟弟做作业，他还不懂。

就是你幫你的弟弟做作業，他還不懂。

Jiù shì nǐ bāng nǐ de dìdi zuò zuòyè, tā hái bù dǒng.

2

a. 要是我有钱，我就不用在图书馆工作。

要是我有錢，我就不用在圖書館工作。

Yàoshi wǒ yǒu qián, wǒ jiù bù yòng zài túshūguǎn gōngzuò.

b. 要是我不工作，我就会有更多的时间读书。

要是我不工作，我就會有更多的時間讀書。

Yàoshi wǒ bù gōngzuò, wǒ jiù huì yǒu gèng duō de shíjiān dú shū.

c. 要是我有更多的时间读书，我的成绩就会好一点。

要是我有更多的時間讀書，我的成績就會好一點。

Yàoshi wǒ yǒu gèng duō de shíjiān dú shū, wǒ de chéngjì jiù huì hǎo yīdiǎn.

d. 要是我的成绩就好，我的父母就会很高兴。

要是我的成績就好，我的父母就會很高興。

Yàoshi wǒ de chéngjì jiù hǎo, wǒ de fùmǔ jiù huì hěn gāoxìng.

e. 要是我的父母高兴，他们就会给我钱。

要是我的父母高興，他們就會給我錢。

Yàoshi wǒ de fùmǔ gāoxìng, tāmen jiù huì gěi wǒ qián.

f. 要是他们给我钱，我就不用工作了。

要是他們給我錢，我就不用工作了。

Yàoshi tāmen gěi wǒ qián, wǒ jiù bù yòng gōngzuò le.

3

a. 如果我是你，我就先跟朋友借钱。
如果我是你，我就先跟朋友借錢。
Rúguǒ wǒ shì nǐ, wǒ jiù xiān gēn péngyou jiè qián.

b. 如果我能借到钱，我就不用工作了。
如果我能借到錢，我就不用工作了。
Rúguǒ wǒ néng jièdào qián, wǒ jiù bù yòng gōngzuò le.

c. 如果我不用工作，我就会有更多时间读书。
如果我不用工作，我就會有更多時間讀書。
Rúguǒ wǒ bùyòng gōngzuò, wǒ jiù huì yǒu gèng duō shíjiān dú shū.

d. 如果我有更多时间读书，我的成绩就会好。
如果我有更多時間讀書，我的成績就會好。
Rúguǒ wǒ yǒu gèng duō shíjiān dú shū, wǒ de chéngjì jiù huì hǎo.

e. 如果我的成绩好，我的父母就会很高兴。
如果我的成績好，我的父母就會很高興。
Rúguǒ wǒ de chéngjì hǎo, wǒ de fùmǔ jiù huì hěn gāoxìng.

f. 如果我的父母高兴，他们就会给我钱。
如果我的父母高興，他們就會給我錢。
Rúguǒ wǒ de fùmǔ gāoxìng, tāmen jiù huì gěi wǒ qián.

g. 如果他们给我钱，我就把钱还给我的朋友。
如果他們給我錢，我就把錢還給我的朋友。
Rúguǒ tāmen gěi wǒ qián, wǒ jiù bǎ qián huán gěi wǒ de péngyou.

4

a. 倘若我是你，我就先跟我的父母借钱。
倘若我是你，我就先跟我的父母借錢。
Tǎngruò wǒ shì nǐ, wǒ jiù xiān gēn wǒ de fùmǔ jiè qián.

b. 倘若他们借给我钱，我就不用工作了。
倘若他們借給我錢，我就不用工作了。
Tǎngruò tāmen jiè gěi wǒ qián, wǒ jiù bù yòng gōngzuò le.

c. 倘若我不工作，我就更努力地学习。
倘若我不工作，我就更努力地學習。
Tǎngruò wǒ bù gōngzuò, wǒ jiù gèng nǔlì de xuéxí.

d. 倘若我努力地学习，我的成绩就会更好。
倘若我努力地學習，我的成績就會更好。
Tǎngruò wǒ nǔlì de xuéxí, wǒ de chéngjì jiù huì gèng hǎo.

e. 倘若我的成绩好，我的父母就会很高兴。
倘若我的成績好，我的父母就會很高興。
Tǎngruò wǒ de chéngjì hǎo, wǒ de fùmǔ jiù huì hěn gāoxìng.

f. 倘若我的父母高兴，他们就会给我钱。
倘若我的父母高興，他們就會給我錢。
Tǎngruò wǒ de fùmǔ gāoxìng, tāmen jiù huì gěi wǒ qián.

g. 倘若他们给我钱，我就用这些钱还他们。
倘若他們給我錢，我就用這些錢還他們。
Tǎngruò tāmen gěi wǒ qián, wǒ jiù yòng zhè xiē qián huán tāmen.

5 (Free response.)

6 (Free response.)

46 Expressing 'both,' 'all,' 'every,' 'any, 'none,' 'not any,' and 'no matter how'

1
a. 我们都喜欢学中文。
我們都喜歡學中文。
Wǒmen dōu xǐhuan xué Zhōngwén.
b. 那些书我都买了。
那些書我都買了。
Nà xiē shū wǒ dōu mǎi le.
c. 那些书都很贵。
那些書都很貴。
Nà xiē shū dōu hěn guì.
d. 学生们都没去上课。
學生們都沒去上課。
Xuéshēngmen dōu méi qù shàng kè.
e. 中文日文我都学。
中文日文我都學。
Zhōngwén Rìwén wǒ dōu xué.
f. 所有的功课我都做完了。
所有的功課我都做完了。
Suǒyǒu de gōngkè wǒ dōu zuòwán le.
g. 他一个字都不会写。
他一個字都不會寫。
Tā yī gè zì dōu bù huì xiě.
h. 我们都不喜欢那个老师。
我們都不喜歡那個老師。
Wǒmen dōu bù xǐhuan nàge lǎoshī.

2
a. 哪儿/哪兒 **nǎr?** b. 什么/甚麼 **shénme** c. 谁/誰 **shéi** d. 什么/甚麼 **shénme**
e. 什么/甚麼 **shénme** f. 什么/甚麼 **shénme** g. 几/幾 **jǐ** h. 怎么/怎麼 **zěnme**

3
a. 我什么电影都不想看。
我甚麼電影都不想看。
Wǒ shénme diànyǐng dōu bù xiǎng kàn.
I don't want to watch any movie.
b. 我什么啤酒都不想喝。
我甚麼啤酒都不想喝。
Wǒ shénme píjiǔ dōu bù xiǎng hē.
I don't want to drink any beer.

c.　我谁都不认识。
　　我誰都不認識。
　　Wǒ shéi dōu bù rènshi.
　　I do not know anyone.

d.　这件事我谁都不想告诉。
　　這件事我誰都不想告訴。
　　Zhè jiàn shì wǒ shéi dōu bù xiǎng gàosu.
　　I don't want to tell anybody about this matter.

e.　谁都不要借给我钱。
　　誰都不要借給我錢。
　　Shéi dōu bù yào jiègěi wǒ qián.
　　Nobody wants to lend me money.

f.　我什么都不想跟你说。
　　我甚麼都不想跟你說。
　　Wǒ shénme dōu bù xiǎng gēn nǐ shuō.
　　I don't want to tell you anything.

g.　哪件毛衣我都不喜欢。
　　哪件毛衣我都不喜歡。
　　Nǎ jiàn máoyī wǒ dōu bù xǐhuan.
　　I do not like any of those sweaters.

h.　我放假什么地方都不去。
　　我放假甚麼地方都不去。
　　Wǒ fang jià shénme dìfang dōu bù qù.
　　I am not going anywhere during the break.

4

a.　我怎么学也学不会。
　　我怎麼學也學不會。
　　Wǒ zěnme xué yě xuébuhuì.

b.　我怎么记也记不住。
　　我怎麼記也記不住。
　　Wǒ zěnme jì yě jìbuzhù.

c.　我怎么写也写不完。
　　我怎麼寫也寫不完。
　　Wǒ zěnme xiě yě xiěbuwán.

d.　我怎么猜也猜不着。
　　我怎麼猜也猜不著。
　　Wǒ zěnme cāi yě cāibuzhāo.

e.　我怎么看也看不懂。
　　我怎麼看也看不懂。
　　Wǒ zěnme kàn yě kànbudǒng.

f.　我怎么想也想不起答案来。
　　我怎麼想也想不起答案來。
　　Wǒ zěnme xiǎng yě xiǎngbuqǐ dá'àn lai.

5

a. 他谁都不喜欢。
他誰都不喜歡。
Tā shéi dōu bù xǐhuan.

b. 他什么事情都不愿意做。
他甚麼事情都不願意做。
Tā shénme shìqing dōu bù yuànyi zuò.

c. 你怎么跟他说话他都不听。
你怎麼跟他說話他都不聽。
Nǐ zěnme gēn tā shuō huà tā dōu bù tīng.

d. 屋子里哪儿都是他的东西。
屋子裏哪兒都是他的東西。
Wūzi lǐ nǎr dōu shì tā de dōngxi.

e. 衣服多么脏他也不洗。
衣服多麼髒他也不洗。
Yīfu duōme zàng tā yě bù xǐ.

f. 他晚上什么时候都在看电视。
他晚上甚麼時候都在看電視。
Tā wǎnshang shénme shíhòu dōu zài kàn diànshì.

g. 你怎么跟他说，他都不关电视。
你怎麼跟他說，他都不關電視。
Nǐ zěnme gēn tā shuō, tā dōu bù guān diànshì.

h. 早上你怎么叫他，他都不醒。
早上你怎麼叫他，他都不醒。
Zǎoshang nǐ zěnme jiào tā, tā dōu bù xǐng.

6

赵太太： 他谁都不想见、什么事都不想做、哪里都不想去、什么东西都不吃。
趙太太： 他誰都不想見、甚麼事都不想做、哪裏都不想去、甚麼東西都不吃。
Zhào tàitai: Tā shéi dōu bù xiǎng jiàn, shénme shì dōu bù xiǎng zuò, nǎli dōu bù xiǎng qù, shénme dōngxi dōu bù chī.
郭太太： 谁都需要时间好好地想想。
郭太太： 誰都需要時間好好地想想。
Guō tàitai: Shéi dōu xūyào shíjiān hǎohaode xiǎngxiang.

7

a. 每天都要遛狗，早上一次，晚上一次。
Měitiān dōu yào liù gǒu, zǎoshang yī cì, wǎnshang yī cì.

b. 每两天浇一次花。
每兩天澆一次花。
Měi liǎng tiān jiāo yī cì huā.

c. 每个星期拿一次信。
每個星期拿一次信。
Měi ge xīngqī ná yī cì xìn.

47 Expressing location and distance

1

a. 医院在城的西南边。
医院在城的西南邊。
Yīyuàn zài chéng de xīnán biān.

b. 中学在城的西北边。
中學在城的西北邊。
Zhōngxué zài chéng de xībĕi biān.

c. 火车站在城的南边。
火車站在城的南邊。
Huŏchēzhàn zài chéng de nánbiān.

d. 银行在城的东边。
銀行在城的東邊。
Yínháng zài chéng de dōngbian.

e. 公园在湖的右边。
公園在湖的右邊。
Gōngyuán zài hú de yòubian.

f. 公园在城的外边。
公園在城的外邊。
Gōngyuán zài chéng de wàibian.

g. 银行在体育馆的北边。
銀行在體育館的北邊。
Yínháng zài tǐyùguăn de bĕibiān.

h. 书店在中学的东边。
書店在中學的東邊。
Shūdiàn zài zhōngxué de dōngbian.

i. 宿舍和中学的中间是书店。
宿舍和中學的中間是書店。
Sùshè hé zhōngxué de zhōngjiān shì shūdiàn.

j. 公园的旁边是湖。
公園的旁邊是湖。
Gōngyuán de pángbiān shì hú.

2

a. 高蕾的右边是饶兴荣。
高蕾的右邊是饒興榮。
Gāo Lĕi de yòubian shì Ráo Xīngróng.

b. 林道余的后头是唐新花。
林道余的後頭是唐新花。
Lín Dàoyú de hòutou shì Táng Xīnhuā.

c. 徐乃康在陈玫玲跟唐新花的中间。
徐乃康在陳玫玲跟唐新花的中間。
Xú Năikāng zài Chén Méilíng gēn Táng Xīnhuā de zhōngjiān.

d. 陈玫玲的左边是王鹏飞。
陳玫玲的左邊是王鵬飛。
Chén Méilíng de zuǒbian shì Wáng Péngfēi.

e. 徐乃康的前边是马嘉美。
徐乃康的前邊是馬嘉美。
Xú Nǎikāng de qiánbian shì Mǎ Jiāměi.

f. 王鹏飞的右边是陈玫玲。
王鵬飛的右邊是陳玫玲。
Wáng Péngfēi de yòubian shì Chén Méilíng.

g. 林道余的旁边是马嘉美。
林道余的旁邊是馬嘉美。
Lín Dàoyú de pángbiān shì Mǎ Jiāměi.

3

a. 房子的前边
房子的前邊
fángzi de qiánbian

b. 两辆车的中间
兩輛車的中間
liǎng liàng chē de zhōngjiān

c. 房子的左边
房子的左邊
fángzi de zuǒbian

d. 那个人的前边
那個人的前邊
nèige rén de qiánbian

e. 桌子上的书
桌子上的書
zhuōzi shàng de shū

f. 右边的房子
右邊的房子
yòubian de fángzi

g. 学校后边的火车站
學校後邊的火車站
xuéxiào hòubian de huǒchēzhàn

h. 前边的那个人
前邊的那個人
qiánbian de nàge rén

i. 猫在桌子上。
貓在桌子上。
Māo zài zhuōzi shàng.

j. 狗在房子的后边。
狗在房子的後邊。
Gǒu zài fángzi de hòubian.

k. 公园里有花。
    公園裏有花。
    Gōngyuán lǐ yǒu huā.

l. 房子里没人。
    房子裏沒人。
    Fángzi lǐ méi rén.

m. 图书馆里有学生。
    圖書館裏有學生。
    Túshūguǎn lǐ yǒu xuésheng.

n. 宿舍里没有猫。
    宿舍裏沒有貓。
    Sùshè lǐ méi yǒu māo.

4

a. 你家离大学远。
    你家離大學遠。
    Nǐ jiā lí dàxué yuǎn.

b. 你家离公园不远。
    你家離公園不遠。
    Nǐ jiā lí gōngyuán bù yuǎn.

c. 你家离火车站远。
    你家離火車站遠。
    Nǐ jiā lí huǒchēzhàn yuǎn.

d. 公园离大学远。
    公園離大學遠。
    Gōngyuán lí dàxué yuǎn.

e. 你家离飞机场很远。
    你家離飛機場很遠。
    Nǐ jiā lí fēijīchǎng hěn yuǎn.

f. 你家离大学有十二公里。
    你家離大學有十二公里。
    Nǐ jiā lí dàxué yǒu shí'èr gōnglǐ.

g. 你家离火车站有五公里。
    你家離火車站有五公里。
    Nǐ jiā lí huǒchēzhàn yǒu wǔ gōnglǐ.

h. 公园离飞机场有二十三公里。
    公園離飛機場有二十三公里。
    Gōngyuán lí fēijīchǎng yǒu èrshísān gōnglǐ.

i. 大学离飞机场有十三公里。
    大學離飛機場有十三公里。
    Dàxué lí fēijīchǎng yǒu shísān gōnglǐ.

j. 你家离飞机场有二十五公里。
    你家離飛機場有二十五公里。
    Nǐ jiā lí fēijīchǎng yǒu èrshíwǔ gōnglǐ.

48 Talking about movement, directions, and means of transportation

1

a. 大学在哪儿？
大學在哪兒？
Dàxué zài nǎr?

b. 到大学怎么走？
到大學怎麼走？
Dào dàxué zěnme zǒu?

c. 从这儿到去大学怎么走？
從這兒到去大學怎麼走？
Cóng zhèr dào qù dàxué zěnme zǒu?

d. 从宿舍到书店怎么走？
從宿舍到書店怎麼走？
Cóng sùshè dào shūdiàn zěnme zǒu?

e. 往左拐吗？
往左拐嗎？
Wǎng zuǒ guǎi ma?

f. 往左拐还是往右拐？
往左拐還是往右拐？
Wǎng zuǒ guǎi háishi wǎng yòu guǎi?

g. 图书馆在左边还是在右边？
圖書館在左邊還是在右邊？
Túshūguǎn zài zuǒbian háishi zài yòubian?

h. 你知道书店在哪里吗？
你知道書店在哪裏嗎？
Nǐ zhīdao shūdiàn zài nǎli ma?

2

a. (1) 从/從 **cóng** (2) 到 **dào** (3) 怎么/怎麼 **zěnme** b. (1) 不起 **bùqǐ**
(2) 不知道 **bù zhīdào** c. (1) 知道 **zhīdào** (2) 怎么/怎麼 **zěnme**
d. (1) 从/從 **cóng** (2) 往 **wǎng** (3) 过/過 **guò** (4) 拐 **guǎi** (5) 走 **zǒu**
(6) 左 **zuǒ**

3

a. 往东走。
往東走。
Wǎng dōng zǒu.

b. 在中山路上往东走。
在中山路上往東走。
Zài Zhōngshān lù shàng wǎng dōng zǒu.

c. 过一个(十字)路口。
過一個(十字)路口。
Guò yī gè (shízì) lùkǒu.

d. 过公园路。

过公園路。

Guò gōngyuán lù.

e. 再往东走。 *or* 一直往东走。

再往東走。 *or* 一直往東走。

Zài wǎng dōng zǒu. *or* **Yīzhí wǎng dōng zǒu.**

f. 在图书馆路往右拐。

在圖書館路往右拐。

Zài túshūguǎn lù wǎng yòu guǎi.

g. 一直往前走。

Yīzhí wàng qián zǒu.

h. 过两个路口。

過兩個路口。

Guò liǎng gè lùkǒu.

i. 在第三个路口往左拐。

在第三個路口往左拐。

Zài dì sān gè lùkǒu wǎng zuǒ guǎi.

j. 那是白湖路。

Nà shì Bái hú lù.

k. 公园在你的右边。

公園在你的右邊。

Gōng yuán zài nǐ de yòubian.

4

a. 我们开进去了。

我們開進去了。

Wǒmen kāi jìn qù le.

b. 我们爬上山去了。

我們爬上山去了。

Wǒmen pá shàng shān qù le.

c. 她跑过来了。

她跑過來了。

Tā pǎo guò lái le.

d. 他们都走出去了。

他們都走出去了。

Tāmen dōu zǒu chū qù le.

e. 我把书拿回来了。

我把書拿回來了。

Wǒ bǎ shū ná huí lái le.

5

a. 我是坐公共汽车来的。

我是坐公共汽車來的。

Wǒ shì zuò gōnggòng qìchē lái de.

b. 我是坐车来的。
   我是坐車來的。
   Wǒ shì zuò chē lái de.

c. 我是骑自行车来的。
   我是騎自行車來的。
   Wǒ shì qí zìxíngchē lái de.

d. 我是走路来的。
   我是走路來的。
   Wǒ shì zǒu lù lái de.

e. 我是骑摩托车来的。
   我是騎摩托車來的。
   Wǒ shì qí mótuōchē lái de.

f. 我是坐地铁来的。
   我是坐地鐵來的。
   Wǒ shì zuò dìtiě lái de.

6   a. dorm: D; b. library: G; c. park: A; d. school: H; e. bank: C; f. bookstore: F

49   Talking about clock time and calendar time

1   a. 十一点半/十一點半 shíyī diǎn bàn b. 1:45 c. 差十分七点/差十分七點 chà shífēn qī diǎn d. 3:15 e. 七点四十/七點四十 qī diǎn sìshí f. 2:20 g. 八点过 一分/八點過一分 bā diǎn guò yī fēn h. 9:25 i. 六点差五分/六點差五分 liù diǎn chà wǔ fēn j. 十二点过十二分/十二點過十二分 shí'èr diǎn guò shí'èr fēn

2   a. 两个星期/兩個星期 liǎng gè xīngqī b. 两天/兩天 liǎng tiān c. 两个小时/兩個 小時 liǎng gè xiǎoshí d. 两个学期/兩個學期 liǎng gè xuéqī e. 两分钟/兩分鐘 liǎng fēn zhōng f. 两个半星期/兩個半星期 liǎng gè bàn xīngqī g. 两天半/ 兩天半 liǎng tiān bàn h. 两分半钟/兩分半鐘 liǎng fēn bàn zhōng i. 两个半月/ 兩個半月 liǎng gè bàn yuè j. 两年半/兩年半 liǎng nián bàn

3   a. 一九九三年七月一日 yī jiǔ jiǔ sān nián qī yuè yī rì b. February 16, 1884
c. 二〇〇三年五月二十三日 èr líng líng sān nián wǔ yuè èrshísān rì
d. March 27, 2005 e. 一九九八年十月五日 yī jiǔ jiǔ bā nián shí yuè wǔ rì
f. August 22, 2008 g. 二〇〇二年一月一日 èr líng líng èr nián yī yuè yī rì
h. September 19, 1916

4   a. 王小妹上星期一买飞机票了。
   王小妹上星期一買飛機票了。
   Wáng Xiǎomèi shàng xīngqīyī mǎi fēijī piào le.

b. 王小妹上星期四游泳了。
   Wáng Xiǎomèi shàng xīngqīsì yóuyǒng le.

c. 王小妹这个星期日回家了。
   王小妹這個星期日回家了。
   Wáng Xiǎomèi zhège xīngqīrì huí jiā le.

d. 王小妹这星期六考中文。
王小妹這星期六考中文。
Wáng Xiǎomèi zhè (gè) xīngqīliù kǎo Zhōngwén.

e. 王小妹下星期日看电影。
王小妹下星期日看電影。
Wáng Xiǎomèi xià (gè) xīngqīrì kàn diànyǐng.

f. 王小妹下星期二听音乐会。
王小妹下星期二聽音樂會。
Wáng Xiǎomèi xià xīngqī èr tīng yīnyuèhuì.

g. 王小妹下星期五看朋友。
Wáng Xiǎomèi xià xīngqīwǔ kàn péngyou.

5 a. 大前天 **dàqiántiān** b. 前天 **qiántiān** c. 昨天 **zuótiān** d. 今天 **jīntiān**
e. 明天 **míngtiān** f. 后天/後天 **hòutiān** g. 大后天/大後天 **dà hòutiān**

6 a. 六点钟/六點鐘 **liù diǎn zhōng**

b. 一个半小时/一個半小時 **yī gè bàn xiǎoshí**

c. 天气不好/天氣不好 **tiānqì bù hǎo**

d. 337号/337號 337 **hào**

e. 一刻钟以后/一刻鐘以後 **yī kè zhōng yǐhòu**

f. 叫旅客马上登机/叫旅客馬上登機 **jiào lǚkè mǎshàng dēngjī**

g. 晚上7:45 **wǎnshang 7:45**

h. 没有 **méi yǒu**

i. 到服务台去办理换机手续
到服務台去辦理換機手續
Dào fúwùtái qù bànlǐ huànjī shǒuxù.

j. 十三个半小时
十三個半小時
shísān gè bàn xiǎoshí

k. 晚上八点钟/晚上八點鐘 **wǎnshang bādiǎn zhōng**

l. 一个小时/一個小時 **yī gè xiǎoshí**

m. 666号班机已经到达了。
666號班機已經到達了。
666 hào bānjī yǐjing dàodá le.

n. 到领取行李处去。
到領取行李處去。
Dào lǐngqǔ xíngli chù qù.

o. 可以。你可以在指定的吸烟区吸烟。
可以。你可以在指定的吸煙區吸煙。
Kěyǐ. Nǐ kěyǐ zài zhǐdìng de xīyān qū xīyān.

7

七月到九月我们得订摄影师、花店、化妆师、九月到十月决定请客名单。十月就得订场地。十一月是订饭店、买礼服。十二月要设计请帖。明年一月记得注册礼物。二月要确认所有预约的项目。三月买戒指，六月要决定座位，和确定典礼流程。

七月到九月我們得訂攝影師、花店、化妝師、九月到十月決定請客名單。十月就得訂場地。十一月是訂飯店、買禮服。十二月要設計請帖。明年一月記得註冊禮物。二月要確認所有預約的項目。三月買戒指，六月要決定座位，和確定典禮流程。

Qīyuè dào jiǔyuè wǒmen děi dìng shèyǐng shī, huādiàn, huàzhuāng shī. Jiǔyuè dào shíyuè juédìng qǐngkè míngdān. Shíyuè jiù děi dìng chǎngdì. Shíyīyuè shì dìng fàndiàn, mǎi lǐ fú. Shí'èryuè yào shèjì qǐngtiě. Míngnián yīyuè jìde zhùcè lǐwù. Èryuè yào quèrèn suǒyǒu yùyuē de xiàngmù. Sānyuè mǎi jièzhi, liùyuè yào juédìng zuòwèi, hé quèdìng diǎnlǐ liúchéng.

50 Expressing obligations and prohibitions

1

a. 现在我们得走了。
现在我們得走了。
Xiànzài wǒmen děi zǒu le.

b. 你一个人在学校，要照顾好自己。
你一個人在學校，要照顧好自己。
Nǐ yī gè rén zài xuéxiào, yào zhàogù hǎo zìjǐ.

c. 你要早睡早起。
Nǐ yào zǎo shuì zǎo qǐ.

d. 别睡得太晚。
Bié shuì dé tài wǎn.

e. 另外，你要按时上课，按时交作业。
另外，你要按時上課，按時交作業。
Lìngwài, nǐ yào ànshí shàng kè, ànshí jiāo zuòyè.

f. 考试的时候别紧张。
考試的時候別緊張。
Kǎoshì de shíhou bié jǐnzhāng.

g. 如果你有任何问题，你应该跟老师说。
如果你有任何問題，你應該跟老師說。
Rúguǒ nǐ yǒu rènhé wèntí, nǐ yīnggāi gēn lǎoshī shuō.

h. 如果觉得不舒服，你应该马上去医院。
如果覺得不舒服，你應該馬上去醫院。
Rúguǒ juéde bù shūfu, nǐ yīnggāi mǎshàng qù yīyuàn.

i. 还有，你得每天给我们打电话。
還有，你得每天給我們打電話。
Hái yǒu, nǐ děi měitiān gěi wǒmen dǎ diànhuà.

2

a. 禁止 **jìnzhǐ** 'prohibit' – spitting b. 勿 **wù** 'do not' – parking c. 免 **miǎn** 'refrain from' – trespassing d. 禁止 **jìnzhǐ** 'prohibit' – taking pictures e. 禁 **jìn** 'forbid' – drunk driving f. 勿 **wù** 'do not' – smoking

3

a. 不可以到处吐痰。
   不可以到處吐痰。
   Bù kěyǐ dàochù tǔtán.

b. 请不要在这里停车。
   請不要在這裏停車。
   Qǐng bù yào zài zhèli tíng chē.

c. 没有事的人不要进来。
   沒有事的人不要進來。
   Méi yǒu shì de rén bù yào jìnlai.

d. 不可以照相。
   Bù kěyǐ zhào xiàng.

e. 喝酒以后不可以开车。
   喝酒以後不可以開車。
   Hē jiǔ yǐhòu bù kěyǐ kāi chē.

f. 不可以吸烟。
   不可以吸烟。
   Bù kěyǐ xī yān.

4

a. 房租：每个月五号以前应当交房租一千两百块。
b. 杂费：房客必须自己付有线电视费用，可是不必付水电费。
c. 宠物：不许养宠物。
d. 规矩：禁止抽烟、十二点以后禁止吵闹
e. 访客：如果访客住超过十五天必须通知房东，如果少于十五天则无须通知。

a. 房租：每個月五號以前應當交房租一千兩百塊。
b. 雜費：房客必須自己付有線電視費用，可是不必付水電費。
c. 寵物：不許養寵物。
d. 規矩：禁止抽煙、十二點以後禁止吵鬧
e. 訪客：如果訪客住超過十五天必須通知房東，如果少於十五天則無須通知。

a. **fángzū:** Měi ge yuè wǔhào yǐqián yīngdāng jiāo fángzū yīqiān liǎngbǎi kuài.
b. **zá fèi:** Fángkè bìxū zìjǐ fù yǒuxiàn diànshì fèiyòng, kěshì bùbì fù shuǐdiàn fèi.
c. **chǒngwù:** Bùxǔ yǎng chǒngwù.
d. **guīju:** Jìnzhǐ chōuyān, shí'èr diǎn yǐhòu jìnzhǐ chǎonào.
e. **fǎngkè:** Rúguǒ fǎngkè zhù chāoguò shíwǔ tiān bìxū tōngzhī fángdōng, rúguǒ shǎo yú shíwǔ tiān zé wú xū tōngzhī.

5

(Free response.)

51 Expressing commands and permission

1

a. 看电视吧！
   看電視吧！
   Kàn diànshì ba!

b. 给你的弟弟打电话吧!
    給你的弟弟打電話吧!
    Gěi nǐ de dìdi dǎ diànhuà ba!

c. 吃饭吧!
    吃飯吧!
    Chī fàn ba!

d. 去看奶奶吧!
    Qù kàn nǎinai ba!

e. 说话吧!
    說話吧!
    Shuō huà ba!

f. 睡觉吧!
    睡覺吧!
    Shuì jiào ba!

g. 回家吧!
    Huí jiā ba!

h. 洗澡吧!
    Xǐ zǎo ba!

2

a. 大家公用的房间可以吸烟。
    大家公用的房間可以吸煙。
    Dàjiā gōngyòng de fángjiān kěyǐ xī yān.

b. 大家公用的房间可以做饭。
    大家公用的房間可以做飯。
    Dàjiā gōngyòng de fángjiān kěyǐ zuò fàn.

c. 可以在自己的房间里看电视。
    可以在自己的房間裏看電視。
    Kěyǐ zài zìjǐ de fángjiān lǐ kàn diànshì.

d. 可以请朋友来自己的房间。
    可以請朋友來自己的房間。
    Kěyǐ qǐng péngyou lái zìjǐ de fángjiān.

e. 房间里不可以吸烟。
    房間裏不可以吸煙。
    Fángjiān lǐ bù kěyǐ xī yān.

f. 房间里不可以喝酒。
    房間裏不可以喝酒。
    Fángjiān lǐ bù kěyǐ hē jiǔ.

g. 音乐的声音不能太大。
    音樂的聲音不能太大。
    Yīnyuè de shēngyīn bù néng tài dà.

h. 房间里不可以做饭。
    房間裏不可以做飯。
    Fángjiān lǐ bù kěyǐ zuò fàn.

i. 垃圾要每天扔掉。
   Lājī yào měitiān rēngdiào.

j. 晚上十点以前必须回宿舍。
   晚上十點以前必須回宿舍。
   Wǎnshàng shí diǎn yǐqián bìxū huí sùshè.

k. 晚上十一点三十关灯。
   晚上十一點三十關燈。
   Wǎnshàng shí yī diǎn sānshí guān dēng.

3

a. 上课别迟到。
   上課別遲到。
   Shàng kè bié chídào.

b. 上课不许吃东西。
   上課不許吃東西。
   Shàng kè bù xǔ chī dōngxi.

c. 上课不许喝饮料。
   上課不許喝飲料。
   Shàng kè bù xǔ hē yǐnliào.

d. 上课以前，把手机关掉。
   上課以前，把手機關掉。
   Shàng kè yǐqián, bǎ shǒujī guāndiào.

e. 上课的时候不可以发短信。
   上課的時候不可以發短信。
   Shàng kè de shíhou bù kěyǐ fā duǎnxìn.

f. 学生不允许晚交作业。
   學生不允許晚交作業。
   Xuésheng bù yǔnxǔ wǎn jiāo zuòyè.

g. 来上课以前，复习课文。
   來上課以前，復習課文。
   Lái shàng kè yǐqián, fùxí kèwén.

h. 有问题请举手。
   有問題請舉手。
   Yǒu wèntí qǐng jǔ shǒu.

4

a. 老师不让我们上课迟到。
   老師不讓我們上課遲到。
   Lǎoshī bù ràng wǒmen shàng kè chídào.

b. 老师不让我们上课吃东西。
   老師不讓我們上課吃東西。
   Lǎoshī bù ràng wǒmen shàng kè chī dōngxi.

c. 老师不让我们上课喝饮料。
   老師不讓我們上課喝飲料。
   Lǎoshī bù ràng wǒmen shàng kè hē yǐnliào.

d. 老师不让我们上课的时候，把手机开着。

老師不讓我們上課的時候，把手機開著。

Lǎoshī bù ràng wǒmen shàng kè de shíhou, bǎ shǒujī kāizhe.

e. 老师不让我们上课的时候发短信。

老師不讓我們上課的時候發短信。

Lǎoshī bù ràng wǒmen shàng kè de shíhou fā duǎnxìn.

f. 老师不让我们晚交作业。

老師不讓我們晚交作業。

Lǎoshī bù ràng wǒmen wǎn jiāo zuòyè.

g. 老师说我们上课以前得复习课文。

老師說我們上課以前得復習課文。

Lǎoshī shuō wǒmen shàng kè yǐqián děi fùxí kèwén.

h. 老师说有问题必须举手。

老師說有問題必須舉手。

Lǎoshī shuō yǒu wèntí bìxū jǔ shǒu.

5

Detective: 坐 zuò!

Detective: 你是江松吧？ **Nǐ shì Jiāng Sōng ba?**

Detective: 说！是谁让你偷哪个花瓶的？

說！是誰讓你偷那個花瓶的？

Shuō! Shì shéi rang nǐ tōu nàge huāpíng de?

Suspect: Nobody asked me to. Can I smoke?

Detective: 这里不许抽烟。不过你可以喝一杯水。拿着！

這裏不許抽煙。不過你可以喝一杯水。拿著！

Zhèlǐ bùxǔ chōu yān. Bùguò nǐ kěyǐ hē yī bēi shuǐ. Názhe!

Detective: 你准备好要写自白了吗？这是纸和笔。写吧！

你準備好要寫自白了嗎？這是紙和筆。寫吧？

Nǐ zhǔnbèi hǎo yào xiě zìbái le ma? Zhè shì zhǐ hé bǐ. Xiě ba!

52 Expressing ability and possibility

1

a. 我会说日语。

我會說日語。

Wǒ huì shuō Rìyǔ.

b. 我很会唱歌。

我很會唱歌。

Wǒ hěn huì chàng gē.

c. 我会跳舞。

我會跳舞。

Wǒ huì tiào wǔ.

d. 我会打篮球。

我會打籃球。

Wǒ huì dǎ lánqiú.

e. 我不会说中文。
   我不會說中文。
   Wǒ bù huì shuō Zhōngwén.

f. 我不会开车。
   我不會開車。
   Wǒ bù huì kāi chē.

g. 我不会用电脑。
   我不會用電腦。
   Wǒ bù huì yòng diànnǎo.

2

a. 你一天能学多少汉字?
   你一天能學多少漢字?
   Nǐ yītiān néng xué duōshao Hàn zì?

b. 这次我一定能考好。
   這次我一定能考好。
   Zhècì wǒ yīdìng néng kǎo hǎo.

c. 我的同屋病了不能去上课。
   我的同屋病了不能去上課。
   Wǒ de tóngwū bìng le bù néng qù shàng kè.

d. 我晚上没事，能跟你们去看电影。
   我晚上沒事，能跟你們去看電影。
   Wǒ wǎnshang méi shì, néng gēn nǐmen qù kàn diànyǐng.

3

A: Do you think he will come tonight? B: I think he will definitely come.
A: But the weather forecast says that there will be a big snowstorm tonight.
B: If it snows heavily, he will not be able to come.

4

a. 他以前会喝很多酒。现在不会了。
   他以前會喝很多酒。現在不會了。
   Tā yǐqián huì hē hěn duō jiǔ. Xiànzài bù huì le.

b. 因为他一喝酒就觉得不舒服了。
   因爲他一喝酒就覺得不舒服了。
   Yīnwéi tā yī hē jiǔ jiù juéde bù shūfu le.

c. 他可以喝可乐，汽水，茶，什么的。
   他可以喝可樂，汽水，茶，甚麼的。
   Tā kěyǐ hē kělè, qìshuǐ, chá, shénmede.

d. 他认为病一好就可以喝酒。
   他認爲病一好就可以喝酒。
   Tā rènwéi bìng yī hǎo jiù kěyǐ hē jiǔ.

e. 他喝了一点酒就觉得很不舒服。
   他喝了一點酒就覺得很不舒服。
   Tā hē le yīdiǎn jiǔ jiù juéde hěn bù shūfu.

f. 他说‘我能喝酒可是我不可以喝酒了。’
   他說‘我能喝酒可是我不可以喝酒了。’
   Tā shuō 'wǒ néng hē jiǔ kěshì wǒ bù kěyǐ hē jiǔ le.'

5

a. 今天晚上你会认识一个美女。她会给你她的电话号码。

今天晚上你會認識一個美女。她會給你她的電話號碼。

Jīntiān wǎnshang nǐ huì rènshi yī ge měinǚ. Tā huì gěi nǐ tā de diànhuà hàomǎ.

b. 你会说中文吗？学了中文以后，你可以去中国工作。

你會說中文嗎？學了中文以後，你可以去中國工作。

Nǐ huì shuō Zhōngwén ma? Xué le Zhōngwén yǐhòu, nǐ kěyǐ qù Zhōngguó gōngzuò.

c. 这个星期六有人会请你吃饭。

這個星期六有人會請你吃飯。

Zhège xīngqī liù yǒu rén huì qǐng nǐ chī fàn.

d. 餐厅旁边有一个小店。吃完晚饭以后，去那里买一张乐透券。你会中奖！

餐廳旁邊有一個小店。吃完晚飯以後，去那裏買一張樂透券。你會中獎！

Cāntīng pángbiān yǒu yī ge xiǎo diàn. Chīwán wǎnfàn yǐhòu, qù nàlǐ mǎi yī zhāng lètòu quàn. Nǐ huì zhòngjiǎng!

53 Expressing desires, needs, preferences, and willingness

1

a. 要 yào b. 希望 xīwàng c. 情愿/情願 qíngyuàn d. 愿意/願意 yuànyi
e. 情愿/情願 qíngyuàn f. 宁可/寧可 nìngkě g. 偏爱/偏愛 piān'ài

2

a. 你：你们毕业以后想作什么？

你：你們畢業以後想作什麼？

Nǐ: Nǐmen bìyè yǐhòu xiǎng zuò shénme?

b. 王明：我想去中国找工作。

王明：我想去中國找工作。

Wáng Míng: Wǒ xiǎng qù Zhōngguó zhǎo gōngzuò.

c. 唐玫玲：我希望有机会念博士学位。

唐玫玲：我希望有機會念博士學位。

Táng Méilíng: Wǒ xīwàng yǒu jīhuì niàn bóshì xuéwèi.

d. 周利：我要找工作。我宁可在国内工作，不愿意在国外工作。

周利：我要找工作。我寧可在國內工作，不願意在國外工作。

Zhōu Lì: Wǒ yào zhǎo gōngzuò. Wǒ nìngkě zài guónèi gōngzuò, bù yuànyi zài guówài gōngzuò.

3

a. 请问，有没有禁烟区的座位。

請問，有沒有禁煙區的座位。

Qǐngwèn, yǒu méi yǒu jìnyān qū de zuòwèi.

b. I'm sorry. We do not have non-smoking seats. Do you want to sit over there?

c. 我希望那边的人不抽烟。我们情愿到楼上去坐。

我希望那邊的人不抽煙。我們情願到樓上去坐。

Wǒ xīwàng nà biān de rén bù chōu yān. Wǒmen qíngyuàn dào lóushàng qù zuò.

d. No problem. There are seats upstairs.

e. What dishes would you like?

f. 我们要两个菜一个汤。希望你们不要放太多味精。

我們要兩個菜一個湯。希望你們不要放太多味精。

Wǒmen yào liǎng gè cài yī gè tāng. Xīwàng nǐmen bù yào fàng tài duō wèijīng.

g. What else do you need? (Do you need anything else?)

h. 我们还要一瓶啤酒，不要别的。

我們還要一瓶啤酒，不要別的。

Wǒmen hái yào yī píng píjiǔ, bù yào biéde.

老大：我宁可擦窗户也不要扫地。

我寧可擦窗戶也不要掃地。

Wǒ nìngkě cā chuānghù yě bùyào sǎodì.

老二：我不喜欢洗床单，谁愿意跟我交换？

我不喜歡洗床單，誰願意跟我交換？

Wǒ bù xǐhuān xǐ chuángdān, shéi yuànyì gēn wǒ jiāohuàn?

老三：我情愿洗床单也不要擦窗户。

我情願洗床單也不要擦窗戶。

Wǒ qíyuàn xǐ chuángdān yě bùyào cā chuānghù.

老四：有没有人要帮我做？我今天得做功课，哪儿有时间洗碗！

有沒有人要幫我做？我今天得做功課，哪兒有時間洗碗！

Yǒu méi yǒu rén yào bāng wǒ zuò? Wǒ jīntiān děi xǐ wǎn, nǎr yǒu shíjiān xǐ wǎn!

老五：妈妈总是偏爱老四，老四的工作比较容易！

媽媽總是偏愛老四，老四的工作比較容易！

Māma zǒngshì piān'ài lǎosì. Lǎosì de gōngzuò bǐjiào róngyì!

54 Expressing knowledge, advice, and opinions

a. 我会讲一点日语。

我會講一點日語。

Wǒ huì jiǎng yīdiǎn Rìyǔ.

b. 我知道图书馆在哪儿。

我知道圖書館在哪兒。

Wǒ zhīdao túshūguǎn zài nǎr.

c. 我认识那个人。

我認識那個人。

Wǒ rènshi nàge rén.

d. 别担心。我认识路，我能找到。

別擔心。我認識路，我能找到。

Bié dānxīn. Wǒ rènshi lù, wǒ néng zhǎodào.

e. 我知道他，并不认识他。
    我知道他，并不認識他。
    Wǒ zhīdào tā, bìng bù rènshi tā.
f. 我认识这个字，但是不知道怎么写。
    我認識這個字，但是不知道怎麼寫。
    Wǒ rènshi zhège zì, dànshì bù zhīdao zěnme xiě.
g. 我知道他为什么不来。
    我知道他爲甚麼不來。
    Wǒ zhīdao tā wéishénme bù lái.

2 a. 看 kàn b. 以为/以爲 yǐwéi c. 想 xiǎng d. 认为/認爲 rènwéi
e. 以为/以爲 yǐwéi f. 认为/認爲 rènwéi g. 以为/以爲 yǐwéi

3 a. 你想问谁就问谁。
        你想問誰就問誰。
        Nǐ xiǎng wèn shéi jiù wèn shéi.
    b. 你想去哪儿就去哪儿。
        你想去哪兒就去哪兒。
        Nǐ xiǎng qù nǎr jiù qù nǎr.
    c. 你想买哪个就买哪个。
        你想買哪個就買哪個。
        Nǐ xiǎng mǎi nǎge jiù mǎi nǎge.
    d. 你想吃什么就吃什么。
        你想吃甚麼就吃甚麼。
        Nǐ xiǎng chī shénme jiù chī shénme.
    e. 你想借多少就借多少。
        Nǐ xiǎng jiè duōshao jiù jiè duōshao.
    f. 你想怎么去就怎么去。
        你想怎麼去就怎麼去。
        Nǐ xiǎng zěnme qù jiù zěnme qù.
    g. 你想选哪门课就选哪门课。
        你想選哪門課就選哪門課。
        Nǐ xiǎng xuǎn nǎ mén kè jiù xuǎn nǎ mén kè.
    h. 你想看哪个电影就看哪个电影。
        你想看哪個電影就看哪個電影。
        Nǐ xiǎng kàn nǎge diànyǐng jiù kàn nǎge diànyǐng.

4 a. 私人汽车太多，造成的交通不方便。
        私人汽車太多，造成的交通不方便。
        Sīrén qìchē tài duō, zàochéng de jiāotōng bù fāngbiàn.
    b. 交通不方便。
        Jiāotōng bù fāngbiàn.
    c. 有车才有面子。
        有車才有面子。
        Yǒu chē cái yǒu miànzi.

d. 我想他没有汽车，因为他认为私人汽车太多了。

我想他沒有汽車，因爲他認爲私人汽車太多了。

Wǒ xiǎng tā méi yǒu qìchē, yīnwei tā rènwéi sīrén qìchē tài duō le.

e. 汽油的价钱高了，但是这并不影响人们买车。

汽油的價錢高了，但是這并不影響人們買車。

Qìyóu de jiàqian gāo le, dànshì zhè bìng bù yǐngxiǎng rénmen mǎi chē.

f. 不买车，尽量使用公共交通工具，汽车，地铁等等。

不買車，儘量使用公共交通工具，汽車，地鐵等等。

Bù mǎi chē, jìnliàng shǐyòng gōnggòng jiāotōng gōngjù, qìchē, dìtiě děngděng.

5

a. 你这样穿别人会以为你已经四十岁了。你应该穿白色的。

你這樣穿別人會以為你已經四十歲了。你應該穿白色的。

Nǐ zhèyàng chuān biérén huì yǐwéi nǐ yǐjīng sìshí suì le. Nǐ yīnggāi chuān báisè de.

b. 我今天的工作做不完，我看我不能跟你一起吃晚饭。

我今天的工作做不完，我看我不能跟你一起吃晚飯。

Wǒ jīntiān de gōngzuò zuòbùwán, wǒ kàn wǒ bù néng gēn nǐ yīqǐ chī wǎnfàn.

c. 我想请教您一些关于中国历史的问题。

我想請教您一些關於中國歷史的問題。

Wǒ xiǎng qǐngjiào nín yīxiē guānyú Zhōngguó lìshǐ de wèntí.

d. 你最好再跟你爸妈谈一谈，告诉他们你心里的想法。

你最好再跟你爸媽談一談，告訴他們你心裡的想法。

Nǐ zuì hǎo zài gēn nǐ bà mā tán yī tán, gàosù tāmen nǐ xīnlǐ de xiǎngfǎ.

e. 你想吃什么就吃什么，随便你。

你想吃甚麼就吃甚麼，隨便你。

Nǐ xiǎng chī shénme jiù chī shénme, suíbiàn nǐ.

55 Expressing fear, worry, and anxiety

1

a. 你不要怕冷。

Nǐ bù yào pà lěng.

b. 别怕那个老师。

別怕那個老師。

Bié pà nàge lǎoshī.

c. 别怕开车。

別怕開車。

Bié pà kāi chē.

d. 你不要怕没有人来。

你不要怕沒有人來。

Nǐ bù yào pà méi yǒu rén lái.

e. 你不要怕你学不会。

你不要怕你學不會。

Nǐ bù yào pà nǐ xuébuhuì.

f. 你不要怕黑天一个人走路。

你不要怕黑天一個人走路。

Nǐ bù yào pà hēitiān yī gè rén zǒu lù.

g. 你不要害怕考试。

你不要害怕考試。

Nǐ bù yào hàipà kǎoshì.

h. 考试的时候你别紧张。

考試的時候你別緊張。

Kǎoshì de shíhou nǐ bié jǐnzhāng.

2 a. 怕 pà b. 恐怕 kǒngpà c. 吓/嚇 xià d. 可怕 kěpà e. 紧张/緊張 jǐnzhāng
f. 着急/著急 zháojí g. 恐惧/恐懼 kǒngjù

3 Participant 1: 怕, 害怕 pà, hàipà

Participant 2: 充满恐惧/充滿恐懼 chōngmǎn kǒngjù

Participant 3: 担心/擔心 dānxīn

Participant 4: 可怕 kěpà

Participant 5: 紧张/緊張 jǐnzhāng

56 Expressing speaker attitudes and perspectives

1 a. 哎 āi b. 啊 á c. 哈哈 hā hā d. 噢 ō e. 啊 à f. 哎 āi g. 喔 ō h. 啊呀 āyā

2 a. 嘛 ma b. 啦 la c. 啊 a d. 啦 la

57 Topic, focus, and emphasis

1 a. 那个饭馆，我不喜欢。

那個飯館，我不喜歡。

Nàge fànguǎn, wǒ bù xǐhuan.

b. 中文课，我觉得很有意思。

中文課，我覺得很有意思。

Zhōngwén kè, wǒ juéde hěn yǒu yìsī.

c. 那个电影，我没看过。

那個電影，我沒看過。

Nàge diànyǐng, wǒ méi kànguò.

d. 这次考试，听说很容易。

這次考試，聽說很容易。

Zhè cì kǎoshì, tīngshuō hěn róngyì.

e. 日本饭，我没吃过。
日本飯，我沒吃過。
Rìběn fàn, wǒ méi chīguò.

f. 汉字，我每天都写。
漢字，我每天都寫。
Hàn zì, wǒ měitiān dōu xiě.

g. 中国的经济情况，我不太清楚。
中國的經濟情況，我不太清楚。
Zhōngguó de jīngjì qíngkuàng, wǒ bù tài qīngchu.

h. 别人的事，请你不要管。
別人的事，請你不要管。
Biéren de shì, qǐng nǐ bù yào guǎn.

2   a. 首先，我们把所有的椅子都搬出教室去。
首先，我們把所有的椅子都搬出教室去。
Shǒuxiān, wǒmen bǎ suǒyǒu de yǐzi dōu bān chū jiàoshì qù.

b. 然后，我们把课桌都搬到教室的后边。
然後，我們把課桌都搬到教室的後邊。
Ránhòu, wǒmen bǎ kèzhuō dōu bān dào jiàoshì de hòubian.

c. 小陈把吃的和喝的放在课桌上。
小陳把吃的和喝的放在課桌上。
Xiǎo Chén bǎ chī de hé hē de fang zài kèzhuō shàng.

d. 小王把地扫干净。
小王把地掃乾淨。
Xiǎo Wáng bǎ dì sǎo gānjìng.

e. 小李把黑板擦干净。
小李把黑板擦乾淨。
Xiǎo Lǐ bǎ hēibǎn cā gānjìng.

f. 小毛把音乐准备好。
小毛把音樂準備好。
Xiǎo Máo bǎ yīnyuè zhǔnbèi hǎo.

g. 你们两个人把 '春节好' 这三个字写在黑板上。
你們兩個人把 '春節好' 這三個字寫在黑板上。
Nǐmen liǎng gè rén bǎ 'chūnjié hǎo' zhè sān ge zì xiě zài hēibǎn shàng.

h. 你们三个人把这两张中国画儿挂在墙上。
你們三個人把這兩張中國畫兒挂在墙上。
Nǐmen sān gè rén bǎ zhè liǎng zhāng Zhōngguó huàr guà zài qiángshàng.

3   a. 除了我以外，别的同学都喜欢上中文课。
除了我以外，別的同學都喜歡上中文課。
Chúle wǒ yǐwài, bié de tóngxué dōu xǐhuan shàng Zhōngwén kè.

b. 除了我以外，他们也去看电影了。
除了我以外，他們也去看電影了。
Chúle wǒ yǐwài, tāmen yě qù kàn diànyǐng le.

c. 除了我以外，我的同学也都去过中国。
除了我以外，我的同學也都去過中國。
Chúle wǒ yǐwài, wǒ de tóngxué yě dōu qùguò Zhōngguó.

d. 除了中文以外，我也学中国文学和中国历史。
除了中文以外，我也學中國文學和中國歷史。
Chúle Zhōngwén yǐwài, wǒ yě xué Zhōngguó wénxué hé Zhōngguó lìshǐ.

e. 除了星期日以外，他星期一到星期六都工作。
除了星期日以外，他星期一到星期六都工作。
Chúle xīngqīrì yǐwài, tā xīngqīyī dào xīngqīliù dōu gōngzuò.

f. 我的同屋，除了足球以外，别的运动都不喜欢。
我的同屋，除了足球以外，別的運動都不喜歡。
Wǒ de tóngwū, chúle zúqiú yǐwài, bié de yùndòng dōu bù xǐhuan.

g. 我每天除了练习写汉字以外，也听录音，复习语法，念课文。
我每天除了練習寫漢字以外，也聽錄音，復習語法，念課文。
Wǒ měitiān chúle liànxí xiě Hàn zì yǐwài, yě tīng lùyīn, fùxí yǔfǎ, niàn kèwén.

h. 这个学校，除了餐厅的饭不太好吃以外，别的都很好。
這個學校，除了餐廳的飯不太好吃以外，別的都很好。
Zhège xuéxiào, chúle cāntīng de fàn bù tài hǎo chī yǐwài, bié de dōu hěn hǎo.

4

a. 这个字一定很难。连老师都不认识。
這個字一定很難。連老師都不認識。
Zhège zì yīdìng hěn nán. Lián lǎoshī dōu bù rènshi.

b. 这个字很容易。连一年级的学生都认识。
這個字很容易。連一年級的學生都認識。
Zhège zì hěn róngyì. Lián yīniánjí de xuésheng dōu rènshi.

c. 我连一个中国朋友都没有。
我連一個中國朋友都沒有。
Wǒ lián yī gè Zhōngguó péngyou dōu méi yǒu.

d. 他不念书。他连图书馆都没去过。
他不念書。他連圖書館都沒去過。
Tā bù niàn shū. Tā lián túshūguǎn dōu méi qùguò.

e. 他不会写字。他连他自己的名字都不会写。
他不會寫字。他連他自己的名字都不會寫。
Tā bù huì xiě zì. Tā lián tā zìjǐ de míngzì dōu bù huì xiě.

f. 小王不喜欢美国饭。他连汉堡包都不喜欢。
小王不喜歡美國飯。他連漢堡包都不喜歡。
Xiǎo Wáng bù xǐhuan Měiguó fàn. Tā lián hànbǎobāo dōu bù xǐhuan.

g. 我不会做饭。我连炒鸡蛋都不会。
我不會做飯。我連炒鷄蛋都不會。
Wǒ bù huì zuò fàn. Wǒ lián chǎo jīdàn dōu bù huì.

h. 他每天都工作。连星期天都工作。

他每天都工作。連星期天都工作。

Tā měitiān dōu gōngzuò. Lián xīngqītiān dōu gōngzuò.

5　a. 我是在波士顿长大的。

我是在波士頓長大的。

Wǒ shì zài Bōshìdùn zhǎngdà de.

b. 我是昨天晚上才回学校的。

我是昨天晚上才回學校的。

Wǒ shì zuótiān wǎnshang cái huí xuéxiào de.

c. 我是跟我的同屋一起回来的。

我是跟我的同屋一起回來的。

Wǒ shì gēn wǒ de tóngwū yīqǐ huílai de.

d. 我们是开车来的。or 我们是坐车来的。

我們是開車來的。or 我們是坐車來的。

Wǒmen shì kāi chē lái de. or Wǒmen shì zuò chē lái de.

e. 我的同屋是从中国来的。

我的同屋是從中國來的。

Wǒ de tóngwū shì cóng Zhōngguó lái de.

f. 他是两年以前来的。

他是兩年以前來的。

Tā shì liǎng nián yǐqián lái de.

g. 他是坐飞机来的。

他是坐飛機來的。

Tā shì zuò fēijī lái de.

h. 我们是在一个晚会上认识的。

我們是在一個晚會上認識的。

Wǒmen shì zài yī gè wǎnhuì shàng rènshi de.

i. 是他让我学中文的。

是他讓我學中文的。

Shì tā ràng wǒ xué Zhōngwén de.

j. 我是昨天晚上跟我的同屋从波士顿开车回学校的。

我是昨天晚上跟我的同屋從波士頓開車回學校的。

Wǒ shì zuótiān wǎnshang gēn wǒ de tóngwū cóng Bōshìdùn kāi chē huí xuéxiào de.

k. 他是两年以前从中国来美国的。

他是兩年以前從中國來美國的。

Tā shì liǎng nián yǐqián cóng Zhōngguó lái Měiguó de.

l. 他是两年以前从中国坐飞机来美国的。

他是兩年以前從中國坐飛機來美國的。

Tā shì liǎng nián yǐqián cóng Zhōngguó zuò fēijī lái Měiguó de.

6

a. i.   你们是什么时候认识的？
        你們是甚麼時候認識的？
        Nǐmen shì shénme shíhou rènshi de?

    ii. 你们是在哪儿认识的？
        你們是在哪兒認識的？
        Nǐmen shì zài nǎr rènshi de?

    iii. 是谁介绍你们认识的？
        是誰介紹你們認識的？
        Shì shéi jièshào nǐmen rènshi de?

b. i.   戒指是在哪儿买的？
        戒指是在哪兒買的？
        Jièzhǐ shì zài nǎr mǎi de?

    ii. 他是怎么求婚的？
        他是怎麼求婚的？
        Tā shì zěnme qiúhūn de?

c. 除了家人以外，我们还请了五十个朋友。
    除了家人以外，我們還請了五十個朋友。
    Chúle jiārén yǐwài, wǒmen hái qǐng le wǔshí ge péngyou.

d. 关于未来，我们打算十二月结婚，明年买房子，后年生孩子。
    關於未來，我們打算十二月結婚，明年買房子，後年生孩子。
    Guānyú wèilái, wǒmen dǎsuàn shí'èr yuè jiéhūn, míngnián mǎi fángzi, hòunián shēng háizi.

58　Guest and host

1

a. 欢迎，欢迎。/ 歡迎，歡迎。**Huānyíng, huānyíng.**
b. 请进。/ 請進。**Qǐng jìn.**
c. 请坐。/ 請坐。**Qǐng zuò.**
d. 喝点什么，茶还是咖啡？
    喝點甚麼，茶還是咖啡？
    Hē diǎn shénme, chá háishi kāfēi?
e. 请再来。/ 請再來。**Qǐng zài lái.**
f. 慢走。**Màn zǒu.**

2

a. host b. guest c. host d. host e. host f. host g. guest h. guest i. guest
j. guest k. host

59　Giving and responding to compliments

1

a. 我说得不好。/ 我說得不好。**Wǒ shuō de bù hǎo.** b. 哪里，哪里。/ 哪裏，哪裏。**Nǎli, nǎli.** c. 真的吗？/ 真的嗎？**Zhēnde ma?** d. 您过奖了。/ 您過獎了。**Nín guòjiǎng le.** e. 不敢当。/ 不敢當。**Bù gǎn dāng.** f. 没什么。/ 沒甚麼。**Méi**

shénme. g. 过奖，过奖。/ 過獎，過獎。**Guòjiǎng, guòjiǎng.** h. 便饭，便饭。/
便飯，便飯。**Biànfàn, biànfàn.**

2

a. 王明：高蕾，我看了你写的文章，好极了。
王明：高蕾，我看了你寫的文章，好極了。
Wáng Míng: Gāo Lěi, wǒ kàn le nǐ xiě de wénzhāng, hǎojíle.

b. 高蕾：写得不好，请多指教。
高蕾：寫得不好，請多指教。
Gāo Lěi: Xiě de bù hǎo, qǐng duō zhǐjiào.

c. 王明：你的描述非常高明。
Wáng Míng: Nǐ de miáoshù fēicháng gāomíng.

d. 高蕾：您过奖了，非常一般。
高蕾：您過獎了，非常一般。
Gāo Lěi: Nín guò jiǎng le, fēicháng yībān.

e. 王明：你的实例说明特别好，我看你很有才气。
王明：你的實例說明特別好，我看你很有才氣。
Wáng Míng: Nǐ de shílì shuōmíng tèbié hǎo, wǒ kàn nǐ hěn yǒu cáiqì.

f. 高蕾：普普通通，没有什么特别。
高蕾：普普通通，沒有甚麼特別。
Gāo Lěi: Púpǔtōngtōng, méi yǒu shénme tèbié.

3

Sample answers:

A. a. 真好 **zhēn hǎo**! b. 哪里/哪裏 **nǎlǐ** c. 没有/沒有 **méi yǒu**

B. 不敢当/不敢當 **bùgǎndāng**

60 Expressing satisfaction and dissatisfaction

1

a. 还可以。/還可以。**Hái kěyǐ.** b. 好极了。/好極了。**Hǎojíle.** c. 还不错。/
還不錯。**Hái bù cuò.** d. 相当好。/相當好。**Xiāngdāng hǎo.** e. 马马虎虎。/
馬馬虎虎。**Mámǎ hūhū.** f. 还行。/還行。**Hái xíng.**

2

a. 糟透了。/糟透了。**Zāo tòu le.** b. 不太好。**Bù tài hǎo.** c. 很差。**Hěn chà.**
d. 非常不好。**Fēicháng bù hǎo.** e. 很差。**Hěn chà.** f. 不太好。**Bù tài hǎo.**

3

a. Friend: How is your dorm?

b. You: 还可以。/還可以。**Hái kěyǐ.**

c. Is the bathroom clean?

d. You: 早上还可以。到了晚上就不怎么干净了。
早上還可以。到了晚上就不怎麼乾淨了。
Zǎoshang hái kěyǐ. Dào le wǎnshang jiù bù zěnme gānjìng le.

e. Friend: Are you used to things?

f. You: 习惯了。时间久了就习惯了。
習慣了。時間久了就習慣了。
Xíguàn le. Shíjiān jiǔ le jiù xíguàn le.

g. Friend: How is the food in the dining hall?

h. You: 还可以。马马虎虎。

　　　還可以。馬馬虎虎。

　　　Hái kěyǐ. Mámǎhǔhǔ.

i. Friend: How is the service in the dining hall?

j. You: 不怎么样。

　　　不怎麼樣。

　　　Bù zěnmeyàng.

4

感谢您为我们填写意见表。您的意见帮助我们为您带来更好的服务与用餐经验。为表达我们的感谢，每个星期我们会选出五位顾客得到本店的 $25礼券。

感謝您爲我們填寫意見表。您的意見幫助我們爲您帶來更好的服務與用餐經驗。爲表達我們的感謝，每個星期我們會選出五位顧客得到本店的$25禮券。

Gǎnxiè nín wèi wǒmen tiánxiě yìjiàn biǎo. Nín de yìjiàn bāngzhù wǒmen wèi nín dàilái gènghǎo de fúwù yǔ yòngcān jīngyàn. Wèi biǎodá wǒmen de gǎnxiè, měige xīngqī wǒmen huì xuǎn chū wǔ wèi gùkè dédào běndiàn de $25 lǐquàn.

请提供您的意见/請提供您的意見
Qǐng tígōng nín de yìjiàn

	好极了 好極了 hǎo jíle	满意 滿意 mǎnyì	还可以 還可以 hái kěyǐ	不太好 bù tài hǎo	糟透了 zāo tòule
用餐环境/用餐環境 yòngcān huánjìng					
食物 shíwù					
服务/服務 fúwù					
整体经验/整體經驗 zhěngtǐ jīngyàn					

你会不会跟朋友推荐我们的餐厅？　　　　□ 会/會 huì　□ 不会/不會 bù huì
你會不會跟朋友推薦我們的餐廳？
Nǐ huìbuhuì gēn péngyou tuījiàn wǒmen de cāntīng?

其他意见/其他意見 qítā yìjiàn: _____

联络方式/聯絡方式 liánluò fāngshì:
姓名 xìngmíng: _____
电子邮件/電子郵件 diànzǐ yóujiàn: _____

61 Expressing gratitude and responding to expressions of gratitude

1 a. 不必客气。/不必客氣。 **Bù bì kèqi.** Don't be polite. b. 哪儿的话?/哪兒的話? **Năr de huà** What kind of talk is that? c. 没什么。/沒甚麼。 **Méi shénme.** It wasn't anything. d. 不谢。/不謝。 **Bù xiè.** Don't thank me. e. 你太客气了。/ 你太客氣了。 **Nĭ tài kèqi le.** You are too polite. f. 不客气。/不客氣。 **Bù kèqi.** Don't be polite.

2 a. 首先，我要感谢我的父母，感谢他们多年来给我的支持。

首先，我要感謝我的父母，感謝他們多年來給我的支持。

Shŏuxiān, wŏ yào gănxiè wŏ de fùmŭ, gănxiè tāmen duō nián lái gěi wŏ de zhīchí.

b. 我非常感激为了使我能够得到良好的教育他们所作的牺牲。

我非常感激爲了使我能够得到良好的教育他們所作的犧牲。

Wŏ fēicháng gănji wèile shĭ wŏ nénggòu dédào liánghăo de jiàoyù tāmen suŏ zuò de xīshēng.

c. 同时，我也要感谢老师们给予我的指导和教诲。

同時，我也要感謝老師們給予我的指導和教誨。

Tóngshí, wŏ yě yào gănxiè lăoshīmen jĭ yŭ wŏ de zhídăo hé jiàohuì.

d. 他们不但传授给我们知识，更重要的是教我们作一个正直的人。

他們不但傳授給我們知識，更重要的是教我們作一個正直的人。

Tāmen bùdàn chuánshòu gěi wŏmen zhīshi, gèng zhòngyào de shì jiào wŏmen zuò yī gè zhèngzhí de rén.

e. 最后，我要感谢我的同学和朋友们，感谢他们的友情和帮助。

最後，我要感謝我的同學和朋友們，感謝他們的友情和幫助。

Zuì hòu, wŏ yào gănxiè wŏ de tóngxué hé péngyoumen, gănxiè tāmen de yŏuqíng hé bāngzhù.

f. 很难想象没有你们我怎么能够渡过这几年的大学时光。

很難想像沒有你們我怎麼能够渡過這幾年的大學時光。

Hěn nán xiăngxiàng méi yŏu nĭmen wŏ zěnme nénggòu dù guò zhè jĭnián de dàxué shíguāng.

g. 大学毕业是新生活的开始，我一定要更加努力地学习和工作，不辜负你们的 希望。

大學畢業是新生活的開始，我一定要更加努力地學習和工作，不辜負你們的 希望。

Dàxué bìyè shì xīn shēnghuó de kāishĭ, wŏ yīdìng yào gèng jiā nŭlì de xuéxí hé gōngzuò, bù gūfù nĭmen de xīwàng.

3 Sample answers:

a. 辛苦 **xīngkŭ**

b. (i) 麻烦/麻煩 **máfán**, (ii) 不好意思 **bù hăo yìsi**, (iii) 不客气/不客氣 **Bù kèqi**

c. (i) 笑纳/笑納 **xiàonà**, (ii) 客气/客氣 **kèqì**

62 Invitations, requests, and refusals

1 a. 好。 **Hǎo.** Okay. b. 可以。 **Kěyǐ.** I can. c. 你太客气。/你太客氣。 **Nǐ tài kèqi.** You are too polite. d. 可以。 **Kěyǐ.** I can. e. 好。 **Hǎo.** Okay.

2
a. 你太客气了。/你太客氣了。 **Nǐ tài kèqi le.** You are too polite.

b. 不要客气。/不要客氣。 **Bù yào kèqi.** Don't be polite. (That's not necessary.)

c. 我试试看。/我試試看。 **Wǒ shì shì kàn.** I'll see what I can do.

d. 恐怕我太忙。 **Kǒngpà wǒ tài máng.** I'm afraid I'm too busy.

e. 现在有一点不方便。
现在有一點不方便。
Xiànzài yǒu yīdiǎn bù fāngbiàn.
It's a little inconvenient right now.

f. 我恐怕帮不了你的忙。
我恐怕幫不了你的忙。
Wǒ kǒngpà bāngbùliǎo nǐ de máng.
I am afraid I am unable to help you.

3
a. 对不起，我不去书店。
對不起，我不去書店。
Duìbuqǐ, wǒ bù qù shūdiàn.

b. 不好意思，我已经有别的安排了。
不好意思，我已經有別的安排了。
Bùhǎoyìsi, wǒ yǐjing yǒu bié de ānpái le.

c. 对不起，我现在得去上课。
對不起，我現在得去上課。
Duìbuqǐ, wǒ xiànzài děi qù shàngkè.

d. 对不起，我今天没有时间。
對不起，我今天沒有時間。
Duìbuqǐ, wǒ jīngtiān méiyǒu shíjiān.

e. 对不起，我现在得去开会。
對不起，我現在得去開會。
Duìbuqǐ, wǒ xiànzài děi qù kāi huì.

f. 我的电话坏了。
我的電話壞了。
Wǒ de diànhuà huài le.

4
Abby: 告诉他你不喜欢泰国菜。/告訴他你不喜歡泰國菜。
Gàosù tā nǐ bù xǐhuān Tàiguó cài.

Cathy: 就说你最近很忙，恐怕没有时间。/就說你最近很忙，恐怕沒有時間。
Jiù shuō nǐ zuì jìn hěn máng, kǒngpà méi yǒu shíjiān.

Emily: 说你会考虑考虑。说你现在不方便说话。
說你會考慮考慮。說你現在不方便說話。
Shuō nǐ huì kǎolǜ kǎolǜ. Shuō nǐ xiànzài bù fāngbiàn shuō huà.

You:

63 Expressing apologies, regrets, sympathy, and bad news

1
a. 对不起。/對不起。**Duìbuqǐ.** Excuse me. b. 不好意思。**Bù hǎo yìsi.** How embarrassing. c. 对不起。/對不起。**Duìbuqǐ.** Excuse me. d. 真抱歉。**Zhēn bàoqiàn.** I really apologize. (I am really sorry.) e. 对不起。/對不起。**Duìbuqǐ.** Excuse me.

2
a. 真可惜。**Zhēn kěxī.** What a pity.
b. 希望你早日康复。
Xīwàng nǐ zǎo rì kāngfù.
I hope your health is soon restored.
c. 那太可惜了。
Nà tài kěxī le.
That's a pity.
d. 真可惜。**Zhēn kěxī.** What a pity.
or
失败是成功之母嘛。
失敗是成功之母嘛。
Shībài shì chénggōng zhī mǔ ma.
Failure is the mother of success.
e. 真可惜。**Zhēn kěxī.** What a pity.
f. 多保重身体。
多保重身體。
Duō bǎozhòng shēntǐ.
Take care of your health.

3
A. c B. a C. b D. b

64 Expressing congratulations and good wishes

1
a. 圣诞快乐!/聖誕快樂! **Shèngdàn kuàilè!** Merry Christmas!
b. 新年快乐!/新年快樂! **Xīnnián kuàilè!** Happy New Year!
c. 恭喜发财!/恭喜發財! **Gōngxǐ fā cái!** Congratulations and get rich!
d. 庆祝新婚。
慶祝新婚。
Qìngzhù xīn hūn.
Congratulations on your wedding.
e. 祝贺开张大吉。
祝賀開張大吉。
Zhù hè kāizhāng dàjí.
Wishing you extraordinary good luck on your great business opening.

f.　祝你生日快乐！

　　祝你生日快樂！

　　Zhù nǐ shēngrì kuàilè!

　　Wishing you a happy birthday!

g.　祝你寿比南山，福如东海。

　　祝你壽比南山，福如東海。

　　Zhù nǐ shòu bǐ nán shān, fú rú dōng hǎi.

　　I wish you a long life and great fortune.

h.　祝你鹏程万里。

　　祝你鵬程萬里。

　　Zhù nǐ péngchéng wànlǐ.

　　Wishing you a promising future.

i.　庆祝结婚纪念。

　　慶祝結婚紀念。

　　Qìngzhù jiéhūn jìniàn.

　　Congratulations on your wedding anniversary.

2　a. No. b. No. c. Yes. d. No. e. Yes. f. No. g. No. h. No. i. No. j. Yes. k. No. l. Yes. m. No. n. No. o. Yes. p. No.

3　A. c B. b C. a D. c

Index

The numbers refer to chapters in which relevant exercises occur. For example, 13 refers to Chapter 13 of this workbook. 13.1 refers to Chapter 13, Exercise 1.